THE **LOST CITIES** SERIES
IS KNOWN AROUND THE WORLD

"An adventurer cuts loose...a cut above most of its genre."
—The Oakland Tribune

"One long tale of quest and adventure, of chance meetings and
inevitable partings, meals relished and hotels endured, camel
caravans caught and buses missed–spun through with his
ecclectic gleanings from obscure works of archaeology,
history and explorers' diaries. Also woven throughout the books,
in a crazy-quilt jumble of innocent awe and hard bitten savvy,
are reflections on the people and places he encountered...
...There is a disarming casualness and a kind of festive, footloose
fancy to his tales that are utterly beguiling."
–The San Francisco Chronicle

"...a tonic...experiences in exotic places the rest of us think
only Indiana Jones visits...it will whet your appetite
and leave you chomping at the bit."
—The Missoulian

"...an offbeat travel guide that is fun to read even if you
don't have plans to duplicate author David Hatcher Childress'
remarkable journey. A thoughtful young man, Childress tells
a good story and his book is lively and interesting."
—The Washington Post

"Explore for lost treasure, stone monuments
forgotten in jungles...and hair-raising terrain
from the safety of your armchair."
—Bookwatch

"A fascinating series of books, written with humour,
insight, depth and an astonishing knowledge
of the ancient past."
—Richard Noone, author of 5/5/2000

Other books in the **Lost Cities Series**:

Lost Cities & Ancient Mysteries of Africa & Arabia
Lost Cities of Ancient Lemuria & the Pacific
Lost Cities & Ancient Mysteries of South America
Lost Cities of North & Central America
Lost Cities of Europe and the Mediterranean

About the author:

David Hatcher Childress was born in France, and raised in the mountains of Colorado and Montana. At nineteen, he left the United States on a six-year journey across Asia, Africa and the Pacific. An ardent student of history, archaeology, philosophy and comparative religion, he has authored numerous articles, which have appeared in publications around the world, as well as several books, including *Lost Cities & Ancient Mysteries of South America, Lost Cities of Ancient Lemuria & the Pacific, Vimana Aircraft of Ancient India & Atlantis,* and others.

Currently, he travels the globe in search of lost cities and ancient mysteries. He also leads small groups of similarly interested individuals to many of these sites, including some of those mentioned in this book. Expedition-tours to lost cities in the Andes, Egypt, Easter Island, a sunken city in the Pacific, and others are run all during the year. For information on Mr. Childress' books, small group tours, or for correspondence directed to him, please write or call:

Adventures Unlimited
Box 22
Stelle, IL 60919 USA

1-815-253-6390

The **Lost Cities** Series:

•LOST CITIES OF CHINA, CENTRAL ASIA & INDIA
•LOST CITIES & ANCIENT MYSTERIES OF AFRICA & ARABIA
•LOST CITIES & ANCIENT MYSTERIES OF SOUTH AMERICA
•LOST CITIES OF ANCIENT LEMURIA & THE PACIFIC
•LOST CITIES OF NORTH & CENTRAL AMERICA
•LOST CITIES OF EUROPE & THE MEDITERRANEAN

The **Mystic Traveller** Series:
•IN SECRET TIBET by Theordore Illion (1937)
•DARKNESS OVER TIBET by Theordore Illion (1938)
•TENTS IN MONGOLIA by Henning Haslund (1934)
•MEN AND GODS IN MONGOLIA by Henning Haslund (1935)
•MYSTERY CITIES by Thomas Gann (1925)
•IN QUEST OF LOST WORLDS by Count Byron de Prorok (1937)

LOST CITIES OF CHINA, CENTRAL ASIA & INDIA

*We are going away again,
this time to Central Asia,
where, if anywhere upon earth,
wisdom is to be found,
and we anticipate that our
journey will be a long one.*

—H. Rider Haggard: *She*, 1887

I dedicate this book to the great Central Asia explorers:
Sir Aurel Stein Nicholas Roerich, Sven Hedin,
Alexandra David-Neel, Nicholas Notovich, Theodore
Illion, Henning Haslund, James Churchward, Roy
Chapman Andrews, Marco Polo and to the Indiana
Jones in all of us.

Lost Cities of China, Central Asia & India
Copyright 1985, 1987, 1991

David Hatcher Childress

Printed in the United States of America

Third, revised edition
 October, 1991

ISBN 0-932813-07-0

Published by
Adventures Unlimited Press
Box 22, Stelle, Illinois 60919-9989 USA

The **Lost Cities Series**:
Lost Cities of China, Central Asia & India
Lost Cities & Ancient Mysteries of Africa & Arabia
Lost Cities of Ancient Lemuria & the Pacific
Lost Cities & Ancient Mysteries of South America
Lost Cities of North & Central America
Lost Cities of Europe and the Mediterranean

TABLE OF
CONTENTS

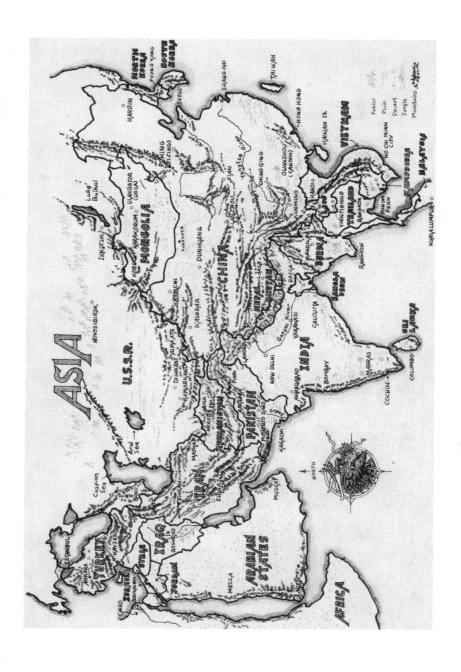

THANKS to Mom, Dad, Linda, Janet,
Dave, Jamie, Mil, Steph and
to *Bill and the Rose Garden Crowd* in
Kathmandu, without their help this book
would never have been produced.

*Every mystery solved brings us to the
threshold of a greater one.*
　　　　　　　　—Rachel Carson

*A Traveller! By my faith you have great
reason to be sad; I fear you have sold your
own lands to see other men's; then, to have
seen much and to have nothing, is to have
rich eyes and poor hands.*
　　—William Shakespeare. "As You Like It."

The Mystic Traveller Series:
•IN SECRET TIBET by Theodore Illion (1937)
•DARKNESS OVER TIBET by Theodore Illion (1938)
•TENTS IN MONGOLIA by Henning Haslund (1934)
•MEN AND GODS IN MONGOLIA by Henning Haslund (1935)
•MYSTERY CITIES by Thomas Gann (1925)
•IN QUEST OF LOST WORLDS by Byron de Prorok (1937)

The **Lost Science Series**:
•THE ANTI-GRAVITY HANDBOOK
•ANTI-GRAVITY & THE UNIFIED FIELD
•VIMANA AIRCRAFT OF ANCIENT INDIA & ATLANTIS
•THE MANUAL OF FREE ENERGY DEVICES & SYSTEMS
•TAPPING THE ZERO POINT ENERGY
•THE BRIDGE TO INFINITY
•THE ENERGY GRID
•THE DEATH OF ROCKETRY

Chapter One

AT THE DOORSTEP OF CENTRAL ASIA:

TALES FROM THE SEVENTH GATE

...for our goal was not only the East, or rather the East was not only a country and something geographical, but it was the home and youth of the soul, it was everywhere and nowhere, it was the union of all times.
—Herman Hesse

He who enters the Seventh Gate may not retrace his footsteps.
— Indian proverb

"Tweee-eeeeet!" The conductor blew his whistle and simultaneously, the great black steam engine blew its mighty whistle. "Come on!" yelled Kyle, running down the platform. "We'll be late for the train!" I shouldered my heavy pack, grabbed the equally heavy duffle bag at my feet, and ran after Kyle.

"So this is India!" I thought, hurrying past pastry vendors and newspaper stands. Porters in turbans and red shirts passed through the crowds of passengers in silk saris and baggy cotton pants with pointed shoes that crowded the platform of Howrah Station, the main train station of Calcutta. It was a world vibrantly alive: a sensory bombardment of sights, smells, tastes, sounds, touches, and fascinating experiences. A chill shot up my spine. How I loved being on the road, heading full speed into another

9

adventure, in another country, in another time. This was India!

Kyle, my traveling companion, was a bearded Mandarin student from Ann Arbor, Michigan, whom I had met at the American English Center in Taipei, Taiwan. Just now, he was racing up ahead of me, trying to find out which carriage we were supposed to be on. He ran up to one conductor, who pointed back down to the opposite end, and so he reversed and came running by me again, shouting, "It's this way!" over the noise of the station and the steam engine. We ran to the other end of the station where a conductor told us that, no, our carriage was on the other end of the train, where we had just come from!

The train whistle blew again, and the train started to move. Kyle glanced at our ticket and then just jumped on board. With a great grunt, I ran for one of the doors, threw my duffle bag on the train, and then jumped on the moving carriage. With a great sigh of relief, I collapsed onto the floor, and then sat there in a state of exhaustion watching the scenery from the open door as we pulled out of the Howrah-Calcutta station, on our way to the Indian-Nepalese border.

As we pulled out of the station, I gazed in awe at the great city of Calcutta—India's largest, with around eight million people—one of the most densely populated cities in the world. It was late afternoon as we pulled out past the small encampments along the railway bed of homeless people who had come to the big city with hopes of finding a job. In the distance was the famous Howrah Bridge, a colossal steel structure spanning the Hooghly River that separated Calcutta from its sister city, Howrah. The bridge, Calcutta's most famous landmark, has come to symbolize the city.

Calcutta was founded in 1860 by the East India Company, and named after the three-hundred-fifty-year-old Kalighat temple in the small fishing village that the British decided would be the site of the new city. From a historical point of view, Kali was the nastiest of the Hindu Pantheon of deities—often symbolized by an eight-armed, frenzied, bloodied woman, with each of her hands holding a bloody dagger.

Kali was the patron deity of the Indian Thugee cult (from which we get our word "thug"). Members of this fraternity of assassins and murderers worshipped Kali in a rather gory way. Generally, they disguised themselves as merchants or wandering holy men and waylaid wealthy travelers,

10

robbing them and killing them as sacrifices to the blood-thirsty Kali. Also known as Phansigars (stranglers) because they strangled their victims, they came into view in the thirteenth century and apparently were quite active in India, especially in the eastern part.

They were finally repressed by the British, who executed some four hundred and twelve "thugs" and imprisoned another three thousand during a campaign which lasted from 1829 to 1848. On one hand, it is doubtful that they were completely wiped out. On the other hand, some scholars claim that they never really existed at all, and that their "society" was simply a fabrication. The Indian government thought they were real enough, though, and even had any suspected thugs (including family and relatives) register so they could be kept under police surveillance, through a Criminal Tribes Act which was not repealed until 1947. The Thugees were the subject of the 1984 movie "Indiana Jones and the Temple of Doom."

Calcutta has changed a bit today. The old Kali-ghat Temple has been turned into a hospital by the famous Mother Theresa, who does a lot of charity work in the city, and it perhaps India's greatest industrial city. But, as I gazed out the open door of the train, I saw a relic of the past: a pedi-rickshaw being pulled by a thin brown man in a loin cloth. Calcutta is the last place in the world where bicycle and motorized rickshaws have not replaced foot-powered ones, largely because of the strength of the rickshaw union in Calcutta.

What was I, a slim, blonde archaeology student fron the University of Montana, doing here in the city of Kali? At nineteen, I was fresh and eager for adventure and mystery. I knew perfectly well what I wanted: to discover the truth about the so-called "Lost Cities" of Asia, to climb in the Himalayas, and to do all the other things I had daydreamed of so heartily during boring classes in school. Then, I'd imagined that my life would be like a beer commercial—I'd keep "grabbing for all the gusto" I could. I wanted to go—everywhere! I wanted to do everything, meet everyone, and I wanted to do it all right away! And now, to my great delight and excitement, it was all happening.

Naturally, I didn't have much money. I had taught English for six months in Taiwan and saved what I could. My parents loaned me some money, then generously gave me some more. But it still wasn't very much, and I would have to travel cheaply, spending from three to five dollars a

11

day. I discovered that it was possible to spend as little as one dollar a day in India and still get by. I lived like any other Asian, traveling by third class train or bus, hitchhiking when I could, and staying in the cheapest hostels, lodges, and flea-bag dives that I could find. Typically, these type of Indian hotels have four to five beds a room: steel-framed boxes with stained, lumpy mattresses on them. It may not sound very appealing, but after a hard day of traveling, I slept well on anything.

Toilets, all over India and Asia, were holes in the floor over which you have to squat. If you were lucky, they would actually flush like normal toilets, but if you didn't stand back, your feet would get wet! Many toilets didn't flush by pulling a chain to a tank overhead, but had to be flushed by pouring a bucket of water down the toilet. Toilet paper was virtually never provided, as most Asians never use it, cleansing themselves by washing with their left hand. For this reason, the left hand is considered unclean, and it is thought impolite to handle or pass food with the left hand.

Naturally, most Westerners are ignorant of this basic common courtesy, and may unconsciously insult their hosts in this way; although, as India and other countries become more and more westernized, it has become more and more acceptable to eat with both hands. Throughout India and parts of Central Asia, most people eat with their fingers, except in China where they use chop sticks, of course. Many travelers carry their own knives, forks, and spoons in the interests of better hygiene (as hepatitis and other diseases are often transmitted by poorly washed dishes and cutlery), as well as their own toilet paper.

§§§

Kyle came up to me on the train and told me that he had found our seat. When we had made our reservations, we could get only one seat on the train, so we would be sharing it during the fifteen-hour trip to Muzafapur near the border of Nepal. I had met Kyle while we were both teaching English at the American English Center in Taipei. Both of us were in the middle of our college educations, and were taking breaks to study and work in Taiwan. When we found that we were both interested in doing some climbing in Nepal, we decided to get together and make the trip to Nepal as a team.

First, we'd flown to Hongkong, then to Bangkok,

Thailand, and on to Rangoon, Burma, where we spent a week. From there, we flew to Calcutta, where we'd landed a few days ago.

Kyle took off his tortoise-shell glasses and wiped the dust off them with his blue cotton shirt. "Well, we have one seat by the window. I found a place at the end of our car where we can store our gear. We can't lock it though, so perhaps we should take turns guarding it."

"That sounds fine to me," I said, glancing out the door at the fiery orange ball that was setting on the distant horizon, over a village of grass thatch buildings and occasional temples. "I'm still pretty worn out from catching the train. I think I'll just sit here by the door for a while and watch the sunset."

"Okay," said Kyle, putting his glasses back on and pulling gently on his beard. "I'll see you back at our seat."

I kept a steady gaze on the magnificent sunset that was flaming in the sky. I could hardly believe that I was really here, here in Central Asia! There was so much to do, so much to see, so many wonders and mysteries to explore.

Southeast Asia has one of the most spectacular lost cities ever discovered: Angkor Wat, glory of the Khmer kingdom, and the largest religious building ever constructed. The royal city of Angkor, apparently built between A. D. 800 and 1200, was lost to the outside world for centuries until it was rediscovered by the French Naturalist Henri Mouhot in 1860. Because of the recent Vietnamese invasion of Cambodia, where Angkor Wat is situated, Angkor is nearly impossible to visit today, since Cambodia (now called the Khmer Republic) has virtually sealed its borders.

So, I would miss Angkor Wat, but there was plenty to see in countries that were open, and many of them raised questions that were fantastic, to say the least. There have been ancient cities recently discovered in India that are thousands of years old. Might they date back to "before the flood," and have been built more than 12,000 years ago? Is there evidence of an atomic war in 9,000 B. C.? What of rumors of vitrified cities and radioactive skeletons from an ancient, semi-mythical Rama Empire? What of even older cities in the Gobi desert, once the site of a vast, heavily-populated civilization? Did the fabled "Abode of the Immortals" exist, or a network of tunnels beneath Tibet linking monasteries and secret underground cities?

I wanted to find out these things, and more. In the

mountain areas of Central Asia were lost monasteries, libraries and kingdoms like Hunza, Zanskar, Mustang, Bhutan, and others. Here were the mysterious Lop Nor desert, center of Asia's UFO mystery, and the strange Bodgo-Gegen and his magic ring: the "Master of the World" who still supposedly lives in Mongolia. I wanted to go to these places, explore them, and bring back some answers. I even wanted to go to the dreaded "Black Gobi," where no one dares to venture, in my pursuit of lost cities and ancient mysteries. This was an adventure that had my name on it, and I was in the mood for a quest.

At the thought of this grand adventure of life and exploration, a terrific grin lit up my face. The wind blew coolly on me as I sat on the floor by the open door, staring out at the sunset. One interesting explorer of lost cities that suddenly popped to my mind was Captain James Churchward, a British officer stationed in India around the turn of the century.

Churchward claimed to have been given some clay tablets by an Indian Priest who taught him how to translate the mysterious, ancient writing that was engraved on the tablets. According to Churchward, who is the only one ever to have seen these tablets, they were written by the Naacals, a white race of people who, according to the ancient Indian epic The Ramayana, were the first race to come to India, some time around 30,000 to 70,000 years ago. They had swarthy complexions and came from Burma. While Churchward called them Naacals, they were also known as Nagas.

Their original home was the "land of their birth in the east," according to the Ramayana, and is thought by Churchward to have been what is called "the Motherland, Mu." This was a continent of sorts in the Pacific Ocean, similar in tradition to Atlantis, though seemingly much older. The Nagas, or Naacals, emigrated, possibly from this continent in the east, settled for some time in Indochina around Burma, and eventually moved to the Deccan Plateau in morthern India where they stayed permanently. In fact, Nagas can still be found in this area today.

According to the Ramayana, the Nagas, also known as "Mayas" (as well as Naacals) in the Indian texts, were "learned architects—they built great cities and palaces." They were also "mighty navigators whose ships passed form the eastern to the western oceans and from the southern to the northern seas in ages so remote that the sun had not yet risen above the horizon." This last expression, according to Churchward, refers not to the actual sun rising, but to the colony of the Nagas becoming a colony of the Motherland, Mu, the "Empire of the Sun."

The Nagas allegedly built their capital city at Nagpur, where the modern city of Nagpur stands today. The last remnants of the Nagas still live around Nagpur, though they are considered a rather primitive culture by the now dominant *Aryans* of India.

Interestingly, a recent archeological discovery that supports these rather fantastic statements is the site of Ban Chieng in northern Thailand. Thai archeologists have uncovered remains of a civilization dating back at least five thousand years, which used bronze tools and jewelry. Up until this find, it was thought that bronze was invented in Mesopotamia a thousand years later! The objects found at Ban Chieng were bronze weapons and jewels, carved ivory objects and pottery, all of them beautifully made, which bear witness to an advanced civilization that has completely vanished. This find indicates that the making of bronze may have originated in the far east rather than in the middle-east, as most archeologists previously thought. Yet, curiously, bronze was not known to be used in China until about 1300 B.C., and in Vietnam it was not used until the Fourth Century B. C. Could Ban Chieng hold remains from the advanced Nagas?

Did the knowledge of bronze manufacturing originate in southeast Asia (or perhaps in Mu, the "Empire of the Sun") and get passed onto the middle-east? In answer to that question, the Ramayana says: "From Burma they established themselves in Deccan, India, from whence they carried their religion and learning to the colonies of Babylonia and Egypt" (!) It was the Nagas who reputedly established the greatest Empire of Asia, the Rama Empire, and the ancient cities of Rama was a definite stop on my quest!

"Your ticket, sir," said the conductor suddenly, interrupting my musings. I glanced up at him and fished into my picket. He was a brown, cheerful-looking man in his forties, clean-shaven and with a twinkle in his eye.

"Here you go," I said, handing him the small piece of cardboard that was my ticket.

"Thank you, sir," he said and continued on his way down the car. Outside, there was still a little glow from the sunset on the horizon, and I meditated silently on it, appreciating the cool wind that was created by the train.

It was totally dark now, and I stared out into the dark night as we rattled northward across West Bengal state into Bihar state. The lights of the villages shone like stars, lighting up the darkness of the Indian plains here and there like miniature galaxies.

I went back to our seat and sat in it for several hours, dozing lightly while Kyle stood by our luggage and the door. He woke me up sometime after midnight, and told me that it was my turn to watch the luggage. I took my place by the door at the end of the carriage, and stared out at the passing villages.

It was still hot and humid, and a new moon was just beginning to rise. Sleeping villages, palm trees, rice paddies, and train stations passed by in the night as I stood gazing into the darkness. Life was good. It felt great to be on the road, moving through the country. Once again, I was in search of cities, ancient mysteries, and most of all, I was searching for my "self," the greater meaning of which had escaped me as a teenager. It was a search into which I could sink my teeth.

The conductor came along again, and stopped to chat with me for awhile. He spoke excellent English, as most educated Indians do; English being the language that essentially unifies all of India. He was a gentle, intelligent man, and seemed keenly interested in America.

"I'd love to go to America sometime," he said. "I've been working as a conductor for twenty years, and have been all over India, but I would like to travel to other countries; America, especially!" His face was somewhat sad as he said that, as if he realized that it would never be.

"Where is it that you are going?" he asked me, removing his blue conductor's hat and brushing it off. The train was very quiet, since it was now nearly three o'clock in the morning.

"I'm on my way to Kathmandu with my friend," I told him. "We're planning to do some climbing in the Himalayas."

"Ah, yes, very exciting, isn't it?" he exclaimed. Just then we pulled into a small station, and the train stopped. "Excuse me," he said, disappearing down the train. I decided to step out onto the platform to have a cup of tea.

The platform was packed with people, which surprised me, given the time of night. Most of them were fighting to get on the train, which had bars across the windows to

16

keep them out. The doors were all locked as well. I walked down to one end of the platform where there was a small tea stall, and had a cup of "chai," the sweet, milky tea that is served all over India and Central Asia. Then I heard the train whistle and headed back up the platform to my door.

As I neared the car, I saw, to my surprise and horror, a huge angry crowd fighting to get on the train, and in front of my door, no less! Standing in front of them all was the conductor, fighting them back and yelling at them in Hindi. The crowd of twenty or more people pushed and shoved, desperately fighting to get on board the train, while the conductor fought to keep them off.

The whistle blew again, and the train lurched once. The conductor spotted me and yelled, "Come on!" With strength derived from desperation, I threw Indians right and left, creating a path through the mass of people. When I got to the conductor, the train was just starting to pull out, but with a mighty heave, I sprang on board! As if we were in in a grade-B thriller, the conductor and I fought back the people and together forced the door closed, locking it as the train started to pick up to a steady clip. We both breathed a heavy sigh, and in a rush of relief, I gave the conductor a big hug.

We looked at each other and laughed at the adventure. "Welcome to India," he said, and turned to move down the carriage.

"Thank you," I replied.

He straightened his uniform and then turned to me. "There just aren't enough trains to serve these areas!" Later, I heard him calling down the carriage, "Tickets, please!" After all, it was all in a day's work.

§§§

By mid-morning we were in Muzafapur, where Kyle and I caught a crowded bus to Raxaul, on the Indian side of the Nepalese border. We were stamped out of India and took a bicycle rickshaw a mile to the Nepalese border town of Birgunj. Birgunj is a small, semi-industrial town in the grassland-terai of southern Nepal. Beyond it lies the first foothills of the Himalayas, and then the intriguing capital city of this Himalayan kingdom: Kathmandu.

When we got through customs and immigration, it was mid-afternoon and too late to catch a bus for the ten hour ride to Kathmandu. There are nearly a dozen small hotels

17

and lodges around Birgunj, most of them near the bus depot where all the buses leave for Kathmandu, and we spent the night in one.

We caught our bus early the next morning. After the lowland terai, the bus was quickly climbing the first foothills of the Himalayas. Soon, the bus was winding laboriously up the switchbacks toward the top of the first pass, going by the many terraced fields and thatch-roofed houses of the local farmers.

Kyle and I had climbed onto the roof of the bus at one of the stops and were enjoying the view tremendously. At the top of the second pass, the Mahabharat Himal, we could see for the first time the main range of the Himilayas in the distance. I was struck by the awe-inspiring sight! Like a long line of white, jagged teeth, the highest and most impressive mountains in the world spanned the horizon as far as one could see from east to west. Mountains rose over mountains, with clouds below them.

Beyond this fortress of rock, ice and snow lay Tibet, vast and forbidding, with an average altitude of sixteen thousand feet. In my romantic youth, I had often day-dreamed of seeing this very sight, the Himalayas, and here they were! It was everything, and more, that I had hoped.

The bus descended down to Chitrang in the Insuli Valley, and we all got off for a stretch and snack. To the north were the snowy peaks of the Ganesh Himal. After a fifteen-minute break, Kyle and I climbed back on top of the bus, and the driver headed up the switch-backs toward another pass, beyond which was the Vale of Kathmandu.

The Himalayas, it is surmised, were created hundreds of thousands of years ago, when the tectonic plate of the Indian sub-continent literally collided with that of the Asian mainland. Where the two plates met they pushed upward, forming the Himalayas and some of the other mountain ranges in Central Asia. These ranges are still rising today, it is believed by many geologists, because of the pressure of the plates against each other. At the top of the final pass into the Vale of Kathmandu, one comes to a small gap in the mountains. This is the "spout" that drained the Kathmandu Valley, which was once a lake.

I slapped Kyle on the back as the valley came into view, with the city of Kathmandu in the distance. "Wowee!" I yelled over the whine of the bus and the whistling of the wind. It was like coming home. Kathmandu was my Mecca, a fabled land in mystical Central Asia where I could find whatever it was I was looking for....

"It's great!" Kyle yelled back. In front of us was the long valley of Kathmandu: green, fertile, and packed with temples, monasteries, other travelers, and Nepalis. The angular pagoda roofs of the temples emerged above the sloping tiled roofs of the old city. We cruised past the small town of Kalimati and into the central bus station, just near the post office. I gave a long sigh of relief. In some way, one of the major goals of my life had just been reached.

Carved megalithic granite blocks with articulation for fitting other large blocks. These gigantic ruins are found at Yarang, Patani, South Thailand, and they have never been excavated. Thai legend speaks of a great empire named Langkasuka.

Structures carved into solid rock inside the entrance to the cave of "King Tak" in southern Thailand. Legend claims that the ancient land of Langkasuka had a capital city named Tambralinga. Thai legend claims that this cave leads to this mysterious city.

THE KING OF THE WORLD?

Is there an underground cave city called Agharti ruled by a Venusian who holds our future hopes?

ALL through the world today are thousands of people who claim to have knowledge of an underground city, not specifically located although generally assumed to be in Tibet, called Agharti, or Shambala. In this city, they say, is a highly developed civilization ruled by an "Elder" or a "Great One" whose title is among others "The King of the World." Some claim to have seen him, and it is also claimed that he made at least one visit to the surface. It is also claimed that when Mankind is ready for the benefits he can bring, he will emerge and establish a new civilization of peace and plenty.

To quote the words of a "witness": "He came here ages ago from the planet Venus to be the instructor and guide of our then just dawning h u m a n i t y. Though he is thousands of years old, his appearance is that of an exceptionally well-developed and handsome youth of about sixteen. But there is nothing juvenile about the light of infinite love, wisdom and power that shines from his eyes. He is slightly larger than the average man, but there are no radical differences in race."

Apparently the ruler of Agharti is a man; apparently he possesses great power and science, including atomic energy machines. Apparently also he is dedicated to bring to us great benefits. Apparently he has power to end warfare on the surface at will. We, the people of Earth, ask: What man can judge another? Wars must end now! Judge not, Great One, lest you be judged. For we ARE ready for peace!

Above: One of the Hollow Earth features that appeared in *Amazing Stories* in May 1946, a magazine edited by Ray Palmer (*right*)

Chapter Two

KATHMANDU, NEPAL:
THE BOWL OF BUDDHA

> When you fix your mind at one point,
> Nothing is impossible for you.
> —*Gautama Buddha*

As we got off the bus, we were immediately besieged by a hoard of eleven- or twelve-year-old kids who were there to drum up customers for their respective lodges. "Hey mister, want a lodge? Only ten rupees a night!" each cried, zeroing in on a traveler. Fortunately, we already had a recommendation from a friend, and knew just where we were going. Soon we were in a bicycle rickshaw, heading north down New Road, the main street in Kathmandu, toward Durbar Square and "Freak Street." Later we walked down "Pig Alley," at dusk back to the Delight Lodge.

There are literally hundreds of cheap lodges in Kathmandu, as the tourist trade, especially among budget-conscious travelers, has been booming since the late sixties. The Delight Lodge, like most of the lodges in Kathmandu, had rooms for about a dollar a night; and a bed in a dormitory for less. The building was a five-story cement structure, modern by Nepalese standards, with clean rooms which sported two wood-frame beds, a table, chair, and curtains. The floor was cold cement: stark, but cheap and efficient. The doorways were low, and you invariably had to duck to get through them. Like other hotels, in Kathmandu and all over Asia, it only had a few bathrooms for the entire hotel, and hot water "at certain times during the day," as the management's notice said. You never really knew when, but early morning was aways a good bet.

Probably, the reason that the Delight Lodge had been recommended to us was that it had a particularly good view from the roof. When the clouds lifted, it was possible to see, to the north, the peaks of the Langtang Himal, twenty-three thousand feet in height. There was also a good view back across the city, as well as of the Temple of Swayambu in the valley to the north.

Kathmandu is a kind of the Amsterdam or San Francisco of Asia. It has lots of young people, a nightlife of sorts, pop music drifting out of the pie shops, travelers in outlandish costumes, plenty of recreational drugs being used, and a quasi-mystical-guru atmosphere. As I learned in the several years that I came and went in Kathmandu, there are a number of cliques around the city; composed of Europeans or Americans that have been living there for years, many with diplomatic jobs. Some of these people have started their own businesses, which by law in Nepal must be fifty-fifty partnerships with a Nepali.

Some people are interested in the Buddhist monasteries and monks in the hills around Kathmandu. Others are into drama or other activities. Mountaineering is a popular hobby of many tourists. Famous mountaineers, including Sir Edmond Hillary, the first man to climb Mount Everest (with Sherpa Tenzing Norgay), can be found sitting at the bars of certain of the more fashionable hotels around the city, or perhaps in the casino at the Soalty Oberoi Hotel.

Kathmandu, while not qualifying as a lost city, is certainly a place of mystery. I was awed by the medieval charm, the many square oriental pagodas, with little shrines and temples at every turn, the constant tinkling of bells, the smell of incense, garlands of flowers on statues, and the sound of unceasing prayers.

Every twisting turn of the stone-paved, narrow streets holds a new wonder: a goddess walking the streets in a silk sari, little bells jingling on her brown ankle; or a straggly-haired sadhu (a wandering holy man), naked except for a loincloth, sitting on the steps of a temple cleaning his chilum, a funnel-type pipe with which he smoked ganja, the Indian name for marijuanna.

Here or there is a Tibetan—perhaps a monk with a shaved head and maroon robes, or a tall, beautiful woman with rosy cheeks and long, braided black hair. On various walls and doorways are the watchful eyes of Buddha, reminding a person of the "enlightened ones" who are ever-present, yet invisible.

In the evenings, the streets are sometimes enshrouded in a gentle, quiet fog with the pagodas or rickshaws peeking out of the mystical gloom. Wandering the labyrinth of streets, you gaze into lighted shops selling groceries, candy, incense, clothing, or food. At some street corners, men are playing music and telling stories from the Hindu epics while a crowd listens intently.

In the morning, there are pigs, goats, buffaloes, and cows in the streets, while school children in blue and white uniforms paddle off to school. Gurka soldiers with their curved kukri knives walk the streets, and Nepali businessmen as well as small crowds of tourists wander the cobblestone markets. It could be the tenth century, or the twelfth, or the eighteenth, or even 1967 in Haight Ashbury. Kathmandu is a timeless city, a city where the ancient past and modern present blend together harmoniously, yet without really changing each other. Kathmandu—a mystical city on the edge of yesterday.

§§§

Kyle and I wandered about the city for several weeks, captivated by the charm and romantic/medieval feel of the city. We bought sweaters made of yak wool, and Tibetan Carpets, then had pie or yogurt drinks in one of the restaurants found on nearly every corner. Looking out of the window, we might see a little girl on the street, dressed in a brown cotton dress and barefoot, her eyes surrounded by black "kohl," making her look like a grade-school Mata Hari.

Once, as I drank a cup of sweet milk tea, "chai," a young girl stopped on the street just in front of me with a worried expression on her face. She set down her books and then pulled up her brown dress. Then, squatting, she had a bowel movement right there on the street. People took absolutely no notice whatsoever of her, and she picked up her books, her face looking somewhat relieved, and paddled off down the street. The teenage boy that was running the restaurant kitchen gave me a knowing look. Kathmandu was such a fantastic place, I thought, I could live here forever!

§§§

Kathmandu also has plenty of fortune tellers, herbal doctors, gurus of one sort or another (Nepali, Indian, Tibetan, and Eruopean), plus other occults of varying degrees of harmlessness. Kathmandu has a reputation for being a very active area for black occults of many kinds, and one should be careful with whom one is asociating, I have been advised. Many "spiritual" guides do not have your best interests at heart: in fact, some may be tools of a stronger power than themselves.

The King of Nepal is an interesting figure, and looks a bit out of place with his black glasses and small physique. He appears more like a computer programmer than the reincarnation of the Hindu God Vishu, which he is supposed to be. "His Auspicious Majesty," as he is called in the newspapers of Nepal, may be seen occasionally on holidays, or perhaps in a parade. His palace is a fairly modern building at the end of Kanti Path Road, but you can't go inside.

One character in Kathmandu that I once had the pleasure of meeting was the "Global Emperor," a Nepali in his fifties who used to frequent Aunt Jane's, a popular restaurant just near New Road. I would generally have breakfast at Aunt Jane's, either by myself or with some friends. With its nice sunny atmosphere, red-checkered tableclothes, and pancake-house- type menu, it was a great place to have a cup of tea, some french toast or poached eggs, and read the *Rising Nepal*, one of the Kathmandu's English newspapers.

One morning I was sitting there with Kyle when we saw an older Nepali wearing an old blue wool army overcoat and a black, conical Nepali hat, which looked something like a Shriner's hat. He was unshaven, and carried a bundle of papers and notebooks under one arm. Like many of us, he was a regular breakfaster at Aunt Jane's and, through the years, as I came and went, I would often find him there. He appeared well-educated and was always very friendly and polite.

Once I asked Gopal, one of the waiters, who this guy was. "Why, that's the Global Emperor!" exclaimed Gopal, with a sardonic smile.

"The Global Emperor?" I asked. "Does he breakfast here all the time? What an honor!"

"Certainly," replied Gopal. To him, it was no big deal to have the *Global Emperor* eating dinner or breakfast here every day. "He is a Rana, of the Nepalese ruling class, and a close relative of the King's. They take care of him, because he is a little loose up in the head!"

"Oh, really," I remarked! After a second's thought I decided it wasn't so strange after all, for him to be the *Global Emperor*, for the King (this man's cousin), believes he is the incarnation of Vishu, one of the all-powerful Hindu Trinity.

The Global Emperor, as we naturally called him, would often make little notes on napkins while having breakfast, and then give them to someone at the restaurant when he left. We got to know him quite well, and he would even wave to me on the street. I found him to be a very convivial person, intelligent and cheerful, and concluded he was preferable to many of the madmen who run other countries. One day he gave me this message.

> See my coronation films
> of the dates New Moon/Full Moon
> via Cinema Adhoc Committee
> Kathmandu and every Foreign Country.
>
> Worship picture of God
> Count the name of God up to eight hours
> Follow picture order.
> Arrest every criminal fit to work.
>
> From!—his Majesty the Great
> Vishosamrat Chakravrah Kaja
> Almighty King—God Vishnu
> Sri Panch Boda Mahraj Douraj
> Bhagwannn Travokyo Birbikram
> Shah Dev God Vishnu!
> Global Emperor Military Dictator
> Patron of the Globe

This was the message passed on to me by the Global Emperor, Military Dictator, and Patron of the Globe, and I thought I ought to let the world in on it, just in case it contained something important that should be known. I have read it carefully quite a few times, searching for a possible secret message of hidden meaning, but could find none. The first stanza obviously (I think) refers to some coronation films of his, released through the "Cinema Adhoc Committee," of which there really is one in Kathmandu, theoretically controlled by the King. The second stanza is more cryptic, but I decided it was a reference to the curious Indian custom of taking a religious story, such as the story of Gautama Buddha or Lord Krishna, and putting it in a photograph-painting form. There would be a hundred or more pictures with captions, showing the story in chronological order. In a temple, visitors would walk around, following the story, and thus, the "Global Emperor" would have us follow his "picture order": presumably the story of how he came to be the Global Emperor. Such a picture order does not exist, as far as I know. The last stanza of his message is naturally his

27

celebrated title, and a long one it is, full of all kinds of Sanskrit-Hindu titles, common in use among Masters of the Age, God-Kings, and the like.

§§§

As I cruised the trekking shops of Kathmandu looking for information on our forthcoming climb, I met a number of the local mountaineers, but none were as colorful as an Australian named John. On several afternoons, John and I went into the local bar and drank chang (a fermented millet-barley beer, popular among the Tibetans and other Nepali). John was husky and rugged, not conventionally good-looking but, like so many mountain climbers who take the sport very seriously, he seemed to have a lot of pent-up energy which gave him a tough mien. He had thick, black hair, and dark eyebrows that almost grew together across his forehead. He possessed a wealth of information about Nepal, the Himalayas and Tibet. One of his favorite pastimes was talking about the lore of the Himalayas over his chang.

John would get into horrible, stupifying drunken binges, in which he became quite violent. Fortunately, I just heard about them rather than actually seeing him in such a state. His violent binges took place when he was drinking one of the popular brands of Nepalese hard liquor such as Kukri Rum, "Joney Wine," (a whiskey of sorts with a label that was cribbed directly from Johnny Walker Red Label), or the local home made liquor: Roxshi. I did enjoy drinking a few changs and swapping stories with him on occasion.

"You know," said John one day, as we drank, "according to Nepali legend, Kathmandu was covered by a lake known as the Lake of Snakes. One day Manjusri, a demi-God from the north, was meditating on the top of some mountain around here and looking out over the lake. He suddenly decided to free the "Valley of the Lake," and, taking his great sword, he cut the mountain in half at the southern end of the lake. The lake emptied into the plains of India, taking all the snakes with it. The Gorge of Chohbar, through which the lake ran, is today a place of pilgrimage and is not far from Kathmandu!"

"Oh, I remember," I said, "We passed it on our way into Kathmandu from the border."

John went on to tell me some of the interesting history of Nepal. "Very little is known about Nepal before the thirteenth century. About as far back as we can go is the birth of Gautama Buddha in about 560 B. C., in the marshlands of Southern Nepal. It was known as Kapilavastu back them, but is now called Lumbini. Nepal only consisted of the Kathmandu Valley in Buddha's time—a state of affairs which lasted until the eighteenth century. Anyway, as a young man, Buddha and his followers would journey from Kapilavastu to "Nepal" as the Kathmandu Valley was called. Buddha seemed like the Kathmandu Valley and its people, who were supposedly descended from the demi-God Manjusri. One legend has it that the temple of Swayambu was created when he turned over his rice bowl when he died..."

"That's interesting," I murmured.

"Nepal has a fascinating history," continued John, gesturing to the bar maid for a flagon of chang. "Most Nepalese before the thirteenth century were of Mongolian-Tibetan stock, such as the Gurkas and the Sherpas. When the Muslims invaded India in the eighth century, Hindus began to pour into the rough foothills of the Himalayas. The present ruling families of Nepal stem from the Rajputs who fled to Nepal when they were defeated by the Mohammedans in 1303 at the battle of Chittor in Rajastan. Since then, there has been a considerable blending of these Aryan Hindus and Mongolian-native Hindus and Buddhists.

"Another interesting episode in Nepal's history was when the Gurkas invaded Tibet in the 1790's. They took quite an impressive army with them into Tibet and sacked Lhasa. Then a Chinese army began to chase them. They headed back for Kathmandu, but got caught on a high pass in a snowstorm. They were in pretty big trouble because a large Chinese Imperial Army was on their tail (Tibet was part of China at that point), plus they had run out of food. However, they had a big yak train, which was loaded down with gold, silver, silk and other loot from Lhasa.

"Well, they were starving, but these Gurkas were Hindus, and Hindus, as you know, are absolutely forbidden to eat beef. They turned to a Hindu priest who was with them, and asked him to decide for them whether a yak was a cow, or what? Well, do you know what that Hindu priest decided? He decided that yaks were a type of deer, and therefore they could eat them! Hah! Deer!" John laughed uproariously over that and I joined in. We were both pretty drunk by now. Yaks are, in fact, just big, shaggy cows, yet even today, it is okay to kill a yak in Nepal, but not a cow.

"So they ate some yaks, survived, and headed for

Kathmandu. The Chinese came after them, of course, and forced them to terms. That was one reason why the Nepalese made a treaty with the British, because they wanted to get some help in their problems with the Chinese." John ended our evening by confessing over his last beer that he was a "hopeless Himalayophile!"

§§§

Kyle and I often rented bicycles and rode out to the nearby towns of Patan, Baktapur, or other places in the Kathmandu Valley. Among the many sights to see in Kathmandu and environs are the Durbar Square Palaces and the Palace of the Living Goddess. The Living Goddess is a young girl who is chosen to live as a goddess until she menstruates and then is cast out to become just another mortal like the rest of us (except, of course, for the King of Nepal, who claims to be an incarnation of the Hindu God Vishnu and ofcourse the Global Emperor...). I have been told that she ofmay marry afterwards, but it is considered bad luck, so they never do. Rather, because they often have no other way of making a living, the ex-goddesses often become prostitutes, wandering the streets of Kathmandu (not what we generally imagine happens to former gods or goddesses)!

The Hanuman Doka is the old Royal Palace and is located in Durbar Square near the Palace of the Living Goddess. Engraved into the wooden walls and trestles of some of the temples in Durbar Square are some very erotic carvings, calculated to make even the most sophisticated person blush.

To the north, of course, is Swayambu, the Bowl of Buddha, built as a replica of Buddha's overturned bowl. Swayambu is said to be a good example of "geomancy," the art of sculpting the landscape to engineer what is called the *World Grid*. Much as Britain has megalithic sites or man-made hills over "power spots," Swayambu is said to be such an artificially created hill over a "power spot." It is sacred to both Buddhists and Hindus, and inhabited mostly by aggressive monkeys. It is unwise to have a picnic lunch up there, as the monkeys will swipe it from you right under your nose. If you resist their marauding, you are apt to get bitten.

Three miles to the east is Pashupatinath Temple, built in 1692, and one of the most famous of all Hindu shrines. Inside is a "Lingam" of phallus-shaped stone, sacred to

Hindus amd symbol of the Hindu deity Shankar, also known as Shiva. However, this is so sacred that non-Hindus are not allowed to enter. Pashupatinath is known as the Benares of Nepal, and it is here that there are cremation ghats (platforms), for the cremation of the dead along the Bagmati River.

A mile further east is Bodhnath Stupa, the highest Buddhist Stupa in the world. Many Buddhist monks live here, and there is quite a colony of Tibetans. The Stupa is famous for its pairs of eyes that stare at you from the four sides of the shrine. Even farther to the east is Bakatapur, also called Bhadgaon, a charming old city with its own Durbar Square and lots of temples.

Patan is back to the west of Kathmandu, has a Durbar Square, and outranks any other city in Nepal for elaborate medieval temples and monuments. There are no less than 1,400 Buddhist monasteries and Hindu shrines in Patan. Not to be missed are Hari Whamkara and the Vishvanath temples in the main square, and the Golden Temple or Hiranya Varna Mahavihar off to the northeast of the Durbar Square. Any way you look at it, there's lots to do and see around the exotic valley of Kathmandu. It's no wonder that it is becoming the major tourist destination in Central Asia.

§§§

Nepal is one of the abodes of the legendary Abominable Snowman, the Yeti; a tall, hairy, man-like ape that apparently lives in the remote mountain fastnesses of the Himalayas and Tibet. It has gained a certain amount of fame in the past fifty years, but while many stories and myths have been collected, not much in the way of "hard" evidence can be found, except for footprints. A hand and scalp of a Yeti, which may or may not be authentic, exist in an accessible monastery near Mount Everest. On one of my treks near Mount Everest, I explored one area of the remote Himalayas where Yetis, the locals said, abounded. You'll hear more about that in a later chapter.

One of the great mysteries of Central Asia that I had wanted to unravel is that of certain secret societies and legends of secret cities and powerful "Masters" that inhabited them. Tales of these mysterious groups and places are contradictory as well as bizzare. There was the "Abode of the Immortals" in western Tibet, said to be the headquarters of "The Great White Brotherhood," the

"Sacred City of Shambala" in the Gobi Desert and the "Underground University of Agartha," probably on the border of Nepal and southeastern Tibet.

Were all of these places the same? Did any of them even exist? My researches into the esoteric lore connected with each turned up many surprising "facts" which will be slowly uncovered throughout the book. My search for the "Abode of the Immortals" was to take me to Western Tibet. My search for Shambala was to take me to the Gobi Desert, and my search for Agartha was to lead me the Mount Kanchenjunga area of Nepal.

The occult groups of Agartha and Shambala are well known in the literature of Central Asia, and among students of the occult. Little other esoteric information is as confusing as the stories of the "Hidden Kingdoms" of Shambala and Agartha.

Information on these two groups is widely varied and contradictory. In some texts, Agartha and Shambala are said to be underground cities, or kingdoms, somewhere in Central Asia where occults live and study. Shambala is sometimes said to be north of Lhasa, possibly in the Gobi Desert, and other times said to be somewhere in Mongolia, or else in northern Tibet, possibly in the Changtang Highlands. Agartha is said to be south of Lhasa, perhaps near the Shigatse Monastery, or even in Northeast Nepal beneath Mount Kanchenjunga, the third highest mountain in the world. Occasionally it is said to be in Sri Lanka. Both have been located inside the "Hollow Earth." Shambala and Agartha are sometimes said to be at odds. In some traditions Agartha is the right-hand path, the "white occult" group, while Shambala is the left-hand path, or "black occult" group. Also, it is conversely said that Agartha is occupied by dark forces and Shambala is the abode of the "Masters of the World" and a place of goodness. [38, 33, 29]

While in Nepal, I turned my attention to the Agarthi. Early tales of Agartha reached Europe with the publication of an obscure book in French, "*Mission de l'Inde en Europe*," by Saint-Yves d'Alveydre, published in Paris in 1885. Later Ferndinand Ossendowski, a follower of Gurdjief, published his book, "*Betes, Hommes et Dieux*" (Beasts, Men and Gods) in Paris in 1924. Using these two sources, "*The Dictionary of Imaginary Places*" has this to say about Agartha:

"AGARTHA, an ancient kingdom in Sri Lanka (although some travellers say that it is located in Tibet). Agartha is remakable mainly because visitors are known to have crossed it without ever realizing it. Unaware, they have probably gazed on the famous University of Knowledge, Paradesa, where the spiritual and occult treasures of humanity are guarded. Unaware, they have walked through Agartha's royal capital, which houses a gilded throne decorated with the figures of two million small gods. Perhaps they have been told (and now cannot remember) that this divine exuberance holds our planet together. If a common mortal ever angered any of the two million, the divine wrath of the gods would be immediately felt: the seas would dry up and the mountains would be powdered into deserts.

"It is probably useless to add (again, visitors will have seen them and forgotten) that Agartha holds some of the world's largest libraries of stone books and that its fauna includes birds with sharp teeth and turtles with six feet, while many of the inhabitants have forked tongues.

"Forgotten Agartha is defended by a small but powerful army, the Templars or Confederates of Agartha."[68]

Agartha would appear a rather fanciful lost city, though many persons attest that it really exists, and most probably in Tibet or Nepal, rather than Sri Lanka. In the last hundred years, a number of travelers and mystics and claimed to have visited Agartha, or at least have had some contact with them.

The Agarthi have been associated with one of the "persons" who claims to be the "King of the World," in a similar, but not so harmless, way as the Global Emperor of Aunt Jane's restaurant in Kathmandu. This "King of the World" is known as the Metatron and the "High Lord of Agartha," the underground kindgom and university beneath Tibet, with its many entrances in the monasteries of Central Asia, and around Mount Kanchenjunga.

According to Ray Palmer and Richard Shaver (author of the "Shaver Mysteries" published in *Amazing Stories* magazine in the late forties), the "Ruler of Agarti" was a Venusian who "came here ages ago from the planet Venus to be the insturctor and guide of our then just dawning humanity. Though he is thousands of years old, his appearance is that of an exceptionally well-developed and handsome youth of about sixteen" (*Amazing Stories*, May 1946).

While the "King of the World" may be here to save us (from ourselves, presumably), other accounts have the Agarti as an evil force of Black Magicians bent on causing chaos and suffering. The Shadow of Metatron is known as a dark force and is identified with Sar Ha-Olam, or Satan, whose name is derived from that of the ancient Egyptian God of the Underworld & evil, Set. [20, 23]

Agartha is also associated with the "Hollow Earth" theories of certain groups. In these, the inside of the earth, which is thought to be hollow, contains the "sacred territory of Agartha." In Nazi occult doctrine, it is here that the Nazi "Supermen" lived. The Nazis hoped to contact these Superman, who were a central part of their own "Hollow Earth/Eternal Ice" ideology. [29]

The theory of the hollow earth was first proposed by the famous seventeenth-century astronomer Sir Edmund Halley, who discovered Halley's comet. He conceived the hollow earth as being composed of three concentric worlds, each supporting life.

Later, other "hollow earth" theories became popular. One slightly warped hollow earth idea—which included the belief that mankind was already living inside a hollow earth whose sun was a ball in the center: half dark, half light—was an important part of Nazi doctrine. This idea was first proposed by Cyrus Reed Teed of Utica, New York, in the eighteen sixties and has steadily gained popularity over the years in certain occult circles. The Nazis apparently believed in two seemingly contradictory ideas: that their Supermen lived in the hollow earth, and that we were already inside the hollow earth. [49]

The Nazis went so far as to make German scientists working for the Third Reich officially declare their belief in a hollow earth. It is a recorded historical fact that the Nazi admiralty sent a naval expedition to the island of Ruegen in the Baltic in April 1942, with the purpose of taking pictures of the British fleet by aiming their cameras upward and shooting across the center of the hollow earth! [49, 29]

Today, many occultists still believe that the earth is hollow and that it is "the Sacred Territory of Agartha," though the idea that we are already inside it seems to have died with World War II. They also believe that most UFOs come from the center of the earth, out of holes at either pole. These holes, entrances into Agartha or the hollow earth, are known as "Symmes holes," named after another American, John Cleves Symmes, who also was keen on a hollow earth and thought it was inhabited. [49] Almost without exception, persons who have formed cults and relayed information about a hollow earth claim to have been in contact with "intelligent astral entities" or "Masters" in Tibet or sometimes outer space, that relay this information to them. Assuming that the earth isn't hollow, which I believe we can safely do, I surmise that these poeple are being purposely misled, probably by the Agarthi themselves through telepathic communication and perhaps mediumship.

If, therefore, Agartha is not the kingdom in the center of the earth, what, then, is it? Here are some more theories:

According to some esoteric traditions, Agartha was the great initiatory university of Asia, and had a huge underground library and a network of tunnels beneath Tibet. In the past, so-called emissaries from Agartha have made fantastic claims: that the population of Agartha was twenty million people and that the library there has information that has been stored for more than fifty thousand years. Supposedly, anyone can study at Agartha and many people are said to drop out of the school, becoming low-life fakirs and fortune tellers. However, no textbooks are allowed to leave Agartha. [33, 38, 20]

In 1947, "Prince Cherenzi Lind, Maha Chohan (Great Leader) and Supreme Regent of the Realm of the Agartha" came to France to meet Michel Ivanoff, an occultist of the period. In Paris, the magazine *Point de Vue* interviewed the "Maha Chohan" (also known as Kut-Humi, or Kuthumi, as he liked to call himself), who claimed to be the director of the Great White Brotherhood as well as the "Supreme Regent of the Realm of Agartha." In the interview, he said that there was an underground kingdom in Tibet, linked with nearly all the monasteries, and that he would personally guide an expedition to Agartha in August of 1948, which he would also finance. He claimed that all beings in the realm of Agartha have their own luminosity, although flash bulbs had to be used to photograph the Maha Chohan. He refused to work any miracles on the grounds that one is never enough (quite true!) and promised to meet with some distinguished French physicists of the day to discuss nuclear physics, but instead disappeared.

He also claimed to wear the *Ring of Genghis Khan* in which was a hydrogen atom "capable of blowing up the whole world"! When the French investigator Robert Charroux gave the Agarthi some bad press for their imaginative claims and unfulfilled promises, he was officially condemned to death by them. Certainly not a very tolerant and loving attitude for the "Masters of the

World," as the rulers of Agartha like to call themselves. [33]

According to various traditions, Agartha has been located in various places besides the hollow earth: in Sri Lanka, Afghanistan, and other places; but I believe that it is most reliably thought to be near the Tibetan border of Sikkim and Nepal. Possibly it is in Tibet, in the region of the Shigatse and Kwen Lun monasteries which are on the Bhramaputra river, to the southwest of Lhasa, or perhaps closer to the Nepal border just near Mount Kanchenjunga, or even beneath it, which could place it in northeastern Nepal. [38, 49, 33]

The area around Kanchenjunga is highly sensitive, being the corner of several international boundaries: those of Tibet/China, Nepal, and Sikkim/India. It is a forbidden area, and trekkers are not allowed into it, though coming into the base area of Kanchenjunga could be possible by trekking up the Arun river valley, which is a rather unique and mysterious area in itself, as it is so deep, and maintains an almost tropical climate even into Tibet. It is largely unexplored and is inhabited by a very wide spectrum of cultural groups. A good place to view Kanchenjunga is Darjeeling, an even better is Gangtok in Sikkim, a formerly independent state taken over by India in the nineteen-seventies.

The Kanchenjunga area is also well-known for Yetis, which adds to the mystery. The famous anomaly investigator John Keel relates in his interesting book, Jadoo,[72] several incidents with Yetis around Mount Kanchenjunga. At one point Keel comes to a strange valley where his guide acts frightened and points to one of the many flowers growing all throught the valley. "It was shaped like a monk's hood, big and hollow, with a tough stem digging into the bare rocks. Unable to understand what he was trying to say, I picked it and started to smell it. He jerked it out of my hands and stomped on it. Suddenly I realized what was wrong.

"Those flowers were nightshade, the poisonous plant whose scent can be fatal! The whole valley was filled with them. We were probably already breathing the dangerous pollen." This "Valley of Death" around Kanchenjunga may be symbolic of Agartha; dangerous and deceptive.

In addition, several legends relate to the idea that the entrance to Agartha is beneath Kanchenjunga. This would be supported by certain Theosophical literature, which seems to locate Agartha in this vicinity. The great Russian explorer and mystic Nicholas Roerich speaks about the mysteries of Kanchenjunga in his story *Treasure of the Snows* in 1928.[69] "In the foothills of the Himalayas are many caves and it is said that from these caves, subterranean passages proceed far below Kanchenjunga. Some have even seen the stone door which has never been opened, because the date has not arrived. The deep passages proceed to the Splendid Valley."

Based on the information I've been able to dig up, my opinion is that the "lost city" of Agartha is either located in caves in the Arun Valley, to the north side of Kanchenjunga, or beneath the Tashi Lumpo monastic citadel in Shigatse, which is less than a hundred miles away. It is also quite possible that both these places are connected by a system of underground tunnels, and this is certainly part of the myth. [29, 21, 38]

§§§

What is the truth about Agartha? Kingdom in the Hollow Earth, gigantic underground University of Enlightened Masters, or cave community of wayward Indian and Tibetan Occultists out to decieve the world? Maybe all or none of the above? Who knows? Yet, my research on the secret societies of Central Asia was certainly not over. I was very interested in the idea that there was indeed a group of enlightened "Masters" who were working hard for the betterment of mankind. Some secret brotherhood of sorts if you will. Did a "Great White Brotherhood" of loving, compassionate and advanced egos exist? I hoped so.

I was sitting with some friends at a cafe in Kathmandu, and we were discussing such topics. Outside, it was raining, turning the wonderous, magical, twisted streets of the city into slick alleys of mud. A tall Alaskan biologist named Mark, who claimed to be a Tibetan Buddhist, had been talking with another friend, Alan, and me about the Shambalists and the Agarthi.

When the rain stopped, and the sun, nearly instantaneously, began to shine, the three of us stepped out onto the streets. In Durbar Square, Alan, a bearded traveler from California, said, "Hey, guys, let me buy you an ice cream cup."

The three of us strode across the square, past a dancing bear with a rope through its nose that danced while his owner, a young man in buckskins and a wool jacket, passed a tin cup for change. "Have you ever noticed the brand names of this ice cream that they sell on the street?" asked

Alan as he paid for our cups.

"Some of them do have funny names," I agreed.

"Yeah, they're too much," laughed Alan, sticking some vanilla ice cream in his mouth. "Look at this brand: 'Shital'. With the other names like 'Baraf' and 'Anil', I think they're trying to say, 'Have some and then find a bathroom—quick!'"

We all laughed hard at the truth of that. Perhaps the Nepal Dairy Association and the private entrepreneurs did have a wild, satirical sense of humor. At any rate, the sunny warm days of Kathmandu couldn't help but put a smile on your face!

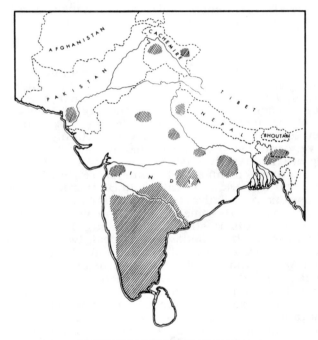

DISTRIBUTION OF MEGALITHS IN INDIA

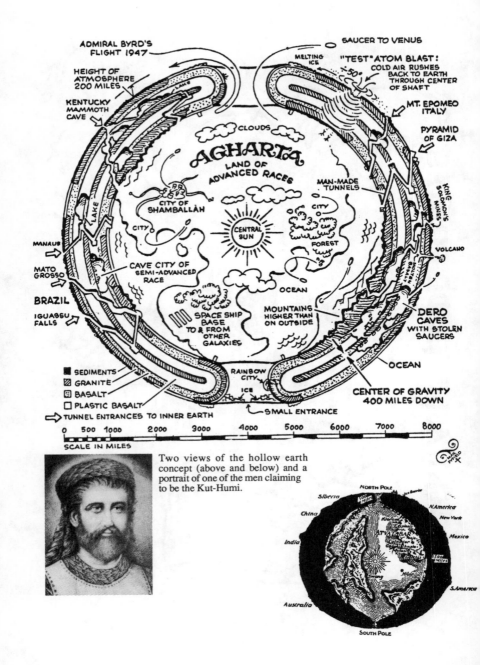

ADMIRAL BYRD'S
FLIGHT 1947

SAUCER TO VENUS

MELTING
ICE

"TEST" ATOM BLAST:
COLD AIR RUSHES
BACK TO EARTH
THROUGH CENTER
OF SHAFT

HEIGHT OF
ATMOSPHERE
200 MILES

KENTUCKY
MAMMOTH
CAVE

MT. EPOMEO
ITALY

PYRAMID
OF GIZA

CLOUDS

AGHARTA

LAND OF
ADVANCED RACES

MAN-MADE
TUNNELS

CITY

KING
SOLOMON'S
MINES

CITY OF
SHAMBALLÀH

CITY

CENTRAL
SUN

VOLCANO

MANAUS

FOREST

MATO
GROSSO

CAVE CITY OF
SEMI-ADVANCED
RACE

OCEAN

BRAZIL

DERO
CAVES
WITH STOLEN
SAUCERS

MOUNTAINS
HIGHER THAN
ON OUTSIDE

IGUASSU
FALLS

SPACE SHIP
BASE
TO & FROM
OTHER
GALAXIES

OCEAN

SEDIMENTS

GRANITE

BASALT

PLASTIC BASALT

TUNNEL ENTRANCES TO INNER EARTH

RAINBOW
CITY

ICE

CENTER OF GRAVITY
400 MILES DOWN

SMALL ENTRANCE

0   500 1000   2000   3000   4000   5000   6000   7000   8000

SCALE IN MILES

Two views of the hollow earth
concept (above and below) and a
portrait of one of the men claiming
to be the Kut-Humi.

NORTH POLE

Siberia

China

N.America

New York

India

ATVATABAR

Mexico

Australia

S.America

SOUTH POLE

Above: Adolf Hitler, who organized searches for the entrances to the Hollow Earth

Right: A sketch of Marshall B. Gardner's concept of the inside of the earth

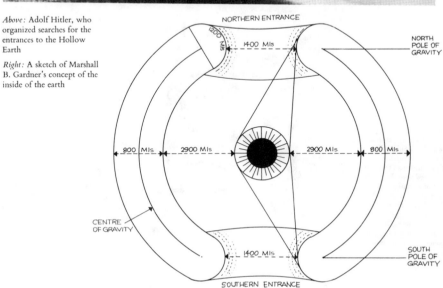

NORTHERN ENTRANCE

1200 MIs

1400 MIs

NORTH POLE OF GRAVITY

800 MIs 2900 MIs 2900 MIs 800 MIs

CENTRE OF GRAVITY

1400 MIs

SOUTH POLE OF GRAVITY

SOUTHERN ENTRANCE

Hitler believed the the earth was hollow and that by contacting special forces in Tibet and the Gobi Desert, he could conquer the world.

Three of the most important
photographs of yeti tracks.
Above: Eric Shipton's
picture showing the size
of the Snowman's footprint
compared with that of the
boot of a climber, and
(*far right*) a line of tracks
taken during the same
expedition in 1951. *Right:*
Magazine cutting showing
the first ever photograph
taken of a yeti footprint.

FOR COMPARISON WITH THE IMPRESSION OF A BEAR'S
FOOT: AN "ABOMINABLE SNOWMAN'S" FOOTPRINT
PHOTOGRAPHED BY THE LATE MR. FRANK SMYTHE IN
THE HIMALAYAS IN 1937.
(*From "The Illustrated London News" of November 13, 1937.*)

Chapter Three

TREKKING IN NEPAL:

HIDDEN VALLEY AND THE LOST KINGDOM OF MUSTANG

...a pilgrimage distinguishes itself from an ordinary journey by the fact that it does not follow a laid-ouplan or itinerary, that it does not pursue a fixed aim or a limited purpose, but that it carries its meaning in itself, by relying on an inner urge which operates on two planes: on the physical as well as on the spiritual plane.
—Lama Anagarika Govinda

Over the many days Kyle and I "hung out" in Kathmandu, partying, resting, sightseeing, and meeting people, we continued to make our preparations for the climb in the Himalayas. We hired a guide named Purna, a short wiry Nepali of Aryan (as opposed to Sherpa/Mongolian) descent, who would take us to "Hidden Valley" near Dhaligiri, and around the Thorong Pass in the Kingdom of Mustang. Purna, it turned out later, was more of a cook than a guide, but at least he did know his way to the Hidden Valley. Purna got us two porters, friends of his, and we bought some provisions in Kathmandu.

We learned, to our dismay, that we hadn't needed to bring all that climbing gear that we'd lugged halfway across the world, for the city of Kathmandu is absolutely chockful of climbing gear and trekking shops that will sell or rent you just about any kind of mountaineering gear you could ever desire or need, at a fraction of the price that you would buy it for in America or Europe.

Indeed, Nepal is the cheapest place in the world to buy climbing equipment, mostly because it is dumped by expeditions, and the Sherpas turn around and sell the gear that expeditions have given them. Nepalese government policy is that expeditions can bring in just about anything they want, duty free, but they can't take it out again.

The only things that are really worth bringing from home are down jackets and sleeping bags, and a pair of good boots that fit well.

We left Kathmandu for Pokhara on a bright Tuesday morning, heading south for an eight-hour drive to Nepal's second city. Pokhara is set in a lovely valley at the foot of Mount Anapurna, one of the highest mountains of the world. You are much closer to the mountains in Pokhara than in Kathmandu, and the early morning view of the towering mountains above Lake Phewatal is spectacular. Machapucre, a magnificent fish-tail mountain, can also be seen towering above the city on a clear day.

Most people stay at the lake where a small tourist colony has sprung up, with lots of little hotels, restaurant and shops. You can stay in the town as well. It has a bazaar that rambles along through town for a good four miles, and makes for interesting shopping. Treks to Anapurna sanctuary and the Kali Gandaki Valley all tend to start with a slow walk through town.

We checked into the Snowland Hotel just by the lake, and had "buff steak"; a chewy water buffalo steak, served with onions, french fries, and salad. We decided to start our trek around Anapurna by going up the Manang Valley first, across Thorong Pass to Muktinath, and then down the Kaligandaki valley to Tukche, where we would ascend to Hidden Valley, and make our climb from there.

To trek up the Manang Valley, one actually starts from Dumre, a few miles out of Pokhara, toward Kathmandu.

It was a hot autumn day as we started along the trail. Kyle and I went ahead, with the porters and Purna following. We wore shorts, T-shirts, and our clunky hiking boots, and each of us carried sixty pounds or so on our backs. Wiping the sweat off my brow, I gazed up at the mountains, all white and icy. Anapurna looked like a big bowl of vanilla ice cream, twenty-six thousand feet high. The thought made me feel a little cooler.

Trekking, like hitchhiking, takes a lot of time. The walk to the village of Manang itself, at the end of the valley, would take a good ten days. Our first night we stopped at Turture, where we read this curious comment in the register book:

"Captain Zap Fan Club meet for a Solidarity meeting with 'Popular Democratic Yeti Liberation Front' in the Demilitarized Zone next Tuesday of the Full Moon!" It appeared that a trekker from California was a few days ahead of us.

For the next few days, we found ourselves trekking through rice fields. Twice a day we would stop for a meal with our porters. We would eat a huge plate of rice, known in Nepali as "baht", with a generous ladle of lentil soup, known as "dahl", served with some vegetables, perhaps spinach and potatoes, on it and these were called "subji" (vegetables). This menu was the staple diet of trek- kers and Nepali alike, and was called dahl-baht-subji. It is also possible to get such luxuries as eggs, chicken, flat chapati bread, popcorn, and oatmeal porridge. I carried with me a gigantic can of peanut butter as a treat for the trail which I had purchased in Kathmandu. Also, we carried some special freeze-dried foods for our ascent to Hidden Valley and subsequent climb.

At one point, we came to a river that needed to be crossed, and gratefully took a dip in the cool water, rinsing off the sweat from a few days' trekking. At night we would always be in some small town (we passed several every day) where we'd get a good night's sleep, and have a glass of roxshi, or their sour chang (Tibetan millet beer). Once you got used to it, it tasted pretty good and was almost a meal in itself.

At midday on our second day, we stopped for lunch along the trail while the porters went on ahead to have lunch at the next town. Kyle and I sat by a hollow tree eating biscuits and peanut butter along with a small pineapple we had bought the day before. A Nepali gentleman approached us. He was brown-skinned and well-worn, and his Aryan-Indian features stood out beneath his multi-colored peaked hat. He sat down near us and produced a small, four-string, hand-carved fiddle. Deftly he sawed a couple of tunes while we ate lunch. We shared what we had with him, and he was on his way.

That night we stayed in a small lodge in Bhote Alar, a small village along the Marsyandi Khola. Kyle and I had a glass of roxshi as the sun went down behind us. We were startled to realize that two pretty Gurung maidens were standing nearby, watching us. They stayed near us for a while, and we chatted amiably with them in our limited Nepali.

After a bit, they left. Shortly after dusk, I was standing in the yard just outside the small, two-story lodge where we were staying. Suddenly, I smelled something funny. Hmmm. It was perfume. I turned to see the two girls standing there, and with them was an older woman. Perhaps the village match-maker, I speculated. Kyle and I were asked to sit on a bench with the ladies, while a middle-aged Nepali named Rajit (who was staying at the lodge, and working for the Nepalese government on some kind of leprosy research project) acted as translator.

Our courtship was short: the girls wanted to know if we were married, how long we would stay in their village, and if we liked Nepali women. They were tall and cute, with bare feet. Their long black hair was braided down their backs; their cheeks were a natural red, and they looked very fresh and pretty. They were probably the chore women of the village, doing laundry and such tasks, and they were dressed in gray wool skirts, with brown aprons and white blouses; all rather old clothes, though clean.

Kyle and I made it quite clear to them that we were bachelors and weren't getting married for a while. We indicated that we did like Nepalese girls, and found them attractive. Then, we concluded our rather formal and curious introduction, and the women went their way.

Kyle and I had our dinner of dahl-baht-subji with a little soy sauce for luxury, and settled back to play cards and drink roxshi. The porters and our guide had gone to sleep. Suddenly, the women appeared again. We invited them to have some roxshi, and play cards with Rajit and us. Rajit was a pleasant fellow who spoke English well, and seemed to take to western ways. The girls declined to drink with us, but stood behind Kyle and me. Apparently, we were on our first date, but Kyle made it clear that he was not interested in any 'dating games'. I had had three roxshis by then, and was frankly a little tipsy. Standing behind me was the tallest and prettiest of the two girls. She asked us for a cigarette, which neither Kyle or I had. Rajit gave her one.

She stood very close to me, smoking her cigarette. I felt quite attracted to her and began absent-mindedly stroking her lower calf, which was bare. She didn't object, and I continued chatting with her and thoroughly enjoying myself. It began to get late, though, and I didn't see us becoming 'serious'. After all, we were all sleeping upstairs in one big room: three people were already crashed out up there.

Around midnight Rajit jumped up and said, "Time to go to bed." He pointed ot the girl whose leg I had been stroking, and said, "She goes with you!"

"What?" I sputtered. "Who, me? Where? You're kidding!"

"No, really," he said, "She will sleep with you in your bed tonight. Upstairs."

Well, I didn't see how that could work, but I supposed it was the Nepali way, at least in the mountains. No one else would mind, they said, and certainly not the charming lady. But, I just couldn't go along with it. "Uh, well, that's great," I stammered. "But, uh, not tonight, I think. Let's do it tomorrow night or something."

Rajit translated for the maiden, who said that was fine with her. We all said goodnight, and I went to sleep, feeling a bit guilty for having led her on.

The next morning we hit the trail bright and early. That

was one town I didn't want to spend two nights in!

A few days later, up the trail, we met some American Peace Corps Volunteers, headed the same way as we were. I told them the story and they were amazed that I hadn't spent the night with the young lady.

"You mean you didn't? Why not? You're crazy!"

I guess they were more savvy than I was about mountain women. I had had visions of something like a shotgun wedding the next morning. Anyway, I was more interested, at that point, in trekking than in getting into trouble.

§§§

I am glad I shall never be young without wild country to be young in. What avail are forty freedoms without a blank spot on the map?
—Aldo Leopold

I lay back at the top of a ridge, exhausted, and looked up at the clouds. We were higher now, and it was cooler, but I was sweating from the strain of the hike. We had been going six days now, and were getting near Chanche, and the narrow gorge that would open up into remote Manang Valley. The porters had gone up ahead, and Kyle and I decided to have a lunch of biscuits and peanut butter along with a handful of trail mix.

We had met another trekker earlier that day, who was on his way to Manang as well. He was an English man named Nicholas, and was traveling with a porter. Forty-five years old, or thereabouts, he had a distinct Oxford accent and sported a gray goatee. He came up the trail just as we started our lunch. "This looks like a good place to rest," he puffed, collapsing on the stone resting spot.

I examined the stone seat—it was a typical porters' resting spot: a bench dug out of the mountain slope, inlaid with flat stones to sit on and some Tibetan "Mani stones" along the back. Mani stones are flat stone slabs, chiseled with the common Tibetan prayer, Om Mani Padme Om, which possibly means "The Jewel Inside the Lotus". Often the prayer is carved as many as a dozen times into each stone.

The interesting thing about this resting spot was that it seemed particularly ancient. Such porter benches are a dime a dozen throughout the Himalayas, but this one had a huge banyan tree growing out of it, indicating that it was quite old. It looked so inviting that one could hardly help stopping here as one came up the trail. I remarked on how nice the resting place seemed.

"This banyan tree is a blessing, offering protection from sun or rain," declaimed Kyle poetically, taking a bite of peanut butter on a cracker.

"This resting place must be thousands of years old," I commented. "Who knows who's been through here?"

"Oh, probably a few Adepts, like Buddha and Jesus," said Nicholas.

"Buddha and Jesus?" exclaimed Kyle. "Do you really think so?"

"Well, who knows?" said Nicholas, biting into an apple. "But both probably trekked through here at one time or another. Buddha, as you may know, was born here in southern Nepal, just south of Pokhara in Kapilavastu, now known as Lumbini. Jesus studied in India for many years. He eventually trekked across the Himalayas on his way to Lhasa, in Tibet. He could have come this way, or possibly by the other side of Anapurna, up the Kali Gandakhi."

"That's pretty far out," I said.

"These mountains are very old, and so are the trails that go through them. Many people have walked here before us. We might be surprised at the persons who have trod these paths in the past. History is, as you Americans say, 'far out'."

We trekked on for some days, crossing the river occasionally on a rope suspension bridge, and then crossing back later up the trail. We hiked up and then down again, staying in some tea shop for half an hour for a rest and a cup of sweet buffalo or yak milk tea. Sometimes at night in the lodges (which were also tea houses), we would have some popcorn after our dahl-baht dinner. A glass of roxshi or chang would mellow us out, and help us stretch our muscles before we went to bed. In the morning, we would always check out our feet, looking for tender spots or blisters, and doctor them up.

Seasoned trekkers often become "back country doctors". The Nepalese know that trekkers usually carry a variety of medicines, so, often they asked the trekkers to fix up some young Nepali with a sore, a headache, or what have you.

When we arrived in the Manang Valley, we planned to stop for the night in Bagarchap. We had to show our trekking permits to the local 'checkpost', which was at Doripani, an hour or so before Bagarchap. There was a small apple orchard there, started by some Peace Corps Volunteer, and we had a couple of big, juicy apples.

Later, that night, just before going to bed, I went out onto the porch of the lodge in Bagarchap to admire the majestic view. The sky had changed from the cloudy mass it had been for the last few days, and was crystal clear. There was a beautiful view of the mountains, white and pure in the light of the waxing moon. I heard a melodic tinkling, and saw a small blue light floating down the path. The light turned almost perfectly along the winding, flagstone street of the village, and with it came the tinkling of a soft bell. I nearly fell off the porch!

Was I witnessing some fairy or even Tinkerbell herself taking an evening stroll through town...? Then a small yak appeared from the shadows, standing quietly with a bell around its neck. I followed the small light, a firefly—the first one I had seen in the Himalayas—down the path to a pasture, where I could do some tinkling myself.

The next day, Kyle and porters had gone ahead on a steep hill, when, to my horror, I was attacked by bees as I struggled up a steep section of the path. It was horrible! I was stung on my side. They just kept on attacking me. I ran uphill with my heavy pack while the bees dove at my face, got in my hair and clothes, and I swatted at them wildly. I ran for dear life, terrified, with the swarm chasing me. I stopped, gasping for breath, and they still kept on attacking. So, I ran on up the hill. Finally, they left, and I collapsed, crying from exhaustion and pain.

I found Kyle a little way up the trail, and he pulled out the stingers. "I don't know what I did to incur their wrath, but I hope I never do it again!" I said forcefully.

We trekked on through a pine forest and past a waterfall with a sign that said, "Stop here and rest awhile". We were nearing the end of the valley, and getting close to the village of Manang itself. We passed a Brazilian guy who told us there was a lot of snow on the pass, and that two trekkers had tried to make it through, got lost about a week ago, and were presumed dead.

We passed an airstrip as we entered the Manang valley. Manang is a strange place in Nepal, somehow set-off and more remote than other places in the country. Manang was given a special autonomous position by the Nepalese government, and Manangis have special passports that allow them to travel and trade much more freely than other Nepalis. As a result, many Manangis are very successful traders and importers, and quite rich, by Nepalese standards.

The CIA apparently built a small airstrip in Manang back in the sixties so that they could fly in supplies to the Tibetan Campa (a Tibetan word for "bandits") guerillas, who were fighting the Chinese when they weren't just being bandits. They were funded by the CIA, who would fly cargo planes for the Campas into Manang, which is very near the Tibetan border. This was stopped in the early seventies.

The Campas were well supplied in the past. They had the latest sophisticated American "Armalite" rifles, made out of graphite. Because they are so lightweight, they proved to be very handy in the Himalayas. (As a comparison, the Nepalese army was generally supplied with antique bolt action rifles.) The CIA was quite keen to harass the Chinese communists who had invaded Tibet in the fifties, and the Campas are feared throughout Tibet for their careless disregard for human life and property. So, the Campas seemed the perfect tool for the CIA.

They armed these bandits, who did indeed occasionally attack the Chinese. However, ultimately the Chinese were too much for the Campas to handle, so they began raiding the easier Nepali towns as well as villages in Tibet, making off with whatever they could. Eventually, with the Chinese army chasing them across Tibet, they headed for a pass into Nepal, where the Nepalese army was waiting to ambush them. As the first of the Campas came through the pass, the leader was shot dead by the Nepali army. The other Campas surrendered. Much better to be taken prisoner by the Nepalese than the Chinese, that was for sure! They were disarmed, thrown into prison, but later released. After all, they hadn't killed any cows (a crime punishable by death). That was pretty much the end of the Campas, or of one group of them, anyway. Some still exist as armed bands in remote areas of Tibet and the Himalayas.

"The CIA won't need this airstrip for awhile," I thought as we walked past it. I supposed Royal Nepal Airways would probably start service up to Manang when more tourists began to enter the area. Manang had just opened the spring before, and so far, only a few trekkers had made their way through.

We had a bath in the small, natural hot springs just outside the town of Chame that night, our first bath in a week. A day later, we arrived in Manang, where we rested for a day, and prepared for a two-day trek through uninhabited country, across the eighteen-thousand-foot Thorong Pass, and down to the pilgrimage center of Muktinath. We sunbathed on the windy terrace of our lodge, and watched the local Tibetans harvesting their barley and millet crop for the winter. That evening, I sat with Nicholas, the Englishman, who had arrived one day behind our crew. We chatted a little, and then Nicholas started to talk about the Bowl of Buddha.

"Buddha was born the son of a wealthy king in what is now Lumbini, Nepal," he said. "In those days, it was called Kapilavastu. His parents sheltered him from the painful truths of the rest of the world. He grew up hardly aware of pain, suffering, disease, and death. Eventually, he married, and lived the life of a healthy, loving, but sheltered prince. Then, one day, he saw an old man on the road who was begging. Looking around, he noticed a dead man, and a man who was very sick. He was very moved by this, and it sparked in him a need to understand why life should be thus; why so many people live lives of suffering. He cast off his princely title and robes, left his family, and began to wander Central Asia and India as an ascetic, searching for greater truths. So the story goes, he fasted for forty days beneath a Bodhi Tree."

Nicholas took a sip of tea. The fire lit one side of his face, casting moving shadows on his sharp but friendly features. He was knowledgable and interesting. When trekking through the Himalayas, one seems to make friends almost instantaneously, with fellow traverers and Nepalis alike. We would often take turns telling our stories around the fires in the frosty tea shops of the Roof of the World; Nicholas' stories were particularly interesting.

He went on, "The word Buddha, or Bodhi, is Sanskrit for intelligence, and so the word Buddhist means 'intelligent one'. As Buddha, (whose real name was Siddhartha Gautama) sat beneath the tree one day, he was given some milk by a maiden. It is also said by some people that he ate of the fruit of the Bodhi tree. At this point, Buddha had a revelation, and from there, according to tradition, the religion of Buddhism was formed. Buddha advocated what he called the middle path. He said that man should balance himself between the extremes. He should neither be an ascetic nor a hedonist. Life was yin and yang, and man should find a happy meduim. Balance is the key."

"Like a friend of mind in Montana used to say," I interjected, "Moderation in all things, including moderation."

"Yes, something like that, I suppose," Nicholas said, stroking his beard. "Buddha said that the way to attain liberation, enlightenment, or whatever you want to call it, is through the Eight-Fold Path, that is: correct belief, correct aspiration, correct speech, right action, right livelihood, right effort, right meditation, and most important, correct thought!

"Buddha eventually became a member of the Brahmic Brotherhood, one of the lesser brotherhoods under the auspices of The Great White Brotherhood. Jesus was a member of the Essene Brotherhood. Buddha was trained in Raja Yoga by the Brotherhoods, which exist secretly all over the world, and his focus was largely on brotherhood

51

between men, and loving your enemies and all people. Raja Yoga is a technique of consciously controlling your thoughts in a positive way, as Buddha suggested, so as to remove all negative thoughts from your mind, and pursue virtuous living."

"That's all very interesting," I said. "What happened to Buddha in the end?"

"Well," said Nicholas, with a mischievous smile, "In the end he died." Then he added, "One legend has it that the last thing he was asked was 'What is the meaning of life?' He took his rice bowl and turned it over in answer. Then he died. Buddhists like to say that the temple of Swayambu in Kathmandu is the representation of the Bowl of Buddha."

Nicholas was fingering a grey seed, about the size of a small walnut. "This is a seed from the Bodhi Tree," he said, handing it to me. "Here, take it." I held it tightly in my hand for a moment. It was the size of a cherry, hard and with little nodules on it. In the firelight it looked orange-brown. I put it in my pocket and went to bed.

We were up early the next morning and after a quick breakfast of Tibetan tsampa, a barley porridge, we were on the trail and heading to Thorong Pass. All day we traversed the hillsides on the eastern side of the valley. We trudged past some yaks and yak pastures, and then past a few buildings that were the last human habitation. After eating lunch in a yak pasture, we continued trekking up into the narrow glacial valley. Around us was a wall of six-thousand-meter peaks, including Chulu and Gundang.

Later in the afternoon we crossed a very nice, new covered wooden bridge across the river, and continued up the glacial scree (loose rock) to a hut on the slope of a glacial circ (a round bowl on the side of a mountain carved by a glacier). The porters and Purna made up a big batch of dahl-baht for everyone. We ate dinner, and then sat by the fire for a short time in the evening before going to sleep.

The porters were up at the crack of dawn, and started a fire in the small fireplace in the hut. It was bitterly cold, and I was reluctant to get out of my sleeping bag. I suddenly recalled quite fondly those sweaty hot days in the lower rice fields... "Here, Sahib," said Karka, one of our porters, handing me a cup of hot tea.

"Thanks, Karka," I said gratefully. I looked at him in the dim light of the early morning. His face betrayed a hard life of portering heavy loads through the mountains. He seemed a good person, I thought; rugged, cheerful, and hard-working. It was indeed a pleasure to trek with him, and I told him so. One of the great things about trekking in the Himalayas is meeting the people, and a fine lot they are. How I loved the mountains, and the people; the crisp air, and the spontaneity of the trail! In a rush of goodwill toward all, I wanted to give Karka a friendly squeeze on the shoulder, but he was already gone.

Several hot teas and some peanut-butter chapatis later, we all hit the trail, heading for the summit of the pass: straight up the scree and switching back and forth up the mountain, then traversing the ridges. We rested beneath a small ledge. I felt this was an ideal time to try the Bodhi Seed, so I stuck it in my mouth and began sucking on it.

We slowly slogged our way to the top, the last thousand feet or so on snowfields. It took us about three-and-a-half hours to go from the cabin to the summit, including our one, short rest. At the top of the pass, there was a large rock cairn (pile of stones), with Buddhist prayer flags flapping around it. We took off our packs, and prepared a quick lunch. Through the wind and cold, I gazed at the spectacular mountains, icy giants reaching to the clouds all around us.

We ate snacks: chapatis and peanut butter and "Nebico" (Nepal Biscuit Company) biscuits, and looked around. Purna and the porters who were carrying our climbing gear and food were getting cold, so they started down the other side to Muktinath. Kyle and I climbed a ridge for a good view of the white mountain to the south and some ice lakes at the base of it.

Kyle finally started down, and after lingering a few more moments at the summit, I started down myself. As I took the first few steps with my pack on, I suddenly felt a tingling sensation in the salivary glands on either side of my mouth. I felt a little light-headed, a feeling that sort of faded on and off as I walked down through the snow in the footsteps of Kyle and the porters who had gone ahead.

It seemed that the Bodhi Seed was starting to affect me. Looking around, the scene seemed more incredible, more beautiful than I had noticed before. The sky was unusually crystal clear, and the peaks to the north and south of me were like pure, white monoliths sticking straight up into the sky. I started to reach out and touch one—they seemed so close. I lost my sense of time and space and my mouth curved into a perpetual grin. Everything around me seemed so wonderful; so fantastic! Life itself became incredible. The fact that I was there made me want to jump up and down and shout with joy! Suddenly, I found myself lost in clouds that blew in from the south, and couldn't see anything. The trail was now loose scree, and quite steep. My walking was slightly impaired, and I knew I was liable to trip if I wasn't careful.

Shortly, I emerged from the clouds, and they were then above me. The district of Mustang lay before me. I saw brown rolling hills to the north: this was Tibet, the high plateau north of the Himalayas. To the west was the great Dhaligiri range, on the far side of the valley. Dhaligiri itself, the fourth highest mountain in the world, reared up into the deep blue sky like some gigantic pyramid. The colors of everything were unbelieveably intense, and shadows of clouds crossed the hills on the other side of the valley in front of me, causing an odd perceptual illusion of the hills being in motion. I had to keep watching the trail, occasionally glancing up at the scene to the west. Several times I stopped to look at the view with awe.

To the north, I could just see the forbidden citadel of Lo Mustang. A walled city, it was the former capital of the Tibetan Kingdom of Mustang, absorbed into Nepal some years ago, and made a restricted area by the Kathmandu government. It still has its king, and has changed little over the years. The French anthropologist Michel Peissel, who speaks fluent Tibetan, visited Mustang in the late sixties and wrote a book about his experiences. The country of Mustang projects out into China/Tibet, and is quite a sensitive area. Trekkers are not allowed to visit there.

As I got lower, the whole valley opened up, and I could see the green fields of Muktinath, a pilgrimage center for Buddhists and Hindus alike. There were still the peaks beyond, and the brown rolling hills of Tibet to the north. There was a strong contrast of colors, colors that seemed to vibrate and change hue. The deep blue of the sky, the clear white of the snows and clouds, the many shades of green on the cultivated fields, the light and dark browns of the valley and hills. Some day, I thought, I am going to die...At that moment, I felt I was ready.

"There you are, " shouted Kyle from the trail up ahead. "You were so far behind, I wondered what had happened to you. Muktinath is just down there, about an hour away."

I tried to speak, but my mouth was too dry. I took a drink from my canteen and then was able to say, "I feel kind of funny."

Kyle and I walked down together to Muktinath, where the porters and Purna were waiting for us. We checked into the Government Hotel, a large, clean, hotel-dormitory where we all spent the night. I didn't feel very hungry, so I stepped outside at dusk to look at the view.

Muktinath is perched high up on a ridge above the Kaligandaki Valley and commands a spectacular view. I stared out at the mountains on the other side of the valley. Clouds were sweeping through the valley to the north into

Tibet, as if it were some kind of freeway. The Kaligandaki does create some unusual weather patterns. In the morning, the air in Tibet streams out through this gap in the Himalayas, and then at about noon it starts to move back in again. The clouds were at the same altitude as we were at Muktinath, and they were streaming at great speed through the valley. They looked like an artist's vision of ghosts coursing through the air.

The next day, we went to see the ancient temple that, each year, many pilgrims trek through the Himalayas to visit. It was a standard, small, square pagoda-style building, and inside it, there was an old lady, who drew back a curtain to expose a rock fissure with a flame coming out of it; and we could hear running water inside it at the same time. This is a holy spot, because the four elements of fire, water, rock, and air come together here at the same time.

Muktinath is also part of Mustang, and because of the temple of the four elements, it is a holy spot for Tibetan Buddhists and Indian Hindus alike. This is about as close to Lo Mustang, the walled city, as one could legally go. I thought about traveling on the high ridges to reach the walled city, but there is a Nepali army garrison stationed there, and they would probably arrest me as soon as I was spotted in the city. There is really not that much to see in Lo Mustang, no mysteries that I know of; it was attractive to me simply because it was forbidden. There is something about places that you are not allowed to go to...you want to go! But for now, I was content with our trek so far and eager for the climb ahead.

Our time was running out. We needed to get to Tukche and up into Hidden Valley soon. We had been trekking two weeks now, and still had a lot ahead of us. We left that day for Jomoson, down on the floor of the wide Kaligandaki Valley, a town with a police post and an airstrip. There are flights to Jomoson from Kathmandu every few days. We also met another climber from Eugene, Oregon: Kevin, a big, blond-haired guy, who had done quite a bit of climbing in the Pacific Northwest, and was more experienced than either Kyle or me. He had been up to Thorong Pass with two friends who had planned to climb one of the six-thousand-meter peaks from the top of the pass. His friends had gotten sick, though, and now he didn't have anyone to climb with. We invited him to join our party, and go climbing in Hidden Valley.

§§§

In Tukche, we made our last-minute preparations for the ascent to Hidden Valley and the subsequent climb, we hoped, of a peak. Kevin hired a porter, and we started up into the mountains from the valley floor during mid-morning of the following day. The porters had an hour-and-a-half start on us, but the trail was easy to follow: steep switch-backs going straight up the sharp ridge to the west of the Kaligandaki.

It was cold. Clouds came in and we could hardly see the persons in front of us. When we finally came to the top of the hill, it was late afternoon. We had caught up with the porters some hours before. Purna found us a small yak hut to stay in, though we also set up our tents. We were cold and exhausted. It had been an especially hard day.

The next day was easier. We traversed up the slopes, and came over one ridge to a fantastic view of Dhaligiri and Tukche peak. We were heading for Dampus Pass, still twenty or so hours' trekking along the summer highland yak pastures, and then into glacial rock scree. We spent another night in a small summer hay hut, burning yak pies for fuel.

As the porters were cooking up our evening meal of rice and lentils, I took a short walk around the camp. Eagles soared above and below us. On the face of Tukche Peak, a twenty-three-thousand-foot ice monster directly across the steep valley in front of us, I could see a small avalanche roaring down. It went rumbling, booming down the side, causing a great cloud of snow which lasted for several minutes. It was a desolate, brutal, beautiful world, where, when the sun set and night came on, the cold became almost unbearable. Shortly after dark, we would climb into our sleeping bags, hoping to warm up. During the night, as I lay in my sleeping bag unable to sleep, I could hear more avalanches tumbling down the mountainside and thought about the adventures to come.

In the morning, I was awakened by the delicious aroma of hot chocolate, made by Karka. We had oatmeal for breakfast, and then our party of seven: Kyle, Kevin and I, plus Purna and the three porters, took off for the summit of Dampus Pass, and Hidden Valley. We reached the top of the pass at seventeen thousand feet, huffing and puffing, by three o'clock. As it was autumn, when there is less snow, the pass, fortunately, was not completely covered.

We continued down the valley to a small sod wall, near a stream, that was reasonably sheltered. Hidden Valley turned out to be rather desolate; an extremely cold and windy place. It was a high Himalayan valley surrounded by a number of peaks, including Dhaligiri, the fourth highest mountain in the world. The ground was a rolling tundra, with some grass visible where there was no snow. One day, we even saw a small herd of deer.

We quickly set up camp—three tents—in the shelter of the sod wall, and made a fire out of yak chips. We sent Karka down to the stream, about five minutes away, to get water in a pot. When he came back, there was already ice formed around the top—it was that cold! According to my map, our camp was at slightly less than seventeen thousand feet.

We stayed there for several days, acclimatizing ourselves to the altitude before attempting one of the peaks. Purna, our guide, was quite sick, and during the entire trip had been of questionable health. He certainly wasn't going to be doing any climbing with us, nor did he appear to want to. It was such a cold, desolate place, I could understand his reasoning. After all, he was only on this crazy trip for the money; he wasn't really having any fun.

There were several peaks around us that we could climb in one day from our camp. We walked around the valley on our two rest days. None of the peaks we were considering would be very difficult on a technical level, but the cold wind and altitude could be a problem. We estimated that about an eighty-five-mile-an-hour wind was blowing off the tops of these peaks. A climber could easily be picked up and thrown off the top, falling thousands of feet into the deep valley far below.

At night, as soon as the sun went down, it got bitterly cold. One night I stood outside as long as I could, watching the sunset. I was in all my wool clothing, and had on my down jacket, down vest, down hood, and wool cap as I watched the strangest wisps of snow and cloud come off the top of Dhaligiri. With the oranges and reds of the sunset, and the gathering dark blue of the night lighting up odd swirls of clouds that took off from the summit, it resembled a giant pinwheel. It was certainly very windy up there, I thought, but awesomely beautiful. Even with all those clothes on, I could only stand the freezing cold for five minutes or so, and then my shivering body forced me into my tent and sleeping bag.

The next morning, we got up early to make our ascent. We had chosen a peak on the other side of the valley that was over twenty thousand feet high. However, we needed an early start and it took us longer to get our act together than we had thought. It was nine-thirty by the time we had had breakfast and were ready to go. It would be just the three of us: Kyle, Kevin and I, on a day hike of sorts. But now it was too late to climb the higher peak on the other side of the valley, so we chose the closest peak to the camp, on a ridge just behind us; a sub-peak of Tukche, with an altitude of just under twentythousand feet.

With our day packs full of extra socks, mittens, food, water and film, we started on the climb. We hiked up the scree slopes back toward the pass, until we came to the snowline at about seventeen thousand five hundred feet. We hiked unroped for a while up the snow fields with our crampons on, until we came to a rock outcropping on the ridge we were following. At this point, we roped up, putting Kyle, the least experienced climber, in the middle between Kevin and me.

It was a steep climb up through this rock gully. I went first, not having to use any ice screws or other protection, and then belayed Kyle up. He, in turn, belayed Kevin. From the top of this rock-cliff, we found a vague snow trail that some other climbers before us must have made. We followed it up the ridge for a while, until we stopped for a rest. After a little water, and some trail snacks, we continued, this time with Kevin in the lead.

From here it was one long snowy hump to the summit, which we could now see. As Kevin and Kyle came over the hump, they were exposed for the first time to the back of the mountain, as the ridge was narrowing as we neared the summit. A sudden gust of wind, blew them off their feet, and sent them sliding over the snow to the edge of the ridge, where there was a drop-off of several thousand feet!

Still not directly in the wind as they were, I braced myself to stop them when the rope pulled tight. Fortunately, I didn't have to, as they were able to self-arrest with their ice axes. We continued on, a little shaken up, leaning hard into the wind. Several times a sudden gust of what Kevin estimated was an eighty-mile-an-hour wind would knock us off our feet. For a couple of hours we continued like this until we reached the summit.

The very last hundred yards or so to the top, we had to literally crawl on our hands and knees. The eighty-mile-an-hour wind blew constantly off the top as we neared it, making it impossible to stand and walk at the same time. Suddenly, we were on the summit! Kevin immediately sank his ice ax into the snow and ice, and tied himself off to it, giving himself about seven feet of rope to work with. Leaning heavily into the wind, he began snapping photographs as though there were no tomorrow. Kyle and I did the same, tying ourselves off to our own ice axes sunken in the snow as anchors. With great effort, I stood up, leaning about twenty-five degrees into the wind.

What a view! I was exhilarated! It was fantastic! Looking

straight east from our lofty throne, we could see the range of the Himalayas stretching out to the horizon. Directly before us, to the east, was Anapurna, a gigantic massif of rock and snow, a mountain we had just trekked around ten days before. In the distance, we could see Mt. Langtang, Mt. Everest, Gauri Shankar, Makalu, and the other peaks of eastern Nepal.

To the north was the Tibetan plateau, all brown and stark with the city of Lo Mustang in the distance. Dry barren hills rolled endlessly away, with occasional peaks, white and sharp, sticking up out of the plateau. Behind us to the west was Dhaligiri, still towering above us like some gigantic pyramid. To the south were the foothills of the Himalayas, Pokhara, Kathmandu, and even the plains of India in the distance. It was an exceptionally clear, beautiful day. I let out a scream of sheer joy as I looked out on the scene.

To my horror, however, I found that I had run out of film, and naturally I wanted some photos from the top. I had a fresh roll in my pack, and kneeling, took it out. It was quite a challenge to change film with an eighty-mile-an-hour wind blowing, and in sub-zero temperatures. I had to take my down mittens off. The film was very brittle, and kept breaking. Eventually I did get it loaded, though I lost about a third of the film.

There was a gigantic cornice at the top, and Kyle crawled over to look at it. When Kevin saw him crawling toward the edge, he cried out, "Are you crazy? Get away from the edge!" But Kyle was already there. In fact, it was quite a dangerous thing to do, as the cornice could have collapsed, and taken Kyle, plus possibly Kevin and I, since we were all roped together, with it.

We were on that summit for only about twenty minutes, and the time flew by fast. Then we began the descent, Kevin leading. It was much faster, though we still had to lean into the wind. We came to the rock-cliff, and Kevin descended, Kyle belaying him. I then belayed Kyle, and descended the gulley myself. We stopped for some pemmican and water, and continued. We returned to the camp at four thirty, and devoured endless cups of chocolate and a can of pineapple juice. After a good meal of rice, lentils, and potatoes, we retired to our tents.

I stood outside my tent for a few moments and looked at the clouds that were coming off Dhaligiri. It was a mountain's mountain. I was glad I was not up there in the ice and wind, on those steep faces. Many climbers had been killed on Dhalgiri, known as the Mountain of Storms, famous for its deadly avalanches. This had been enough for me.

Later, as I lay in my sleeping bag, I heard the sound of a massive avalanche sweeping down the mountain. I was safe and warm in my bag. It felt good to be alive!

§§§

It took us a few days to make our way back to Tukche and the Kaligandaki Valley. Our porters were pleased as punch to be leaving Hidden Valley, and, generally speaking, we were ready to move on, too. As we reached the summit of Dampus Pass again on our way out of Hidden Valley, the porters lit some incense at the small rock shrine on the very top of the pass. There were already some prayer flags and a few cairns up there. The porters said some prayers, lit the incense and soon we were back on the trail. It was interesting that the porters, who I believed were Hindus, would partake in this Buddhist ritual, but here in the Himalayas, no one seemed to distinguish between religious creeds very much—which was nice.

After arriving in Tukche, it took us another week to get back to Pokhara and then to Kathmandu, where, of course, we pigged out at the many restaurants around Durbar Square. I hadn't found any lost cities, but I had found something else. It seemed as if another part of my life had been completed. Coming to Kathmandu and climbing in the Himalayas had, in some way, been my lifetime goals up until now. My mind was now free to pursue things perhaps more difficult and important...

Chapter Four

CROSSING THE HIMALAYAS:

CALL OF THE YETI

Those Himalayas of the mind
Are not so easily possessed;
There's more than precipice and storm
Between you and your Everest.
　　　　　　　—C. Day Lewis

After a couple of weeks' rest in Kathmandu, Kyle flew back to the United States with Kevin. By then, I felt restless, ready for another trek. I wanted to go into the Langtang region, just north of Kathmandu, for a while during the winter. So, I promptly got a trekking permit and took off by myself into the mountains. I hoped to come into Yeti country and perhaps catch a glimpse of one of the fabled creatures.

I trekked for several days up the Trisuli Valley, with Langtang Peak, an icy, white giant, looming majestically over the Valley in the distance. I spent two nights in the town of Dumche at a little lodge, resting an ankle which I had slightly twisted one day on the trail and headed off the next day for the town of Shabru, but made poor time. I ended up spending the night in a small village just near Shabru, sleeping on the floor of a Tibetan family's house.

I had met a young Tibetan girl on the trail just as I entered the village, and she invited me to her home for tea. She was clean, well-groomed, and pretty. The house was a one-room, grass-hut dwelling, centered around a fire. The family had a mother in her late thirties, who always kept her breasts uncovered in order to nurse her youngest, an incredibly dirty child of two. The child seemed like a crawling germ dispensary; I was careful not to handle him or things that he touched, as thoughts of hepatitis, dysentery and other diseases raced through my mind.

Her other child was a boy of about seven who, like many children in this part of Nepal, was dressed in rags. He was a porky fellow and rather charming. He seemed quite fascinated by me, and would often exclaim, "Ah-gee-gee!" This, I supposed, was the Tibetan equivalent of "Gee whizz!" The father came in at dusk, a hard-working, woodcutter type who was quite friendly. I had two glasses

61

of chang, wincing at the sour taste, and kept my eye on the well-dressed teenage girl, who watched me with equal interest. To my dismay, she did not live there, but eventually left to go home. I waved her a reluctant farewell as I watched her go.

After a dinner of barley flour (tsampa) and potatoes, we all went to bed. The family took their clothes off and got under a pile of wool blankets and skins. There was absolutely no embarrassment on anyone's part. I slept in my sleeping bag. In the morning, after thanking them for their hospitality, and bargaining a little over the price of my stay, I was off. The mother made me some extra Tibetan breads, flat, fried pancakes, for the trip. It was a dismal cloudy day, not one that seemed very good for trekking.

Within an hour I came to Shabru, the last village before the town of Langtang. From Shabru to Langtang was a good two days' trekking. One long days' trek from Shabru was a cabin in the woods known as the Lama Hotel, and it was there that I headed, after a cup of tea in Shabru, to spend the night.

I trekked all day, stopping several times to rest and making tea once on my stove. I passed two New Zealanders on the trail, the only foreigners I had seen so far, and they said I had a way to go to the Lama Hotel, and that it was about an hour past the river, which I hadn't yet reached. I trekked on in the slow drizzle that was starting.

I came to the river as the light of day grew dimmer. I passed several good campsites, but had no tent. I figured that if things got bad, I could bivouac beneath a rock overhang, but then, it was probably only a little farther to the Lama Hotel...

I trudged on. It got darker and darker and started to rain in earnest. I got out my flashlight, but the batteries were dead; it must have switched on while in my pack. I had my poncho on, but by this time it was completely drenched. I plodded wearily on; it had been more than an hour since I had passed the river, the hotel couldn't be much farther!

By now, it was so dark I couldn't see the trail anymore, or even my feet. Gazing carefully through the darkness to the trail beneath me, I kept going. There was no place to camp, as I was on a steep hillside. I could hear a stream rushing down far below me, sometimes quite close. By using perhaps, some sort of ESP, I managed to stay on the trail and keep plodding along, my feet getting totally soaked. I had no choice. Several times I stumbled, but managed to catch my balance each time before falling. It was raining hard and I was miserable. Where was that damn hotel anyway!

I lost the trail once, and had to retrace my steps to find

it. Several times I came to a railing on the trail, and could hear the stream rushing on through a gorge several hundred feet below me... I was nearly about to give up—I couldn't go on like this, a blind man trekking through the Himalayas— when suddenly I thought I saw a faint light in the distance. It flickered and then was gone. My energy was renewed. Up ahead, I was sure, was a warm cabin and companionship. I staggered on blindly. The light was gone, but I knew that that cabin must be there. Suddenly, the light appeared directly in front of me, faintly illuminating a dark, wooded house.

The cabin was warm and filled to the brim with laughing, drinking Tibetans, hot food, hot drinks, a fire, and dry bunks. Raising their cups of chang (millet beer), the Tibetans were toasting each other and playing cards... they seemed only mildly surprised when suddenly the door burst open, rain and wind swept into the room and a dark figure stood in their doorway, staring in wonder at the scene. I had made it!

I staggered into the room and dropped my pack. "Come in! Come in!" they yelled in Nepali. Gratefully, I took off my poncho, and they took me to another room where there were bunks. The next thing I knew, I was drinking hot tea, eating potato soup and sitting by a fire. There were about a dozen men sitting around drinking and playing cards. It felt so good to be there, I almost wept. Never had I thought I would feel such joy at seeing the faces of these people around the fire. Life was indeed an adventure.

Two days later, I trudged, wet and tired, into Kyanjin Gompa. I had rested a day at the Lama Hotel, and then gone on the next day. At the end of Langtang Valley is the village of Langtang and just beyond it is a monastery, Kyanjin Gompa, with a new cheese factory built with aid from the Swiss. Glaciers poured down into the yak pastures at the end of the valley. A few miles up past the gigantic ice blocks that crashed down onto the snow-covered fields was Tibet, but to get there one had first to negotiate a relatively low pass at seventeen thousand feet or so.

I met an Australian couple, a blond-haired, bearded accountant named Adrian and his friend Brenda, an auburn-haired, attractive grade-school teacher. They had a guide and porters, and were going over the mountains to the lakes of Gosainkunda and the Helambu region. They invited me to go with them. We trekked back to Shabru, passing through the town of Langtang and the Lama Hotel. From Shabru, it was a steep climb through the mountains to a long, high ridge. We camped the night in a deserted Buddhist monastery at Phantang Ghyang. Then it was more uphill trekking in absolutely deserted country to the three alpine lakes of Gosainkunda.

In the summer there are normally quite a few Buddhist and Hindu pilgrims that come to these lakes, but in the winter they are completely deserted. We found three empty buildings to camp in, and, having brought some wood up with us from down below, built a fire. The lakes were quite beautiful, and at fourteen-thousand feet, rather high in the mountains. This is not really very high for the Himalayas; however, we were not in the main range, but the range just south of it. Just to the north of the last lake was a jagged peak of about seventeen-thousand feet in altitude.

That night, we watched the sunset, a beautiful deep-orange sunset that seemed to last for hours. It reminded me of the Tibetan tale of the demi-god Milarepa, who, after drinking at a tea house in Tibet, did not have enough money with him to pay the bill. As he didn't have a good reputation for fair dealing, the establishment refused to give him credit, and so did the other patrons.

Milarepa stood up in anger, drew his dagger, and threw it into the shadow of the setting sun, stopping the sun from setting. He proclaimed that if someone did not pay his bill, he would hold the sun where it was. For several days, the sun did not move, until finally the other patrons decided they had had enough, and paid his bill. Milarepa then took his dagger out of the ground, and the sun finally set.

So it seemed to us, that the sun would not set. Brenda, Adrian, and I sat there for what seemed hours, watching the deep oranges of the sky, meditating on the blending, beautiful colors, waiting for an end that, as we sat there, never came. I listened carefully for the call of a Yeti, figuring this must be a good spot for them....

Suddenly, we heard a loud, "Ga-wah-oomp!" Was this the call of the Yeti I had been waiting for? We were quite startled. The sound was very loud, but had seemed to come from within the lake. The ice and snow that completely covered the lake shook and vibrated with the noise. We walked over to the lake and stood mesmerized, and presently the sound came again, echoing along the hills. I half expected some huge prehistoric dinosaur to come bursting up out of the lake, but none did. There seemed to be a large gas reservoir beneath the lake that was gradually being released. Perhaps a natural fissure came in at the bottom of the lake, bubbling up in huge effervescence. After all, we'd heard that the lakes were supposed to be sacred, though we didn't know why.

After a cold night, with the "Ga-wah-oomp!" sound coming from the lake, we slogged on over a short pass, and then trekked across the mountains at around twelve-thousand feet for an entire day. The trail was good though there was some snow, but fortunately, Adrian and Brenda's guide knew the way. We eventually came to a large rocky overhang where we built a fire and camped for the night. The next day we walked on to Melemchigoan and spent the night; it was the first town we had seen in the five days since we had left Shabru.

It was one more easy day to Tarke Ghyang, the main town of the Helambu region, and home of a large Buddhist monastery. It was our fortune that we arrived at the town just as one of the elder women of the village had passed away, so we were able to witness her funeral celebration. As one Sherpa told me while I stood outside the Gompa, or large temple building, she had died three days before, and they were just about to celebrate. There would be eating, dancing, drinking roxshi and chang, and singing. It was to be a real party, and the family of the deceased was giving it.

"According to Tibetan tradition," the Sherpa told me, stroking his thin beard, and glancing toward the mountains to the north with his almond-shaped eyes, "The spirit, or astral body, of the deceased will enter the Bardo, or as I believe you call this in English, the Astral Plane. For forty days she will wander the Bardo, until she finds her place there, or is, perhaps, reborn." He was a tall fellow, thirtyish, who spoke English remarkably well. He was actually not of this region, but from the Solu Khumbu- Mount Everest region, and had gone to one of the New Zealand schools that Sir Edmund Hillary, the first man to climb Mount Everest (with Tenzing Norgay), had set up.

The Sherpa went on, "The celebration will start later this afternoon and continue all night. You may take part if you like." His voice suddenly lowered, "Be careful here, though, the poeple of this region are not so friendly. They are known all over Nepal for their devious ways. Be wary, and do not bargain too hard over prices. It is not wise to accept chang or roxshi from strangers here, either. Some tourists, and other strangers, have been poisoned by the locals! About a year ago, some tourists died here. We found out that they had been slipped some poison in their drinks and then they were robbed, their fingers cut off to get their rings. Afterward, they were left to the elements!"

"Really!" I said. "Is it safe to attend the funeral this evening?"

"Oh, yes," he said, "It is pretty safe, but do not go to strangers' houses. Where you are staying with your guide and porters is safe. Do not worry. Still, there have been many unfortunate incidents here at Tarke Ghyang, including violent fights, so just be careful."

I thanked him for his advice and then walked back to the home where we were staying. It was interesting that these

Tibetans should celebrate death, rather than mourn it. I visualized a funeral in Southern Europe with everyone dressed in black, complete with hired mourners wailing and mourning their loss. Here, everyone celebrates, not out of disrespect for the deceased, but out of love for them and life! I'm sure the departed would rather have it this way.

I found what the Sherpa had told me about the Bardo or Astral Plane interesting. I knew from my own research that the Tibetan Book of the Dead, or Bardo Thodol, as it is known in Tibetan, is read to the departed person for forty days after they have died. "Bardo Thodol" means "Book of the Bardo," or, in other words, "Book of the Astral."

According to the Bardo Thodol, a person, upon leaving the physical plane at death, meets a "being of light; and is attracted to that being. The person then wanders the Bardo for some time, seeing colors and lights, often meeting other people. The person makes their journey through the astral plane by those colors that they are attracted to. There is some psychological evidence to support such ideas. Persons who have had near-death experiences often report seeing a being of light coming to meet them, and many psychologists feel that they can tell a great deal about our characters by our color preferences.

The home we were staying in was very nice, a beautiful wooden house with a nice kitchen with of copper pots, and a clay-and-stone stove, several rooms, a porch, and more. All the houses here seemed to be just like it, and were a far cry from the grass huts I had stayed in back near Shabru.

Adrian, Brenda, and I went down to the Gompa where the party was just getting started. We sat outside with the women for a while, drank tea, ate rice cakes and meat, and listened to them chant. Brenda and I then settled back to drink some roxshi with the men. As it got dark, the men went inside in the Gompa. We followed them in and I sat down next to Brenda. There was music: huge drums were beaten in a fast rhythm, and there were cymbals and crude horns.

The music was quite exciting, and even more so when a cute Sherpani of about twenty came and sat next to me. She looked me in the eyes and smiled—she had probably had a glass or two of roxshi. She then put her hand on the inside of my leg and began stroking my thigh. I was pretty embarrassed, and told Brenda, who was sitting next to me, what was happening. She laughed, and then I realized that I was the only male sitting on this side of the room. It appeared that the men and women were kept separate. I hated to leave the charming young lady who was sitting next to me, but the local custom dictated it.

I moved to the other side of the room, and stood near a

window with a Swiss guy, one of the few other travelers in town, who I had met earlier that day. The room was now utterly packed with about one hundred and fifty people. At a table in the middle of the room were fifty or so of the elder men. Many of them were so-called "Lamas" or teachers, as the word literally means, but in this instance were "elders," since none were monks from what I could see.

The Swiss guy and I were quitely sipping our roxshis and watching the ceremonies when suddenly two of the Lamas at the head of the table began to fight. They slugged and pushed each other quite violently, and then stood up, still fighting. At this point, all hell broke loose in the Gompa, and everyone stood up and began fighting. There had been a great deal of drinking previously, and many people were quite drunk. Men were fighting and running out of the Gompa. A few even drew their kukris—long, curved hatchet-like swords. Things were definitely getting out of hand. I looked at the Swiss guy, and then we looked at the crowd that was scrambling out the door. In an instant, we both leaped out of the window, which fortunately was on the ground floor, and into safety. People sometimes get carried away at these Central Asian funerals, I decided as I searched for the young Sherpani I had met earlier in the Gompa, hoping she had gotten safely away......

§§§

Destiny is not a matter of chance,
it is a matter of choice.
It is not a thing to be waited for,
it is a thing to be achieved.
–William Jennings Bryan

After only a few more days of trekking, we were back in Kathmandu. We had ridden on top of a bus late one afternoon from Panchkhal, at the end of our trek. As usual, we pigged out for the next few days in Kathmandu, eating pizza, pies, yogurt, shakes, and the like at the many restaurants and pie shops in Kathmandu. I got another bed at the Delight Lodge, and pretty much rested for a couple of weeks. It was a good chance to do some reading, writing, painting, and go for picnic bicycle trips.

Then, I got restless for another trek, determined this time to head into real Yeti territory. After receiving another extension on my visa, I decided to try and trek over the Rowaling Himal to the Mount Everest area. I put some notices around town asking for a trekking partner, and within a week I had hooked up with a young man from

British Columbia named Jeremy. Both of us were anxious to go off trekking, me for the third time, he for the first. Our planned trek was a difficult one. We would have to cross Trashi Lapsa Pass at 18,885 feet, which was famous as an area where Yetis had been sighted. According to my reference, A Guide Book to Trekking in Nepal, "only experienced alpinists should attempt this route, and even then only if the entire party, including porters, is equipped for severe conditions and cold, with food for four or five days. Ice axes, a climbing rope, and crampons are necessary."

Well, my crampons had been stolen out of the hotel and Jeremy did not have any. In fact, not only had my crampons been stolen, but so had my boots. Instead, I had a pair of Indian Army canvas rubber shoes, to make the trek in. Jeremy wasn't an experienced mountain climber, and I wasn't all that experienced either, for that matter. But both of us knew the dangers, and were mentally prepared. We bought provisions, and decided to get a rope in the Rowaling Valley, and hire a guide there as well. Soon we were ready for the biggest trek of all, into Yeti country!

§§§

I awoke at five-thirty in the morning and sat up attentively in the pre-dawn darkness. It was drizzling a little, and thunder could be heard rolling down the hills. Shiva rolling thunder, I thought, lying there quietly. Then suddenly it began to pour and lightning flashed. A deafening blast of thunder rattled the windows. It began raining very, very hard. A regular cloudburst, I thought, as I got up to dress. I was supposed to meet Jeremy at six-thirty at the Annapurna Lodge on Freak Street, and we would then go to the Post Office to catch the seven o'clock bus to Barabise, near the Tibetan border, to begin our trek to the Rowaling Valley.

I did some last-minute packing. I was staying in the dormitory of the Delight Lodge, and there were a couple of other people in the room besides me. I went over to the window, opened it and stood there in the darknesss for ten or fifteen minutes watching the rain. It was a rather poor day to begin our trek, I mused.

Just as the rain was starting to let up, and I was collecting my things to go, an attractive, brown-haired Dutch traveller in the bed next to mine sat up, letting her covers fall around her waist. She wore a loose halter top, but nothing else. Propping herself up on her side, the covers draped over her thighs, she looked at me and then out the window.

I realized I was being impolite, but I couldn't take my eyes off her. A smooth line of beautiful, tanned skin ran from her torso down to her knee. She looked incredibly delicious and wonderful. I wanted to take a bite....

"You are going?" she asked, somewhat wistfully.

Really. "Where was I going, anyhow?" I asked myself. "What was I looking for? Not Yetis, really..." I wanted to crawl into bed with her, that's what I wanted to do. I looked back at the pre-dawn darkness of Kathmandu. The rain had slowed to a drizzle now. "Yes, I am going to Everest," I said.

I can't remember if she said anything after that. She just lay there in bed. I watched her for a while. In retrospect, I think I must have been crazy. It had stopped raining rather suddenly. Jeremy was waiting for me.

I shouldered my pack, gave her one last glance, said "Adieu," quietly and left. In a moment, I was out on the street, walking through the winding, misty streets of Kathmandu. It seemed as if the air had been purified by the rain. I felt good. In the distance I heard a faint sound, and immediately imagined that it was the call of the Yeti.

I met Jeremy, and we boarded the bus just in time. By noon, the old, wooden-seated bus, full of chickens, barley farmers, mattresses and a goat, arrived in Barabise, a small town on the Chinese-built road to the Tibetan border. The border town is Kodari, and beyond it is Chinese-administered Tibet. The road eventually goes on to the Tibetan capital, Lhasa. Most people trek to Everest by starting at Lamusangu, the town just before Barabise on the same road. The trek is a little longer, but much easier, not requiring any mountaineering skills.

We got off to a late start that first day, took the wrong trail, and spent the night in a deserted house while it rained outside. For a while, Jeremy and I sat outside on the porch, and played musical instruments while we watched the flashes of lightning. Jeremy was tall and thin, a youthful, blond-haired biology student from central British Columbia, and was here in Central Asia on his way home from Australia, after visiting a girlfriend there. I looked at his youthful clean-shaven face as he played the recorder, blowing softly into it. Occasionally a lightning flash would illuminate his face and the terraced rice fields outside. Then all would be pitch black again.

I blew into my Chinese harmonica with great gusto, if with little musical skill. It seemed that at least the first few days of our trek would be interrupted by thundershowers.

We trekked on the next day, past the many grass hut farm houses, and newly sprouting fields. It was now springtime in the Himalayas. We ducked into a tea house for lunch just as a thunderstorm began. It was over by the time we were ready to hit the trail again. We spent the night in a Gompa just before the Ten Sing La pass, a 10,890-foot pass that would take us into the Tamba Kose Valley. There were quite a few porters waiting there, all intending to cross the pass in the morning. We slept on the porch of the Gompa with a "pack" of porters and a goat.

The next morning, we were up at 5:30 with all the locals. We trudged up the trail to the pass in the thin morning air. As I neared the top, I looked down at the valleys below, seeing the rhododendron trees in bloom with their red, pink and white blossoms and the sheep grazing in the high alpine fields. "It's great to be here!" I thought. We started down the trail on the other side of the pass. It was turning into a warm, sunny spring day.

We met some Sherpani porter girls on the trail, the same ones with whom we had eaten dinner the night before. They asked us to stop and rest with them. We talked in Nepalese for a while. I changed into my shorts, and they showed us how to take a rhododendron blossom and suck the nectar-dew out of it by biting off the end and sucking.

We had quite a good time sucking rhododendron blossoms and laughing with these pretty, charming young ladies. Their hair was long, black, and braided. Their cheeks were a natural rosy color and their oriental features very beautiful. They wore the typical Tibetan woven wool skirts and colorful, rainbow-patterned aprons. They usually wore gray or black cotton blouses, with some jewelry—turquoise and coral set in silver—as necklaces. There was a natural, country-girl beauty about them, and Jeremy and I found them quite attractive. Apparently, they also found us attractive, each of us blond-haired and fairly well-built, and shouldering a heavy pack, just as they were.

Women are quite liberated in the Himalayas. Tibetan and other Himalayan peoples are among the only societies in the world that practice polyandry, the marriage custom of women having more than one husband. A woman may marry two brothers, for instance, as one man is often trekking through the mountains for months at a time. It is also common for men to exchange wives if they should be having marital problems, hoping that a swap will improve their domestic arrangements.

As I sucked in the nectar from one of the blossoms, I was trying to figure out how to say in Nepali, "Let's go for a roll in the hay," to one of the tall girls standing next to me, feeling my blond curls. But I never did.

The next few days were like a sunny, dreamy romance in the mountains. We wandered from village to village, eating with the local people, sleeping on their porches, drinking chang, napping in fields of wild flowers, and wondering at the awesome beauty of the mountains. At every turn of the trail, there was some new, incredible scene. A blue, misty sea of ridges and peaks were visible in the distance. A frosty, giant behemoth loomed on the horizon somewhere, beckoning to us. It was wonderful.

I mused about trekking. For me, it was the good life. Somehow, trekking helped me to put my life in perspective. Walking, in itself, is a good meditative technique. A poem I wrote one day on the trail sums up my feelings about trekking:

> Trekking seems to be a good
> Allegory for life.
> It's one step at a time
> To the highest peak.
> Some paths are steeper
> And more difficult
> Than others.
> It's easy to get lost
> And take the wrong trail:
> Often difficult to get back
> On the right trail,
> As that path is even steeper.
> When faced with a choice of trails
> One is often inclined to take
> The lower, easier one,
> But the higher, more difficult way
> Is that which will bring
> The trekker to his final destination.

§§§

One day I was sitting on the porch of someone's house, looking at the sunset. A whole crowd of people came to watch me for about twenty minutes as I gazed at the sunset. This area of Nepal is not very often traveled by foreigners, and in fact, has no lodges or tea shops like other trekking routes in Nepal. The people watched me, wondering, I suppose, what I was doing there. It was really the same thing, I thought, my observing them, and their watching me. We were both looking for unique experiences in our own ways.

On another night we were given a room to sleep in. In the middle of the night I woke up and could hear some sniffling, as if someone were crying. The room was quite dark, and I coudn't see anything. "There is someone in this room, Jeremy!" I said, rather alarmed.

"Why do you say that?" he asked.

71

"Because I can hear them sniffling," I said.

"It's me!" he exclaimed, and it was, as he had picked up a cold on the trail. He sniffled all night and I found it rather hard to get back to sleep.

The next day we came to Thare, a "Shiva Sanctuary," where innumerable tridents (the symbol of Shiva) were all piled up inside a grass-roofed shed. There was a fence around the structure, and the whole thing appeared quite strange. Some of the tridents were large with little cups on them while others were small "quickies." Shiva, or Shankar, as he is also called, is often depicted as having a blue complexion, symbolizing divinity. He wears a leopard-skin loincloth, carries a trident and lives in the remote mountains of the Himalayas. Shankar is also the patron god of the ganja smokers in Asia, and is often depicted smoking a chilum.

Mount Kailash in Tibet is said to be his favorite haunt. It's a pyramid-shaped peak that many Hindu and Buddhist pilgrims go to each year, although the political barrier now between India and China makes it more difficult. Mount Kailash has been said by certain mystics to be the "Crown Chakra" of the world, or, in other words, the center power point of the earth. I took a photo of the Shiva Sanctuary, gave Shankar a nod, and headed up the trail.

Eventually, we started up into the Rowaling Valley, a long, steep, and remote valley just to the south of Gauri Shankar, a sacred mountain to Hindus and Buddhists, and another reputed dwelling place of Shiva. It is so sacred that the Nepalese Government has refused permission for any mountaineering party to climb it, therefore, its twenty-three thousand foot summit remains unclimbed.

As we came up a hill one morning after spending the night in Simigoan, we suddenly saw two westerners in a small yak hut just off the trail. We waved to them, and they called out to us in German accents, "Have you any medicaments?" We approached them, and one of the young men (who turned out to be Swiss) was lying in a sleeping bag and informed us that he was sick.

I got out my Medicine For Mountaineering book, which I always carried with me when I trekked, and checked out his symptoms. The sick one, named Hans, was actually a medical student himself and could speak English. His companion, a tall dark-haired youth, was named Baer, and did not speak English at all. Hans had woken up that morning with pain in his abdomen, and was unable to walk. I carefully read the chapter on abdominal pains and checked him by probing in the region. Everything pointed to one thing—appendicitis! That was a very serious ailment to have in such a remote mountain area, and could prove fatal. I administered some tetracycline, an antibiotic that has been known to cure appendicitis, and then Jeremy and I debated about what to do.

We had passed a radio station the day before, and it seemed that the best thing was to call for a helicopter to evacuate Hans. Jeremy would take some food and water and go to the Army outpost/radio station, and I would stay and watch Hans. Baer was perfectly healthy, but seemed a little confused about what to do. Since he spoke no English or Nepali, he was at a distinct disadvantage.

Jeremy took off, and I helped Hans as best I could. He was in great pain, he said, but was quite calm. Baer and I set about collecting wood and preparing a signal fire for the helicopter, which might come later that day, depending on how fast Jeremy could get to the Army Post. Hans said he was cold, even though he was wrapped up in several down sleeping bags and a down jacket, and in addition, it was a warm, beautiful day. "You're the first people we have seen on our trek," said Hans, gritting his teeth. "It is so fortunate that you came along today...oh, oh, the pain!"

All day Hans lay there, unable to move. The helicopter did not come that day, and we could only wait. Wait. It struck me that he could die at any time; in fact, several times I expected that he would: he was in so much pain.

During the night a hail storm broke violently on us in the open-sided yak-hut. In the morning Baer and I prepared things for the helicopter rescue. Hans said that the pain was gone, but he still could not move. That meant one of two things: first, that the tetracycline was working and he was getting better, or more likely, that his appendix had burst, and he might die within the next twenty-four hours if he did not get to a hospital. Just then we saw the clouds lift and heard the drone of a helicopter.

I had put my orange sleeping bag on the roof of the hut, and ran to light the fire. Baer poured some kerosene on it, but it didn't really catch. I then tossed some gasoline from my stove onto it. Just as we got the fire going, and I was waving a red scarf, the helicopter flew over us, and on up the valley. They hadn't seen us! We spent some time building up the fire, and then the helicopter came back. We signaled it, and they saw us. They circled us twice, and then landed right on the hillside in front of the hut.

They cut the engines and a Swiss paramedic and two Nepali pilots jumped out. They commanded me to put out the fire because of the flammable fuel in the chopper. They got Hans on a stretcher, and took him to the helicopter. I helped them load him on. They told Baer he could go, too, and he ran to get his stuff. "Don't worry," said the Nepali pilot to me, "We'll have him in a hospital in Kathmandu in less than an hour."

"Thank God," I said, and glanced over my shoulder at Gauri Shankar. In a sudden rush and flurry of wind from the gleaming blades, the chopper was off, lifting precisely and swiftly into the air, then speeding over the hills west to Kathmandu. In moments it was gone, out of sight.

I turned around to see an old Nepali porter sitting on the hill just behind the yak hut. He must have been watching the whole thing. For a long time, he just sat there and stared at where the helecopter had landed. He had surely never seen anything like that before. The world was, indeed, wonderful and strange! Eventually, he nodded to me, and I nodded back. Then he moved into the shadows.

§§§

Jeremy arrived back at the hut at one-thirty. He had gotten to the radio station from the hut in only two hours the day before. We decided to spend the rest of the day there and rest. At sunset, we walked back down the hill to get a good view of the sunset over Gauri Shankar. We ended up climbing a gigantic Himalayan oak, and watching the sunset from about forty feet in the air.

From our camp it was one long day's trek to Beding, the first town in the Rowaling Valley. We had to negotiate some very tricky portions of trail. Some parts were tiny log bridges built into sheer cliffs, not something for acrophobiacs. In Beding, we stayed with a Sherpa family for two nights, and made arrangements for the crossing of Trashi Laptsa Pass. We would need a guide, a tent, a rope and supplies. All that could be found in Beding, we were assured.

We clinched a deal with a Sherpa who had worked for the 1975 Japanese Everest Expedition as a high-altitude climbing Sherpa. That was good enough for us! He also had all the equipment needed for the trek. His name was Lhakparinjy, but we called him Lhak for short. We left the next day for Nan, the last town of the Rowaling Valley. Here we would wait one day for Lhak and another Sherpa who would accompany us to the top of the pass, as this was the deal we'd made with Lhak.

Two days later we were camped at the foot of the moraine at the western end of a high-altitude lake known as Tsho Rolpa. It is a huge basin, with a fairly large lake in it, beyond the last of the summer yak pastures. We pitched the tent on a sort of windy beach by the lake, and prepared a fire using yak chips. We were finally in the icy, high desolate reaches of the Himalayas: Yeti Country.

In the glow of the fire that evening, Lhak turned to me.

"Tomorrow we must leave very early, and cross this section between the lake and the mountain." He pointed over his shoulder to the north. There, next to the lake, was a twenty-two thousand foot peak. We could not see the summit, as we were too close to it. All we could see was a nearly vertical wall that seemed to go straight up from the lake for thousands of feet. "Much danger of falling rock there," he continued. "Too dangerous to cross in afternoon. Morning good, rock still frozen."

I nodded. The pass was practically straight in front of us. Looking toward the end of the lake to the east, I could see the gigantic ice fall coming down from the glaciers in the moonlight. We would have to negotiate that ice fall to gain the pass. I heard the crashing of an ice block falling some distance away. It sounded like a ten-ton freight car being smashed to bits.

I had read extensively about the search for Yetis in this area. Yetis are usually described as standing from six to ten feet tall, and having reddish-brown hair. A huge sloping head sits atop massive shoulders and and a barrel chest. The creature does not have much of a neck. Yetis got the name "Abominable Snowmen" in 1921 when the first British Everest expedition, led by Colonel H. W. Howard-Bury, sighted a number of large man-apes, or "men in fur coats," moving in single file along the ice above the expedition. The expedition found footprints in the snow that were quite large, and distinctly resembled a human footprint. The Sherpas told Colonel Howard-Bury that the creature was the "Mehteh Kangli," or "Man-beast of the snowy mountains." When the Colonel telegraphed the incident to his aides in Calcutta, the name of the creature was garbled and came out as "Metch Kangli," which a Calcutta columnist, trying to make sense from the words, deciphered as "Wretched Snowman," or as he later put it, "Abominable Snowman." [39]

Since the late eighteen-hundreds, there have been literally hundreds of references to Yetis and sightings of the creatures themselves or of their footprints. Legends from the native peoples of Central Asia, from the Karakorams across the Himalayas to Northern Burma, in Tibet, Nepal, Sikkim, Bhutan, Assam, China, Mongolia, and the Soviet Union, talk about these creatures. Supposedly, they are incredibly strong, and can uproot trees and lift large boulders. They live in caves in the high, inaccessible mountains; being very shy of humans, whom they avoid at all costs. They are herbivores—they do not attack human beings, or animals for that matter. [18, 32]

Tibetan Lamas often speak of the Yetis, and in 1922, the Head Lama of the Rongbuk Monastery in Tibet offered to show British General C. G. Bruce a valley nearby where the Yetis might be seen to frolic. Oddly, Bruce, who was more interested in climbing Mount Everest, at which he failed miserably, declined to take the Lama up on his offer. Later, in 1958, monks at the Rongbuk Monastery claimed that Yetis had destroyed a sacred rock monument overlooking the monastery. [39]

The famous British explorer, Eric Shipton, made Yetis famous, and has discovered and photographed their footprints on several occasions. Once, in 1951 near Gauri Shankar, near to where we were at the end of the Rowaling Valley, they found a trail of enormous human-looking footprints in fresh powdery snow. They followed the trail until it disappeared in a rocky moraine. Some sceptics have suggested that the gigantic footprints found are those of bears, or perhaps monkeys, or even men which have melted in the sun, becoming larger, and somewhat distorted. Footprints in fresh powdery snow, however, cannot be explained away in this fashion. [32, 18]

Once, at Thyangboche Monastery, in the nineteen fifties, just on the other side of Tashi Lapsa Pass, near Mount Everest, a creature, described as a Yeti, came out of the forest and loitered around the wall of the monastery. Monks threw food at it, and it became something of a begging nuisance. Finally, the head Lama ordered it driven away, so the monks got out their cymbals, gongs and horns, and drove the creature back into the forests.

Yetis, apparently, can be quite dangerous. Many Sherpas and Tibetans feel that it is extremely bad luck to meet a Yeti, and that to just look at one can mean death. In 1949 a Sherpa herdsman named Lakhpa Tensing was torn apart by a Yeti in the bleak pass of Nangpala, one of the highest passes in the world, and not far from us in the Rowaling.[72]

Interestingly, Yetis have very often been sighted in the Kanchenjunga region (an area with a certain aura of mystery already, with the supposed entrance to the underground world of Agartha located here) and are sometimes, in that region, called "Kanchenjunga Demons."[39, 14]

I asked Lhak if he believed in Yetis. He looked at me, the fire casting an eerie, orange glow on his face. "Every man who lives high in the mountains, like the people of Rowaling, believes in Yetis," he said firmly.

"Will we find any Yetis up there, Lhak?" I said hopefully.

"Yetis," he mused, turning his face toward me. He was big and rugged. His face was scarred and tough. Now in his late thirties, he looked he had led a hard and wild life, fighting a lot (and winning, too, I imagined). He wore a wool hat and a blue nylon jacket that the Japanese had given him. "To meet a Yeti you must be spiritually pure." He looked at me hard. "Perhaps we will meet a Yeti," he said. "You and that one," he nodded to Jeremy. "Maybe you are ready to meet a Yeti. There are many here. I have never seen one, but I have heard them before."

I supposed that Lhak meant that since just looking at a Yeti would be deadly, most people did not see them and live. Only a spiritually pure person could see a Yeti, up close, and live.

Before going to bed, I took a walk down to the lake. It was cold, and it had snowed for the past two days. The pass looked ominous, and a cloud of fog and sleet hung over it. It was hard to imagine any living creature, except perhaps birds, living here. Tomorrow we would gain the ice fall, and camp on the glacial plateau above it. Then we would go on to the pass the next day.

We were up early the next morning. After a quick breakfast we packed up and prepared to go. There were four of us: Lhak, Jeremy, and I, plus a young Sherpa kid, maybe eighteen, who would accompany Lhak on the way back as he would only take up to the top of the pass. We started off, rounding the lake, walking on the scree piles between the lake and the wall of the mountian. Just as we got to the other side of the lake, we heard a loud boom.

Stopping and turning, we saw, to our horror, a huge avalanche come sweeping down the mountain and over the cliffs. Frozen with fear, we couldn't move, and simply watched in horrid fascination as a hundred tons of snow completely wiped out the area we had just walked through and filled the glacial lake with snow! A huge cloud of snow billowed up, and created a brief snow storm. It was tremendous, powerful, and deadly. Had we started our journey ten minutes later, we would all have been swept up in the avalanche and killed. A giant avalanche can build up a force of eleven tons per square foot. Even the air pushed in front of it can flatten buildings, and it is quite capable of burying its victims under tons of snow!

Jeremy looked at me, rather distraught. "That was a pretty close call," he said, his voice strained.

I tried to speak, but my mouth had gone dry. Lhak broke the silence by announcing that we had better get going. "Very dangerous here," he said, re-stating the obvious. He continued on, up scree cliffs, toward the ice fall. To our left, rocks were continually falling down, so we had to be constantly on our guard. For five hours we climbed through the rock and snow to what Lhak had called the "high camp," a small boulder outcrop just at the foot of the ice fall. We had lunch here, and then decided to go the "extra high camp" another three hours away, on top of the ice fall.

We ascended the steep terrain up the side of the ice fall,

and then Lhak had to cut steps down a steep ice slope. We then used the rope, belaying each member of the team up the ice. Dorje, a young porter, went after Lhak, slipping and falling about forty feet and dropping his load. Jeremy went next, with me belaying him. I went last, without a belay, and fell the last ten feet or so, landing on my feet and then falling over onto my pack. We then ascended an ice gully for an hour. At one point it was filled with perfectly round balls of ice, about the size of bowling balls. The whole experience had taken on a strange, surreal quality and our near brush with death had made everyone a bit dreamy.

Looking to my left as we ascended one bit, I saw towering blue-green seracs, big blocks of ice, standing forty feet tall above me, ready to come crashing down at any moment. As I stopped to look at them, I heard Lhak call from the lead, "Hurry! Much ice danger!" With a surge of adrenaline, I picked up my pace.

Eventually, we made it to an ice wall that was about thirty-five feet high. It was a sheer, vertical wall of ice and we had to ascend it somehow. Lhak attacked it with his ice ax, cutting steps, and clawing his way up for twenty feet. Then he came tumbling down. "I can't do it," he said and turned to me. "You go!"

I looked at the wall, but knew I couldn't do it. My footwear wasn't stiff enough; I was just wearing tennis shoes. Now was the time for the crampons that we didn't have. I looked at Jeremy, who had on a good, stiff pair of mountaineering boots. "You can do it, Jeremy," I said.

I don't think so," he demurred, "but I'll try." And try he did. By valiant effort, he managed to hack and claw his way up about two-thirds of the wall. Then, he couldn't go any farther, but he had gone too far to come down. I grabbed my ice ax and scrambled about fifteen feet up the wall. Grabbing an ice knoll, I swung the ax in just above Jeremy's right knee. It was a good swing and the point went well into the ice. Holding the ax, Jeremy was now able to put his right foot on the adze, the back of the ax, get a good foothold, step up, and make it to the top! We all cheered, and I jumped down to the bottom. Jeremy belayed Lhak up with the rope and then Lhak took over, hauling up all our packs and then the porter, Dorje.

I was last. "Do you want the rope?" asked Lhak from the top of the wall.

I looked at him. "Does a Yeti pee on ice?" I asked sarcastically. "Of course I want the rope. Throw it down!" We all howled with laughter, more than the joke deserved, as we released the tension of the day.

We now found ourselves on a vast glacial plateau of about seventeen-thousand, five-hundred feet. It was covered with fresh snow and loaded with crevasses. We roped up and slogged along the glacier for quite a while. It was getting late and starting to snow. An hour later, in the last dim light of the long day, we pitched the tent, and happily climbed in. We were exhausted, and it was all we could do to make dinner.

Jeremy was shivering, although he said he wasn't cold. I guessed he was getting sick, perhaps from the high altitude. Fortunately, I felt fine, and went outside to relieve myself. It had stopped snowing and the moon was just appearing from behind some clouds. All around us were frosty, towering peaks, and the glacial plateau that stretched on into Tibet, which was just a few miles away. It was beautiful. Just as I was about to go back into the tent, I heard a faint seagull-like sound of high pitched chirping, in the distance, from Tibet in the north. Was this, finally, the call of the Yeti?

§§§

I didn't sleep very well that night, and woke early the next morning. My canvas shoes were completely frozen, so I wore plastic bags inside them to keep my feet warm and semi-dry. It was a beautiful day, without a cloud in the sky. About a foot of fresh snow had fallen during the night, and leaving the tent, we began hiking to the top of the pass. Lhak carefully packed up everything inside the tent, and tied it securely. "Because of Yetis," he said very seriously. Both Jeremy and Dorje weren't feeling too well, and walked behind, while Lhak and I roped up and walked ahead of them. We began to go up the steep incline to the saddle between two peaks. The snow got deeper and we slogged up a steep snow slope to the summit. To the left was a rock wall, and to the right a steep snow/glacial slope that we walked up.

Just below the final hundred feet to the pass, Lhak went back to check on Jeremy who had fallen far behind us, and I roped up with Dorje, who had caught up. The last bit was hard ice and I took my ice ax and cut steps up it. Suddenly I heard someone calling me from the top of the pass. I looked up, and wondered if I had gone mad. Was I seeing snow nymphs? There was some lady up there!

"Yoo-hoo!" she called in English. As I neared the top, the woman spoke to me, saying she was by herself and wondering if there was more ice beyond this! It was like a mirage. What in the name of Shiva, Brahma, and Vishnu was this lady doing up on top of this pass at nineteen thousand feet by herself!?

I paused for a reality check. Yes, I was okay. The crisp

high-altitude air and soaring peaks around me told me I was not dreaming.

She was standing on the other side of a large crevasse, which both my guide book and Lhak had warned us about. I could see it clearly as I walked up to her. I started to say, "What are you doing up here..." when suddenly, I fell into another, hidden, crevasse!

I was falling through space! The weight of my pack pulled me backwards and I landed with a thump on my pack, with it cushioning my fall of about thirty feet. There had been a second crevasse covered with snow in front of the one she was standing behind. I had stepped right into it!

Meanwhile, the guys up on top were pulling on the rope, which was tied around my waist. I was okay, as the pack had taken most of the impact of the fall. I looked around me, and saw your standard crevasse with several false bottoms. I had landed on the first shelf, and the crevasse continued to go deeper. I could not see the bottom, but it narrowed considerably as it descended. I struggled to my feet, and used the ice ax to steady myself, then walked a few feet up a sloping ice ramp to the top of an ice pinnacle using my ax for balance. Still Dorje, and now Lhak, the powerful Sherpa, were pulling on the rope. They didn't know if I was just hanging, or whether I was all right or not. I could have been hanging above a seventy-five foot hole in the earth for all they knew.

"Slack!" I yelled. "Give me some slack; I'm all right!" I kept yelling at them, as they were strangling me with the rope around my waist.

Then I saw Jeremy's familiar face peer over the crevasse. "I'm all right, Jeremy," I yelled. "Give me slack!"

"Slack!" yelled Jeremy. "Slack!" And after a time I finally got some slack. They lowered an end of the rope down, and I tied it to my pack. They pulled up, and I slipped out of the straps. Then came the hard part, getting me out. Everyone got on the end of the rope to haul me out. I passed up my ax first, and then shouted, "Pull!"

The three of them pulled with all their might, and I tried to wedge myself in the walls and chimney-climb my way up the crevasse. Several times I slipped and was left hanging in mid-air, with the rope incredibly tight around my waist. I was just getting near the top when the rope got caught in the ice on the edge of the crevasse. I was hanging, they could no longer pull me up. I groped for footholds, handholds, anything! It seemed so hopeless. God help me, I thought. Then I gained a foothold, but then lost it, falling again into space.

I started to cry. "I won't go down there again!" I sobbed.

Frantically I fought for a hold. Finally, I jammed my right knee into the ice, wedging my back against the other side. It worked. I held fast. They handed me my ice ax, and told me that the rope was jammed over my left shoulder. I hacked awkwardly with the ax at the ice. Mightily, Lhak pulled on the rope. It came free, and they dragged me to safety on my back. I lay there sobbing and gasping in the snow. On the other side of the crevasse was the lady, shooting photos of the whole thing.

I could hear Lhak saying over and over, "You very lucky. You very lucky...."

I had a splitting headache, and it wasn't just from the altitude. I took two aspirin, and then listened to the woman tell her story. She was from Arizona, and was up here by herself. She had spent the night in a snow cave just near the summit, and wanted to go down to Beding. We all decided that she should go back with the Sherpas, and we could go on alone, as planned, to Namche Bazaar. Using a belay on both sides, Jeremy and I crawled on our bellies over a snow bridge that spanned the crevasse, after we had the woman pull the packs over. We then belayed her as she went over the other side in like fashion. We had already paid Lhak, and so we said goodbye.

It took us several hours to plunge-step down the other side. The views were magnificent, and by late afternoon we were at a small village in the uppermost yak pastures. On the descent, my left shoe totally disintegrated, and I had to tape it up with surgical tape. The next day we went on to Namche Bazaar, the capital of the Solu Khumbu/Mount Everest region. Here, for the first time in weeks, we found hotels, shops, and hot showers. One hotel even had chocolate cake.

We rested for several days in the town at a place called "The International Footrest" which had several people staying there. Jeremy was quite ill, and eventually went to a New Zealand doctor in the area, who diagnosed him as having high-altitude sickness, conjunctivitis (an eye infection), dysentery, and hepatitis! Boy, he was one sick guy. I was surprised he had made it as far as he had. Like our friend Hans, Jeremy was going to have to be flown out. When I went to see him off, I looked at him and shook his hand warmly. What a trip it had been! I felt truly grateful that both he and I were alive. He smiled and stepped onto the plane. "Goodbye, Yeti chaser," he said.

Me, I felt fine now, but on cold nights when I stood out on the porch of the lodge I was staying in, I could still faintly hear, far in the distance and high in the mountains, the call of the Yeti.

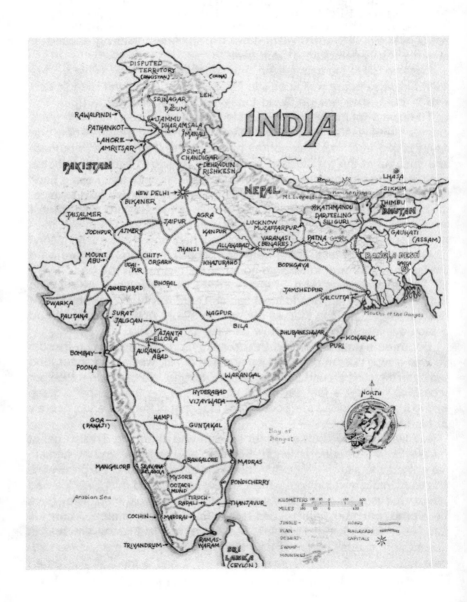

This famous iron pillar of Delhi can be found near the city center. Though it is thousands of years old, it has never rusted.

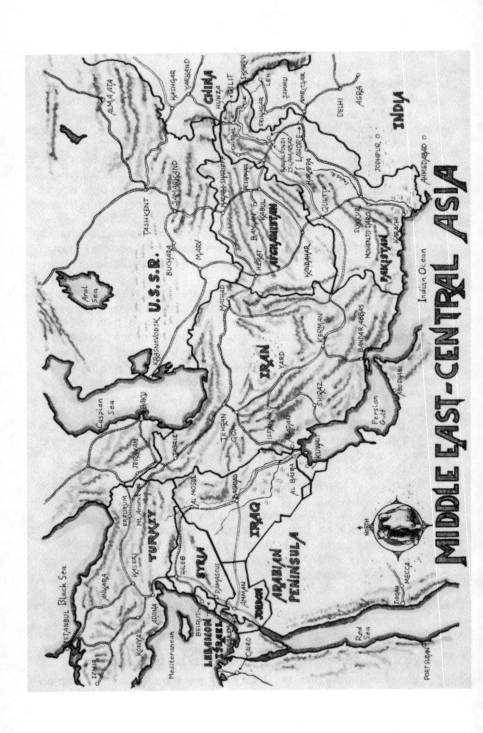

Chapter Five

NORTHERN INDIA:
KRISHNA AND THE TAJ MAHAL

Who sees all beings in his own Self,
And his own self in all beings,
Loses all fear.
When a sage sees this great unity
And his Self has become all things,
What delusions and what sorrow
Can ever be near him?
–The Isa Unpanishad

After an obligatory visit to Mount Everest, I trekked on back down to Namche Bazaar. Interestingly, Mount Everest is not officially the highest mountain in the world anymore. A recent expedition to Mount K2 in northern Pakistan confirmed that this mountain, once officially the second highest mountain in the world, is actual several feet higher than Mount Everest. The Nepalese government is sure to protest such a find! Another mountain in Tibet known as Amne Machin has also been claimed to be higher than Mount Everest, but no one, except the Chinese government, has taken this claim seriously.

I caught a flight back to Kathmandu from the airport at Lukla, a days trek from Namche Bazaar. As usual, I pigged out on the delicious food at the restaurants and pie shops, until I was so stuffed that I literally lay in my bed groaning. The next morning, though, I felt fine, and on a sunny spring Kathmandu morning headed out from the Delight Lodge, across Durbar Square to the Royal Bank of Nepal. My parents were going to send me some money, as I was broke in the middle of Central Asia. This seems to happen a lot to young travelers. They inevitably spend, or lose, all their money and end up writing home.

For citizens of many nationalities, it's possible to ask your Embassy to send you back to your country, which they will usually do, revoking your passport until you have paid for your passage. The American, Canadian, British, and other "Commonwealth" countries will almost always do this. The French government will not do this, however, and because of French compulsory military service, many Frenchmen escape to India rather than go into the military, much as Americans went to Canada or Sweden during the Vietnam war.

A few hundred dollars was waiting in my name at the bank. I collected it in traveler's checks, and feeling pretty good, headed back to the hotel. It was a warm, sunny spring morning, and I was walking along in a pair of faded jeans, a T-shirt, and tennis shoes. My steps fell lightly along the dusty pavement. I felt good. There were some children playing in the square and an old man played a Nepali lute. The souvenir sellers were just setting up their wares: rice prints, prayer wheels, little brass knick-knacks; it felt good to be alive. That feeling, however, was to be short-lived.

I suddenly began to feel cold all over. It was an intense, frigid feeling that struck to my very bones. I began to shiver uncontrollably. My whole body ached horribly, everywhere, all at once. I felt that I was losing control of my muscles; I could hardly move. All this happened in but a few minutes. It was as if someone had come up behind me and clobbered me with a dull instrument. One minute I felt great, the next I felt as though I was knocking at death's door.

"God, I'm dying!" I thought, as I struggled to walk. I couldn't imagine what was happening to me. I suppose I was turning rather pale or something, as a few people passing by gave me funny looks. It took all the strength I could muster to walk the two blocks back to my hotel. Totally exhausted, still shivering and aching uncontrollably, I threw myself onto the bed and passed out.

I awoke twelve or thirteen hours later, and although I was completely covered, I was still chilled and I ached everywhere. I took some aspirin, drank some water, and went back to bed, this time getting into my extra-warm Himalayan sleeping bag. For three or four days, I stayed in bed, drinking tea and hardly going anywhere. I suppose I should have gone to a hospital, but I was used to taking care of myself.

Slowly, I got better, made it out to some restaurants and was soon back to a fairly normal health. It was then, when I was taking a piss in a vacant lot as men will do, even in the full light of day, that I noticed the color of my urine. It was dark brown! I looked at my eyes carefully in a mirror: they were yellow! I had infectious hepatitis, and of course, I had contracted it from Jeremy! It is highly contagious, takes about two weeks to incubate, and can kill you. If I wasn't in such good health from trekking all through the Himalayas, I would have been much more incapacitated than I was. I went to see a doctor in a hospital. He took one look at me, and diagnosed hepatitis on the spot.

"Nothing we can do for you," he said. "There is no known medi- cinal cure for hepatitis except rest and avoiding fried foods, alcohol, cigarettes, and other things that affect your liver. Consume a lot of glucose and related foods and most of all, take it easy."

"Thanks, Doc," I said. I was feeling much better, but my urine was still a dark color, my eyes yellow, and my energy way down. But I wanted to get going back to India. A friend had told me about the Tibetan Medical Center in Dharamsala, Northern India, where it was reputed they could cure hepatitis and other ailments with herbs.

Three days later, I was hitching down to the Indian border, on top of a truck filled with cardboard cartons of something or other, plus a few passengers. The truck, a huge, Indian-made TATA diesel, with a Mercedes motor—common along the motorways of India and Nepal—bounced and squealed along the twisting mountain roads down to the dusty hot Indian plains. When I arrived in Birgunj with the sunset in the west, I took a bicycle rickshaw to the Indian customs post. I ducked in the passport office, and when I came back my rickshaw was gone, my luggage was on the ground, and my camera had disappeared. "Well, if that don't beat all," I thought, gritting my teeth. I spent several hours at the police station, talking with policemen who didn't really give a hoot. I filled out some forms. They said I'd probably never see my camera again, and they were right. I could have hung out there for a week, or even just a couple of days trying to find that rickshaw driver, but I thought, What's the use?

I decided to go on that night to Muzafapur where I could get a train to Varanasi. The buses, as usual, were hideously crowded. I opted to ride on top. It was great for a while. I sat cross-legged with the luggage, accompanied by a couple of old men, heads wound in turbans, three sweaters on to keep warm. It got progressively colder later in the night. Later the mechanic, a teenage kid who rode in back and took tickets, came up and told us all to get back inside the bus, perhaps because we were coming to a police check.

I didn't understand at first, and resisted going down into that sardine can of a bus. The kid got somewhat impatient with me. He managed to get the old men down, and I followed slowly. I still wasn't feeling all that great and was moving laboriously. I had just started down the ladder when the kid gave me a shove and said, "Let's move it, foreigner," in Hindi. He shoved me a bit harder, perhaps, than he had intended to, and I lost my grip on the top of the ladder and fell the entire distance, about twelve feet, and landed on my back in the road!

"Oh, hell!" Once again, I was aching all over. Was my arm broken? I hoped it was just strained, but I couldn't move. "Don't tell me I'm paralyzed..."

The kid leaped down. "Sorry, sorry," he said in Hindi. He and the old men helped me into the bus, and someone actually gave me a seat. In a dizzy tizzy, I slumped into the seat. Shortly we were barreling through the night.

I dozed fitfully. There was a sudden scraping, careening, lurching and screaming that woke me up. The bus ground to a halt, and everyone poured out of the bus: through the windows, out the doors. In seconds the bus was empty except for me, stunned, hurt, confused, still in the back of the bus. "What's going on?" I wanted to say. Moving my aching body, I got up and hobbled outside. Everyone was standing around the bus. It was off the road, in a small ditch, leaning heavily to one side.

"What happened!" I demanded in English of an intelligent looking older gentleman standing near me.

"The front tire came off as we were doing sixty down this dirt road," he said in a thick Indian accent. "The tire just took off and went into that field," he pointed in the direction that the tire had gone. "Buses don't go very well with only three tires, isn't it?" he stated matter-of-factly.

Boy, today just wasn't my day. The driver came over to us and said something to the man.

"He says they can't find the tire. It must have really traveled far," said the man in English. "I suppose we'll have to wait for another bus, isn't it?"

I thought I might cry. I ached all over, my camera, which I had bought for three hundred dollars only six months before, was gone. I was tired and wanted a bed. I should have never have gotten up this morning...

Another bus came along within the hour, and we all got in, making an already crowded bus doubly crowded. Within another hour we were in Muzafapur, and I walked down to the train station. While checking the schedule, I suddenly noticed a tall European sitting in the second-class waiting room. I went over to him and discovered he was from New Jersey. He'd been in the Peace Corps in Malaysia for two years, and was also headed for Benares (Vanarasi), as I was. We chatted for a while. By now it was nearly midnight; the railway station was pretty much deserted. I walked out onto the platform to get some tea when a station worker came up to me, and asked, in English, where I was going.

"To Benares," I said, taking a sip of tea.

"Oh, well, then," he nodded, taking his white cap off and scratching his head. He was in his late twenties, had a thin brown face, a friendly grin and stringy black, greasy hair. His teeth were stained red from pan and beetle nut. "There is a freight train going to Benares tonight, otherwise you'll have to wait until the morning." He pointed to some freight cars on the other side of the yard. A steam engine, black and oily, was just being coupled with the cars. "Most of these cars are empty: just climb in one. The train will leave in fifteen minutes."

I thought about it for a second. Hmm. Why not? Hop a freight train! Sounded like a good idea. "Okay," I said. "Thanks, I'll do it."

"It will be free for you, sahib," he said, looking at the ground. "Do you have some baksheesh?"—meaning a tip, although it also means a bribe or sorts.

"Oh, sure," I said. I reached into my pocket and pulled out a rupee coin. Handing it to him, I said sincerely, " Thanks." He looked at me with his big, sad, brown eyes. His eyes told me this was not as much as he was expecting. I reached into my pocket and took out all of my change, another couple of rupees' worth. "Here you go," I smiled. He smiled too, and left cheerily. I went back to mention all this to John, the Peace Corps volunteer from New Jersey. He was all for it, and decided to go with me, so we collected our backpacks, and headed quietly for the cars at the end of the station.

We boarded the train, just as the whistle blew, climbing into a box car with some empty crates in it, and happily, some benches. I was feeling better at this stroke of luck, and smiled to myself as the train pulled out of the station.

Riding trains in India, if they are not too crowded, and you have a seat, is really a lot of fun. This huge network of trains is even more incredible when you consider that they pretty much run on time. In a country like India, it's even more surprising. Probably Britain's most significant contributions to Indian civilization are this impressive railway network, the second largest in the world; and a bureaucracy that is cluttered in miles of red tape.

The British really had a great fascination for trains, but the British people were not so crazy about them at first. In 1864, in response to an outcry against trains, the British Parliament passed a law which limited steam-driven vehicles to a speed of 4 mph in the country and 2 mph in the city. Indian trains, nowadays at least, travel somewhat faster than this, but not much...still, it is the best way to travel around the country. Hitchhiking, unfortunately, is not especially good in India. There are few private vehicles, and what there are will inevitably be full. Trucks too are crowded, and will charge you, anyway. India is really a vast country, and trains, slow and crowded as they are, are the most comfortable, expedient, and cheapest way to travel about. Flying, by the way, is expensive, but first class on an express train is about the same.

I was sitting there on the floor, looking out at the night, watching the lights of villages like stars and galaxies in the sky as we drove by, thinking about trains, India, the Himalayas, Central Asia...suddenly I heard a noise. I looked around. John the tall, lanky Peace Corps person was fast asleep on one of the benches. There was some motion behind some of the crates. Then a man appeared. He was in his fifties, had long gray hair and a long gray beard. He was dressed lightly, in the standard loose cotton clothing of wandering holy men of India. His garments were faded yellow and he carried a small satchel. There were two white painted lines on his brown forehead, and he wore a necklace of "bodhi beads."

I looked at him for a moment. "Namaste," I said.

"Namaste," he said to me, smiling. He looked me over carefully. "Are you American?"

"Yes," I said. "I'm on my way to Benares. Where are you going?"

"In that direction," he said. He seemed like a friendly person. For someone who looked kind of like a bum, he spoke English pretty well. But, then, the Hindu Holy men of India, known as Sadhus, had few material possessions.

"How do you speak English so well?" I asked him. We both stood up, and moved to sit on one of the benches.

"Oh, I used to be a clerk for the Department of Transportation down in southern India. English is used in much of the government work here in my country," he said.

"You used to work as a clerk? How did you become a wandering holy man?" I asked.

"In India, we have certain traditions," he said. His face was weathered and kind. His eyes shone beneath bushy eyebrows. "According to Hindu tradition," he said, "There are four major periods of a man's life. The first is as son and student. In this period we learn the basics of life. The second phase is as worker- businessman, earning a living and learning about economics in a practical, involvemental way. The third phase is as husband and father. The last, and most important phase, is as a 'Sadhu'. One gives up his job, his wife, his family, and his worldly goods, and travels about. Wandering from temple to temple, living off the land, his life becomes an extended pilgrimage. It is time, now that his children are adults and his wife is no longer interested in sex, that he discover the subtleties that lie beneath the surface of the whither and why of existence."

"Wow, that's great!" I exclaimed. "It's funny, but lately in Western countries, the young people, after getting out of high school, instead of going onto the business-worker phase of life, are going into the 'wandering pilgrim' phase. I seem to be in that phase myself." I then went on to tell him about my recent experiences. As I related them, I became depressed again, the physical and mental aches came back. I moved into my "Why me?" attitude.

"You are filled with self-pity," said the pilgrim. His eyes seemed as if they were on fire, or perhaps it was just the reflection of the moon outside. John stirred around and moaned once on the bench. "You are in fact an incredibly lucky person! Open your eyes and look around you! Can you see the suffering of people around you? Not just that of the beggars and unfortunates, but also that of the businessmen and wealthy materialists. Most people live their lives in a living hell. Their greed and self-pity is truly a shame. They can never be happy. They are ignorant. They do not know the simple secret of life. Know yourself. Love yourself. Love all persons. Love God. Love is everything. See yourself as all persons. In *God*, there is *Unity*. If you see yourself in all things, what sorrow, what self-pity can there be? You own nothing, therefore you cannot lose something you do not have. You are from nowhere, therefore you are at home everywhere. When you are one with all mankind, how can there be hate and bitterness? When everywhere you look, you see goodness and love then you will know your heart is right."

We were silent for a while. What he said made a great impact on me, and affected me strongly. He was so right. I was incredibly lucky, and I had no right to feel sorry for myself. "Besides," he went on, "you are responsible for the things that happen to you in your life. There is no such thing as an accident. Everything that has happened to you, you have earned or have brought into your environment in order to learn an important lesson from. Keep your eyes open and your heart full of love, and you will learn many things in this life. It is the purpose of creation, that mankind learn about himself. We are all striving towards perfection, whether we know it or not. Some, unfortunately, though they are striving for perfection underneath, are on a downward spiral into the depths of despair. They are caught by the evil ones who would destroy all that is good. Be wary, and protect yourself with Love."

This was a lot to think about, and certainly set me back on the right course, as far as I was concerned. It was if this old man had spun me around a couple of times, and plopped me back down, having rearranged my head. As dawn broke, the pilgrim gathered his satchel, and prepared to alight into the train yard. "Thank you, " I said sincerely.

"No thanks to me, thanks to God and you. We are one! Goodbye!" and he was gone, walking carefully across the

91

tracks. I watched him disappear into the early morning mist, thinking to myself, "who was that masked man?" Then John tapped me on the shoulder asked if we were in Varanasi. We jumped down from the car and were off into the train station, where we had breakfast in the railway restaurant.

The excellent restaurants which can be found in almost every railway station are cheap and serve pretty good food. Their breakfasts are the best in India, I always thought. Typically, when getting off an overnight train I would have breakfast at the stations while studying my guide book to whatever new town I was about to enter.

Benares, also known as Vanarasi, has been described as a "city that is a prayer." It is probably one of the oldest cities in the world. For thousands of years, Hindus have been praying and meditating by the banks of the Ganges River, the most holy river in India, a country where everything seems to be holy. It is here that every orthodox Hindu wants to be cremated, and you can see the bodies being burned daily on wooden platforms, called cremation pyres, on the steps, known as ghats, that lead down to the waters. Aside from visiting the many temples and shrines, it is quite a thrill to take a boat trip at dawn on the Ganges.

Another important and interesting sight in the Benares area is Sarnath Park, only five miles out of the city. A deer park where Gautama Buddha once preached to his followers more than 2,500 years ago, it is a pleasant, peaceful place. The Emperor Ashoka erected a huge stone stupa here three hundred years after Buddha's transition, and this can still be seen. It is reputed to contain some relics of Buddha as well.

John and I checked into the Tourist Bungalow near the railway station. We hung around Benares, sometimes called "India in miniature," for a few days, and then he was off to New Delhi. I met three Australians, two men and a woman, all on their vacations from "Uni," the slang Australian word for "University." We all decided to share a room and went down to the ghats together one day. We were sitting there on the steps, all in our shorts, T-shirts, flip-flop sandals and smiles, watching the boats go up the river and the bodies burning, when suddenly this kid walked up to us. He was a Brahmin, one of the priestly caste, a mere ten years old, and seemed rather cocky.

Singling me out, he looked me straight in the eye, and said in English, "You should come and bathe in the river." This was rather strange, I thought, as there were four of us sitting there. Washing in the Ganges is a rather religious thing to do as well, as theoretically all of your sins or negative karma, as the Indians proclaim, would be washed away.

Well, feeling slightly wild and crazy, I said, "What the hell." I walked down to the water with him, and walked down the steps. The water was brown and dirty. Standing up to my knees, still on steps, I couldn't even see my feet. I walked down till my chest was covered, having taken my shirt off, but kept my shorts on. The kid was with me. Someone handed me a bar of soap, and I began washing. The whole thing seemed rather auspicious, a boy-priest or close enough, coming up to me and asking me to wash all my sins away....

I made one mistake though. I got my whole head wet, actually submerging myself entirely in the water, at the insistence of my boy-priest. I didn't drink any of the water, mind you, but it did get on my lips, in my nose, in my ears....That night, back in the hotel, I suddenly felt something coming on, and it wasn't pleasant.

I made a mad dash for the bathroom. Fortunately there was one in our room, something that is uncommon in most cheap Indian hotels. I spent the rest of the night alternately shitting and throwing up. Boy, was I sick! I still felt horrible the next morning, and decided to go on a three-day fast.

I took it easy for the next couple of days, going out to Sarnath Park one day, which was a much-needed afternoon of peace and relaxation. It really is quite peaceful, and with a little imagination, it is easy to see Gautama Buddha sitting with some of his followers teaching the eight-fold path of right thinking and right actions right there in the grass among the deer that are still roaming the park.

§§§

Benares (Varanasi) is sometimes said to be the oldest extant city in the world, and may well be a city so ancient, it was part of the semi-mythical Rama Empire. One curious thing about Benares and the Ganges River is that, while hundreds of bodies as well as untreated sewage and other refuse is dumped into the Ganges, tests of the water show it to be astonishingly pure and "perfectly balanced" without harmful germs or toxins. Why the river should remain unpolluted is still a mystery. Some investigators have gone so far as to theorize that in antiquity, certain secret and forbidden temples, still existing today, were built on the banks of the Ganges, especially in Benares and the vicinity, with a highly sophisticated method of purifying the river: radiation! 53 While this is mere wild conjecture (and even whether the water is actually as "balanced" and pure as claimed is disputed), it is a theory that adds to the air of mystery of the "city that is a prayer." Certainly it is true that thousands of people bath daily in the filthy water, but do not become sick (myself excluded).

The city has plenty to see. One morning, quite early, Robyn, the short, black-haired Australian woman, and I were standing down by the ghats waiting for the sunrise. People were sleeping in the temples, some of them beggars, wrapped in oily rags, some were Sadhus, the naked-loincloth holy men that wander India, often hard to distinguish from beggars. Fifty feet away from us, we could see and smell a body being cremated beginning to really combust. I could smell the scent of burning flesh, and there were several fires just going out. Priests were just then bargaining with a family about a cremation for a relative.

According to Robyn, who had been to India twice and studied one summer in Benares, the priests had quite a racket going here, raising the price and quality of the sandlewood, bargaining over the cost of each verse of holy Sanskrit scripture to be recited while the body burned. And last of all, the cost of a guard to watch over the body until it was completely burned to ashes. This was necessary, as the rumour goes, she said, because some people believed that a few of the beggars were rising above conventional morals, and were eating human flesh!

"God," I exclaimed, "that can't be true!" Robyn insisted that it was true, and I have since read it elsewhere.19

Just then, the sun rose in the east, above the river, a gigantic, red flaming fireball out of the dust. A crowd of pilgrims had gathered, and they began bathing and chanting... it was dawn on the Holy Ganges in Sacred Benares.

One night, the four of us lay in our beds in the large room at the hotel and could not sleep. One of the guys, a stocky, brown-haired fellow named Eric, wanted to light a cigarette but we discovered that we didn't have any matches. It was quite late, about 2:30 in the morning, and everything was closed.

"Wait, the train station is only a few blocks down the street and will still be open," I said, and volunteered to go. Within minutes, I was out on the street. The fresh air was good for me, and I couldn't sleep anyway. There was full moon out, and it was a hot, sultry night. There was not a soul on the street I noticed, as I began walking toward the railway station. The streets were made of dirt, had no sidewalks and were full of potholes and strewn with garbage.

After I had gone a block or so, I heard a noise behind me. I glanced over my shoulder; it was a pack of dogs. There were five or six of them, mangy and hungry, scavanging the empty streets for food. These semi-wild dogs can be dangerous, and certainly liable to carry a score of diseases including rabies. I started to walk a little faster. With a sudden yelp, they spotted me, and to my horror, started after me barking ferociously.

"Holy shit!" I cried aloud (an appropriate expression in a city where everything is holy), and took to my feet, running as fast as I could down the street toward the train station. The dogs, barking loudly, came after me with a vengeance. My own fear must have spurred them on. Fortunately, they were a block-and-a-half behind me, and I could see the light of some small vendor in front of me, near the train station. Train stations are open all night in India, and there is always someone selling sweet milk tea, or "chai," as it is known throughout Central Asia, and always a few people sleeping on the platforms.

Running as fast as I could (which turned out to be much faster than I would have thought), I headed for the shack, with the dogs close on my heels. They gained on me and were about to catch me when I made it to the shack, a small cigarette stand that sold snacks and other little items to travelers. Gasping for breath, I ran inside and slammed the door shut behind me. Inside was a brown-skinned Indian, an older man, who was half asleep. "Namaste," he said, jerking awake. I could hear the dogs barking outside. My hands and voice were shaking as I reached for a box of matches.

"Just came for a box of matches, " I said in my best Hindi. I stayed there for a while talking with the old guy. I bought a packet of coconut cookies and ate them, sharing them with the vendor. When I looked outside, the dogs were gone. After buying another packet of cookies, I took off, heading back to the hotel.

Warily looking out for the dogs, I walked briskly down the street. As I neared the hotel, to my horror, I saw that the pack of dogs was huddling right in front of the door of my hotel! Those bastards, I thought, and in desperation I picked up a handful of rocks. My adrenaline surging, I ran, screaming and yelling at the top of my lungs, straight at those dogs! As I neared them, I threw the rocks, scattering the dogs into alleys and down the street. In the confusion, I was able to duck into the hotel. "Whew," I said when I got back in the room. "The midnight walks around here can be rather exciting!"

§§§

A couple of days later, the four of us split up. Two of the

Australians, Eric and Robyn, went off to New Delhi. The other, a tall, bearded, pleasant archaeology student—also named David—from Canberra, accompanied me to the world's largest fair, the Khumbu Mela, or "Great Fair."

The Khumbu Mela is held every twelve years in Allahabad, about seventy-five miles from Varanasi. Every twelfth fair, according to astrologers, is the most auspicious. The last of these was in 1833, exactly 144 years before the one we were to attend. So, this was another twelfth, and thus highly auspicisous, fair, and it would attract a great many pilgrims. Many Hindus would seize the chance to go to this fair to wash away their sins or negative karma, as they do in Varanasi. But, Allahabad is more sacred because there is a confluence of three sacred rivers here: the Ganges, the Yamuna, and a third, invisible, underground river called the Savarati.

David and I each had a seat on the bus, and were soon rolling across the Indian plains to Allahabad. As we neared the city, there were several checkpoints and people were inspected for vaccinations. At the Khumbu Mela twelve years ago, about twenty-thousand people died in a cholera epidemic, and at the one before that, several thousand had died in an elephant stampede. Security was tight this time, as the Indian government was taking every precaution to ensure the safety of the pilgrims.

We entered the grounds of the fair, and wandered around the many stalls and vendors on our way to the river. There were innumerable tents set up all over the place: government tents of various kinds, private organizations' tents, religious organiza- tions' tents, and restaurant tents. David and I ended up at the Sai Baba tent. Sai Baba is a curly haired, rotund, jovial "Holy Man" from central India, who keeps a low profile and is known for working miracles. He wasn't attending the fair at the time. His followers were friendly and hospitable, and invited us to stay for the night if we liked. We left our bags there, and wandered down toward the confluence of the rivers.

What a sight it was! There were literally millions of people gathered around; bathing, chanting, moving through the sea of bodies doing their thing. According to the Guinness Book of World Records, an estimated twelve million, seven hundred thousand peple were at the month-long fair at its height, and a total of twenty million attended over the entire month! This is the largest crowd ever assembled in one place in history according to Guinness.

David and I waded through the infinite hordes to try and find the confluence of rivers so that we could bathe. After hours and hours, we gave up, and fought our way back through the sea of red and yellow turbans, perfumed black hair, and ecstatic people waving their arms in the air—the chant "Hari Krishna, Hari Rama!" could be heard everywhere.

Back at the Sai Baba tent, the Sai Baba people gave us a dinner consisting of lentils (dahl), spinach (subji) and flat breads (chapatis). Then we watched a very old movie of Sai Baba. In the film, which broke no less than twelve times during its thirty minutes, Sai Baba produced ashes—piles of them—out of a rather small vase, and did a few other assorted tricks, such as producing watches out of thin air, which he handed to people. These "tricks" are generally known as mental precipitations, assuming they are genuine. Of course, they could have been merely sleight of hand, although that seemed out of the question in the case of the piles of ashes from the vase. This "black ash" is said to materialize underneath Sai Baba's fingernails, and comes out in quantities that are genuinely astounding.

Sai Baba does have the best reputation of any guru in India, but he is not a guru in the usual sense of the word. He lives quietly and simply in a small village in central India, and does not ride around in Rolls Royces or surround himself with acolytes, luxuries, palaces, or the like. Nor does he fly off around the world preaching his message of brotherly love. He does, however, have a sizeable and earnest following.

He is said to be the reincarnation of a previous Sirdi Sai Baba, a man who was born a Moslem in central India, studied with a Sufi saint in the mid-eighteen hundreds, preached brotherly love, and eventually became a sort of saint for Muslims and Hindus alike, which was an incredible accomplishment, considering the tremendous rift between the two religions, especially in central India. Even today there are constant religious riots in many areas between Hindus and Muslims.

The first Sai Baba died in the nineteen-twenties, and said that he would come back shortly. This present jovial miracle worker claims to be his reincarnation, lives in the same area, and does not look at all like the previous Sai Baba. However, reincarnation doesn't suggest that two different incarnations of the same ego would look alike, anyway. Reincarnation, the continual rebirth of a person's "soul" into human vehicles, should not be confused with "transmigration of souls," which is the entirely different belief that human souls can transfer into animals or insects. Personally, I had good feelings about both Sai Babas and was happy to be sharing the hospitality of their followers.

After dinner and the movie, a handsome electrical engineer from Munich, one of the few other foreigners that we saw at the fair, told an interesting story. "I went to a big gathering in Andhra Pradesh," he said, glancing at a cheap picture of Sai Baba on the wall. "I was standing in the back of the crowd, watching Sai Baba on stage. He was producing gray ash out of thin air, stuff like that. I was so far away, though, I could hardly see what was going on. I thought to myself, "I wish that I could get up closer so that I could really see and talk with Sai Baba. Ach, it was incredible," he said, his eyes bright.

"Suddenly, Sai Baba called out to me, 'You there in back, you, the German fellow, come on up here!' I couldn't believe it: he read my mind! He had the people clear the way through the crowd—there were thousands of people there—and, completely stunned, I walked up to him on the stage. 'You wanted to see me clearer; well, here I am!' he told me. He produced a watch out of the air, gave it to me, talked about the infinite power of love and the mind, and then I went back."

The young German's face was aglow when he exclaimed, "It was wunderbar! Here, see, I still have the watch! Look!"

He stretched out his left hand. There was a watch, all right: a Rolex watch, in fact, not some Indian "cheapie." Hmm. I looked at David. David looked at me. It is a strange world, indeed.

We spent the night on the ground in the tent, and awoke at five o'clock in the morning. We had a few cups of tea, and then headed down to the river in the pre-dawn darkness. It was considerered to be most powerful to bathe at dawn. We found our way to the confluence, where there were already a few million people wading about. We took off our shoes, rolled up our pants, and waded in. All around us people sang and chanted, "Hari Krishna, Hari Rama!" which is Hindi for "Hail Krishna, Hail Rama," two heros of classical Hindu mythology, and rather divine personalities.

Chanting "Hari Krishna!," the people would throw themselves into the water, completely immersing themselves, and believing they were erasing all their bad karma from this and all their previous incarnations. If this indeed occured, they would not, they thought, have to reincarnate anymore, and could live the rest of their life wave in Hindu Heaven: Samadi (or Nirvana, as the Buddhists call it). David and I got caught up in the whole scene; it was wonderful and quite inspirational. We sang "Hari Krishna, Hari Rama," with everyone, and flung ourselves into the water, reveling in the occasion.

Then a huge flaming orb, awesome and magnificent, began to rise out of the murky dust, bring life to the world. I, David, and the millions of pilgrims performed our salutations to the sun, as we stood there in the middle of the river, all eyes transfixed by it.

Stunned, almost in a state of shock from the mystical intensity of the experience, we headed slowly back to the tent. David was off to New Delhi that morning, and I was on my way to the Taj Mahal in the afternoon. I waved goodbye to him at the station, and then retired to the railway restaurant to write in my journal. Our experience would make us friends for life.

Within a few hours, I was riding on a train, with a third-class reservation to Agra, seventy-five miles south of Delhi, and the home of the Taj Mahal. Across from me were some other foreigners: some French hippies, a German girl and a Swedish guy. I was exhausted from the day, and crawled up into my top bunk early, to reflect and finally, to fall asleep.

The next morning, a bright sunny day, we were still chugging along across northern India. I climbed down, packed up my sleeping bag and took my seat in the open compartment. At the next stop, I went to get some tea, and when I came back, some soldiers were going through the train, searching people. A burly, brown-uniformed soldier asked to look at my luggage.

"Sure, " I said, opening my pack for him. "What are you looking for?" He said nothing, but glanced inside, sticking his hand down in for a moment. He then turned to the French hippies across from me who looked more interesting, and certainly more nervous.

"Open your bag," he ordered one. There were other soldiers on the train, and they were searching everyone. One of the Frenchmen, a thin, scraggly fellow in his twenties, with a black, sparse beard, reluctantly opened up his carpet bag. The soldier dug into it and came out with a bag of marijuana. The Frenchman rolled his eyes, and I thought, "Oh, no!" The soldier looked at it, and then tossed it to the floor.

"Oh, that's all right," he said in English. He dug some more, and came up with a clump of black tar wrapped in plastic. Opium! I thought for sure this "French Freak" was in trouble now. "That's all right," said the soldier, "no problem here," and he started to go away.

"Wait!" I said. "What are you looking for, anyway?"

He turned and gave me a look as if I were daft. "Why, alcohol, of course!" he said. "This is a dry state!"

I looked at the Frenchman, who was sighing with relief. We both laughed as he rolled a joint. It is true. Alcohol is considered a much more serious drug in India than marijuana or opium. Both drugs are sold in government shops around the country, especially in Varanasi, Agra, and Rajastan. Booze, however, is severely frowned upon in much of India, and in many states is completely illegal.

I took a rickshaw from the Agra train station to a hotel a friend had recommended to me, the Mumtaz Mahal. Rickshaw peddlers, whose life consists of peddling the bicycle rickshaws for people, will try to get you to go to certain hotels, and will even offer to take you there for free. This is because they will get a commission if you stay at one of these hotels and the commission is generally greater than a normal rickshaw fare (usually only a few rupees). This is all fine, as long as you're going to a hotel that pays commission. Otherwise you may find you'll have problems getting a rickshaw.

I checked into the hotel, and took off to see the Taj Mahal. This graceful piece of white marble architecture is indeed breathtaking to behold. It is probably India's number-one tourist attraction, and it's one of the few world sites in which, no matter what your expectations, you won't be disappointed. Its shapely onion domes, graceful minarets and intricate latticework were built by Shah Jahan from 1630 to 1648 as a mausoleum to his fourth and favorite wife, Mumtaz, and possibly to himself, although he had plans to build an identical structure in black marble on the opposite side of the Jumna River. The two would have been connected by a silver bridge, and Shah Jahan, "King of the World," would perhaps have rested in the black Taj. As it is, the second building was never built and Shah Jahan lies entombed with Mumtaz in a vault beneath the building. There is an oblong reflecting pool in front of the Taj which adds to its pristine beauty.

Taking off my shoes, I went inside the building. Jewels and verses from the Koran decorated the walls. The echo inside was incredible. I recalled that, some years ago, jazz flutist Paul Horn recorded an album inside the Taj, taking advantage of the superb echo. Actually, the best time to visit the Taj Mahal is before, during or just after a full moon. It is open to the public on those evenings, and the light of the moon on the Taj is an awesome sight (however, because of the recent Sikh violence and terrorism in India, I understand that the Taj is no longer open at night).

There are other things to see in Agra as well: the massive sixteenth- century Red Fort is right near the Taj; it took eight years to build. There is the Ram Bagh, a Mogul garden, Akbar's Tomb and the Jama Masjid. A popular day excursion is Fatepur Sikri, an abandoned city built in 1659, twenty-three miles west of Agra. Emperor Akbar had to abandon it because of its poor water supply.

Agra, I was told, is also famous for its prostitutes, but it wasn't obvious to me. I was soon on the Taj Express to Delhi, a fast train ride that only takes a few hours. On the way from Agra to Delhi, one passes through the ancient city of Mathura or Muttra, on the banks of the Jumna River. This is one of the oldest cities in India, in an area rich in archeological remains. It was a cultural center of great reknown in ancient times and the legendary birthplace of Lord Krishna who played in the nearby Vrindaban Forest.

Krishna's kingdom spread across northern India and Pakistan, with its capital in ancient Dwarka, on the coast in Gujerat, just near the Pakistan border. Dating at Mathura has established it as at least 3,500 years old, and probably much older. It is likely that Mathura was one of the Seven Rishi Cities of the Rama Empire, though not as devastated and abandoned as many. As there is an existing, thriving city on the ancient spot today, it makes archaeological exploration rather difficult.

Nearby is the ancient Rama Empire city Ayodhya, Rama's former capital city The Ramayana says that "Rama ruled the earth...one age of the world ago." An age in Hindu Yuga is generally said to be 6,000 years, and the poet-philosopher Valmiki was generally thought to have written the Ramayana about 2,000 BC, therefore would be atleast 8,000 years old. Dr. Kunwarlal Jain Vyas of India believes that the ancient Rama Empire dates back to the Manu period, about 31,000 BC.

As a modern, united India comes into the decade of the 1990s, the last few moments of our current Kali Yuga, or dark age, the nation was in severe political and religious turmoil directly related to the *Ramayana*, Rama and his capital city, Ayodhya. Since Ayodhya was the glittering capital of a golden age of India gone-by, a modern Hindu revival has threatened to split India in two and plunge the country into civil war.

TIME magazine ran a special story on Ayodhya and Rama in its November 12, 1990 issue: "Militant Hindus marching on the town last week were bent on reclaiming what they believe to be Rama's birthplace, a site now occupied by a dilapidated mosque. If Moslems note that their shrine has stood there for centuries, Hindu revivalists cite as proof nothing less than divine lightning and the appearance of a mysterious black icon.

"Supposedly, it was on the night of Dec. 22, 1949, that a thunderbolt struck Ayodhya and an eerie light emanated from the rear of the Babri mosque's central prayer hall. A bystander, so the story goes, witnessed the brief appearance of a child at the light's source, a spot where later investigation discovered a black stone *murti*, or divine likeness. In Hinduism, Rama was not just a celebrated warrior and king; he was an incarnation of *Vishnu the Preserver*, one of the trinity of supreme gods. As such, his victorious labors in pursuit of Sita—aided by the ingenious

Hanuman, magical king of the monkeys—ushered in a golden age of righteousness known as the Ram Rajya.

"As the Ramayana describes Ayodhya, it was a palatial metropolis of broad avenues, brilliant gardens and mighty walls. Historically, however, the site of present-day Ayodhya became a mini-Jerusalem, a holy place for many faiths where the Buddha's legendary Toothbrush Tree grew and where a Jain saint was born. In the 16th century, Islam arrived. The commingled armies of Babur, a Central Asian warlord, swept down from Afghanistan to found the Mughal dynasty in northern India. And in 1528, Mir Baqi, on of Babur's commanders, established in Ayodhya the Babri mosque, named for his emperor.

"It stands today as one of the religious world's strangest hybrids: a triple-domed Islamic edifice with statuary portraying Rama inside, an outer courtyard reserved for Hindu devotions and, beyond that, a high-fenced,barbed-wire security perimeter monitored by closed-circuit TV. The mosque was declared off-limits in 1949 following the reputed appearance of the child Rama. In the wake of gruesome Hindu-Muslim massacres accompanying the partition of British India in 1947, a local magistrate feared that the incident would inflame animosities. Many Hindus continue to accept the vision as a miracle, but others, with backing from the police report, say that Hindu militants sneaked inside the mosque, placed the *murti* in its strategic niche and then spread a supernatural tale.

"Wonders aside, defenders of the site as Rama's birthplace point to what they call hard evidence: column sections in the mosque that predate its construction and feature ornaments in a much older Indian style. As believers see it, these formed part of an ancient Rama shrine, one superseding, perhaps, the original temple of legend that was built of black stone fetched from Lanka by Rama's simian lieutenant.

"Moslems opposing the campaign to remove the mosque dismiss such claims and have won support from some prominent historians and social activists. Last year a report by 25 distinguished Indian historians found what Romila Thapar, a scholar on ancient India, called "really no evidence" suggesting that the site is one of great antiquity linked to Rama. She added, "There is also no record of the destruction of a temple." In the panel's view, the mosque's Hindu or Jain structural elements could have been collected from ruins elsewhere.

"The dispute is under review by the state high court. Whatever the facts, however, to militant Hindus the birthplace theory is an article of faith. Since a court granted them access to the site in 1986, they have intensified their movement to build a new temple after relocating the mosque or, failing that, destroying it. In the words of Murli Manohar Joshi, one of the movement's top ideologues, Rama "is not a Hindu god but a national hero, and every Indian irrespective of his religion must accept that."

As militant Hindu groups marched on Ayodhya to demolish the mosque and build a new shrine to Rama, the Indian army blocked roads into Ayodhya, battles with the police occurred in which at least 80 persons were killed and Lal Kishen Advani, the political head of the Bharatiya Janata Party (BJP) was arrested by the end of November, 1990.

Advani actually toured India raising support for the new temple to Rama in a "flying chariot" from the Ramayana; that is, a *Vimana!* It was not a real *Vimana*, of course, but a wooden model with swans as a visual representation.

While the glory, history and incredible technology of the ancient Rama Empire of India is missed by most journalists and western educated "Indi-ologists," most Hindus in India are firm believers in the reality of Rama, his exploits and Ayodhya as the former capital city.

§§§

I stepped out of the train station into a hot, dusty Delhi afternoon. Beggars and rickshaws, many of them motorized, loitered about the parking lot. Delhi is a big sprawling place. There's lots to do here, most of it in Old Delhi. Climbing up one of the minarets of the Jama Masjid (Great Mosque) gives you a bird's eye view of the city. The Red Fort just across the park makes a good afternoon's outing, and offers an excellent sound-and-light show in the evenings. Legend has it that it is connected by a secret tunnel to the Red Fort in Lahore, hundreds of miles away! And, there's the Qubt Minar, a magnificent 238-foot victory tower built in the thirteenth century by the first Muslim conquerors of Delhi. Delhi has plenty of musuems and markets to wander through, too, and it is the best place in India for official business, like receiving money, obtaining visas or passports, or purchasing Indian Rail Passes, which are an excellent value.

Nearby is the famed Iron Pillar, generally believed to date from the fourth century A. D. but said by some scholars to be over four thousand years old. It was built as a memorial to a king named Chandra. It is a solid shaft of iron sixteen inches in diameter and twenty-three feet high. What is most astounding about it is that it has never rusted even though it has been exposed to wind and rain for centuries! The pillar defies explanation, not only for not having rusted, but because it is apparently made of pure iron, which can only be produced today in tiny quantities by electrolysis! The technique used to cast such a gigantic, solid iron pillar is also a mystery, as it would be difficult to construct another of this size even today. The pillar stands as mute testimony to the highly advanced scientific knowledge that was known in antiquity, and not duplicated until recent times. Yet still, there is no satisfactory explanation as to why the pillar has never rusted! [43]

One of the most bizarre tales of lost cities to come out of India is the story of the adventurer Graham Dickford, who came to the attention of the British Indian authorities in 1892. Dickford was picked up in a state of collapse and taken to a hospital. Half-dead, completely bald from natural causes and covered with terrible burns, he stammered out a fantastic tale. He and seven companions had discovered a mysterious valley, presumably deep in the jungles of northern India. According to natives, there was a temple there filled with amazing treasures. Instead, the treasure-seeking adventurers found incredible horror. All of Dickford's companions were killed and the dying man spoke deleriously of a "great flying fire, shadows in the night, and ghosts that kill you by looking at you." His story grew more and more incoherent, interrupted by strangled screams, and within three days he died in agony, crying out and struggling with such violence that the Indian attendants reportedly fled in terror.[43]

The valley that Dickford reported become known as the "valley of the seven dead men," and the Indian government sent an expedition there in 1906. Two members died on this expedition and the survivors reported that it was infested with deadly poisonous snakes and plants and that "if one struck a match, there was a terrific roar and flames shot from one end of the valley to the other." The two explorers who died had been investigating a "funnel-shaped hollow in the ground when they suddenly staggered and fell to the ground, dead."

A second expedition in 1911 claimed the lives of five of seven members. The two survivors, standing at a distance from the five, suddenly saw the others spin around, then collapse as if struck by lightning. Eight years later, a third troop of explorers went to the valley, where they found seventeen human skeletons. Three of the members suddenly jumped, for no apparent reason, over a rocky cliff and were killed.

The whereabouts of this deadly valley are kept secret by the Indian government in New Delhi, lest foolhardy people venture in. Scientists have suggested that one cause of the strange phenomena may be natural gases of an inflammable or nerve-paralysing kind, or blasts of carbonic acid gas. [43]

Whether or not there actually is some sort of ancient structure in the valley, I do not know. The story may have been made up by the natives to rid themselves of some pesky British adventurers by sending them into a valley known to be strangely deadly. At any rate, it is not a place that tourists are likely to be allowed into in the near future!

§§§

I was soon on a train heading north. My money was running out, and I still had hepatitis to some degree. My urine was still like "Karma Cola," my eyes yellow, my energy not quite up to its usual high standard. I decided to go to the Tibetan Medical Center in Dharamsala, Himachal Pradesh, Northern India. I took an overnight train to Pathankot, and then an all-day bus to Dharamsala. With my pack, I walked up the winding streets to the town of McCleod Ganj just above Dharamsala. It was like a little Tibetan village, nestled in the Himalayas, the glaciated peaks of the Chamba Himal behind the village.

I checked into the Kailash Hotel, one of the small hotels that lie along a three-block-long strip. I got a bed for a whopping three rupees a night, about thirty-five cents. It was quiet, peaceful, and a whole lot cooler than Delhi! It was a very Tibetan place as well, a sort of little Tibet. When the Chinese took over Tibet in the fifties, the Dalai Lama, Buddhist secular ruler of Tibet, and his entourage fled to India, where they set up a government in exile here at Dharamsala/McCleod Ganj. Even today, the Dalai Lama, fourteenth and last of the Dalai Lamas of Tibet, according to their own ancient tradition, still lives in a small palace here in McCleod Ganj.

After a pleasant nights' stay in the Kailash Hotel, I tripped down to the Tibetan Medical Center a few blocks away. A small building with just a couple of rooms, it is run by the exiled Tibetan government. I sat in a small waiting room. The center was hardly more than a wooden shack. After a middle-aged Tibetan lady and her son had seen the doctor, it was my turn to go in.

The doctor was a tall, beautiful Tibetan woman, who looked about forty, though perhaps she was older. She was wearing a dark-brown traditional Tibetan dress, with a silk blouse and rainbow-striped wool apron. Her long black hair was tied up behind her head in braids and she spoke English. I told her that I had had hepatitis in Kathmandu some weeks ago and had been very sick.

In Tibetan fashion, she took my right hand and felt my pulse, listening quietly for several long minutes. She then did the same for my left hand. Tibetan doctors normally diagnose patients by listening to what they say are twelve pulses coming from the organs of the body, six on each wrist, each coming from a different organ.

Afterwards, she told me that I still had hepatitis, and that my liver was weak. She said that she would prescribe some herbs for me that would clear up whatever symptons I had. Smiling gently, she directed me to the pharmacy which was the next small building down. I thanked her and offered to pay, but she said there was no charge.

At the pharmacy, some young monks, wearing maroon-colored robes and with their heads shaved, filled my prescription. The room was no more like a little booth, full of shelves lined with large glass jars, each filled with little brown pellets the size of small gum balls. My prescription was three different kinds of herbal pellets to take, one each morning, noon, and night, a different kind each time. I looked at them a trifle skeptically: they could have been deer droppings for all I knew. The prescription cost me about fifty cents for a weeks' worth of pellets. Feeling slightly better already, I headed back for the hotel.

I talked with the proprietor of the hotel that night, watching him limp around the kitchen as I sat in the restuarant area having a bowl of thukpa, a Tibetan noodle soup. He patted his leg, the one that made him limp, and told me how he was trained by the American CIA as a Campa guerilla, to invade Tibet and fight the Chinese. He had been training as a parachutist in Agra, when he had landed wrong and broken his left leg just above the ankle. He put it up on the table and showed it to me. It was quite swollen and the jump had been seven years ago! "That's how it goes," he said, "so I gave up being a parachutist and guerilla fighter and became a hotel owner." Good idea, I thought.

Over the next couple of days, I took my tablets and attended classes at the Tibetan Educational Institute. A class of thirty of so western students sat on cushions in a roomy, wooden room. A Lama came in and the class prostrated itself before him as a sign of respect. He spoke in Tibetan, reading from a text, while his words were translated into English by a young, shaven monk in yellow robes. The Lama was sixty or so, wore yellow robes and glasses, and seemed to be an extremely kind and serene person.

He spoke of karma. "When one indulges in non-virtuous activity, it is like a poison, and although the consequences do not show up immediately they will show later." He spoke of a group of persons that were attempting to help mankind. "They are Sanjay, the enlightened ones. Their wisdom may see everything without obstruction. I am always in a place that is understood by the enlightened ones. By pondering first one can be saved from non-virtuous actions. One must be conscious that the enlightened ones are everywhere and know our every action. We must always keep in mind the enlightned ones. By remembering the enlightened ones we can stop all non-virtuous action. Remember Sanjay and the Great White Brotherhood. Call on them if you need help. They are always there to help you. Remember Sanjay!"

Within four days, my urine was back to normal and my eyes were their natural color. I felt completely cured, but continued to take the rest of the pellets. I was healthy! It was something of a miracle cure, as Western medicine has no treatment for hepatitis at present, although gamma-globulin shots are sometimes given as a preventative. Doctors are divided on its effectiveness. My doctor in Montana had recommended that I not get one, as they only last three months, and your resistance is lowered when it wears off.

That night at the hotel, as I drifted off to sleep, I remembered the Lama, admonishing us to "Remember Sanjay and the Great White Brotherhood!"

That electricity was known to the ancients is proved by these electric batteries from the first century B.C. now in the Bagdad Museum in Iraq.

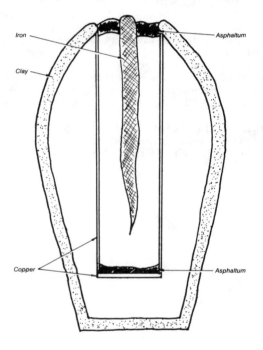

Baghdad Battery. Willard Gray of the General Electric High Voltage Laboratory produced the sketch above based on the specifications of the 2000-year-old Baghdad battery. With the addition of copper sulfate, acetic acid, or even citric acid, this battery will produce an electrical current. In the *Grand Dictionaire Universal du 19th Siecle* the French archaeologist Auguste Mariette writes that while excavating in the area of the Great Pyramid at a depth of 60 feet, he discovered gold jewelry whose thinness and lightness "make one believe they had been produced by electroplating."

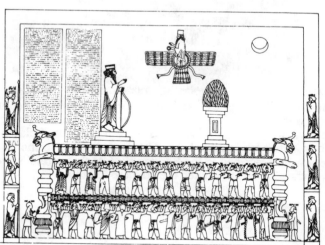

Part of the relief at Persepolis. Note the bearded man on the Winged Disc. Probably a representation of Zoroaster, it has been variously suggested that Zoroaster is arriving on a *vimana* or it is representative of a Sun Disc much as in Egyptian Atonism.

Remains of the ziggurat at Birs Nimrod (Borsippa), south of
Hillah, once confused with the 'Tower of Babel'. The ruins are
are crowned by a mass of vitrified brick work, actual clay bricks
fused together by intense heat. This may be due to the horrific
ancient wars described in the Ramayana & Mahabharata, although
early archaeologists attributed the effect to lightning.

A drawing by the French artist Flandin and the archaeologist Coste
of the trilingual cuneiform inscriptions at Gehistun, as seen from
the Hamadan-Kermanshah road. Their semi-inaccessible position
is well illustrated.

An aerial view of the ancient megalithic ruins of Takht-i-Suleiman, the Throne of Solomon. Takht-i-Suleiman is a round mesa with a spring fed lake from which two rivers spring. Ancient ruins and fortifications surround the mesa. Legend says that King Solomon landed his airship here while on his way to Central Asia.

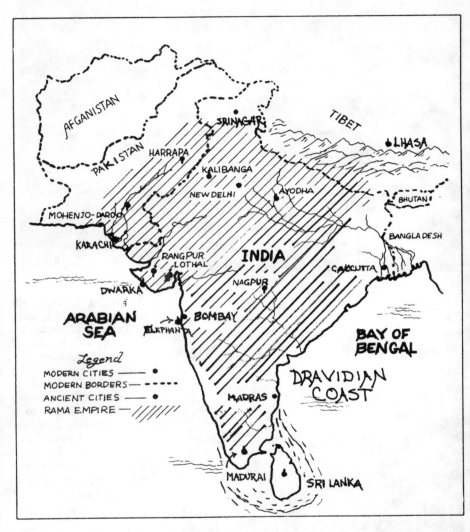

A map of the Rama Empire showing a few of the ancient cities in respect to modern India and Central Asia.

Chapter Six

KABUL TO CENTRAL AFGHANISTAN:

SMUGGLERS OF THE KHYBER PASS

Neither do I burden a camel
Nor do I carry a camel's burden
Neither do I rule, nor am I ruled.
Neither do I have anxieties about the
Past, the Present, or the Future.
Fully I breathe, fully I live life.
—Saadi of Shiraz

Since I didn't have much money, I decided to make a bee-line for Afghanistan, going to Amristar from Dharamsala. At the Indian-Pakistani border, I met a tall, lanky, fuzzy-haired British fellow named Danny. Danny was about six foot two, had a brown Afro, and wore black plastic glasses and green-striped jeans. All in all, he tended to stand out in a crowd.

"Where are you heading?" I asked him after we had both been through Pakistan Customs and our train was pulling into Lahore Station from Amritsar.

"Afghanistan," he said. "How about yourself?"

"The same," I told him. "Have you been there before?"

"Yeah, I was there for a little while on my way to India, three months ago. And you?"

"I came from the far east," I said. "I used to be an English teacher in Taiwan. This will be my first time in Afghanistan." He seemed like a pretty nice guy. I'm always happy when I meet up with someone congenial that I can travel with for a while. We got to Lahore Station and checked out the trains for Peshawar, on the Afghan border. There wouldn't be a train until later in the evening, so we had the rest of the afternoon to wait.

I went out and looked around the station, while Danny watched my pack for me. I had an ice cream cone, which tasted heavenly in that dry heat, and went to the Ministry of Youth, located near the station, where I got a student reduction on my railway ticket to Peshawar. Since I had a student reduction, Danny and I decided to travel by second class, instead of third.

Danny and I caught our train to Peshawar at nine-thirty in the evening. Unfortunately, there was only one second-class car on the whole train, so we didn't have a seat for the first two hours. I sat on my back pack and stared out a window for a while, until, at last, quite a few people piled out at one stop. Danny and I each grabbed a seat for the rest of the trip. I was awakened at one point in the middle of the night by a violent thunderstorm, with lightning flashing in the distance, revealing trees, houses, and dark stormclouds.

We arrived in Peshawar during mid-morning and took a horse-drawn carriage straight to the Afghan Embassy, where we got our visas for seven dollars each (a lot of money for us poor travelers). We checked into what was then the main travelers' hotel in Peshawar, the Rainbow Lodge. I imagine it was the most popular of all travelers' hotels in Pakistan, being right on the main drag to India. In those days of the Great Hippy Trail from Istanbul to India, most travelers passed right through Pakistan, just like Danny and I, preferring to spend their precious time and money in Afghanistan or India. I had wanted to go to the former "Rishi Cities" of the Rama Empire, some of which were in Pakistan, but would have to skip them this time, largely because of lack of funds.

We didn't see much of Peshawar this time around, and little did I know I would be back. After we got our visas at the Afghan Consulate, we showered, had a bowl of vegetable rice in the restaurant downstairs, and read some Captain Marvel comics. I played a game of chess with another traveler from Britain. Tired from the train ride from Lahore, I went to bed early.

Danny and I were up early the next morning, and immediately headed down to the bus station where we caught a local bus to Landi Kotal, a famous smugglers' town on the Khyber Pass. As usual, the bus was full, but, undaunted, we climbed up on top. Along with a dozen local Pushto tribesmen, we held onto the luggage rock and large bundles of goods wrapped up in blankets as we wound our way up the pass. We passed fort after fort as the bus climbed up the steep, barren mountainside. Often the road ran along cliffs with a sheer thousand-foot drop. Many of the forts had rather large cemetaries outside them, a grim reminder of when this was the frontier outpost of Britain's greatest colony. Many a Bengal Lancer and Gunga Din had caught some hot lead from mountain tribesmen during the frequent wars.

To this day, the people in this area are fiercely independent, and the Pakistan government rules over them in only the most cursory fashion. Landi Kotal, the famous smugglers' town on the summit of the pass, is in fact a nomans'-land where anything goes. Basically, no laws are enforced in Landi Kotal (drug laws in particular are ignored), nor are taxes levied. It is probably the biggest and most well-known smugglers' town in the world.

As we came to the town, after passing the last and biggest fort of them all with a memorial to the Khyber Rifles on it, we could see another, more rugged, road winding down in a valley below us.

"That's the smuggler's road down below us," said a bearded, rugged-looking tribesman sitting on top of the bouncing bus with us. Like most men along the Khyber Pass, he wore a turban, a long strip of cloth wound around his head, and a sort of pyjama suit consisting of a shirt with extra-long tails, and matching brown baggy pants. His English was pretty good, and he had a wrinkled, friendly face. "New Japanese tires come up this road, supposedly on their way to Afghanistan, and then are just brought back to Pakistan down the smuggler's road. You can buy anything in Landi Kotal; and I mean anything!"

It sounded wild, I thought as we climbed down from the bus in Landi Kotal, the end of the line. It didn't look like much of a town— small cafes, some cement buildings here and there, lots of low brown mud and brick buildings could be seen. Small Japanese pickups, American Jeeps, and a few buses were visible on the streets. There were quite a few people milling about, mostly men in turbans and brown or gray "pyjama suits." Most men were carrying rifles of one sort or another, with gun belts across their chests. No sooner had we collected our packs (we were the only foreigners to be seen) when a couple of young men came up to us.

"What do you guys want? Name it. Anything," one of them said to us. He looked about twentyish, had no turban covering his black hair, and his face showed a light "five o'clock shadow."

"We're just on our way to Kabul," I said.

"Yeah, sure," the other guy said. "Hey, look, how about a couple kilos of hash?"

"Oh, no, thanks," I said, shouldering my pack and looking around.

"Okay, heroin then. Cheap. How many kilos do you want?"

"Heroin? No, thanks. Look, we really have to catch a bus to Kabul..."

"A machine gun, then, some grenades? Here look at this!"

"What?" said Danny, suddenly interested. "What is that?"

The kid's patter picked up. "Just step over here. Cheap."

The dealers led us into a small open cafe right there on the street. The two kids ordered us all some tea.

"Look at this," said the kid in the cream-colored pyjamas.

He produced what appeared to be a ball point pen. "It's a gun," he said. Unscrewing it, he showed us how it worked. You placed a single twenty-two caliber bullet in the pen, and then it was fired by pulling back on a spring-loaded clicker on the back end, which would lock into place. That was the firing pin. To fire the pen gun, one then pressed down on the pocket clip, firing the bullet. This handy little zip gun, fired at close range, could be very deadly. Even close up it looked just like a Parker Pen. "Only fifty rupees," he said, which was about five dollars.

"That's interesting," I said. "But we've got to get going."

"Do you want it?" said the other kid.

"No, I don't think so," said Danny.

"Go ahead, take the zip gun," said the first kid.

"No, thanks," I said. "We've got to go."

"Don't you think it works? It works, man. Here, I'll show you." And he suddenly produced a bullet, which he started to load into the pen.

"No, don't do that," I said, standing up quickly and picking up my pack. "Really, we believe you. Please don't load that gun...let's get out of here, Danny!" I shouted.

"Wait, man, let me show you!" called the kid emphatically, running after us, loaded Parker Pen in his hand. Luckily we saw a small pick-up taxi just pulling out on its way down the Afghan side of the pass. We ran for it. It had already started rolling. We threw our packs in back and jumped in, slightly out of breath.

"Wait, wait!" shouted the kids.

"Is this truck going to the Afghan border?" I asked a bearded tribesman sitting in the back of the truck. He looked at me, perplexed. He must not speak English, I thought.

"Yes," said another man. "It's just a few miles down the road."

"Thank God," said Danny. "I thought we were goners back there."

"Really," I agreed. "Those things are dangerous; they can go off just like that!"

Our little adventure on the Khyber pass had come to an end. At least we had made it alive, unlike some foreigners before us....

§§§

We went through both borders in a flash. Neither the Pakistanis nor the Afghanis were very concerned about what we might be bringing into their country, or out of it for that matter. We changed some money with a money changer and boarded a bus for Jalalabad, on the road to Kabul. We rode on top of the bus again, getting a great view of the country before us. I immediately decided that I liked Afghanistan. It was mountainous, dry and barren. Men wore long brown, black, or blue shirts and baggy pants, with large turbans; carried big knives, long rifles; and generally had a cartridge belt on them somewhere. Though their appearance was as rugged as the country they lived in, they seemed to have a sense of humanity and were quite friendly.

In Jalalabad, we had a delicious lunch of kebabs, rice, and flat, fresh bread with sesame seeds on it. The town was full of mud brick buildings, with wooden verandas that created shade for the numerous tea drinkers, and other old men who sat around in the restaurants all day. As Danny and I sat drinking our tea, I watched two soldiers, dressed in torn, faded uniforms, walking down the street holding hands.

"Now, that's something you don't see every day—two policemen holding hands like that," remarked Danny.

"That's for sure," I said. Throughout the Arab world and most of Asia, in fact, it is common to see two men or perhaps two women holding hands and walking down the street. But rarely, virtually never, in a Muslim country, does one see a man and a woman holding hands. This would be considered scandalous. Women were not readily seen at all and the few that appeared on the streets were entirely covered by chaderis, long garments, like sheets draped over the head, with a meshes of lace to look through. One could not see women's faces, nor any part of their bodies except their hands.

A Moslem man may marry up to four women, according to Koranic law, as long as he can support them all. He may then divorce any of these by simply saying, "I divorce thee," three times. A women does not have this privilege, which would irk most females back in the States. A man must be careful how he looks at a woman as well. He is allowed to look at a passing woman twice, but not three times. The first time he may look at her by accident as they are passing, then he may look at her a second time if he thinks it was his mother or sister, but to look at her a third time would be considered very rude.

It has been said that the Koran forbids women to show their faces in public. However, the Koran only says that women should be modest. The practice of wearing veils is thought by some scholars to come from early Christians in Lebanon, who wore veils. Possibly the Moslems later picked up this habit from them. At any rate, it is rare to see a woman in Afghanistan or Pakistan, for that matter, except beneath a chaderi. Men, however, are more free, and often quite affectionate among themselves.

We decided not to stay in Jalalabad, although there were a few hotels around the market, and to head straight to Kabul that same day. It was only about one o'clock, and Kabul was an hour or two away. We got another bus, this time riding inside. It was a pleasant ride. Transportation in Afghanistan was surprisingly cheap and comfortable. The buses are mostly Mercedes buses, and the main roads are paved and smooth. Just before getting to Kabul, we passed through the incredibly scenic and steep Kabul Gorge, the road winding up along sheer cliffs, the river thousands of feet below. One wrong turn, and we would have all plunged to our deaths. As we emerged at the top of the gorge, we were in the Kabul Valley, nestled in the Hindu-Kush mountains. Shortly, Danny and I found ourselves at the central bus station in the eastern area of Kabul.

We got a motorized cycle rickshaw to take us to Chicken Street, the main tourist street of Kabul. There are a number of cheap hotels around Kabul, especially in the Chicken Street area. We ended up at the New Nuristan Guest House, which was at the northern end of Chicken Street, near the Iranian Embassy, on a friend's recomendation. Our hotel had a great little courtyard, where on cool, clear nights, we would sleep outside. As it was summer, it was scorchingly hot during the day, and also warm at night, so most people, especially the Afghanis, would sleep outside on the wooden strung-rope beds with cotton mattresses on them. One would generally lie on the bed in one's clothing, without even a sheet in the early evening, but toward morning, it would get chillier and one would use a sheet or light blanket.

There is good shopping along Chicken Street, especially for leather goods. Plenty of nice restaurants, too, serve mutton shish-kebabs, rice, salads, delicious flat bread, and apricot pies for a few cents. Danny got his hair cut and headed out of town for Herat and Iran on his way back to England.

I met up with a New Zealand woman named Karen, whom I had first met in India, and she moved up into the dormitory with me. I busied myself by getting an Iranian Visa and collecting mail. In those days of pre-Khomeini Iran and pre-Russian intervention in Afghanistan, my visa to Iran was free and good for multiple entires for five years. Boy! I had never gotten a visa like that before. "They must really like Americans in Iran," I mused as I walked down Chicken Street to find a restaurant.

One day after a big meal and several apricot and strawberry pies, I found I wasn't feeling too well. I had a tremendous amount of gas in my stomach, and was burping and farting something terrible. I made it to a pharmicist who gave me some pills for giardias (a type of amoebic infestation) and went back to the guest house where I finally threw up. I collapsed on my bed in the room, practically dead from the Chicken Street Shits.

I felt a lot better in the morning. Karen and I went out for tea and then decided to take a bus to Bamian, a hundred and forty miles northwest of Kabul, one of Afghanistan's "lost cities," and a fantastic mysterious place in the remote mountains of the central provinces. Within seven short hours our mini-bus was rolling up the long green valley to Bamian, which was also one of the most important Buddhist Pilgrimage centers in the third, fourth, and fifth centuries.

Famous for its Buddhist frescoes and rock-carved Buddhas, Bamian was a resting place for the early caravan trains between Balk and Peshawar. It became a place of pilgrimage after Buddhism was firmly established in northern India and Afghanistan. A vertical cliff rises abruptly from the valley and is honey- combed with a number of caves which possibly date form the same era. As we stepped off the mini-bus and looked across the valley at the cliffs, I was stunned. Carved into the rock, a brown sandstone, were two Buddhas, both enormous.

I blinked hard, and looked at them again. Because of the searing summer heat, there was a veil of rising hot air that gave the view a certain surreal aspect. I had the illusion that I was looking at a gigantic screen, with these cliffs and ten-stories-tall standing Buddhas projected like a faded cinema-scope print. The largest of the statues, officially the tallest Buddha in the world, is 174 feet tall, while the second one is about 115 feet tall. The cliff itself is a huge monastery. Windows and stairways could be seen all up the walls and it was possible to walk up to the top of the tallest Buddha through the rooms of the monastery.

According to certain esoreric tradtions, Bamian existed long before the fourth century A.D., and supposedly, like many other ancient cites, it was found intact, this time by a band of Buddhist monks who moved into it. This is quite possible, in my opinion. The statues are said to be "imperishable witnesses" to a secret doctrine left by Atlanteans who took refuge in Central Asia some ten thousand years ago. The statues and a network of caves behind them supposedly represent the work of the deities of these Atlanteans, much in the same was as the Easter Island statues are said to represent a "Glory of days gone by." 31

Oddly, the gigantic statues have no faces at all, and do not seem to have been defaced by the Moslems, since the cuts are as smooth as if made by expert workmen. One theory, now widely accepted, holds that the Buddhists apparently covered the original statues with plaster to transform them into Buddhas. This theory would then date the statues and monastery at before the fourth century AD.

D. by hundreds, even thousands of years. Here, monks lived for centuries collecting ancient records which were largely destroyed when Islam spread throughout Central Asia, especially along the Silk Road, into China. [33]

In the Lemurian Fellowship lesson material first published by the Lemurian Fellowship of Ramona, California in 1936, they state that several thousand Atlanteans were airlifted out of Atlantis in aerial vehicals known as "Vailxi" just prior to cataclysm that destroyed the small continent circa 10,000 B.C. These people then supposedly became the Aryans, who later invaded Iran, Afghanistan and Northern India, bringing with them the Vedas and Vedic culture. Could they have built Bamian?

Bamian and its caves are also frequently connected with the legends of Agartha. [54, 75] In Mysteries of Ancient South America, Harold Wilkins says, "Among the Mongolian tribes of Inner Mongolia, even today there are traditions about tunnels and subterranean worlds which sound as fantastic as anything in modern novels. One legend—if it be that!—says that the tunnels lead to a subterranean world of Antediluvian descent somewhere in a recess of Afghanistan, or in the region of the Hindu Kush. It is a Shangri-la where science and the arts, never threatened by world wars, develop peacefully, among a race of vast knowlege. It is even given a name: Agharti. The legend adds that a labyrinth of tunnels and underground passages is extended in a series of links connecting Agharti with all other such subterranean worlds! Tibetan lamas even assert that in America—it is not stated whether North, South or Central—there live in vast caves of the underworld, reached by secret tunnels, peoples of an ancient world who thus escaped a tremendous cataclysm of thosands of years ago. Both in Asia and America, these fantastic and ancient races are alleged to be governed by benevolent rulers, or King-archons. The subterranean world, it is said, is lit by a strange green luminescence which favours the growth of crops and conduces to length of days and health."[54]

Fantastic as it may seem, such a cave system does apparently exist throughout the Andes. It is well known in Peru, was used by the Incas, probably built thousands of years ago, and well documented. Wilkins devotes an entire chapter in his 1947 book to these "Atlantean Tunnels" as he calls them. The Peruvian government has sealed many of the entrances, but there are still occasional expeditions. I have actually seen several entrances and been inside portions of these tunnels (see my book, *Lost Cities &*

Ancient Mysteries of South America).
Does such a similar cave system exist in Central Asia? It occurs to me that it may well. Do the caves lead to some underground city of Agartha? Not necessarily. These tunnels, if they exist, may have been built thousands of years ago by Atlanteans, and are now incorporated into the mythology of hidden kingdoms and subterranean worlds. It is apparent, however, that Bamian with its caves and giant statues, is the main site in Afghanistan that is linked with the legend of Agartha.

Whether Bamian was actually built by Atlanteans, I had no way of knowing, though it seemed doubtful to me as I gazed in wonder at these colossal images. Still, I had no doubt that these ruins were older than the Greco-Buddhist culture of 1,500 years ago, but then there was a lot of history under the bridge since the theoretical sinking of Atlantis. The covering of the statues with plaster was quite obvious. Who had built these massive relics of an unknown civilization? They will, perhaps, always remain a mystery to their investigators.

Both Buddhas were wearing monk's robes, with concentric folds, which is typical of Greco-Buddhist statues in Central Asia. On the floor of the valley are many mud brick peasants' huts, over which the cliffs, rooms, and Buddhas loom. There are several hotel guest houses and restaurants near the small bus station. To the east of town is the impressive Red City, a ruined fort on top of a hill.

As Bamian is one of the central tourist spots in Afghanistan, there are several good hotels there, or at least there were at that time. I decided to check into the Caravan Hotel, where I got a bed in a room with three other people, French and Italian travelers, for thirty Afghanis, which was less than a dollar. Karen met a friend, and went off with her to the lakes of Band-i-Amir, several hours away by truck.

Just nearby was Bangladesh's Restaurant and Hotel, which was a little more expensive than the Caravan Hotel. They served good food at both hotels, as is generally the case in Afghanistan, including excellent kebabs, rice pilaf, chicken, bread, eggs, and apricot pies. (Afghanistan is not a vegetarian's delight as India, Nepal, and China can be. Meat is very much the staple, and is served at every meal. Vegetables are not so common, as the country is extremely arid, so the variety is rather poor).

Afghanistan has always been a strange, rugged and inhospitable place. It stands at the crossroads of Central Asia. Many an army has marched through the land-locked country that is slightly smaller than Texas in size. The Russians weren't the first country to march into Afghanistan; historically, the Afghans have been constantly invaded and often conquered by foreigners. Their history, like that of Iran, reads like a "Who's Who" of Conquering Armies.

Persia conquered Afghanistan in the early fifth centuty B.C., just about the same time that Zoroaster, the founder of Zoroastrian Religion, was born in Azerbijan. Zoroaster, like the other great teachers of Central Asia, was born about 600 B. C. and was a contemporary of Buddha, Confucius, Mahivira, and Lao Tzu.

Zoroaster's philosophy of good thoughts, good words, and good deeds became very influential in the rise of Persian civilization after he persuaded the King Vishtaspa to accept his philosphy. King Vishtaspa then spread Zoroastrianism by force throughout the Persian Empire. The general precepts of Zoroastrianism, which included reincarnation, karma and correct conduct, were put into the Zend Avesta.

Alexander the Great invaded Afghanistan in 330 B.C. One of the Afghan provinces, Bactria, broke away from the empire in 246 B.C. and became independent, governing northern Afghanistan for several hundred years. Eventually, the Moslem Arab armies conquered most of Afghanistan in the seventh century. Turkish-speaking tribes from north-central Asia invaded Afghanistan during the nine-hundreds through the twelve- hundreds.

Finally, as the icing on a long, bloody cake, Ghengis Khan and his Mongol hordes swept through Afghanistan in 1220 and practically wiped out the male population. Mongol leaders ruled Afghanistan until the seventeen-hundreds when the Persians re-conquered it. The Afghan tribes united for the first time in 1747, and revolted against the Persians. Ahmad Shah became the first ruler (or Shah) of Afghanistan.

The British and Russians then began vying for power in the young medieval state. The British invaded once in 1839 from India, on the pretext of doing it before the Russians could. They withdrew, but invaded again in 1878 to install a new, more favorable Shah. Meanwhile, the Khyber Pass was the British Colonial Indian frontier, where the Afghans and British constantly harassed each other. The Wakhan Valley was created as a funny extension to the northeast of Afghanistan to separate the huge super-powers of Russia and British India.

More recently, there has been coup and counter-coup in Afghanistan. In 1973, King Mohammed Zahir Shah was overthrown in a bloodless coup by his brother-in-law General Daud. Afghanistan stopped being a monarchy and became the Republic of Afghanistan. The only fatality in the coup was that of an over-excited tank commander who backed his tank into the Kabul River and was drowned. A counter-coup in 1987 estab- lished a "leftist," pro-Soviet government. Since the Russian "intervention" in Afghanistan, things have changed considerably because of several more coups. Tourists are now rarely allowed into the country, and travel there is dangerous, especially if you are caught in a bus that is ambushed by Afghan mujaheddin or "holy warriors."

When I traveled in Afghanistan, the civil war had yet to come, but it was still a dangerous place for the traveler. I wanted to head into Central Afghanistan, to some lakes known as Band-i-Amir. I decided to pay the charge for the two-hour ride in a pick-up truck from Bamian going west, instead of hitchhiking, as there were very few vehicles going there. I piled into the back of the pick-up with a half-dozen Afghanis and a few tourists, and by mid-morning we were off over the Hindu-Kush mountains.

It was a bouncy, dusty ride, there not being any real roads in the area. In the distance were the snow-capped peaks of the Shah Fuladi range rising over sixteen thousand feet. My companions, clean-shaven Afghanis, were wearing their typical extra-long shirts and matching baggy pants. One fellow, an un-turbaned clean-cut guy with light brown hair and blue eyes asked me where I was from in faltering, but decent, English.

"The United States of America," I told him. "Where are you from?"

"The Republic of Afghanistan!" he announced. Many Afghanis have very light complexions, being Aryans, not Arabs. "How do you like Afghanistan?" he asked me over the rumble of the truck.

"Nice country," I said. "I like Afghanistan very much. It is very wild."

"Yes, we have a very wild country. The people are, too."

"I have heard that. Is it dangerous for a foreigner to travel in your country?" I asked him as we hit a big bump and were all thrown into the air. Just then, we stopped for a tea break in a little village along the road. I got off and went to a small tea shop, the young Afghani joining me. The country was high, mountainous, bleak, brown and treeless. Still, people scratched out a living in these remote valleys. This one had a four-wheel drive road going by it, at least.

Answering the question I had asked earlier, he replied, "Yes, it can be dangerous for foreigners in Afghanistan. You should be careful. It is especially dangerous for women here. Are you married?"

""No," I said. "Should a woman travel around in Afghanistan?" Many did, I knew, tourists and so on. Of course, I thought of Karen who was traveling with another woman and was in Band-i-Amir right now.

"Well...." he said, "I would not let my wife, if I had one. The men of Afghanistan do not like it. They think that the foreign women who come here are prostitutes. They have no shame. Many of them are very foolish, too. They do not respect our customs, or understand that they are in danger here. The Afghanis are very proud people. In other Moslem countries, Iran or Turkey, they might rape and kill a woman whom they thought was a prostitute, as they think of many foreign women. But in Afghanistan, we are too proud to rape such a woman. We would just kill her. It is a disgrace to rape a woman."

I took a long sip of my tea and stared into his blue, friendly eyes. "That's very considerate of you," I said, ironically.

"We are civilized, in our own way," he went on. "I would never do any of these things. I am not a violent person. "

"Are you married?" I asked him.

"No, I just told you. It is expensive to get married in Afghan- istan. One must pay a dowry of twenty thousand Afghanis, that is four or five thousand of your dollars," he said, taking a sip of tea.

"That's quite a bit of money, " I said. "Where do you get it? Afghanistan is a very poor country. It would take a heck of a long time to save up that much money.

"I save my money. Perhaps my father will help me. I am studying to be an engineer in Kabul, so my salary will be higher than most people's in my country. Still, it takes a long time to save up the money for a dowry. Most men will be in their late twenties or early thirties by the time they have saved up enough money."

"That's a long time to wait. In the meantime, do you date?"

"Date?" he laughed. "Certainly not! We hardly get to see a woman, except our mothers and sisters, until we are married."

"Really!" I exclaimed. "That sounds rough!"

"When you don't know what you are missing," he said, finishing his tea, "You don't miss it."

We paid for our tea, and were climbing into the back of the Ford pickup. "We just have to wait," he said. "In the meantime, we have young boys...."

Three men or "gods" are apparently hovering in a flying machine above a half-moon in this cylinder seal from the British Museum in London. On the left is an unexplained rocket-like object.

A common Assyrian symbol found on cylinder seals and other reliefs. It may show an ancient *Vimana*

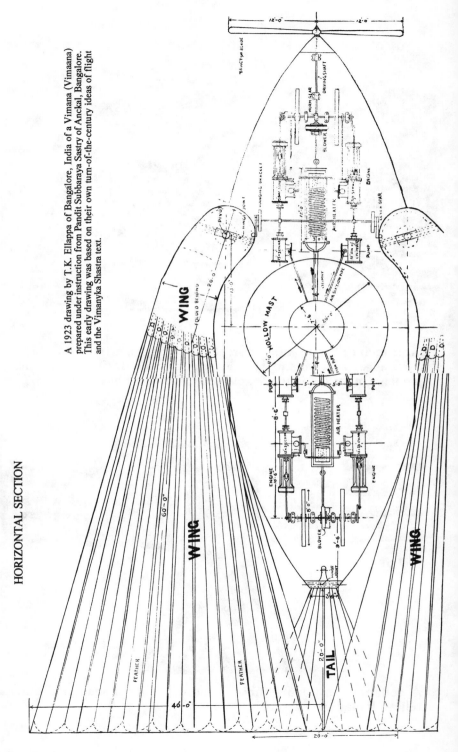

SHAKUNA VIMANA

HORIZONTAL SECTION

A 1923 drawing by T.K. Ellappa of Bangalore, India of a Vimana (Vimaana) prepared under instruction from Pandit Subbaraya Sastry of Anckal, Bangalore. This early drawing was based on their own turn-of-the-century ideas of flight and the Vimanyka Shastra text.

Chapter Seven

BALKH TO EASTERN AFGHANISTAN: THUS SPOKE ZARATHUSTRA

I should like to know what a man
who has no knowledge has really gained,
And what a man of knowledge
had not gained.
  –El Ghazali, *Persian philosopher*

I was tired and dusty when we arrived at Band-i-Amir, a tiny little tourist town in the middle of the central Afghan arid mountains. Looking down from the hill as we pulled into the town, I could see two long blue lakes cutting through the mountains. I gasped at the sight. They were the deepest, most vibrant colors of blue I had ever seen. The contrast with the brown desert and mountains around them made them look like gigantic lapis lazuli jewels in the dusty land. The lakes are not well known at all, and no one knows how deep they are, as no one has found a bottom yet. There are several of these lakes, linked like sausages, long and narrow, like some incredibly deep canyon filled with liquid color.

I spent the next couple of days exploring around the lakes. There were a number of little guest houses there, such as the Band-i-Amir Guest House or the Caravan Guest House, an affiliate of the one in Bamian. I met Karen again at breakfast. She had been there two days already, and was leaving that day. It was good to see her, and I was glad to see that she was all right.

I walked down to the natural earth dam between the first two lakes. There were several cascades leading down to the small pond where one could swim. The water in the lakes was absolutely ice cold, but in the shallow pond, the sun could warm the water up slightly. As I sat there by the lakes, once again eating apricot pie and gazing out into the vast, empty desert-hills beyond, I noticed an Afghan watching me from the top of a hill near the lake.

He was dressed in a long, black flowing robe. A black turban wound around his face and two cartridge belts crisscrossed his chest. He held a large rifle in his hand and stared at me intently. Uneasily, I finished my pie and walked back to the tourist village.

I met a Dutch physicist the next day, and we took a walk just before sunset that evening, climbing up a steep hill overlooking the lakes and the snowy Hindu-Kush in the distance. As the sun went down, the lakes became black with traces of blue or green along the edges. The sunset created a dull orange-brown glow all about the horizon of the high desert and seemed to illuminate the plateaus and cliffs in a curiously surrealistic manner, lending an awesome beauty to the scene.

To the west, the cliffs and rock formations were subtly silhouetted in this mystical shroud. I felt transported to another time, cast into the middle ages, a time of magic and hope, terror and darkness. The physicist had just been explaining to me about how nothing really exists, not atoms anyway. They are neither here nor there, have no real location and cannot be defined. Atoms are just empty space, yet vibrating to create the illusion of matter. As the shadows moved about the cliffs and hills I felt I was losing my grip on reality. Colors began to swirl and blend into each other, sucking me into them.

"Say, that's some sunset, eh?" said the physicist.

Like a rubber band, I was snapped back into the fourth dimension. "Yeah, really." I managed to say. We hiked down the hill in the growing darkness and went back to the tourist village for some tea and more apricot pie. Sometimes it seemed Afghanistan was like a phantom country, one that didn't exist on our own time plane. It certainly did not belong to the world of turbo-charged jets, space craft and silicon chips. Thank God.

Late the next morning, I was off in a pick-up to Bamian, bouncing in the back with a half-dozen Afghanis and a half-dozen traveling foreigners. I sat down next to a French woman, whose English boyfriend was on the other side of her. I was tempted to catch a different truck out when I noticed her scant clothing, but found that this would be the only vehicle out of Band-i-Amir that day. She was only wearing a pair of very short shorts and a tank top that nicely exposed her shoulders and cleavage. She was quite stunning and would have been well received on the Riviera, but after all, this was Afghanistan. She was obviously unaware of the conventional mores of this area of Central Asia.

The truck took the roads slowly; still, we were tossed about. In the distance we could see nomads on their way north. Their camel hair tents, called yurts, were set up. Camels and goats, as well as the famous Karakul sheep, grazed on the sparse vegetation. Meanwhile, the Afghan men on the truck were burning holes through the rather oblivious female tourist. I tried to look away, gazing at the scenery. Finally, she got a bit uncomfortable about the stares she was receiving, put a sweater on, and covered her thighs with a bandana. It was quite hot, but she must have been getting the message....

Suddenly the truck overheated, and we had to stop. We all got out and walked around. I wanted to get away from everyone and walked over to the crest of a hill, while the driver started to work on the machine.

An Australian fellow I had met in Band-i-Amir came up to me. "Boy, I'll tell you, mate," he said, "Those Afghan guys back there would kill that girl, I mean *kill* her, if there weren't so many foreigners in that truck. They know we'd never let them." He was rolling up a cigarette with some Afghan cannabis in it. Lighting it up, he said, "I don't suppose you picked up one of those little Parker Pen Zip-Guns they sell on the Khyber Pass for five dollars, did you? We may need it!" With that, he laughed and then took a puff. Life was, indeed, horrific and comical at the same time.

We made it to Bamian all right, and I spent another night at the Caravan Hotel, planning to hitchhike north to Mazar-i-Sharif the next morning.

"No, you'll never make it," said the manager of the hotel. "The truck drivers will never give you a lift. Better to go back to Kabul and take a bus from there."

"Maybe I can get a bus from Caricot on the main road to Mazar-i-Sharif," I said.

"No," he told me, "All the buses are full. Really, you can't get a bus to Mazar-i-Sharif from here or there, you must go back to Kabul!" he said adamantly.

It was the old you-can't-get-there-from-here routine. The manager was very friendly and helpful and concerned that I would get stuck in some small town, or perhaps he was worried about my safety, but wouldn't say so. And so I took the bus back to Kabul, waving good-bye to the giant statues of Bamian, and checked into the New Nuristan Guest House again. Just as I got there, diarrhea struck me. I made a mad dash for the downstairs bathroom, but it was locked. I was in dire straits, and dashed up to the bathroom upstars, but it, too, was occupied! I felt like crying, and then—after shitting in my pants—I did cry. Western men, I was once told by a psychologist, should cry more, so it was ultimately good for me...or so I told myself.

That night, I dragged my rope-strung bed out into the courtyard and sat with the owner, a pleasant, hospitable Afghan, and chatted with some of the other guests at the hotel. I turned to one Afghan to ask him what he thought of

America, then discovered he was an American Peace Corps volunteer from New Jersey, who dressed and looked just like an Afghan!

"America wasn't so bad," he told me, "But I like Afghanistan better."

I smiled and looked up at the moon, a great yellow orb in a black cloudless sky with a myriad of stars. It made me feel much better.

A Canadian traveler was playing his guitar and he was quite good. Lying back on my bed in the warm evening, and watching the clear, starry sky, I drifted off to sleep. The lyrics of the song he was singing echoed in my head:

"Won't you please read my mind,
Be a gypsy.
Show me what I hope to find
Deep within me.
But if you can't find my mind,
Please be with me...."

§§§

The entire next day, I was on a comfortable Mercedes bus, zooming north of Kabul on paved roads, toward Mazar-i-Sharif, the capital of Afghan Turkestan, a city famous for its great mosque. It is three hundred eighty miles to Mazar-i-Sharif, and the journey takes the best part of a day. Transportation is quite efficient and comfortable in Afghanistan, especially compared to India. Here the buses are large, comfortable and uncrowded. Cheap, too. Memories of the horrible crowds of India, pushing for a space on the train or bus, all faded away as I leaned back in my seat.

Mazar-i-Sharif is a town of 75,000 people or so, but has only a couple of hotels. I stayed at the Balkh Nights Hotel, the main traveler hotel, and the nicest of the hotels in Mazar-i-Sharif. It had a large courtyard, where nearly everyone slept during the hot summer nights underneath that superb Central Asian sky. They charged a dollar a night and it was more than worth it.

After a pleasant night out under the stars, I wandered around the city. Dusty and hot, it had wide streets, some scatterred shops, and a restaurant here and there. For a town of 75,000, it didn't have a whole lot to see. The Blue Mosque in the center of town was fantastic, however. A place of pilgrimage for many Moslems, the building has a huge entrance arch and twin domes, and is decorated with glazed mosaics of cobalt-blue and turquoise. It was dedicated to Ali, the fourth Caliph and brother-in-law of Mohammed, the man who started the division between Sunni and Shiite

Muslims. It was so incredibly hot that afternoon, that as I walked back to the hotel, I would duck into little sweet shops and have "Afghan slushes" (shaved ice with some noodles and sugar cane syrup) every block or two.

That night there was a wedding in the courtyard of the hotel. There was singing, dancing, and astonishingly, even women without veils. An English chap named Colin and I watched from the balcony of the second story, observing the wedding or gazing at the canopy of stars.

The next day, Colin and I decided to go out to one of the great lost cities of Afghanistan and Central Asia, once called the "Mother of Cities": the great Balkh. Known more recently as Wazirabad, Balkh is one of the most ancient cities in the world, and its origins date back to the very beginnings of time. Zoroaster, of Zarathustra, was born here in Balkh around 628 B.C. He founded the Zoroastrian religion, which is all but dead today. Balkh was part of the Persian Empire in the first millenium before Christ, and the capital of Bactria, an independent state before and after.

In 330 B.C., Alexander the Great's armies marched across Persia defeating the Persian King Darius III, who fled and was murdered by his own followers. Alexander marched into Bactria and its capital, Balkh. Here he married Roxanne, a Persian/Bactrian princess, and then continued into northern India. Bactria then became a Greek state, though many Persian officers were incorporated, serving in the army and government. When Alexander's troops refused to go any farther in India, they returned through Bactria and Persia to Babylon where Alexander mysteriously died, probably from poison. Bactria remained a Greco-Persian state until it declared independence in 240 B. C. About the same time, the Greeks in Bactria invaded India again, occupying it as far east as Pataliputra (Patna).

Balkh remained the capital of a powerful Greco-Roman state until around 120 B.C., when it fell to a nomadic tribe from Central Asia, the Sakas, and did not rise again as a state. It was out of Balkh, and northeastern Persia, that the Magi, the three wise men, came to visit the infant Jesus in Bethlehem. They were Zoroastrians, well-versed in the arts and sciences of astronomy and astrology (which were one and the same then) and, according to legend, they noticed the "signs of the heavens" that foretold the birth of Jesus.

Balkh was later taken by the Arabs in 653. By then it was also the birth place of a Sufi saint, Jelaluddin Rumi. It was still a mighty and wealthy city in those times. It rose to become a center of learning in Central Asia. Marco Polo came through Balkh on his travels and described the city as famous for its "many beautiful palaces and many marble houses." The end of Balkh came swiftly and violently. In

1221 Ghengis Khan and his Mongol hoards attacked the city and killed every living creature within the city walls, and totally razed the once-magnificent center of knowledge into a smoldering pile of dust and ashes. One Chinese historian that visited the city after the Mongols attacked was surprised to see a cat still alive in the smoking ruins!

It was a half-hour local bus ride out to the village on the edge of the ruins. There was quite a nice old mosque at the village, and a pleasant park, where a vendor sold shaved ice. Some kids were trying to sell some coins, the rumor being that they were from the period of Alexander the Great.

The ruins of Balkh were beyond the village on an absolutely desolate, dry plain. Mostly all that was left were the walls of the old city, and the foundations of buildings inside. However, there were still some pretty tall towers and portions of the battlements, all made out of brown, mud brick. The wind blew hard over the dry land and battlements. Colin and I stood in silence over the last remains of a great and ancient civilization, now turned to ruins.

"Dust, " said Colin under his breath, echoing my thoughts.

"It's like the end of the world," I commented.

Colin tossed his shoulder-length blond hair, and adjusted his wire-frame glasses. "You know," he said, "this is where Zoroaster first preached his message."

I knew of Zoroaster, or Zarathustra, as he is also known, but was not very familiar with his message. "What did he have to say?" I asked.

"Like all great sages, Zoroaster taught that good thought, correct deeds, good words and clean living, in the sense of not hurting other people, were the keys to higher consciousness. Like Jesus, he was said to be born of a virgin. His book, the Zend-Avesta, contains may good hygenic laws, long before these was such a thing as hygiene. In that, it's much like the Kosher Laws of Hebrews, which given the habits of the time, were very good advice. The Zoroastrians did not separate the sciences of astronomy and astrology—they were interchangeable—and they were very proficient and knowledgable in these areas."

Colin and I had to turn our backs to the strong wind that was blowing dirt across the brown, dusty plain. "It's funny," he said, "but the Zoroastrians had, as part of their doctrine, a struggle between good and evil. The Dead Sea Scrolls, written by the Essenes, a Jewish sect to which some scholars say Mary and Joseph belonged, also tell of the same cosmic battle between the 'Sons of the Light and the Sons of the Darkness'."

"Sounds kind of like 'Star Wars'," I said as we walked back to the village. "Whatever became of these Zoroastrians, and of Zoroaster himself, for that matter?"

"Apparently, Zoroaster was killed at the age of 77 during an invasion of Persia by the Turanians. Possibly he was even crucified by them, though no one really knows for sure. Some say he journeyed to the Valley of Immortals in western China, the same place that Lao Tzu was said to have gone. Zoroastrianism continued strong for a thousand years, but later corrupted...."

"Like all great teachings, it seems," I interupted.

"Yeah, I guess so," Colin agreed. "Zoroastriansim later mutated in the west and became known as Mithraism, a popular cult in Rome in the first century A.D. Many Zoroastrians continued to live in Persia and worship their deity, known as Ahura Mazda, who was symbolized by fire. When the Moslems invaded Persia in the seven hundreds, those Zoroastrians who were absolutely devoted to their religion fled to India, and now live in Bombay. They are called Parsis, their name coming from the Persian province of Parsa. There are more than one hundred thousand of these people living in and around Bombay today. There are also a few fire worshippers today in Iran, called Ghebers."

"So is that what Zoroastrianism has degenerated into," I said as we stood at the bus yard near the park, waiting for a bus back to Mazar-i-Sharif, "a bunch of fire worshippers?"

"Probably not what Zoroaster really had in mind. The Magis too, eventually earned a bad name, having degenerated into a bunch of sooth-sayers and crooked astrologers. The word *magic* is derived from the Greek word *magi*, and originally meant the 'works of Magi'," said Colin as we got our seat on the bus. "It would seem that the Zoroastrians may have succumbed to the 'Sons of Darkness'."

Colin decided to hitch the northern routh to Herat from Mazar-i-Sharif, a tough, long route, without paved roads or regular bus service. I thought about it, but it was so damn hot, I didn't know if I could take the heat in the back of a truck during the afternoon. I decided to check out the local Buzkashi games, a wild game where two teams of reckless horsemen compete for the honor of skewering a headless young goat (Buzkashi means 'goat game'), carry it around a post and then drop it in front of the judges at the starting point. It is a no-holds-barred game and quite a spectacle. There don't seem to be any real rules, and it can be quite dangerous, even for spectators.

It is not uncommon for someone to be trampled or otherwise hurt during the games. It's tremendously exciting, of course, and is played mostly in the north. Mazai-i-Sharif is the main place its played, but it's also played in Kunduz or Maimana. Unfortunately, I learned that it is only played in the winter, the summer months being too hot, I suppose.

I took a bus, which left at four o'clock in the morning, back to Kabul and arrived in the late afternoon on Chicken Street. I checked back in at the New Nuristan Guest House and ordered a pot of green tea and some cookies to have in the courtyard. As I sat, leaning back in a wicker chair, I suddenly saw my friend, the Dutch physicist that I had met in Bamian a week earlier.

"Hey, how are you?" I called.

"Hello! You'll never guess what happened!" he said, walking up to me, his black hair still wet from a shower. He had an English-Afghan newspaper in his hand. "Look at this." He showed me the newspaper. A story at the bottom of the page read, "Woman Shot in Band-i-Amir." "You know what happened?" he said. "A Magic Bus from London on its way to Kathmandu came to Band-i-Amir, just after you left. I was getting ready to leave myself and go back to Bamian, when I heard the story. These two English girls went down to the watering hole between the two lakes, and were swimming, either in the nude or with bathing suits.

"As they came out of the water, there was an Afghan guy standing there, all dressed in black: a robe, black turban, and of course, a rifle. He started shooting at the girls, and killed one of them. The other girl threw rocks at him and ran before he could get her! Not all this is in the newspaper, I heard it while I was in Band-i-Amir. Just got back a couple of days ago!"

"My God, that's terrible!" I exclaimed. And I suddenly remem- bered the Afghan I had seen when I was there, watching me eat my apricot pie. I guess I got lucky, though he was probably just after women.

"Some women just don't know how dangerous this country is. Afghanistan isn't exactly sourthern California," said the physicist.

The next day, I wrapped up my affairs in Kabul, and prepared to head west, to Kandahar, Herat, and Iran. I was careful about pigging out on kebabs, bread, salad, and pies this time. One must watch what one eats in Afghanistan, as Zoroaster's laws of hygiene are no longer in effect. I stopped in at the American Library in the afternoon, where I was treated to the nicest sight I had in all Kabul: an unveiled young women. She was working at the desk, was about seventeen and ravishing. I was captivated by her long black hair, ebony eyes, and wonderful smile.

"May I help you find something?" she said, as I stood staring at her in a dazed fashion. In a country where the women must, by custom, be covered from head to toe, this was such a treat. And if she was any indicator, Afghan women were very beautiful. No wonder then keep them locked and covered up!

"Oh, uh," I stammered, "do you have the *International Herald Tribune* ?"

"Just over there, with the magazines," she smiled. Tripping over a chair, I went for the magazines, and sat there for a while reading and secretly watching her. I suddenly recalled the Islamic adage that you should not look at a woman more than twice. I knew she wasn't my sister....

§§§

After one more night at the New Nuristan, sleeping outside under the cloudless desert sky, I was on my way to Kandahar in south-central Afghanistan. It is about a seven-hour bus ride to Kandahar from Kabul. I arrived at Kandahar in the early evening. I hadn't had dinner, so I looked around, and eventually ended up eating at a cafe called "Your Bakery." They had brownies, and good Afghan yogurt, which is available all over the country, and which I found was good for stomach upsets. I had originally planned on spending the night, but all the hotels seemed full.

What the heck, I thought, I'll just take the night bus to Herat, as I didn't really feel that there was that much to do in Kandahar, anyway. I had heard one horror story about Kandahar. It seems a couple of French Hippies were "hanging out" in the city when some of the local mujaheddin rode in out of the Registan desert to the south. These mujaheddin were not the "Holy Warriors" that are fighting the Russians, in fact, the Russians hadn't even entered the country yet. They were more like bandits, and quite fanatical Muslims, believing, as traditional mujaheddin do, that infidels, or non-believers, should be killed, for Mohammed had once said that it was not wrong to kill "unbelievers." I guess the mujaheddin took him very literally. These French Freaks were enticed to a hash party by the mujaheddin, while a few of their friends refused the invitation. The ones who went were never heard of again. Central and southern Afghanistan are pretty wild areas in a pretty wild country. One had better watch one's step, even when the country is not at war.

I wandered around Kandahar for a while waiting for the bus to leave for Herat. There is a market on Saturdays, a town square, camels, and perhaps, here and there, a few mujaheddin drinking green tea in a restaurant-tea shop, waiting to cut the throat of some infidel. Eventually, my paranoia, and conversely my boredom, regarding Kandahar got the best of me, and I caught the midnight bus to Herat.

I got on board the red Mercedes bus after paying a dollar seventy-five cents for the seven-hour ride to Herat, near the Iranian border. There weren't too many people on the bus. It was all native men, and each person had two seats to themselves. In the back were quite a few empty seats, and I took one near the window. We were soon on our way through the desert. Looking out the window, I saw millions of stars lighting up the Afghan sky.

After an hour, we stopped at a small town. A large Afghan male got on the bus. He was well over six feet tall with a black grisly beard, and was dressed in a gray cloak, and carrying a small bag. I watched him from the corner of my eye as he walked down the aisle. Then, to my absolute horror, he decided to take the seat next to me in the back of the bus! I couldn't believe it! With all the empty seats in the bus, why did he have to sit next to me? I seriously considered moving, but there was no place to move to where I would not be sitting next to someone else. All those horror stories of Afhganistan, about random killings, homosexuality, and fanatical religious beliefs, flitted through my mind. Calming myself, I placed my small day pack between us so that he wouldn't try anything funny.

I decided, as the night went by, that I had caused this to happen to me simply because I was afraid it would happen. As a friend once told me in Kathmandu, you are constantly attractiong things into your environment mentally, good things as well as bad. Fearing that something will happen is likely to make it do so.

I was grateful when we arrived in Herat, without incident, at seven in the morning. I checked into the Ariana Hotel, following a friend's recommendation. I was so early that I had to wait until mid-morning to get a room, as they were waiting for people to check out.

"How is this hotel?" I asked one American as he came down the stairs.

"It's a circus, you might say!" he laughed, and took off.

I wondered what he meant by that, as I collected my pack and proceeded to my room. Well, it turned out that there was, in fact, a circus staying at the hotel.

Herat was once the intellectual Mecca of Central Asia. A well-known "hang out" of Sufis back in the Middle Ages, Herat had a great mosque, begun by Ghiyat al-Din Sam in 1200 A. D., which was destroyed twenty years later by Ghengis Khan. Later, it was rebuilt and restored many times. When the people of Herat revolted against the Mongol rulers in the thirteenth century, killing Ghengis Khan's men at the garrison, Ghengis, testy fellow that he was, rode against Herat with eighty thousand men, beseiged the city for six months, and left only forty people alive!

The mosque of Herat is not quite as splendid or colorful as the Blue Mosque in Mazar-i-Sharif, but it is the second best, many scholars say, in Afghanistan. Just nearby is the ancient citadel of Herat, built by Alexander the Great in the fourth century B. C.

Herat is Afghanistan's second city. Though much older than Kabul, its population is only a third of Kabul's at one hundred thousand. I spent a couple of days looking around Herat, and did some shopping, buying some sandals, a pair of loose cotton pants, and a leather belt with a secret zipper pocket on the inside. On my last day, I walked to the outskirts of town where there were some minars: four minarets standing in the desert known as the Mussalla Complex. As I looked around at these ancient structures, I suddenly saw Colin. It was good to see him. He had had a good, but hot, ride through northern Afghanistan on his way here, he told me. It had taken him several days to make the journey. We decided to go to a tea shop for a respite.

We chatted about our journeys. I told him about the woman being shot in Band-i-Amir. He told me about an Australian guy who was murdered and castrated on the street here in Herat, very late at night a few weeks ago. In fact they had even imposed a curfew which was still in effect. Oh, well, neither of us was particularly worried.

An older Afghan at the next table wanted to talk with us. He seemed to be about seventy, had a long, grey beard, and wore a pair of brown baggy pants and matching long-tailed shirt.

"How do you like Afghanistan?" he asked, the standard opening line.

"Fine," I said.

"Sure," said Colin. "It's a wonderful place."

"Oh, thank you," said the old man. "We are a poor country."

"How do you like Americans?" I asked out of curiosity.

"We like Americans," he said. "They build roads for us. The road from Kabul to Herat was built by the Americans, I believe."

"Don't the Russians build roads in Afghanistan?" said Colin.

"Oh, yes," said the old man, his bushy grey eyebrows rising. "They have built more roads than the Americans. They built the nice road that comes from the Russian border down to Herat. But there is something funny about that road, you know."

"What's that?" asked Colin and I together.

"Well, the kilometer markers read from the Russian border to Kabul backwards. It makes sense if you are driving from Russia to Kabul, but not if you are an Afghan.

Funny, those Russians," he said. "They just do the strangest things...."

Colin and I looked at each other. The Russians had made their mileage stones to read for an invading army coming from the border, so it would know how many kilometers it was from Kabul or Herat.

"It seems," said Colin, as we finished our green tea, "that we are leaving the country just in time...."

According to Oriental tradition, this portrait of Jesus was painted
by Anan, secretary to King Abgar V of Edesse in Syria.

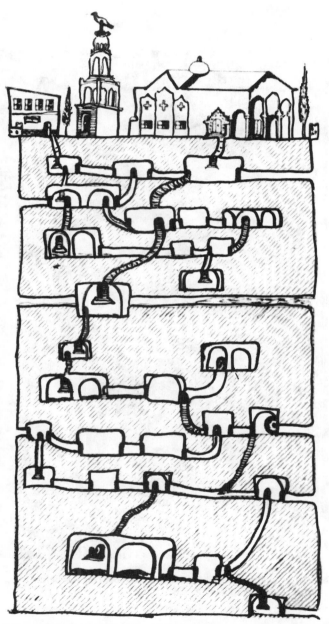

The underground city of Derenkuyu in central Turkey.

Chapter Eight

THE CASPIAN TO TEHRAN:

A JIHAD SWEEPS IRAN

All religion, as theologians and their opponents understand the word, is something other than what it is assumed to be. Religion is a vehicle. Its expressions, rituals, moral and other teachings are designed to cause certain elevation effects, at a certain time, upon certain communities. Because of the difficulty of maintaining the science of man, religion was instituted as a means of approaching truth. The means always became, for the shallow, the end, and the vehicle became the idol. Only the man of wisdom, not the man offaith or intellect, can cause the vehicle to move again.
  – Alauddin Attar, Persian philosopher

I took a mini-bus out of Herat to the Iranian border the next morning. Only fifty miles or so from Herat, I was passing through Iranian Immigration. They discovered that my cholera vaccin- ation was six months out of date, something that had slipped by the Nepalese, Indians, Pakistanis, and Afghans. But the Iranians were too thorough to let it slip by them. I was afraid that they would tear my pack apart looking for contraband, something that would have taken hours. There is a very impressive display in the customs building of places where they have found contraband on travelers (inside the soles of shoes, gas tanks, backpack tubing, etc.) To my relief (not because I was smuggling, but because I didn't want to have my pack dismantled) they passed me through customs without a second glance. They did, however give me a cholera shot, free and on the spot. I had never been too concerned with such stuff, and would often let my shots expire, especially cholera shots, which are supposed to be received every six months.

A French doctor had told me once, "They are totally useless, and won't stop you from getting cholera." He then asked me if I really wanted the shot, as I had gone to him

141

"Not especially," I said, as they often make you sick for a day or two.

"Then, I'll just validate your International Health Card," he said. "If I gave you a shot, I'd just have to open a new bottle of vaccine, anyway." This may give the traveler some indication as to the effectiveness of cholera shots!

I met several people at the border: a woman, who was a lawyer in Argentina, a couple of Italian hippies, and an English fellow who had been teaching in Tehran for two years, and had just taken a vacation in Afghanistan. Everybody piled into a bus and headed for Mashad, the capital of Khorasan Province in northeast Iran. Mashad was about a hundred and fifty miles away, and we got there at dinner time.

"Mashad, in Persian, literally means 'Place of Martyrdom', a reference to Imam Reza, the eighth patriarch of the Shia Muslim sect, who was poisoned here in the ninth century," said Philip, the Englishman I had met who was teaching English in Tehran. We were chatting over dinner that night in Mashad. "There is a memorial for him right here in Mashad, the Imam Reza Shrine, the holiest place in Iran to Muslims."

"What is the difference between the sects of Islam, anyway?" I asked, helping myself from a bowl of beans in a tomato-mutton sauce. "All this Sunni Muslim, Shia Muslim stuff and then some sect called the Ishmaelis?"

"Basically," said Philip, munching on pita bread, "The Sunnis are the fundamental sect of Islam, and the most numerous. They believe that when Mohammed died, God's revelation to man was finished. Everything, therefore, stands on the Koran and Mohammed's works, there is nothing more. The Shias believe, however, that God's revelation to man was not finished with Mohammed, but was continued by Mohammed's successors, including his brother-in-law, Ali.

"Ali was known as the Imam, and continued to reveal God's word, supposedly. There was then a succession of Imams, all in a hereditary fashion, directly descended from Mohammed. This chap who's buried here, Imam Reza, was the ninth Imam in this succession. However, according to the Shiites, after the twelfth Imam, they no longer appeared in physical bodies, as they had before, but only existed in the spirit form, so to speak. This is the difference between the Ishmaeli sect and the Shia sect; the Ishmaelis still believe that the Imam takes a physical form, and is present on earth. He is still a direct descendant from Mohammed, and is known as the Aga Khan."

"The Aga Khan!" I said. "Yeah, I've heard of him. Where does this Aga Khan live?"

142

"The Aga Khan is from Bombay, India, but lives in London. Most Ishmaelis live in Pakistan, India, and East Africa, among the Indian immigrants. There are little pockets of Ishmaelis here and there around Arabia, but it's mostly popular in the Indian sub-continent. There are many Shiites there, too. Iran is almost entirely Shiite, while most of Arabia and North Africa is Sunni. They often don't get along too well, either. Like the Catholics and Protestants in Northern Ireland, they focus on their differences. The twelfth and final Imam yet to come will appear on the 'Day of Judgement' and is called The Mahdi," said Philip as we finished and paid for the meal. The Day of Judgement, I thought, could be coming soon, considering the state of the world.

Mashad, a city of over six hundred thousand, is one of the biggest cities in Iran. A large old city, it is dominated by the Imam's Shrine, has a new cement jungle downtown, and some cheap hotels close to the bus and railway stations at a couple of dollars a night for a bed. There isn't a whole lot to keep travelers occupied here. It is the terminus of the railway from Tehran, and quite near the Russian and Afghani borders.

The Italians, the Englishman, a couple of Pakistanis, and I spent the night in some nameless hotel, each getting a bed for two dollars in a room with six beds and a table. There happened to be a religious festival going on in Mashad at the time, and the next morning, Philip told us it would be impossible to get a bus into Tehran from Mashad. But we could take a bus to Bojnurd and get a bus from there.

"That's okay," I said, "I would like to hitchhike, anyway."

"It would be better to take a bus to Bojnurd, about four hours from here, and start hitchhiking from there. It could be a little difficult to hitchhike out of Mashad at this time," Philip said. We all grabbed a bus, and were soon roaring off through northeastern Iran.

We reached Bojnurd at noon, and I decided to start hitching, as my funds were quite limited, and Iran was much more expensive than Afghanistan. The others took a bus on to Tehran, leaving me behind.

I looked up and down the road. I was waiting for a lift to Tehran, or its environs. I had taken a city bus out of Bojnurd onto the main highway that went to Tehran, and was now waiting for a lift. A couple of trucks had passed me, but I hadn't been waiting too long, when a big truck, a Tad-Iran Mercedes, came around the corner. I started jumping up and down, and waving my right arm down the road. My gestures were wild and exaggerated. I wanted that guy to stop!

He came to a screeching halt just past me, and I grabbed my pack, then ran up to the cab. Without saying anything, I opened the door, threw my pack up and inside, and climbed in. We were off.

"Where are you from?" asked the driver as he shifted gears. I took a breath and looked over at my benefactor, noting his youth, his English, his short, brownish-black hair and brown plastic glasses. He seemed like a nice guy.

"I'm from America," I said. "Where are you going?"

"Tehran," he said, looking down at my pack. "Are you traveling around the world?"

"Not really. I'm just coming from Afghanistan. Today is my second day in Iran."

He handed me a bag of pistachios. "How do you like our little country so far?"

"Well, I can't really say yet. But I've heard a lot about Iran; how do you like it?"

"Well...." he said. Perhaps he did not feel free to speak. The Shah was still in power at the time and had his dreaded SAVAK agents everywhere. One never knew when a knock on the door would mean imprisonment and torture for "treason." "Iran is growing very fast, " said my driver, "We are going at full speed to become like the European countries. The Shah is a very powerful man. You see, here in Iran we have a dictatorship. One must be careful what one says about the government. The Shah declared that 'There is plenty of room in our country for complete freedom, but there is no place in our country for treason.' It is hard to determine what is treason. These SAVAK people are terrible, and they are everywhere. If they get you, then no one will ever see you again...." He was quiet for a moment, and staring out the window at the road.

"How do you know that I'm not a SAVAK agent?" I asked.

"You are too young, and you are American. We like Americans, but some people feel bitter about America, because it supports the Shah."

"Hasn't the Shah made a lot of progressive reforms for women and improved the economy?" I asked.

"I suppose so. Many people, especially the older ones, are very conservative. They say that Iran is changing too fast. They want to return to the old ways."

It was true. There was such a big difference between Afghanistan and Iran it was like taking a three-hundred-year leap out of the Middle Ages into the twentieth century. Iran looked like a strange combination of old and new. The Shah had said, "You people in the West find it hard to believe us when we say that in ten years we will be another

France or Germany. But I can assure you it is no exaggeration: Our young people will inherit a different country." Iran was certainly rushing into the twentieth century at such great speed that you could almost say they were out of control. Most Iranians were suffering from some form of "future shock."

The scenery was mountainous and rugged. There were many farms and cultivated fields in the valleys, the number of farms increasing as we got near the Caspian Sea. The Caspian Sea is not really a sea, but, in fact, is the largest lake in the world, covering over forty-three thousand square miles, and more than four times as large as Lake Superior, the second largest lake in the world. From the Caspian Sea comes one of the world's most expensive foods, caviar, produced from the eggs of the sturgeon that live in the lake. Iran's main caviar-producing town is Bandar-e-Pahlavi, further to the west.

We barreled on through the night. It was a twelve-hour trip from Bojnurd to Tehran, and we finally arrived at the capital city just after midnight. I thanked my driver warmly as he let me off in downtown Tehran near the Amir Kabir Hotel. A large hotel, and cheap, the Amir Kabir has for years been the stopping-off rest spot in this big, modern city for hitchhikers and travelers on their way to India. I got a bed in a room with two other guys for two dollars, and crashed out for the night.

One out of every ten Iranians lives in Tehran, a city where the contrasts of Iran are the most pronounced. For example, across the street from the multi-million new municipal hospital is an open sewer! Traffic is one huge snarl beneath the 148-foot tall Shahyan Tower, the unmistakable symbol of Tehran. One could consider it the Eiffel Tower cum Arc de Triomphe of the middle East. Dedicated in 1971, it is a gigantic cement thing that twists and turns on two legs like some misshapen "gumby doll" while traffic flows between the two "legs."

Iran takes its name from the Aryan invaders that came out of Central Asia some three to five thousand years ago to conquer much of Asia Minor and Northern India, hence the name Iran (Aryan). Like Afghanistan, Iran was on the main trade route between the west and the east, and its history (like Afghanistan's) reads like the "Who's Who" of invading armies. It seems that anybody who was anybody invaded Iran at some time or another. In the sixth century B.C., Cyrus the Great conquered all of Asia Minor. He ruled this huge empire, including Palestine and later Egypt, from his famous capital, Takht-e-Jamshid, "The Throne of Jamshid," named after a legendary Aryan king. The Greeks called the city Persepolis, "City of Parsa," hence the Greek

145

name of Iran: Persia.

But empires were made to be conquered, and Alexander the Great had a "great" time marching his armies across Persia in 330 B. C. They torched Persepolis, and ruled the country for eighty years. The rest of Persia's history is one of invasion after invasion. After the Parthians and Romans had invaded the country, the Arabs moved in, bringing the new religion of Islam with them to replace the Parsis (Zoroastrian) religion. They also introduced the Arabic alphabet, and Persia became a great center of science and learning not just for the Islamic world, but for the entire west, including Europe.

Eventually, Genghis Khan and his hoard of merry Mongols swept through the country, destroying many cities and killing millions of people in their fervor to create the world's biggest empire ever, the Mongol Empire. Later, after the Turks and Afghans had invaded the country, Russia invaded in 1826 so that it could have an outlet to the Persian Gulf. A subsequent treaty determined Iran's present northern boundary with Russia. Not to be outdone, the British declared war on Iran in 1856, after the Persians had seized Herat in Afghanistan.

In 1926, an Iranian army officer named Reza became dissatisfied with the weak government of Ahmad Shah, and marched his troops into Tehran and seized control of the government. He became Reza Shah Pahlevi, founding the Pahlevi dynasty. During World War II, the British and Russians forced the Shah to resign, as he insisted on remaining neutral in the war. His son, Mohammed Reza Shah, became the new ruler.

§§§

I wandered the streets of Tehran, down to the central bazaar, a nine-mile covered labyrinth of some six thousand shops selling spices, leather, bread, gold, lighter fluid, you name it. Here I met a young woman from Washington, D. C., who was traveling with her husband. I had been introduced to them at breakfast that morning at the Amir Kabir. For some reason, I was incredibly attracted to this woman, who I now saw without her husband. She was pretty, of slight build, but my attraction to her was something else. It quite mystified me, but there was a certain quality about my feelings that I had never had before, and especially with someone I had just met and had only had a few words with.

"Hi," I said, walking up to her at a bakery. "Out shopping?"

"Yes. My husband is at American Express for the day. I'm just out for a stroll. What are you doing?" she asked, smiling. I guessed she was about thirty; she and her husband were on their way to India.

"Oh, just being a tourist," I said. "May I walk with you through the bazaar?"

"Of course," she laughed. And we strolled through the streets, tasting pastry, bargaining for souvenirs, and talking.

"You know," she said, "A person in Washington, D. C., once told me a kind of odd thing. He was a guy I'd met who said he had great psychic powers, and also bragged that he was a great lover."

""Oh, yeah?" I asked, laughing, as I dodged a girl in a long black chaderi who went running past.

"Well, he was fat, and rather unattractive, and besides, I was already married. But he told me a curious thing. He said that Hitler was some kind of 'anti-Christ', and that another 'anti- Christ' was living in France. And that he was some Iranian guy!"

"Really!" I said. "What made him think that?"

"I don't know. But he said the guy's name was something like Komanee."

"Komanee," I said under my breath. "Hmm, I've never heard of that name."

"Me neither,"she said. "It's just something kind of strange I seem to be remembering since we got to Tehran."

I realize now that it was indeed strange that we should have had this conversation. Khomeini at this time was already well into his secret campaign to oust the Shah. Iran was certainly ripe for his takeover as well. The Shah of Iran, who called himself Aryamehr, "Light of the Aryans" and Shahanshah, "King of Kings," was nothing if not terribly conceited, cruel, and naive. In his book, *The White Revolution of Iran*, he had predicted that in the future man would wage war only on social evils, not on his fellow man. Khomeini had carefully plotted his campaign against the Shah focusing, ironically, on social evils. No Iranian could have ever imagined the terror that would grip many Iranians with the overthrow of the Shah, and the triumphant return of Khomeini. For every step the Shah had taken forward in westernization for Iran, Khomeini took it two steps back, into the dark ages. Iran was turned overnight into a fundamental religious state that ruth-lessly wiped out its opponents, and those that did not adhere to its codes.

In retrospect, it is interesting to compare the philosophies of one anti-Christ with another. I know that Hitler believed that the earth was hollow, and inside it lived a race of supermen, dwelling in "eternal ice." The Aryans were supposedly the ancient descen- dants of these supermen, and were destined to rule the world, as superior beings. (Khomeini doesn't believe in hollow earths or supermen to my knowledge, but is the fountainhead of a new fanatical religion of suicidal martyrs who will kill and terrorize the world at his whim. This thought produces a rather frightening picture.) Other esoteric tradition relates that the Aryans were the descendants of Atlantis, airlifted into Central Asia, to what is today Western China, as this was considered a safe area during the cataclysm of circa 10,000 B. C. that sank Atlantis. It wasn't until another climactic change occured that the Aryans moved out of this area into Persia and India around 4000 B. C.

"We'd best head back to the Amir Kabir," said the woman from Washington, D. C. It was a short stroll back to the four-story hotel. We stopped outside my room for a moment. I suddenly thought again about my uncanny attraction toward her. It was something mystical, wonderful and overpowering. I looked deep into her brown eyes, and she reached over to brush her short black hair back from her forehead. Suddenly, I had my arms around her. Both of our faces were red from embarrasment, but she didn't pull away, nor did I let her go.

"I'm married, " she said, still blushing.

"I don't know what's gotten into me," I said. "I...I can't help myself. I'm so attracted to you, and I don't know why."

"Yes, there is something going on here," she said. "I'm also very attracted to you. I'm not sure, but I think...I think perhaps, we might be what they call 'soul mates'. Have you ever heard of that?"

"I don't think so. But I think I know what you mean."

"I really must go. It was nice talking to you today. Goodbye," she said, and pulled away from me. She ran up the stairs to her room. I stood there for a long time looking at the stars. What was getting into me?

§§§

Do not regret the past
And do not worry about the future.
—*Dhun-Nun* , *Sufi*
philosopher

I spent a few days in Tehran, getting a feel for the city, and doing a few errands like going by American Express to get my mail. I shared a room at the Amir Kabir with a French guy and a sailor from New York City who bragged that he could say, "I want oral sex," in nine different languages.

Iran has a number of mysteries, and even a few "lost

148

cities" which are worth looking into. Persepolis is by far the greatest and most well-known site of antiquity to be found in Iran. Started by Darius the Great, probably around 520 B.C., it was soon well- known throughout the western world as one of the great cities of its time. The Apadana Audience Hall was one of the largest enclosures ever built, and the city itself was built, supposedly, on divine influence, after Darius' father, Cyrus, was converted to Zoroastrianism. Most of the work was later completed by Darius' son, Xerxes.

Persepolis attracted scholars and people from all over the world. In the Book of Esther in the Bible, it says that when the candidates for the Persian queenship were assembled by King Artaxerxes, they were brought to the royal harem and there they were treated for "six months with balm and six months with spices." When Alexander sacked and burned the great city in 331 B. C., it is said that it took no fewer than thirty thousand mules and camels to carry the treasure home to Greece. There is still a great deal of Persepolis to be seen today, and it is located in southern Iran, just near the city of Shiraz.

Iran's mysteries hint at the splendor and level of civilization that this part of the world evolved. Incredibly, there are a number of electric batteries in the Bagdad museum, found in 1938 by the German archaeologist Wilhelm Konig. These are earthenware jars with necks covered with asphalt and iron rods encased in copper cylinders. Inscriptions apparently indicated they were from Parthia, part of the Sassanid Empire, which included Iran and parts of Iraq. In tests, they produced electric current, and were apparently used for electroplating. Electroplated objects have been found around Bagdad and other areas of ancient Babylon and Persia.[62] Ancient batteries and electric lamps have been reported in ancient Egypt, India, Greece, Central America, and even in remote areas of New Guinea and Indonesia, as well as South America and Tibet. [31] Thus, it seems that electricity was known to the ancients.

How old is civilization in Iran? According to most historians, the Elamite civilization in southwest Iran is the oldest, dated as beginning around 3000 B. C. However, a civilization called Tepe Yahya was found in southern Iran in the Soghum valley. It is believed to be part of the Elamite kingdom, and stone tablets found there proved to be receipts for imported and exported goods, indicating that Tepe Yahya was already a trading center around 4000 B. C.

At Shahda, southeast of Tehran in the Dasht-e-Lut desert, a necropolis of red clay pots, believed to have been coffins, was found, though no bodies or remains were found in them. These dated from around the same period, or possibly earlier. Some of the pots were inscribed with an unknown writing. Excavation of the site has just begun, but it is already believed to be a cultural center of some importance, though it is of an unknown civilization. The area is quite desolate, and occasionally floods, which might have wiped out many traces of civilization. It would seem that the climate was quite different at the civilization's time, as present conditions are not very positive to the growth of a community. [51]

According to some sources, mainly ancient Indian records, the Nagas, who inhabited Central India, at one point emigrated by ship up through the Persian Gulf and into southern Iran and Iraq. They brought their scientific knowledge and culture with them, founding, among other places, Babylon.[8] Could the ruins at Shahdad be a Naga settlement? Could they have been the ones that brought the knowledge of electricity from India into Iran and Iraq? Much of the legends of the great cataclysm or "flood" come from Babylonian sources. That some change in the earth's land masses and seas has occured can be evidenced in the ancient Sumerian port city of Ur, which today lies buried in sand far from any river or shore.[71]

Iran, being situated at the crossroads of Asia, may well have been a center for world travel. In Atlantean times, many cultures, according to Indian and esoteric sources, flew in cigar-shaped airships, similar to zeppelins. King Solomon of Jerusalem is said to have had a "heavenly car" in which he often flew, according to the oldest of the Ethiopian scriptures, the Kebra Nagast. [34] Throughout the Middle East, as far as Kashmir, are mountains known as the "Thrones of Solomon," including one in northwestern Iran, a flat-topped mountain called Takht-i- Suleiman (Throne of Solomon). It has been conjectured that these may have been landing bases for Solomon's airship, left over from Atlantis or the Rama Empire of India, I suppose.

Nicholas Roerich testifies that throughout Central Asia it is widely believed that Solomon flew about in an airship. "Up to now, in the people's conception, King Solomon soars on his miraculous flying device over the vast spaces of Asia. Many mountains in Asia are either with ruins or stones bearing the imprint of his foot or of his knees, as evidence of his long-enduring prayers. These are the so-called thrones of Solomon. The Great King flew to these mountains, he reached all heights, he left behind him the cares of rulership and here refreshed his spirit." [69]

Incredible as it may seem, the old Sassanid town of Ardashir Khurra, located near ancient Persepolis, was a city divided in four quadrants. At the center was an eighty-foot tower, hollow inside, but without doors, windows or steps. (The Sassanids ruled Persia just after the time of Christ, and were the last native rulers of Persia, though the towers may be older than their dynasty, as the town appears to have been built around the tower.)

Archeologists are mystified as to why anyone would build such an impractical tower, and yet there is one that is identical at Zimbabwe Ruins in southern Africa. The great tower there is about the same height, has no doors, windows or stairs, and is also hollow inside! Archeologists are just as mystified by this tower, and interestingly, the ruins are also associated with King Solomon's Gold Mines of Ophir! Furthermore, both towers are associated with "flying men." Did King Solomon have some flying vehicle with which he flew to Tibet? With whom did he meet there? Given the many stories of flying vehicles from the ancient Indian epics, this is not so unusual. Mountains with ruins on their summits exist all over the world, such as the "thrones of Solomon." Were they landing pads for flying vehicles similar to zeppelins? It is a strange world, full of strange stories, legends and ancient mysteries. Sometimes, indeed, "truth is stranger than fiction!"

George Sprod: 'Solomon Visiting Sheba', cartoon (from Sir Leonard Woolley, *As I Seem to Remember*, George Allen & Unwin Ltd, London 1962)

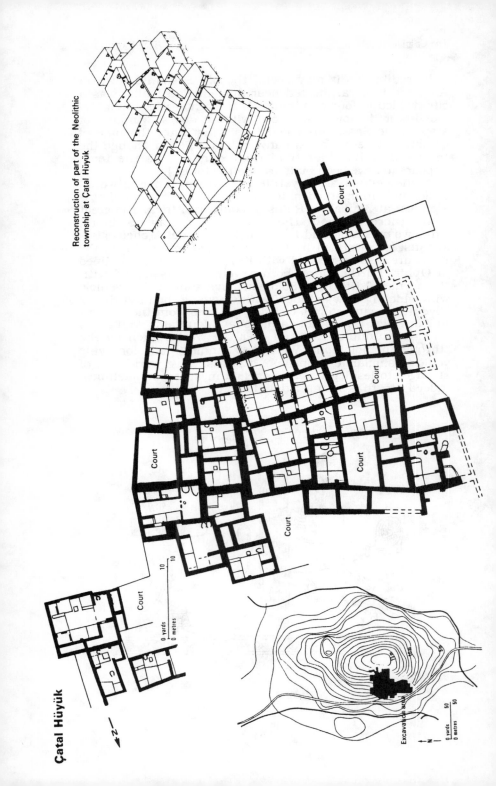

Çatal Hüyük

Reconstruction of part of the Neolithic township at Çatal Hüyük

Court

Court

Court

Court

Court

Court

Excavation area

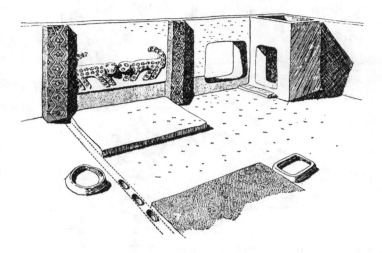

North and east walls of the Leopard Shrine at Çatal Huyuk, 9,000 years old, in Turkey. This leopard motif is identical to that used in South America at Samaipata in Bolivia and other places.

Restoration of the east and south walls of shrine VI.14 at Çatal Huyuk. Bulls' and rams' heads are modeled in relief and a ladder is on the right. These ladder cities were identical to the Pueblo cities of the American Southwest, though thousands of years earlier.

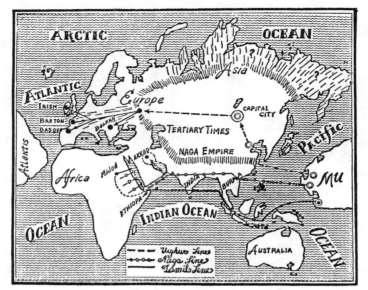

James Churchward's drawing of the dispersion of tribes from the ancient Pacific continent called variously Mu, Lemuria or others. The Naga Empire allegedly founded the Rama Empire.

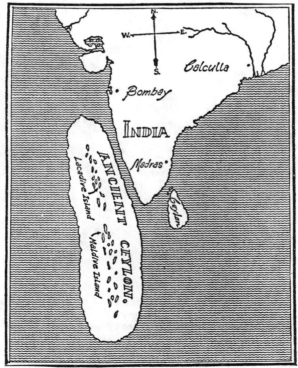

Churchward's drawing of ancient Ceylon, which is instead a large island that includes the Lacadive and Maldive Islands.

Chapter Nine:

TABRIZ INTO ASIA MINOR:

MOUNT ARARAT AND THE CULT OF THE ASSASSINS

I mean those to whom traveling
is life for the legs.
The traveler must be born again on the road,
and earn a passport from the elements,
the principle powers that be for him.
He gives no rest to the sole of his foot,
and at night weariness must be his pillow.
—Henry David Thoreau

Time was running out, and I decided to head for the western border and Tabriz. Hitchhiking out of Tehran, I caught a lift with a truck driver who spoke only a few words of English. He was pleasant enough, and took me right into Tabriz. A serious man in his thirties, he had, as so many Iranians do, a heavy "five o'clock shadow." I gathered that he was married and had two daughters, but no sons. He seemed rather depressed when he told me that. We stopped once, and he bought me a soft drink at one of the roadside shops. Iran is one of the world's largest producers of pistachio nuts, and they are cheap, too. I bought a big bag, and had them for lunch.

He let me off in the central market of Tabriz, the carpet capital of Iran, and one of the oldest cities in the country. As I walked down the street with my pack, looking for a hotel, a young man in his twenties, came up and asked, in English, if I was American.

"Yes, " I said. "Are you from Tabriz?"

"Yes, I am, " he said, smiling. "Can I be of service to you?"

"You certainly may. Could you please help me find a hotel? Maybe the cheapest hotel in Tabriz?"

"Hmm," he said. "There are some hotels over here, just near the bus stand; let's check them out." We walked down to the bus stand, and checked a few hotels in that vicinity, most without English names. We finally settled on one that cost a dollar-fifty a bed in a dormitory room with five other people. The beds were clean and simple, with a blanket neatly folded on the end. A couple of old guys with gray hair and beards were napping on the beds at one end.

It was just getting dark, and my new friend and I went out for dinner. We found a small restaurant and went inside, choosing our food cafeteria-style from the hot steel tray on the counter. We talked about Iran and America for a while. He was dressed in jeans and a T-shirt that said AMERICAN BICENTENNIAL, and wanted more than anything to go to America. He showed me around town, and we talked about girls. He had never been on a date, but said it was theoretically possible to meet a girl at a movie, or something. In the big cities, it was much easier than in the country, where people were naturally more old-fashioned.

The next morning I was at the truck depot, where I met another English-speaking Iranian who said he would help me get a lift to Tabriz. He was hitchhiking out of town himself, in the same direction. We found a truck and got in, but then the driver changed his mind for some reason, and told us to get out. We then decided to catch a mini-bus to the next town. We cruised along in this little eighteen-seater bus, picking up people along the way and letting them off, often in the middle of nowhere. The scenery was dry, mountainous and rugged; small villages of low adobe-style houses dotted the landscape.

My Iranian friend got off at a village, and told me to get off at the next crossroads, as the bus would be turning off the main road to Tabriz. The bus let me off, and then I stood there in the middle of a desert crossroads, with absolutely nothing in sight except a few gnarled, old trees on the horizon near a rocky outcrop of hills. I chewed on a cucumber as a few cars passed, all going in the opposite direction. It suddenly occurred to me that this was the territory of the ancient cult of the "Assassins," a secret order—and perhaps a branch of the Shiite religion—that was founded by Hassan Sabah late in the eleventh century.

Hassan maintained his cult in the secret fastness of his mountain fortress, called Alamut, nearby. Members of the Assassins (an Arabic word meaning "Hashish eaters") would ruthlessly exterminate their political oppoonents. They became quite a political power, and grew strong all over Persia and Syria. Eventually, toward the end of the twelfth century, the Syrian branch of the Assassins separated from the Persian sect. The crusaders came into contact with this branch, and introduced the word assassin into European languages.

The Assassins' power was finally checked by those intrepid invaders—the Mongols—who made a special point of destroying them in Persia. Hulagu Khan attacked the fortress of Alamut in 1256, a castle said to be an "earthly Paradise," an idyllic citadel with rivers of honey, beautiful maidens, and culinary delights, where assassins could revel in all sensual pleasures before going out to do their dastardly deeds. This usually preceded their own demise, as they inevitably killed themselves. The idea, apparently, was to give them a taste of Paradise while still alive, so that they knew where they were going when they martyred themselves for the cult.

Finally, Ghengis Khan's men, as they rode across Central Asia into Asia Minor, leaving a trail of destruction behind them, again attacked the Assassin fortress of Alamut, after the first attempt had failed. Ghengis Khan knew all about the Assassins and was determined to put a stop to them. He attacked them full-force and surged over the walls, destroying the terrible power of a cult whose name still lives as a word in our vocabluary.

The Syrian branch of the Assassins met a similar fate at the hands of the Bibars, the army under control of the Mameluke Sultan of Egypt. Only scattered groups of the Assassins persisted. These are said to still exist today, mostly in northern Syria and parts of Iraq, Western Iran and Eastern Turkey.

The assassins perhaps live on under the guise of another secret society known as the Illuminati. The Roshaniya or "Illuminated ones" surfaced in Persia in the sixteenth century. They believed that they were inspired by special divine revelation, or illumination. A strong faction of this group evolved in the mountains of Afghanistan and controlled a considerable amount of territory from their mountain strongholds. They called themselves mystical warriors, but their enemies, the Moguls of India, called them assassins and bandits.

Eventually the Moguls, distant descendants of the Mongols (who had broken the power of the assassins) brought down the Moslem Illuminati. By the mid-seventeenth century, the sect had been thoroughly defeated and dispersed. Yet, fifty years later, the Illuminati surfaced again, this time in Germany. The Bavarian Illuminati was started in 1776, but shortly went "underground." About the only link between the Bavarian Illuminati and the Moslem Illuminati and the Assassins, is that the German sect claimed that the Prophet Mohammed was one of their initiates, an unusual thing for a secret society in the West to do. [73] The Illuminati is said to survive today, attempting to control the world behind the scenes in much the same way as the assassins: political manipulation, assassination and deception, but that is another story....

§§§

These were not pleasant thoughts to think at a lonely crossroads, and when a truck finally came along, I did a little wild dance to get him to stop, jumping up and down, waving down the road, and then stabbing downward with my right hand. It worked! He stopped, and took me to the next town, Maku, and from there I caught a mini-bus to the border, or more accurately, to the last little town before the border. I had to walk about a mile up a hill to what was the real border on a small pass.

This little corner of Iran is just near Mount Ararat, the 16,945 foot mountain that is the cornerstone of the borders of Iran, Turkey, and the USSR in Asia Minor. It was getting pretty late in the afternoon, as I hiked up the road toward the border posts. I then recalled that a couple of Canadian travelers back in Kathmandu had warned me not to get caught at night on the Turkish side of the border, as it was an especially lawless and crime-ridden area.

Eastern Turkey is notorious for having some of the most dangerous and deadly people in the world. Police and law enforcement are virtually non-existent. Trucks on their way to Iran travel in convoys, and do not travel at night. They stay in armed truck stops overnight that have guards with automatic weapons to keep away the bandits and highway robbers that infest the roads all through Eastern Turkey.

The two Canadians, who had been driving Magic Buses between Amsterdam and Kathmandu for years, related this grisly tale: "A few years ago, three French guys were camping out on Mount Ararat, just sleeping outside in the warm summer. In the morning the guy who was sleeping in the middle woke up, and to his horror, he found that both of his friends had been decapitated during the night! Their heads were completely severed. The Turks had just done it as a joke. As a joke! They knew that the guy in the middle would wake up in the morning and see his friends dead...boy, they've got a weird sense of humor, those Turks. Yessireeee...." the Canadians had told me.

Thinking of that, I tore off a piece of bread and munched it as I came to the border post. The story was possibly true, or at least I'd heard others that were quite similar. Also, there were the assassins....it was getting chilly, and the afternoon was turning a cold gray. I turned my collar up and tried to think nice thoughts. I'd just catch a bus into Erzerum, best not to try hitchhiking in this area....

I was checked out of Iran without much ado, and then got

stamped into Turkey. Customs could care less what I had in my pack, and just waved me through. The Iranian side of the border was a police post, with some new cement buildings. When I stepped out into the Turkish side, I was surprised to see only one small, rundown shack that was the immigration building. There was nothing else except a little outdoor tea stall, and a half-dozen rather unsavory characters loitering about a dirty, makeshift parking lot.

I walked up to a man in a greasy apron with a four-day beard, who was running the little tea stall. "When's the next bus to Erzerum?" I asked.

He looked at me for a moment, then took a toothpick out of his mouth. He glanced around at some of the suspicious characters who were sort of hanging around and then said, "Sorry, the last bus just left. You'll have to spend the night."

I'm sure my face paled visibly. What I had been warned against, what I had feared, was happening! I gave myself a knock on the head. This will teach you to attract negative things into your environment, I told myself. By fearing that bad things would happen, I had brought them upon myself. I made a conscious decision to control my thoughts better in the future. Meanwhile, I appeared to be in a bit of a mess, and thought I'd better extricate myself, but fast. I glanced around. There was no hotel or anything here, just a lot of poor, scroungy-looking Turks loitering around, waiting to move in for the kill, so to speak. Then, behind me, I noticed a silver BMW sedan parked by the border barrier.

I walked over to it, and looked inside. No one was in it. Just then, a tall young German man, with long brown hair and cowboy boots, came out of the small immigration post. "Excuse me," I said, walking up to him, "but are you heading west by any chance?"

He looked at me. "Yes," he said.

"Uh, well, do you think you could give me a ride?" I tried hard not to sound as desperate as I felt.

"Ya, sure," he said in his German accent. "But first I have to find my knife. One of these bastards took a hunting knife out of my car while I was sitting in it! They're great thieves here. Dangerous, too. You shouldn't hang around here if you can help it!"

"Yeah, I know!" I said fervently, and offered to help him recover his knife.

After hassling around with various people around the border, and offering some cigarettes as bribes, he got his knife back, and we were off. In the fading light of the afternoon, we could see Mount Ararat in the distance, a huge snow-covered, cone rising up into the sky. A very high mountain for this part of Asia at nearly 17,000 feet, it towers a good five-thousand feet above anything else in the vicinity. The Bible says that the mountains of Ararat were the resting point of the Ark after Noah had braved the cataclysm.

Incredibly, there is quite a bit of evidence to support the idea that there is some sort of huge ship on or near Mount Ararat, and many books and articles have been written on the subject. Ararat is quite a treacherous mountain with storms and blizzards occurring nearly every day. The first person to reach the summit in recorded times was the German physician Dr. Friedrich Parrot in 1829.

Noah's Ark, as described in the Bible, was a huge ship: 450 feet long, 75 feet deep, and 45 feet wide. Scientists have proved it to be an incredibly stable craft. It remained the largest, most stable vessel ever known until its size and ratio were almost duplicated in 1844 in the ship "Great Britain." It wasn't until 1884 that a ship larger than the Ark (as described in the Bible) was built: the Eturia, a Cunard liner. Marine architect George Dickie used the same ratios as the Ark (length to depth to width) in the design of the U.S.S. Oregon, which the Navy considered the most stable battleship ever constructed. It was the flagship of the American fleet for awhile. It was one seventh smaller than the Ark. Tests on models of the Ark have shown that it could easily withstand 200-foot waves without capsizing![16]

"Noah's Tomb" is a real place in the Lebanese mountains, and the Ark has been sighted literally hundreds of times. Why has no one ever conclusively brought it to the world? Assuming that it exists at all, it would periodically be covered and uncovered by the large glaciers of the mountain, depending on the temperature and snowfall of each year. Legend has it that pilgrims traditionally would climb part of the way up the mountain to scrape bits of tar off the old shipwreck for good luck, the last reported incident of this kind occuring about 700 B.C.

Among the many "Noah's Ark Stories":

•In 1840, there was a violent earthquake in Eastern Turkey and an expedition checking for damage discovered a gigantic wooden ship high on the mountain.

•In 1876, British statesman Sir James Bryce climbed Mount Ararat alone and returned with a five-foot piece of lumber, partially petrified.

•In 1887, Prince John Joseph Nouri ascended the mountain and found a gigantic ship wedged in the rocks and ice. He came to the U. S. with the idea of exhibiting it in the 1893 Chicago World's Fair, and wanted investors...this may have been but an elaborate hoax to make some easy money.

•In 1916, Russian aviators sighted the Ark, and a year later sent an expedition of a hundred soldiers to take measurements and photos of the vessel. The material was lost a few years later during the Russian revolution.

•In 1902, George Hagopian was taken to visit the Ark by his uncle, and gave incredibly detailed descriptions of it. He claimed that he actually walked on the roof of the Ark.

•On July 6, 1955, French engineer Fernand Navarra found the Ark at the bottom of a deep crevasse on the mountain. He took photos of timbers and beams in the ice and of a glacial lake at the bottom of the crevasse, and brought back a hand-hewn and squared structural beam that has been carbon dated as being at least 7,000 years old.

There have been many other reports, including satellite sightings and aerial photographs of "Ark-like" shapes on the mountain. Today, because the mountain lies in such a politically-sensitive corner of Turkey, Russia, and Iran, it is difficult to get near the mountain. There's also the problem of the unfriendly Kurds and other xenophobic locals. Interestingly, the impression of what appears to be the shape of a 450-foot ship has been found on a mountain twenty miles north of Ararat. Frequently photographed by air, expeditions have found traces of wood on the sides of the formation, indicating that such an object may have once been there and since sunk down in solidified and frozen mud. [9]

Ark investigator David Fasold said in an interview with Charles Berlitz that the Ark (one of many in the Ararat Mountains, according to him) is located in the Akyayla Range where anyone who goes there can see it. It is located at latitude 39° 26.4" N and longitude 44° 15.3" E and is 11.3 kilometers southeast of the town of Dogubayazit. Fasold also believes that the ancient ship is actually a reed boat covered by a bituminous substance such as asphalt with pumice and other catalytic agents, a sort of cement vessel, making it appear to be made of stone. [70]

The idea of the Arks of Ararat being reed boats is particullarly fascinating in light of the research done by the famous Norwegian archaeologist Thor Heyerdahl. In his latest book, *The Maldive Mystery*,[71] Heyerdahl makes a number of interesting finds and theorizes that a group of ancient seafarers once sailed all over the world, in *reed* ships. He believes that reed ships were used by the ancient Indians, Sumerians, Egyptians, and others. Evidence and actual use of reed ships can be found in Easter Island, Peru, Lake Titicaca, Gujerat, the Maldives, the Nile, Morocco and many other places. Heyerdahl has sailed several reed ships across both the Atlantic and the Pacific.

So-called Arks have been reported all over the world, from the Middle East to South America. Flood traditions and legends similar to Noah's Ark persist from nearly every ancient culture; the Babylonian "Epic of Gilgamesh" and Armenian legends give very similar accounts. Most likely there really were dozens of Arks. Perhaps they were just normal sea-going vessels of their time, carrying cargo from Atlantis or other areas, when suddenly a cataclysm hit and they found themselves "surfing" the two-hundred-foot tidal waves of some devastating geological upheaval. The ships that survived got washed up on the higher mountain ranges of those land areas that were not submerged. In this scenario there could be several "Arks," one on Mount Ararat, and others on the mountains around it, and in many other places as well. After all, mountains are the natural refuges from the world's legendary floods.

Today the CIA and the KGB take too much interest in Mount Ararat and the Ark, often funding expeditions on the pretense of investigating the Ark just to spy on each other in this politically sensitive part of the world. It has even been suggested that the Russians have gone so far as to dismantle the Ark, and that they hide the most exact information on it, knowing that its discovery and media exposure would tend to cause a religious revival in the "atheistic" communist countries! [9]

§§§

As we drove around the western side of the mountain, which was all white with snow and beautiful as it caught the bright rays of the last sunshine that broke through the heavy, gray clouds, the German, whose name was Bruno, told me what he was doing here. He had bought the car from his father, and had driven it to Tehran to sell it, having heard that one could make quite a tidy profit by sellilng a Mercedes or BMW in Iran. However, he had made the mistake of taking a two-door sports car, rather than a four-door family car. In Iran, two-door sports cars are heavily taxed and not easily sold. So, he was on his way back to Munich, to return the car to his father.

I asked him if he would stop the car for a minute, so I could take a photograph of the mountain. He stopped and I got out to take a photo. "Oh, no!" he cried. "You'd better get in fast!"

I turned and looked. About five children with rocks were running across a field toward us at full gait. "Let's go!" said Bruno. "If you stop at any of these small villages, the children will come out and throw rocks at you. If you should accidentally hit one of them, it is better not to stop, but to keep on going. The villagers will kill you if you run over somebody, even if it wasn't your fault!" He was throwing cigarettes out the window as he spoke. The children stopped throwing rocks to scramble for the cigarettes. I admired the clever ruse that Bruno had developed to save the paint job on his father's car.

We drove on, heading west. We stopped for tea in a little cafe by the road, and drank sweet, black tea from miniature beakers, and then hit the road again. Later, we stopped at a cafeteria and had dinner. Bruno was pretty keen to get out of Eastern Turkey, and we practically drove all night, stopping at two in the morning for gas, and then again at 4:30 to sleep. He parked in a field, and we reclined the seats and snoozed.

Some children woke us up around ten that morning, peering curiously in at us through the windows. We had passed Erzurum, the main town in eastern Turkey, during the night, and were now somewhere around Erzincan. Getting up and looking around, we saw that it appeared we'd parked right in the middle of an opium poppy field. Bruno started the car, afraid that the kids might scratch it, and we were off again.

Bruno let me off later that day in Kayseri, smack-dab in the middle of Turkey, and in an area formerly known as Caesarea. I'd had two options: to continue west with Bruno to Ankara, the modern capital of Turkey, or to take a more southern route through ancient and fascinating Cappadocia. I chose to stay the night in Kayseri, and head south.

I checked into the Kayseri Oteli right on the main square in town, and went out to get a bite to eat. There are a couple of hotels in town, all quite reasonable at one or two dollars a bed. The next day, I headed south to Urgup. Near here are rock churches and monasteries built into hundreds of small volcanic cones, dating from the fourth to the thirteenth centuries, complete with frescoes of scenes with Christ. It was funny to walk through the dusty valley, staring at these miniature volcanoes with windows and doors, many of them still inhabited. In fact, some of them had television antennas on top of them.

I spent a night in a small guest house in nearby Urgup, in a little room with a comfortable bed for a dollar.

This odd area was formed by successive eruptions of now- extinct volcanoes that have left a plateau covered with volcanic tuff. The soft rock was transformed by intense erosion into a haunting, surrealistic landscape of cones, columns and canyons. These cones were then hollowed-out by man to create the unique churches.

Turkey has its share of mysteries and lost cities. Perhaps the most interesting mystery, aside from Noah's Ark, is that of the Hittites. The Hittites were a people of

Central Turkey (known as Anatolia in ancient times) that are best known historically as the first people to make use of iron. In Egypt, Hittite iron was more valuable than gold. The Hittite capital was Hattusas, now known as Bogazkale, and it was protected by a massive stone wall thirty- three-and-a-quarter miles around. Said to have been built around 1800 B.C. (though possibly much older), it consisted of stones that were, in some cases, twenty-six feet long and twenty feet thick!

The Hittites had an extremely authoritarian system and obeyed an aristocracy whose foreign origins remain unknown. They wrote their records on tablets in cuneiform, a popular script of the time, usually using their own language, Hittite (or Kanisic). However, they sometimes wrote in Babylonian, and in other languages, including languages not related to Hittite.[51]

What little is known about the Hittites, an extremely war-like though inventive and productive group, leads some historians to believe that they were the Hyksos, the foreign invaders or "Shepherd Kings" that invaded and subdued the Egyptians, not once, but twice. The first time was in remote pre-history, before they had their capital at Hattusas. They immigrated down the Arabian peninsula, crossing the Red Sea into Ethiopia, where they later entered Egypt and built the Great Pyramid at about 4000 B.C., under the direction of their "foreign aristocracy." They peacefully took over Egypt, and then suddenly left upon the completion of the Great Pyramid. Some Hittites emigrated to Britain, others to Palestine and Anatolia, which explains how both the British and the Hebrews inherited what is called the "Pyramid Inch," which is incorporated in the Great Pyramid.[46]

In 1800 B. C. the Hittites ruled a powerful federation of states in Central Turkey. They moved in on Egypt again, conquered the Pharoah Ramses II, and ruled Egypt for a century, introducing the horse-drawn chariot, foreign ideas, and a cognizance of the outside world. They were finally expelled again from Egypt, and withdrew back to their capital at Hattusas. They were at the height of their power in the twelfth century B.C. when they were attacked by an unknown power and their capital destroyed. [22 47 51]

The final destruction of the Hittites is a bizarre ending to an already odd history; not only was the capital sacked and burned down, but the brick houses of Hattusas were subjected to such intense heat that their bricks fused! This kind of phenomennon is known as vitrification, and is not isolated just to cities of the Hittites.

One theory is that the Thracians and Phrygians, peoples from what is now northern Greece and western Turkey, attacked the Hittites together and may have used what was called "Greek Fire" on the cities. Greek Fire is a mysterious substance whose chemical nature is not known, but which was used in a number of military campaigns in antiquity and the early Middle Ages. It was generally thought to be made of pitch, phosphorus and other chemicals, and one version of it was known to burn under water, and was therefore most notably used in naval battles, being flung at enemy ships by catapults. The "Greek Fire" used asgainst the Hittites, however, must have been entirely different. There are no known substances, according to historians, that the ancients knew of that could produce such intense heat as to fuse bricks, stone, and whole cities!

While vitrified fortresses made of stone exist in many parts of the world, especially in Scotland, Ireland, and India, it has been surmised that only the blast of an atomic weapon could cause such a fusion of rock and earth! About the only other phenomenon that man can think of that would produce the kind of heat necessary to fuse bricks or stone would be an intense volcanic eruption, or possibly some bizarre sort of comet or meteorite, perhaps similar to that which hit Siberia in the early part of this century. There is another form of theoretical weaponry called Scalar Waves, a form of "beam weapon" that was invented by Nikola Tesla, inventor of alternating current and three phase motors. These radio frequency "Scalar Howitzers" are reputed to be able to fuse rock or disintigrate it (see our *Lost Science* series[89]). They can also be used to create caves or tunnels. Another term often used for this little known technology is "ultra sounds." Was such a technology used in the dim beginnings of our history? When Joshua blew his trumpet and the walls of Jericho came tumbling down, was he using ultrasounds?

Another theory is that the mysterious "sea peoples" (usually thought to be either Minoans or Phoenicians) who threw the entire Eastern Mediterranean into confusion around 1200 B. C. may have wiped out the Hittites, with, I suppose, some diabolical weapons that fused their cities. At any rate, it is not known who conquered the Hittites, how they did it or what happened to the Hittites or their conquerors after this puzzling chapter in the history of Asia Minor. It is known that that the Lydians succeeded the Hittites, but they apparently weren't the ones that stamped them out. [11, 13, 51, 53]

It was long thought that the first cities were those of the Sumerians, built around 3,000 B.C. when recorded history as we know it began. Now, with the excavations at Biblical Jericho and Catal Huyuk in Turkey, we can push that date back 4,000 years! Excavations in the late 1950's revealed that walls, fifty feet down beneath the ruins of Jericho (now in the West Bank of Israel/Jordon) had been built around 7,000 B.C.

Similarly, the bee-hive city of Catal Huyuk, discovered in south-central Turkey in 1961, has been carbon dated at before 6,500 B. C.! There being no stones in the vicinity, the people, apparently farmers, used mud bricks to build a compact city that was clustered together and had no streets. Buildings, and the city itself, were entered via ladders that extended from the rooftops, which provided an excellent defense system for this early citadel. Pieces of carpet found in the ruins were of such high quality that they compare favorably with what we have today.

Catal Huyuk caused something of a revolution in the archaeological world, though not much is known about it yet. It seems likely that its population was between six and ten thousand and as yet, only one acre of a thirty-two acre mound has been excavated. It is also interesting to note that "leopard motifs" at Catal Huyuk are identical to motifs found at the mysterious lost city of Samaipata in the Bolivian jungles of South America! [43, 51]

Another lost city worth noting in central Turkey is Nemrut Dagi. It is a ruined city standing at the peak of a mountain. Around the site are the enormous heads of once thirty-foot-high statues that have been toppled by earthquakes. Built by order of the king of Commagene, Antiochus I, they are statues of the king himself, of the Greek Gods Apollo, Hermes, and Helios, the Greek hero Hercules, and the Persian Gods Mithras and Ahura Mazda. The statues were built around the first century B.C., and a horoscope is featured on one bas-relief with the stars in the position of July 7 of the year 61 or 62 B.C. Because of the high earthquake activity in the area, very little excavation has been done, and the burial place of King Antiochus with his treasures remains to be found. [51, 22]

§§§

The next day I headed south, to the underground cities of Derinkuyu and Nevsehir Kaymakali which are near Gorme. The underground cities were built by Christians living here in Central Anatolia around the second century A. D., as protection from pagan Arab raids. The cities were inhabited until the twelfth century, and at one time had a population of fifty to sixty thousand.

At the cities, I met Ben, an archaeology student from the University of Chicago, and Rene, a Frenchman. We took a tour through Kaymakali, dodging through small passageways that led down, down, down. The whole place was riddled with catacombs and nooks that go down nine stories, but tourists are only allowed to go down five. When we were on the fifth level below the surface, the guide said that we were 85 meters (200 feet) underground! The Christians who had built this incredible city were called troglodytes by the local guides, although the name really means "cave men." The underground city even had a discoteque that the tourist bureau had put in, though no one seemed in the mood to dance. Perhaps it was too stuffy.

Ben, Rene, and I decided to hitchhike together to Nigde, and we got a ride with a couple of Turks who were on their way to our specific destination. They didn't speak any English, but were quite friendly, and even stopped the car along the way for a picnic, producing bread, cheese, melons, nuts and beer. They were both in their thirties, clean-shaven, and cheerful, friendly fellows, who seemed to enjoy the company of a small group of travelers. Ben took off his black, plastic glasses and laid them on the checkered cloth; Rene opened another beer. "This, *mes amis,* is the life," he sighed.

"Hitchhiking in Turkey is fun," said Ben, smiling and brushing back his brown hair.

"Here's to our charming hosts!" I toasted, raising my beer toward the two Turkish gentlemen next to us. They understood completely, and raised their glasses, too. The sun shone down on us. It was a beautiful day. Our hosts even left us to go into the next town and get more beer and wine.

I lay back in the sun with a slice of melon. It seemed like years ago that I was caught on that gloomy day on the border of Iran and Turkey. Things had certainly improved since then. I reflected on how fortunate I had been to get the ride. If the Tibetan Lama back in Dharamsala was correct, then my thoughts were directly influencing my life, and positive mental attitide was as effective as negative thoughts in affecting the outcome of events in my life. I thanked Sanjay and the Great White Brotherhood for a good time.

Ben, Rene, and I spent the night in a small hotel in Nigde and then Ben and Rene headed south to Antakya, where they were going to meet a friend near the bus station.

I hitched west, heading for Konya. I got a ride with a Turkish family in an antiquated old station wagon whose paint job had been replaced with rust. They were nice and friendly, but didn't speak English. "*Sprecten se Deutch?*" asked the father. Many Turks speak German, as quite a few Turks go to Germany to work in the factories or such. In fact, the city with the second largest population of Turks, after Istanbul, is Berlin!

I don't speak German, and so wasn't able to converse with this family. Mom had a scarf on her head, typical of Turkish women, and the kids, two little boys, were wearing T-shirts that said "Disneyland" with a picture of Mickey Mouse on one and Donald Duck on the other. They let me off in Konya, the former capital of the Seljuk Sultans from the twelfth to thirteenth centuries, and the religious center of Turkey.

Here the most important sight is the Tekke, the monastery of the Whirling Dervishes, now officially the Mevlana Museum. Ataturk crushed the semi-heretical order years ago, but the order's founder Mevlana (a Sufi Saint), buried in the Monastery in 1273, draws many pilgrims each year. I checked into the Hotel Konya, taking a bed in a triple-bed dormitory for about a dollar.

Konya is a pleasant, old-fashioned city, the oldest contin- uously inhabited site in Turkey. Whirling Dervishes still dance here in the first half of December, whirling around in order to create a "divine ecstasy." Myself, I was off to Istanbul. Deciding to hitchhike, I was on the road out of town before I knew it. I caught a short ride in a pick-up truck twenty miles or so along the road to Istanbul, and there I was, once again, standing on a dusty crossroads, with not a house, person or vehicle in sight.

Traveling across Central Asia, at this point in time, was fun, albeit somewhat dangerous. Once into Central Turkey, however, I felt much safer. Turkey from here west was pretty "civilized," unless of course you happened to get caught smuggling drugs. If you've seen the movie "Midnight Express," you know Turkey can be something out of your worst nightmares.

It just so happened that the next vehicle to come along was a big Mercedes bus, about half full, heading for Istanbul. They automatically stopped for me, even though I wasn't trying to get them to stop. After all, I was standing there on their side of the road, in the middle of nowhere.

"Jump in," said the bus driver in English. I did. Hitching wasn't too good that morning, anyway, and it was a long way to Istanbul. I took a seat on the bus, and the conductor told me it would only cost about three dollars to Istanbul. More expensive than hitching, but faster, I thought as I fished into my leather pouch.

The next day, I was sitting in the famous "Pudding Shop" in Sultanahmet, near the Bosphorous Straits in Istanbul. I had arrived in town late the night before and was staying at a nearby hostel, called the *Yucel Tourist Hostel*. The Pudding Shop is the hangout for travelers on their way to or from Asia. It is a cafeteria-restaurant, serving beer and, of course, puddings. It is generally full of all sorts of interesting people, and has a bulletin board for messages.

Turkey is a mixture of East and West, and Istanbul is the city that exemplifies this idea the most. Once the capital of the Christianized Eastern Roman Empire, Constantinople (now Istanbul) later became the capital of the powerful Ottoman Empire. Istanbul is the only city in the world to bridge two continents. For the hitchhiker on his way to Central Asia, it is the road-head of Asia, and full of interesting sights.

One interesting part of the city is the area known as Sultanahmet, on the European side of the Bosphorus. Here you will find many fantastic museums, the old covered bazaar, and the beautiful Blue Mosque, known as Sultanahmet Camii.

The Topkapi Museum has one of the most incredible collections in the world, and even people who don't like museums enjoy spending a few hours here. The weapons room has medieval armaments you never knew existed, as well as full suits of armor from all over the world. You can visit the Harem, see the jewel collection, and even the hand and head of John the Baptist.

Archives at the museum hold such interesting documents as the famous Piri Reis map which shows South America and Antartica in incredible detail before they were discovered! Another document tells of the firing of a manned rocket over the Bosphorus in the year 1633! The rocket, fueled by gunpowder, flew a thousand feet over the water and then the pilot launched himself on a hang-glider! Wright Brothers, eat your hearts out!

Saint Sophia, the Church of the Divine Wisdom, was completed by Justinian the Great in 537. It was a masterpiece of architecture back then, and is still considered one of the truly great buildings in the world today. It was turned into a mosque by Sultan Mehmet II (hence the name for this area of Istanbul: Sultanahmet) and is now a museum.

I took a long draught of my cold Turkkish beer at the Pudding Shop. Iran and Afghanistan were still open at that time, and the great Hippy Trail with its Magic Buses to India was still stretching across the continent. Travelers of all sizes, shapes, and nation- alities were making their last-minute preparations for the over- land route to India and the hippy Mecca of Kathmandu. I sighed. I was already missing Nepal and India. It seemed I had hardly scratched the surface of the lost cities and mysteries of Central Asia, let alone of myself. Finishing my beer, and ordering another one, I vowed to return!

View of the cave-temple at Bhaja, near Poona.

Entrance to the mysterious cave-temple on Elephanta Island.

The massive, rock-hewn entrance to Karla Temple between Bombay and Poona, painted by Henry Salt in 1804. It is a Buddhist Temple, believed constructed in 80 BC.

Louis Jacolliot (1837-1890), the French writer who first spoke of a lost continent in the Pacific named *Rutas* and the existence of a secret underground university in India or Tibet named Agartha. He stands here at the entrance to one of the temples at Ellora in Western India.

Chapter Ten

BOMBAY AND WESTERN INDIA: GURUS AND LOST CITIES

With every true friendship
we build more firmly the foundations on which
the peace of the whole world rests.
—Mahatma Gandhi

Stepping out of the airport terminal after arriving from the Sultanate of Oman in Southern Arabia, I knew immediately that I was back in India. Taxi drivers flocked around me. "Here, take my cab," one would say. "No, take my cab!" another would say. It's nice to be wanted, but in India, it can be a real pain. I jumped into a three-wheeled motorized taxi, forced the driver to turn on the meter (which most drivers will tell you is broken) and we sped off, in a cloud of carbon monoxide, toward the heart of Bombay.

"Where to, Sahib?" asked the driver, a large fat man in a greasy sport shirt and a *bidi* (a small conical cigarette) in his mouth.

"The Salvation Army, please," I replied, and leaned back in the seat. Actually, it's nice to be back in India, I thought, even if it does mean the incessant crowds. It had been several years since I was in the subcontinent, and this was my first time in Bombay. In the past three years I had been traveling in Africa and Arabia, working in the Sudan and Capetown, sailing in the Indian Ocean, and was now returning to India for a year, on my way to the Far East and China. "Ah, the smells, sights, and sounds," I sighed, "the sensory bombardment of Mother India...."

"What's that you said?" asked the driver, turning around for a moment to look at me.

"Huh? Oh, nothing, " I said. "I'm just glad to be back in India."

"Been here before, Sahib?" The driver made a quick cut in front of a speeding bus, almost ran over a cow that was wandering the street, and hit a pot hole all at the same time, jerking me to attention from my dreamy state.

"Yeah. It's been a couple of years, though," I said, putting my hand on my green internal-frame pack. It was going to be one of those "wild rides of Mr.Toad"–type trips into downtown Bombay, I could tell.

"Well, things have changed a lot since you were last here," he said, swerving hard to avoid a pedestrian.

"India? Change?" I returned. "This country has hardly changed in five thousand years!"

"No, things have changed!" he yelled back. "For one thing, Indira Gandhi is no longer the Prime Minister. Now the Prime Minister is Moraji Desai! Do you know what he does? He drinks a quart of his own urine every day! Can you believe that, drinking a glass of your own piss every day?" He slowed down for a cow, honked his horn, and then sped up with a jerk.

"Why does he drink a quart of his own urine?" I yelled at him over the din from the engine.

"He's a health nut! Has some really strict vegetarian diet and drinks his own piss!"

"That doesn't sound so healthy to me. Does everyone do that in India?" I asked, as a joke.

"Are you kidding? No way! Lots of people do, I'll say that, but not me. No, never! I don't want to be THAT HEALTHY!"

I leaned back and laughed, closing my eyes; I didn't want to watch the crazy traffic anyway. Ha, I must be back in India. Where else would the head of state drink his own urine?

India is just about the most interesting country in the world, according to the people with whom I've spoken. It seems to elicit very strong reactions from people: either they really like it or they really hate it: no in-betweens. India's new Prime Minister, Moraji Desai, had been elected in 1977, just after I had left the country, and he certainly does drink his own urine, according to articles I've read in several publications, including TIME Magazine. People had become rather disenchanted with Indira Gandhi from 1975 to 1977 because of her "Emergency Declaration" and rather dictatorial political tendencies toward suspending civil liberties. She would throw political opponents in jails, and was even convicted of illegal activities in connection with her own election. It is also worth noting that Indira Gandhi is not the daughter of, nor related in any way to, Mohandas (Mahatma, or "Great Soul") Gandhi, who led India to independence from the British. She is the daughter of Jawaharlal Nehru, India's first Prime Minister, and friend of Mahatma Gandhi. Indira just happened to marry a man whose last name was Gandhi, and so the confusion arises. Moraji Desai was not destined to be the Prime Minister for long. He was ousted by none other than Indira Gandhi herself in the next elections, shortly after my return to India. Desai himself had been imprisoned by Gandhi in 1975 so it was no surprise when he ordered a series of investigations into her alleged abuses of power. (Indira was assassinated by some of her own Sikh officers in the fall of 1984, an event which shocked the entire world.)

India should not really be thought of as a country. It is a continent, somewhat like Europe. India is a confederation of states, and each of these states is very different from the others. The one thing that really holds India together is Hinduism, and this in itself is a problem. Of the twenty-some states in India, most of them have their own separate language, and often their own script, though Hindi is the official language. Their culture, language, script, civil laws and such are all different. If you travel by train, you will usually find two Indians speaking together in English, because it is the only language they both understand! Of the 250 known alphabets in the history of language, fifty are still alive today and half of these are in India. As many as 1,652 languages and dialects are spoken by India's eight hundred million people. Only 38% speak the official language, Hindi. English is an associate language, and very widely spoken, probably as much as Hindi.

"Here you are, Sahib," said the driver, pulling up to the curb in front of the Salvation Army.

"Great," I said, grabbing my pack, paying for the ride, and nodding to the driver. "Thanks!"

"Anytime, Sahib, anytime!" and he gave me a toothy grin. "Would you like a nice girl? Young!"

"Oh, no, thanks, I'm trying to quit," I said jokingly as I walked away. Inside, I was lucky to be able to get a bed, as the Salvation Army is often full. Bombay is India's second largest city, after Calcutta, and is the "Hollywood of India." India makes more films than any other country in the world, including the U.S., and Bombay is the center of the industry.

Once a slipper-shaped island full of malarial swamps, Bombay was ceded to Portugal by the Sultan of Gujerat in 1534 and then passed on to the British in 1661 as a dowry to Charles II of England and Catherine of Bragana. The British drained the swamps and transformed what was once a tiny fishing village into the "Gateway to India," and Britain's piecemeal acquisition of India gained with this important foothold.

With six million people, sprawly Bombay is the most "westernized" of India's cities. Bombay has plenty of hotels, but they are the most expensive of all of India's cities. By western standards, they are still inexpensive, but when you are used to getting a hotel for a dollar, six or seven dollars for a room seems rather high.

There are a number of things to do in Bombay, such as going to the Prince of Wales Museum or seeing the Elephanta Caves on an island six miles from the Gate of India. There are six enormous caves, supposedly dating back to the eighth century though tradition indicates that they are much older.

The caves are hacked out of solid rock and the roof of the largest cave is 130 feet high and supported by immense pillars. The caves contain awesome statues of Hindu gods. They are quite a mystery. It is not known why or by whom such a colossal religious shrine was built on this isolated little island, nor how the builders could accomplish it with the primitive tools that people of that time were said to have had. [17]

Esoteric Brahmanic tradition relates that these caves were once linked to underground tunnels whose secret entrances could be found at Elephanta (though no such enterances have been found), and to the Ellora and Ajanta Caves to the northwest of Bombay. These tunnels were supposedly built by the Nephilim, or "men of the golden age" who, I suppose, also theoretically built the caves. [54]

One of the more interesting things to do is go to the Parsis Five Towers of Silence. When the Parsis (ancient followers of Zoroaster) fled Persia in the eighth century to escape religious persecution by the conquering Islamic armies, many of them came to Bombay's environs and the areas north of Bombay such as the city of Surat. Of course, there was no Bombay at the time. They brought with them their sacred fire and kept it burning in consecrated places. They do not believe in cremation or burial of their corpses as it pollutes the earth and fire, both of which are sacred. They therefore dispose of bodies by putting them on high platforms to be devoured by birds of prey. These platforms are the Five Towers of Silence, and can only be seen from a distance.

As Bombay is the center of India's booming movie industry, many travelers go to the studios and work as extras, since the Indians always need a few Europeans in their movies. Pay is moderate, and it can be a lot of fun. It's also fun to catch a movie here in Bombay, but the cinemas can be crowded as Indians love to watch movies and there are very few televisions, so tickets should be bought in advance, if possible. Otherwise, scalpers sell them outside the theater.

Another interesting excursion is to the "Red Light District," called *Cages*. Here, women sit behind bars, waiting for customers. Many prostitutes are actually transvestites, and a large portion of them eunuchs. The area extends around the Foras Road area. According to tradition, if a devout Hindu dreams of Yellama and Bahuchara, the goddesses of eunuchs, he is obliged to join their group, called the Hijra, or third sex, and be castrated. Volunteers these days are few & far between, so, unfortunately, the Hijra have taken to kidnapping young boys and emasculating them. The Indian press has had quite a hey-day with this.

§§§

My first day in Bombay, I walked from the Salvation Army to Church Gate, the business center of Bombay, to see the Tourist Bureau. It all seemed so familiar: the teeming masses of people surging toward me as I crossed the street, all going in the opposite direction. I fought this wave of beings, desperately trying to get to the other side of the street before the light changed. It was like a being a swimmer caught in a riptide and trying to get ashore. Gasping for breath, I barely made it in time as the autos, all Indian-made cars looking like forties-style Studebakers or Nashes, came surging into the square.

Bombay is known for its con artists. I read about one famous con on the bulletin of the Salvation Army, which involves having you change travelers' cheques for an Indian merchant who wants to get money out of the country. It's all very complicated, and usually involves another tourist who is part of the con. You might be sitting in a coffee shop and another tourist (at the time he was a young man from Scotland) tells you he's made plenty of money helping an Indian businessman out. He makes it sound real appealing and it seems as if you will make a few hundred dollars. You take his advice and the next thing you know you have lost all your money. The note on the bulletin board at the Salvation Army told of someone, the writer, losing $600 in this scam!

As I walked down the street out of the Tourist Office, an Indian came up to me. He was dressed well, wearing a white shirt and cotton slacks, and spoke English perfectly.

"I'll give you two hundred dollars if you will change some of my money into travelers' cheques for me. I have American dollars, but Indians are not allowed to take the money out of the country," he said as we walked down the street. "I'm opening a silk shop in Montreal and want to get $50,000 out of the country. I'm just going now to meet an English chap who did it for me yesterday. Come with me to the coffee shop..." It was awfully tempting. Two hundred dollars would go a long way in India, a tidy profit for sure. Then, suddenly, I remembered the notice at the Salvation Army. Travelers' cheques...English tourist...coffee shop...I realized it was the con the note at the Salvation Army had talked about.

I looked him in the eye. "Sorry, " I said, "but I don't have time now. Goodbye." And before he could say another word, I turned and headed up another street. Seeing how my attitude suddenly changed, he split too.

The next day I was walking around town and another man came up to me, and began talking to me on the street. He said he was from Goa, an ex-Portugese colony south of Bombay. "Would you like to see a Saudi slave market?" he asked.

"A Saudi slave market?" I said. "That sounds interesting."

"It's just down the street," he said, pointing. "Saudis come here and buy young girls for two to four thousand rupees." (That's three to five hundred dollars, quite a tidy sum in a country where the per capita income is about $165.) We walked for blocks down the street and he took me to a Hindu cremation place.

"Where is the slave market?" I asked.

"It's too far," he said, and showed me the cremation rooms, which were rather interesting. Afterward, as I started to leave, he asked if I could loan him some money. "I'll pay you back tomorrow," he said.

Well, I had had enough of that. The guy must have thought I was awfully gullible. He was not nearly so slick as the first man; there was no Saudi slave market, not here at least.   Still, many con artists and thieves in India are fiendishly clever. They also steal passports, which can be worth hundreds of dollars.

Shortly, I boarded a train out of Bombay going to Poona, only a few hours away to the east. I was going there as that's where India's most trendy Ashram, that of "Bagwan Rajneesh" was located. I had heard so much about it, some good, some bad, I felt I should check it out personally.

Just south of Poona is the small town of Shivapur. Here there is a mosque dedicated to the sufi saint *Qamar Ali Dervish.* In front of a one-story building with a neatly painted facade of one door and two windows is a green lawn on which lies a large granite boulder weighing about 55 kilograms (aprox. 120 lbs). Occasionally, when visitors come to see the stone, the mula of the small mosque will ask exactly eleven of them to circle the stone, each placing their right index finger on the stone. Then, chanting "Qamar Ali Dervish" in loud ringing tones, an incredible thing happens!

The stone defies gravity, and rises about 2 meters (six feet) into the air! The heavy granite boulder hovers in the air for about a second and then comes down with a thud so that the participants have to mind their feet. There is another smaller stone weighing 41 kilograms, and it requires nine people, chanting the same words. This demonstration takes place almost every day of the year, as long as there is the exact number of people to touch the stone.[53]

That evening I was sitting in a small restaurant near the Rajneesh Ashram drinking a Guru Lager Beer and reading the *Times of India* and my guidebook. The newspaper had an interesting item with the headline "DEAD MAN FOUND LOITERING IN DUBAI." Dated July 27 with a UNI news service label, it read: "The police are searching for the identity of a man, said to have died two years ago, who was found roaming in Dubai (United Arab Emirates) recently. About two years ago, Khalef Khadem Al- Dhahr of Khor Rakkan village in the northern province of the United Arab Emirates died and was buried. The cause of his death was not known. A few days ago, he was found loitering in the Dubai cemetary. He was naked and apparently mad. Al-Dhahr's father is positive that the man is his 35-year old son whom he buried two years ago."

"Hmm, life is strange," I muttered to myself, and took a long draught of my beer. I turned to my guidebook. "Poona was once the capital of the Mahratta Empire from 1750 until it surren- dered to the British in 1817. The gateway to the fortress of Purandhar near Poona is built on a foundation of solid gold. The fifty thousand gold bricks in the foundations would be worth over five hundred million dollars...."

"Whew," I thought, taking another swig. Looking up, I saw that I had been joined by a European person in a purplish-red gown. Most people who came to Poona, after all, were here for the Ashram, and the devotees, thousands of them, all had to wear red, or orange, or purple. Many people came from North America Europe, Australia, or Japan to experience it.

"Where are you from?" I asked the orange-clad person sitting across from me.

"California," he said. He looked like a nice guy, and had a long, neat brown hair and a beard. On his neck he had a "Bodhi Bead" necklace, small round brown seeds with a picture of the bearded Rajneesh in a wooden oval frame hanging at the end of the necklace.

"I guess you are a follower of Rajneesh," I said

perceptively.

"Yeah, a *Sunyasin*," he replied. "Have you come to receive the light?"

"The light? Oh, I'm just here for a couple of days to check the place out, you know. What do you think of Rajneesh?" I asked.

"He's the *Master of the Age.* You know, they have a Master of the Age every two thousand years," he replied with enthusiasm. "He's wonderful. I'm sure he's the greatest guru in the world. Since I've come here, I've really become a different person!"

"That's nice," I said. "Is Rajneesh around? I'd be interested to see him."

"Well, he usualy does a morning puja (prayer sesssion), but he's been sick the last couple of weeks. His health isn't so good. So we haven't seen him for awhile."

"Oh, really?" I said. "What's his problem?"

"Well, he gets sick really easily. He's also got a lot of allergies. He's never had chicken pox either, so if there's an outbreak in the ashram he usually goes into hiding until it's all over."

"Hmm," I said. "If he's the Master of the Age, why doesn't he heal himself and create perfect health for his body?"

"Beats me. That's a good question. I'll have to ask him some time... God has an answer for everything."

"God?"

"That's what Bhagwan means—God. We call him *God* a lot."

I finished my beer and stood up. "I think I'd better go. If *God* is sick, I should get to bed early. Thanks for the conversation."

"Anytime," said my orange friend.

The next morning, I was off bright and early to visit "God" and his ashram. I felt a little funny, because everyone was in colorful red or orange clothes except me and a few other misfits. I had never felt so conspicuous. The ashram is a large estate, walled in and guarded by burly orange-clad guards with walkie-talkies and electric stun-batons. They are also black belts in Karate, I was told. I was searched as I entered. At the reception office I bought an all-day pass for the activities of the day. I made it to the Tai Chi Chuan class, which was a lot of fun, and then to Bhagwan's discourse, which was actually a video tape of a previous one, since he was sick and in retreat.

Bhagwan, or Rajneesh, I should say, looked to be about fifty years old, with long blackish-grey hair and a long beard. Like his followers, he wears a red robe. He discoursed on Eastern philosophy and told a few jokes: "All

insititutions are bad, and marriage is an insititution...."
"What did Jesus say to the innkeeper as he threw a couple
of nails on the table? Can you put me up for the night?" His
voice had a flat monotone quality, and although he
delighted his followers with his jokes, he never laughed
himself. "Why don't I laugh at my own jokes?" he asked.
"Because I've heard them all before!"

He often dropped names of great philosphers, Buddha,
Confucius, Jesus, Lao Tzu, and then put them down. He
billed himself as the *Master of the Age* and he had a certain
charisma about him, but, lying there on the floor of the
"Great Hall," I found myself drifting off, and eventually fell
asleep. I was awakened at the end of the video to see a
rather strange sight. Rajneesh was performing his "energy
dharshan" while his followers, in the tape, chanted. He
stuck out his right hand to various devotees and touched
them right between the eyes, pressing their foreheads with
his fore- finger, his hand vibrating. The person he was
doing this to was apparently in ecstacy. People gathered
around chanting. He would do this to a person for a minute,
and then move on to someone else. For some reason, the
sight of this was rather disturbing to me.

I had lunch in the ashram cafeteria, clean and plastic,
like some college cafeteria in the U.S. Food was simple,
vegetarian, and expensive, about the same prices as in
America, and as expensive a place in India as you might
find. After lunch, I attended a few more classes, some
Kundalini and Nataraj Meditation, with music and
dancing—rather fun. I browsed in the book store, had some
mango ice cream at the milk bar, and then attended the
Music Group, where some Westerners played guitars and
sang pop-type music that had a good rhythm. "Bhagwan,
your grace—straight to my heart, straight to my heart!" we
all sang. We also did some familiar old pop songs: George
Harrison's "My Sweet Lord," and Steven Stills' "Find the
Cost of Freedom." I found it quite enjoyable and
inspirational in its own way.

It was dark by the time I walked back to my hotel. I
stopped in at a restuarant for a snack on the way. I was
sitting at a table with a person who was dressed in blue
jeans, the only other non- purple person besides myself in
the restaurant.

"Well, what's a blue person like you doing here?" I asked
him, making conversation.

"Oh, just came by to check it out," he said. "I'm on my way
to Auroville in southern India." He was clean-shaven,
American or Canadian, I guessed, in his thirties with light
brown hair and a sparkle in his eye. When I asked him

what he thought of Rajneesh and his ashram he said, "Well, Rajneesh is an interesting guy. He was the Debating Champion for all India back in the late fifties when he was in college at Benares Hindu University. He went on to get a degree in philosophy and then decided to go into the guru biz. He's terribly egotistical, as you have probably noticed. Like many gurus, he gets people into sex. It's a hang-up most westerners, and Indians, too, for that matter, need to work through. That's why they all have to wear those red colors: red corresponds to the lower, sexual chakras, and stimulates a person sexually....."

"Like the Lady in Red," I said, "or Red Light districts?"

" Yeah, right," he said, and laughed.

"Gee, I saw him do a strange thing on the video tape," I said, taking a sip of mango juice. "Something called an energy dharshan."

"Oh, that," he said, a bit disturbed. "Yeah, that's something a lot of gurus do these days. He's working with the person's third eye (that spot where the pineal gland is in the forehead), stimulating it, and putting the person in ecstasy. It's another of the body's chakras. It is better that you not let someone do this to you," he warned. "Your third eye will open when it is naturally ready. It is better not to have this kind of artificial stimulation. With your third opening artificially by Rajnesh, you will be irrestibly attracted to him, and he will have power over you."

Hmm, it was all pretty interersting. The guru business in India and everywhere was booming. (Rajneesh and his ashram moved to Oregon, where they created something of a ruckus. In the end, after some internal intrique, "Ma Guru," one of Rajneesh's close aids, skipped the ashram, Antelope Ranch, with several million dollars. Rajneesh was arrested and deported. He returned to Poona, and died in 1990) Lots of these guys become very wealthy: Rajneesh certainly was. I lay back in my bed and started to drift off to sleep. Rajneesh: a comedian, a jerk, an invalid, a guru.

§§§

One of the great "lost cities" of India was discovered in 1819 by a British army officer who was out hunting a panther in central India. These were the famous Ajanta caves, and nearby are the equally famous and splendid Ellora caves. Lost to the world for two thousand years, the Ajanta caves were supposedly carved out of solid rock around the second century B. C. and are in a rather remote part of India, but well worth the trouble of a visit.

From Poona, I took a bus to Aurangabad, near the Ellora

Caves. Here, there are twelve Buddhist, seventeen Hindu, and five Jain cave temples strung out along a cliff facing west. Ellora is theoretically more recent than the Ajanta caves. They are dated circa 500 A. D. and may have been being inhabited and added to for five centuries. The most remarkable of the temples is the Kailasa, which had been described as "certainly the noblest Hindu memorial of ancient India." It is quite impressive; dedicated to Shiva, it is carved entirely out of one gigantic outcrop of black volcanic rock—an estimated two hundred thousand tons of rock arduously chiseled away to create a hewn rock gateway, pavilion, courtyard, and assembly hall.

I spent the night at a small government rest house in Ellora. Very few tourists actually make it out to the Ellora and Ajanta area, and the guest house was rather unused to having visitors. The next morning it was a three-hour bus ride to the site of the Ajanta caves, famous for their Buddhist frescoes, generally depicting the life of Buddha. There are twenty-nine caves altogether, carved into a rock cliff that is well hidden. It was here that hundreds of Buddhist monks lived and worked. A certain mystery hangs over these magnificent frescoes. They have a richness of color and glow with a depth that is highly sophisticated and unusual. The artists used some unknown type of special luminous paint that makes the paintings stand out and come alive. When the lights are turned off, gradually the figures on the wall appear to be three-dimensional as if they were made of marble. The secret of the fantastic effect obtained by clever deployment of this luminous paint is no longer known.

Both Ellora and Ajanta, along with Elephanta and other ancient ruined cities of India, were said to have hidden entrances in them that opened into the subterranean world of tunnels under Asia. These tunnels, hundreds of miles long, were supposedly connected with the tunnels in Tibet. In ancient Brahmic tradition, they were built by the Nephilim who lived on an island in the Gobi desert when it was a sea. These tunnels were their only link with the outside world. [54]

No trace of such entrances has ever been found at Ellora, Ajanta, or Elephanta, though there apparently are such tunnels in the Andes Mountains, collectively known as the Tunnel of the Inca (Socabon del Inca), which apparently run for hundreds of miles through Peru, from Lima to Cuzco and farther west, while another branch runs south to the Atacama desert in Chile. Parts of these tunnels have been explored, and their entrances have supposedly been blocked up and the vast remaining treasure of the Incas stored inside. These tunnels in South America were apparently not built by the Incas as they lacked the technology. It is surmised that they were actually built by the Atlanteans some ten to fifteen thousand years ago. [54]

I suppose that Atlanteans would build such tunnels (assuming that they really exist) for easy travel, much as there are many tunnels in the Alps and other mountainous areas, and possibly also for military purposes of one sort or another. Today, it has become quite popular for governments to hollow out mountains and rock cliffs to create underground cities and submarine bases. Take for instance the NORAD command center, located inside Cheyenne Mountain in Colorade Springs, or the Soviet submarine bases discovered by the Israelis in Lebanaon that were hollowed out of cliffs, and other so-called secret underground cities in Australia, New Zealand, South Georgia Island, and other areas.

Still, I really had to wonder, as I walked around the caves of Ajanta, just what was the truth of this underground tunnel business in Central Asia and India? I had my doubts. Still, it is possible that certain tunnels, built by Atlanteans, or their contemporaries (rather than by a bunch of weirdos living underground, or nasty spacemen from a dead planet), do exist around Tibet. There's certainly a lot of talk about them, and where there's smoke, there's quite often fire! I concluded, however, that it was unlikely that any tunnels emerged here at the caves, as they aren't particularly big or deep.

Still, maybe a secret stone door, like in some Indiana Jones movie, was at the back of the cave. I pushed hard on the wall. It didn't budge. Oh, well, at least you can't say that I didn't try....

§§§

Shortly I was on a train heading northwest. I had wrangled a reservation on a third class sleeper in Jalgaon by slipping the conductor ten rupees (about a dollar). We traveled all day, and next morning, I hoped, we would be in Ahmedabad, the largest city in Gujerat, and sixth largest in India, at over one-and-a-half-million people. As I got off the train the next morning, I met a French traveler named Maurice, and we decided to look for a hotel together.

Ahmedabad is a prosperous industrial city, famous for its textile industry. Hotels are not especially cheap here, and as in Bombay, the cheaper hotels are also often full. Walking out of the railway station toward the Great Mosque, one will pass a number of inexpensive hotels.

They were all full when Maurice and I tried them. We kept going down the street, asking people at the hotels if they knew of a hotel that wasn't full. We finally got rooms at a rather out-of-the-way place called the Neelama Guest House near the General Post Office. We each took our own single room for 12 rupees, or $1.50 a night. A common bed in a dormitory was 5 rupees, or about sixty-five cents.

There really isn't much to see in Ahmedabad, and most people end up there either because they are transiting through Bombay or Rajastan, or because they want to visit the Gandhi Ashram. Gandhi spend most of his later life in Ahmedabad, and it was here that he started his famous ashram, the Satyagraha (Soul Force) Ashram.

It was founded in 1917 and it has a small museum of his few personal effects plus a photographic history of his life and the Independence of India. It was from here that Gandhi started his historic 1930 Salt Tax March to Dandi, 241 miles away on the coast. Gandhi and his followers walked to the salt flats where Gandhi took a pinch of salt and ate it, thereby breaking the British Salt Monopoly Law. He was arrested, and the rest is history.

Maurice and I went out to the Gandhi Ashram and spent the day. It is a group of low, whitewashed huts in a peaceful setting among trees beside the river. Some people still live there. Leaving the ashram, Maurice remarked, "This is wonderful. If only Europe had a leader like Gandhi-ji." (Ji is a title of respect.)

Returning fully inspired from the ashram, we visited the Great Mosque in the center of town. Built in 1424, the mosque is famous for its swinging minarets, possibly built three hundred years before the present mosque. They are more than sixty feet high and twenty feet apart. When a group of visitors reaches the top of a minaret, the guide goes to the top of the other and, grasping the railing, begins to swing the minaret. Immediately, the other minaret begins to sway, often to the alarm of the guests.

Theoretically, this is accomplished by the communication of vibration from one minaret to another, though no one has figured out the secret yet. In fact, an inscription in front of the minarets reads, "Swinging towers. Secret unknown." Certainly, they are amusing, but more importantly, they stand as testimony to the ancient sciences of antiquity.

We had a nice dinner of rice, curry, vegetables and yogurt, and a banana milkshake at the Gandhi Cold Drink House, and then went to see a typical Indian movie: combination musical-tear jerker-comedy-romance-high action and a touch of the supernatural. The movies are silly to us westerners, but the Indians love them.

Just south of Ahmedabad is another of India's great lost cities: Lothal, one of the Seven Cities of the Rama Empire! According to ancient Indian and esoteric tradition, the Rama Empire was started at least fifteen thousand years ago. Churchward believed that the Nagas, or Naacals, had come into central India from Burma, according to certain records, more than twenty-five thousand years ago, before the sinking of the great continent in the Pacific known in ancient Chinese and Indian chronicles as the "Motherland, Mu."[8]

When new arrivals came to India after a great cataclysm had sunk Mu, the Rama Empire was formed by the aristocracy of immigrants, many of them exceptionally advanced in the "quality and development of Mind," that is, they had great mental powers.[8]

The Rama Empire, according to ancient doctrine and archaeological information, stretched from the Indus Valley in what is now Pakistan, across western India, Gujerat, and the plains of the Ganges. It may have also included southern India. A number of the advanced cities of the Rama Empire have been excavated, most notably the well-known and amazing cities of Mohenjo-Daro and Harappa in Pakistan. These cities are about five thousand years old according to traditional archaeologists, and about twelve thousand years old according to those scientists that subscribe to what is known as "cataclysmic geology." These cities are especially remarkable because of their highly sophisticated water and sewage systems, plus the neat grid pattern of the cities. These things point to a highly advanced civilization.

The lost city of Lothal is eighty kilometers south of Ahmedabad on the Arabian Sea, and is laid out in chessboard fashion, much like Mohenjo-Daro and Harappa. It has the same sort of sophisticated drainage system, and the houses have bathrooms and fireplaces. Only discovered twenty years ago or so in the late fifties, it is not as well excavated as those cities in Pakistan.

Interestingly, the port is quite a distance from the Gulf of Cambay across large dry mud-flats. Even the local river is too far to send flood water into the basin. Here, we have a port city that is not near any water! It is obvious that some major geological change has taken place since the heyday of Lothal. At the very least, the level of the world's oceans has dropped considerably since it was constructed. What could have caused that?

Thor Heyerdahl also noticed that the entrance to the port had been closed, so that larger sea going craft could no longer enter the harbor. What was the reason for this? Heyerdahl also believes that the ships used at Lothal were large reed ships—just like Noah's Ark, Lake Titicaca, Easter Island, and Egypt![71]

I stopped in at Lothal for a day on my way south to Palitana. I was determined to find out more about the ancient Rama Empire, and a trip to Pakistan would be necessary for that.

I took a train south to Palitana, spent a night in the Government Rest House and then checked out the eleventh century Jain fortress-temple on top of Shetrunjaya Hill. Called Palitana Temple, it is an imposing, magnificent fortress made out of stone and intricately carved. It is perhaps the most sacred place in India for the Jains, a Hindu sect started by the Saint Mahivira who was a contemporary of Buddha.

Jains in general are ascetics, many of the men (the priests and monks, anyway) do not wear clothes, and they are very strict vegetarians. In fact, Jains believe that all life is so sacred they think it is a sin to kill anything, even an insect. Jains sometimes wear a scarf over their mouths, so as not to accidentally breathe in and harm some hapless bug! There were many Jain pilgrims at the temple, climbing the stairs to the temple at the top of the hill, many of them wearing the cotton scarf across their mouths so as not to breathe in a little flying critter.

I took a night train back to Ahmedabad, having had a two-day excursion from the city. To my surprise, Maurice was still hanging out at the Neelama Guest House, having gotten a little sick. We had dinner together, and he bought a ticket south to Bombay, feeling that he needed to get back on the road again.

I rested the next day, and prepared to leave for Mount Abu in Rajastan. I went with Maurice to the train station, to wait for his train south for Bombay. I saw his train off at dusk, while mine would not leave for a couple of hours. The sun, a hazy red ball, was setting behind a water tower, and the station was filled with smoke from the coal-burning engine. The platform was full of the flotsam and jetsam of India. I wrote this poem:

> A smokey black stallion snorts
> And stands on the rails,
> It's taking us down
> On the Evening Mail
> People sleeping on the platform...
> ...An old man sipping tea.
> Staring from a corner
> I thought I saw Gandhi-ji.

Soon, my train too was snorting and chugging its way past the dusty villages of western India. I leaned back in my seat. For once I was traveling first class, though Mount Abu was a relatively short trip. The rest of the train was full and a businessman at the railway station had bought my watch, so I had some extra rupees to blow. First class carriages are closed compartments, unlike second or third class. Second class was actually phased out in the mid-seventies, leaving only two classes. However, there is third class reserved, which is in reality second class, as opposed to third class unreserved. There's even an air conditioned class, which is a deluxe first class available on a few trains (if you are thoroughly confused, it is only because it is thoroughly confusing)...most budget-conscious travelers travel by "third class reserved" in India.

I had bought a Bombay Sunday paper, and even had a couple of *Goldwater Lager* beers to quaff on the trip. In Rajastan, there is complete prohibition of alcohol, so this would be my last chance to enjoy the amber brew. I took a gulp of my Goldwater Lager, and read the paper. "Dead Man Gets Up from Pyre" was one headline.

With a second gulp of beer, I read the news story: "An eighty-year-old man, declared dead yesterday by a doctor at Badnera, near here, got up from the pyre to the great delight of the family. The octogenarian fell suddenly unconscious at his Sindhi Colony residence and the doctor, who was summoned immediately, pronounced him dead. As the last rites were being performed, the old man got up from the pyre."

An Indian gentleman entered my compartment. He was dressed in a business suit, and was clean-shaven and neat. He was in his forties, I guessed, and he wore sandals, which I thought contrasted nicely with his suit. I read him the news story of the dead man getting up from the pyre. "Strange, isn't it?" I said.

"Oh, not so," he objected. "Such things happen all the time. One wonders if it is the incompetence of doctors or the enigmatic nature of death and life. Scientists tell us that a man is dead when his heart stops beating, his lungs quit breathing and his brain waves cease. Such a person is legally dead. This is known as clinical death and were you to be in such a condition, you would naturally be shipped off to a morgue, and likely cremated or buried within a day or two. But in every country of the world, patients are continually waking up in morgues and on funeral pyres. Even in graves!"

"Really!" I exclaimed. Actually, from what I had read in the past, this was true. One famous book by British biologist Lyall Watson, *The Romeo Error*, talks from a scientific point of view about our inability to distinguish between life and death. There are countless stories of persons waking up in mausoleums or coffins, and several inventors have gizmos out on the market for people who are frightened of being buried alive, bells and such to ring from inside your coffin. One recent Mexican inventor was buried alive three times and finally patented his own device for telephoning or ringing people from the coffin. "Wouldn't be buried without one," he was heard to comment.

"There are Yogis in the Himalayas, north of Rishikesh, who can stop their hearts, breathing, and brains as long as they want!" said the Indian gentleman across from me. I offered him a glass of beer, but he was a teetotaler. "Some French scientists came once to do some tests on them, and hooked up all kinds of scopes and such to these Yogi chaps, who then went into their meditation. By gad, they were dead! Or so the scientists declared—clinically dead for hours. But of course they weren't dead, and the yogis were in perfect control. That's life for you," he concluded, "mysterious and confusing."

"But fun," I added, folding up my paper.

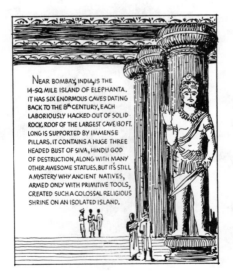

NEAR BOMBAY, INDIA, IS THE 14-SQ. MILE ISLAND OF ELEPHANTA. IT HAS SIX ENORMOUS CAVES DATING BACK TO THE 8th CENTURY, EACH LABORIOUSLY HACKED OUT OF SOLID ROCK. ROOF OF THE LARGEST CAVE 130 FT. LONG IS SUPPORTED BY IMMENSE PILLARS. IT CONTAINS A HUGE THREE HEADED BUST OF SIVA, HINDU GOD OF DESTRUCTION, ALONG WITH MANY OTHER AWESOME STATUES. BUT IT'S STILL A MYSTERY WHY ANCIENT NATIVES, ARMED ONLY WITH PRIMITIVE TOOLS, CREATED SUCH A COLOSSAL RELIGIOUS SHRINE ON AN ISOLATED ISLAND.

The levitation of the stone at Shivapur.
Photo courtesy of Andrew Tomas.

Chapter Eleven

RAJASTAN TO SOUTHERN INDIA:

FIREWALKERS OF THE GREAT INDIAN DESERT

Kill, therefore, with the Sword of Wisdom
The doubt born of ignorance that lies in thy heart.
Be one in self harmony, in yoga,—
And arise, great warrior, arise!
–Krishna to Arjuna, Bhagavad Gita, 4:42

In the dark of the next morning, we arrived in Rajastan. I got off the train at Abu Road, the railhead nearest to Mount Abu. I had an early breakfast at the railway lounge and then took the first bus up into the mountains. The road was so rough and windy one Indian vomited on the way up from motion sickness. Mount Abu is quite a popular little resort for Indians, though not many foreigners go there. It is a pleasant little town, perched high above the Great Indian Desert on the top of the mountain.

Stepping off the bus and shouldering my pack, I looked around. There are dozens of hotels to choose from, though it took me quite a while to find one, as I had so many choices. I settled into the *Tourist Camp Hotel*. After a shower, I headed out into the streets. Mount Abu seemed a pleasant place, though rather touristy. Fortunately, it was the off season. I walked through the small market, full of gift shops, restaurants, sweet shops, and the like, down to the lake. Legend has it that Brahman himself dug out this lake with his fingernails. It is small and picturesque. Honeymooners rent rowboats and go out on it. I took a stroll around the lake and down to Honeymoon Point on the other side, where one could look right off the mountain and down to the desert below. It was quite an impressive sight.

I met a young German traveler, of medium height and build. He had a youthful, brown beard, and wore loose cotton clothing, the only other traveler in town besides myself. We decided to go watch the sunset together at Sunset Point. I had earlier asked an Indian tourist what there was to do in Mount Abu. "Oh, watch the sunset," he told me.

Well, he was right. Watching the sunset was the most popular pastime at Mount Abu, and just about everyone turned up to see the sun, an orange flaming orb, sink into the dust of the Thar Desert (Great Indian Desert). The view from the top of Mount Abu is spectacular, and sunsets themselves are one of the great joys of life. It lasted a long time, the sky turning a multitude of colors, ever so slowly. It became rather chilly after the sun had gone down, so the German and I walked back into town.

We stopped in at the Spiritual Museum, a small place run by the Indian Raja Yoga Foundation. There was a small picture display, and we walked around in the two-room building. As I stood there after looking at the displays, a man in a white cotton shirt and pants came up to talk with me. He was an Indian in his forties, with short hair and a cheery smile. He introduced himself as the curator of the museum. The German came up and joined us just as the curator and I got to talking about Raja Yoga.

"Yoga is Sanskrit for *union*, " said the man. "Raja, as in Rajastan, means *kingly*, therefore Raja Yoga means *Kingly Union*. Unlike Hatha Yoga, Tantric Yoga, or the many other forms of Yoga, Raja Yoga does not require the practitioner to do any physical exercises, nor to chant a mantra or such. Of all the forms of yoga, we believe it is the highest."

"Is that right?" said the German. "I've read quite a bit about Yoga. How is Raja Yoga different from the others?"

"The method of Raja Yoga is to gradually increase the frequency of your spiritual vibrations through character uplift, mental and emotional refinement, and basic good living. It is a mental technique, a form of thought control. It's personal control of your own thoughts, done by yourself.

"Here at the Raja Yoga Foundation, we believe positive thinking is very important. By consciously being aware of your thoughts, cutting out negative thoughts, consciously thinking positive thoughts, and keeping a positive mental attitude, you can reach great heights of health, prosperity, happiness and mental powers that you never thought possible!

Your thoughts are very important; just as important as your actions. Negative thoughts, attitudes and consciousness will drag us down, and ultimately destroy us. Many diseases are in fact caused by negativity, although germs, viruses and microbes are very real. But our bodies' natural defenses keep them under control unless they are weakened by negative attitudes. Fear of contracting a disease will thus often bring it into our environment.

"Furthermore, Raja Yoga provides natural protection to a person when his break-through to astral clairvoyance occurs. In a sense, he will be such a good person that no harm can come to him. Raja Yoga is intended to turn persons into literal saints by controlling their thoughts; by only allowing good thoughts!"

"What about other forms of yoga?" asked the German. "Don't they lead a person to clairvoyance?"

"Yes, indeed," said the gentleman, smiling. He was rather tall, I remember thinking: six foot three or so. His hair was thinning out. He seemed an exceptionally cheery person and was very articulate. "Most other forms of yoga will lead a person to clairvoyance, and at a faster rate as well. They can be, however, quite dangerous, and do not ensure that the practitioner is a good person.

"Black occults can and have gained the Astral Plane while conscious through these means. However, when one forces his way into the Astral Plane, he will come in at the bottom of the plane, where those persons of especially low, negative thought vibrations are accumulated. One will meet the person at the very bottom of the Astral Plane, known in yoga as the 'Dweller at the Threshold.' This Ego, a human, mind you, is so vile and horrible that he will appear as the most hideous monster imaginable, and usually drives the aspiring yogi insane. Believe me, it is a very frightening experience. I wouldn't want live through it myself. Raja Yoga, however, naturally protects a person. Your spiritual vibration will bring you into the Astral Plane at the same level as your own thoughts, which by that time, are naturally of high quality."

He put his hands on our shoulders. "You, like everyone, have much to learn. Be aware of your thoughts. Be positive. You are continually attracting into your life those things that you dwell on. Attract positive things into your life by having positive thoughts. What you fear, you will attract to you. Then you will either have to deal with it, and lose your fear, or keep running away. But you can't run away forever. Your fears will follow you."

It was getting late. We thanked the man for his discussion of Raja Yoga, bought a few books and left. We had a late dinner in a restaurant in the central market. The German suggested that we sit outside on the terrace, where they had a charcoal barbeque that was cooking shish-kebabs. We sat there for a while after dinner, and finally left when the next restaruant started a music war with our restaurant. They battled it out for a while, each turning up its stereo. "Om, Shanti Om!" boomed out of ours, while the other's rang, "Baat Ban Jai!"

We tripped out into the night. It was late. We took a walk down by the lake, and then decided to have a cup of tea before retiring. We stopped at a small tea house and went inside. Taking a seat, I looked around. It was a typical Indian teashop: a small shack with a few tables, a kitchen of sorts to one side. The stoves were kerosene pressure stoves, like coleman camp stoves. It was dark, and rather oppressive. A young boy hardly ten was watching the place. His father was in the back, cooking. The German looked at his watch. It was almost midnight. "That kid should be in bed," he said. We ordered two teas, and talked for a moment.

I watched the boy, noticing that he seemed very quiet and sullen, and looked very tired. Child labor is very common all over Central Asia. This poor kid probably didn't get to go to school, but rather worked from sun-up to the wee hours in this restaurant, while other children played and studied at school. The thought of this kid's hard life stirred a number of emotions in the depths of my being. I looked at him with great sympathy. He was a waif, in dirty old cotton clothes. He seemed to be in fair physical health, despite his glumness. "What's your name?" I suddenly asked in English.

He perked up immediately. I actually saw him smile, and could almost hear him think, "Is this foreigner interested in me?" "Lochan," he said.

"How old are you?" I asked cheerily.

"Nine years old." His English was good. I suppose he picked it up from working in the restaurant. I asked him if he would like a tea, and then bought him one. He came back with his tea. I put my arm around him. We chatted about Mount Abu, and I told him a little about America. It was a great pleasure watching him light up, a smile on his face, a light in his eyes. Later, as we left, tears came to my eyes. It was such a messed-up world. Life, especially for children, could be torture. It seemed important to brighten this child's life. I felt I had to make as much of a difference as I could in this world. Better interactions with the people around me seemed like a good start.

The next day, I took a late afternoon bus back down to Abu Road, and then a night train to Jodhpur in central Rajastan. I had the day to spend in Jodhpur and would take a night train to Jaiselmer. I stepped into the Railway Restaurant for breakfast, walked across the room, wide and spacious, to the desk, and ordered some poached eggs, toast, and milk. I saw what looked like a European sitting at one of the tables reading a newspaper. There was hardly anyone else in the restaurant. I decided to go and sit with him.

I took a seat. "Mind if I join you?" I asked.

"Be my guest," said the man in a German accent.

I sat down and looked at him as he put down his newspaper. What I saw made it difficult for me to keep my composure. He was about thirty, I suppose, and of normal build. However, he had apparently been in some auto accident, because his face was completely burned off. His entire face was a mass of scar tissue. He wore wire-rimmed glasses, and had a little bit of nose left, as well as about half of each ear. Some of his hair was still there, and he wore it shoulder length. Large patches of hair had been taken from the top of his head and grafted onto his cheeks to create sideburns of a sort. He had no lips or eyebrows, and his hands, or what was left of them, were terribly burnt.

It was a particularly uncomfortable situation for me since, as a teenager, I had seen a news documentary about a young boy in America who had been badly burned, and it affected me strongly at the time. Since then I have had a certain fear not only of being burned myself, but of dealing with persons who were terribly burned. Trying to be philosophical about it, I decided now was as good a time to deal with my feelings as any. We chatted for a bit. He was going to Jaiselmer, too. I got my breakfast, and took a big gulp of milk. He was very German, and got to talking about Buddhism. It was something that he was especially interested in. I asked him about Hinduism and Taoism, and other Eastern philosophies.

"No! Buddhism is the way!" he stated adamantly. "It is the philosophy for me. I'm not interested in anything else!" It seemed to be a touchy subject for him. I decided he must be under a lot of mental stress, perhaps due to his physical state, which appeared to have happened recently, though I could never bring myself to ask him about it.

I excused myself and went off for a day's touring of Jodhpur. Jodhpur has one of the best old forts in Rajastan, a state noted for its great, scenic forts. Perched on a bluff overlooking the city, it is quite impressive. Inside is a museum, well worth visiting. One painting that I found particularly amusing was entitled, "Opium Eaters Frightened by a Rat," with a dozen thin, wide-eyed and wasted opium addicts in their paranoia coming upon a rat with their daggers. The rat was backed up against a tree, preparing to meet its doom. The grimaces on the faces of the opium eaters were so distorted, it was like a cartoon.

After wandering about the museum I stopped at the ramparts of the fort to look out over the city below. Vultures and hawks were soaring about on the air currents looking small animals to swoop down on. ("Watch out chipmunks!" I wanted to yell.)

I shopped for a while and then took a night train on a

dead-end line out to far western Rajastan, Jaiselmer. It is here that the Indian government tested its atom bomb, and there is a large airforce base somewhere in the vicinity. Jaiselmer itself is a fascinating town; very medieval, full of camels, castles, small tea shops, and bushy-bearded, orange-turbaned, desert-dwelling Rajputs.

When I awoke early the next morning, it was still dark, but I was the only one left on the train. Slowly I got up. It must have been five in the morning and we were already in Jaiselmer. Being the last one off the train, I noticed that the station was virtually deserted except for one person squatting on the platform selling tea. I had a cup and he pointed the way into town, as we were out on the edge of the desert somewhere. As I walked the half-mile or so into town, yellow streaks began to form on the eastern horizon. It was quite chilly. Dawn broke just as I got into town; on the western skyline was Jaisel Castle, its towers stretching up to the sky. With a great shout of joy at this romantic sight, I leapt over a sleeping camel—once again on the road to adventure in the Great Indian Desert!

Shortly thereafter, I checked into the Hotel Tourist Home, a small hotel with five or six rooms in a courtyard. Its card said, "Comfartable and Chipest Stay," which was probably a misprint, although their food did create a lot of intestinal gas!

The next few days I wandered about the town, and met an old friend from Bombay, a tall, thin, bearded Aussie named John. We bummed around together and watched an incredible sunset from the roof of his hotel, the Golden Hotel. We explored the fort, which had a small city inside it with narrow winding streets, and a market. "Charming," was one of John's favorite comments. He showed me his Indian rope trick, a simple magic trick with string which never ceased to amuse people at tea shops. We'd have cardamon tea at our favorite tea shop, John would show his trick, and in the evenings I read *Marco Polo's Travels.* I walked John to the train station one night, as he was heading out. There was a wedding processsion on the street as we walked by. They stopped to play us a tune. There was an entire band, and several scores of people, with the groom riding a horse, and the bride nowhere in sight.

I met another friend, Bill, whom I had met before in Kathmandu. Bill was heading out that afternoon, but he told me, over a cup of tea, an interesting story about a time that he had been in Jaiselmer some months before at the Jaiselmer Fair:

"They were doing firewalking," Bill said. He had blonde, sandy hair, and a blonde beard. He was an electrical engineer from Ohio. "I went with some friends to see the show. When we got there, there was a big pit, about ten feet by ten feet square, filled with red hot coals. Presently, a couple of yogi guys, naked except for loin cloths came up to the pit and stood there." Bill took a sip of his cardamon tea and went on, "They then began to jump over the pit, and eventually, there were three of these guys jumping onto the hot coals, barefoot too, and jumping out! After they did this for a while, one guy jumped right into the pit, picked up a handful of coals, then threw them in the air. Soon they were all in the pit, playing around in the hot coals, throwing red hot coals around, even putting them in their mouths and spitting them out! I couldn't believe it!"

Bill was starting to perspire just thinking about it. I was listening intently as he went on, "After they left, I talked with my friends for a bit, and then I wanted to check out the fire pit, so I walked down to the pit from the bleachers where we were sitting, and do you know what? It was so hot, I couldn't even get close to it! I couldn't get within ten feet of that pit—it sends shivers down my spine just thinking about it. It gave my reality paradigm a workover!"

I walked Bill to the train station, and sent him on his way. What a great story! Firewalkers are well known in Fiji, and other South Sea Islands, and here in India, they can be found, too. What an experience!

The next day I moved into the *Golden Hotel,* because it had such great sunsets. There was a nice dormitory there, and Bill had been the only one staying there, and was now gone. I had seen the German with a burned face in some of the restaurants, but he was staying in some other hotel. I was avoiding him because I felt uncomfortable around him. I came back from lunch that day to find someone's back pack on the bed next to mine. Later in the evening, I came back to the dormitory to find, of course, that the burned German, the person I had been avoiding, had moved into my dormitory!

I took a deep breath. There were four beds in the room, but there was just him and me. He was folding up some of the clothes on the bed. "Well, hi!" I said, swallowing hard. The very thing I had been carefully avoiding had happened. What I feared most had become reality. I resolved to meet this challenge, knowing that, as the man at Mount Abu had said, we have to face our fears sometime. Now was such a time for me.

For three nights we shared the dormitory, and we became quite close friends. He turned out to be a nice person on a serious spiritual quest; an engineer, who had been traveling around India for several months. We had dinner together occasionally. After a few days it no longer gave me the creeps to sleep next to him, and I found that I could look him right in the face and sincerely be his friend.

My last day in Jaiselmer, I met a petite and charming English gal at the *Gaylord* restaurant at lunch. She was new to India, and by herself. We walked about town for the day, inside the fort and around the graveyard. She went into a jewelry store while I sat outside and did my newly-learned Indian rope trick for a crowd of enthusiastic kids and old men. They gave me a piece of opium, which I casually popped into my mouth. Alcohol is completely forbidden in Rajastan, but opium and ganja are sold in government shops and completely legal. Most Rajastani men, it seemed, were into opium to one degree or another. It has a medical use as an anesthetic and as a cure for diarrhea, as it naturally paralyzes the colon. I had had a touch of diarrhea that morning, so took the opium. Oddly enough, I felt no effect from it, except that it constipated me.

My afternoon romance with the British lass carried on. She was a school teacher, and quite charming. We watched the sunset together from the roof of the Golden Hotel, and then she went off to her hotel, saying she would meet me for dinner. I was, unfortunately, leaving later that night to go back on the train to Jodhpur

I walked around town a bit, and went back to the hotel. The German guy had left me a note saying that he would be at a certain restaurant. It was almost time to go and I was faced with the problem of either saying goodbye to the English lass or the German who had been my nemesis. I decided that it was more important to see the German. I found him at the restaurant and we had a nice farewell. I was so grateful to have faced this fear; one of many. As the train pulled away from the station I thought of the charming English girl. Why didn't I stay in town with her? Perhaps that was another fear I needed to deal with....

As I left by train, I wrote this poem for the city in the desert:

> Jaiselmer
> Where they're still talking
> About my Indian Rope Trick
> I listened to the twang
> Of a desert violin
> And drank the music
> With Cardamon tea.
> Afterwards I had my knife sharpened
> And on the whole street
> No one had change for a rupee.

Jaiselmer
Where the men stare
From behind their turbans
And bushy moustaches,
With the glazed eyes
Of opium eaters.
The Great Indian Desert
Blows past them
And their shops
To the starry night beyond.

§§§

From Jodhpur, I could either have spent the night in the Government Tourist Bungalow, or gone on to Udaipur. I decided to do the second. Udaipur, the "City of Sunrise ," became the capital of Rajastan after the old capital, Chittorgarh, had been sacked for the third time by the Moghuls in 1567. The Rajputs, fierce Hindu warriors, put up the most resistance to the invading Muslims that were moving in and conquering India at the time. Many battles were fought on the dusty plains of Rajastan, usually with the Moghuls winning.

It was during these fierce wars that the peculiar Hindu practice of Suttee got started. Suttee requires a Hindu widow to throw herself onto her husband's funeral pyre in grief, commiting suicide because she cannot go on living without him. This was started by one Hindu princess who, in the sixteenth century, decided to kill herself by jumping onto a pyre, rather than marry the conquering Moghul Emperor who had just defeated her husband's army on the plains below the Chittogarth Fort. Her entire entourage, some fifty or so ladies-in-waiting, followed suit, throwing themselves in the bonfire.

This became quite the rage in India for years, the women imagining themselves as deeply spiritual, throwing themselves on their husband's pyre. It was expected of them in many places and became quite a problem, continuing to this day. The Indian govenment has made it against the law to commit Suttee, which has cut the practice down somewhat. But one can still occasionally see a widow running screaming to her husband's pyre, wailing in grief, and before anyone can stop here, she's out of the frying pan and into the fire, so to speak.

A few hours' train ride north of Udaipur is Chittogarth, former capital of Rajastan and birthplace of the tradition of Suttee. I spent a night there at the Tourist Bungalow, and took a trip around town, organized by the Tourist Bureau. The Chittor Fort, where most of the battles were fought, is

199

very impressive. It is situated on a plateau with excellent natural defenses, and a mini-city inside that the Moghuls sieged for months.

That night on my way north to Ajmer, I had to bribe the conductor with five rupees to let me sleep on the floor of a third-class compartment, because I couldn't get a reservation. In the morning it was a two-hour bus ride from Ajmer to Pushkar, where there is a special desert fair once a year in November.

I hit town in the afternoon at the height of the fair, and POW, insane city! It was incredible: millions of people, many of them with their camels, all camped out and doing their thing. There was a carnival, complete with ferris wheels and other rides, hawkers, games, camel races, and motorcycle daredevils.

During the fair, tent hotels spring up all over the place, including the Pushkar Hotel and the Tourist Hotel. Most of these hotels are full of travelers from all over the world. I met a doctor from San Francisco named Ben, and we wandered about the fair for several days.

It was sensory bombardment of the highest degree. Crowds flowed through the streets, pushing everyone in front of them; a huge human wave. There were snake charmers and beggars on the streets asking for "baksheesh" (handouts), young women in bright red, yellow, or orange saris, with bells on their feet and rings in their noses, chewing sugar cane and giggling. The men were all wearing their big, colorful turbans; the crowd was a sea of yellow, red, orange, and blue turbans. Ben and I ate hot peppers dipped in batter that looked like corn dogs. After eating one of these "hot" dogs, we would look for a cool yogurt drink (*lassi* in Hindi) to cool off our tongues.

We dodged the occasional aggressive cow that wandered the streets and got to the central carnival area. There we saw the daredevil motorcyclist in the "Death Well," a large wooden well in which the morotcyclist rode horizontally to the ground, his centrifugal force keeping him from falling! I rode on the ferris wheel with an old man in a white turban who was having the thrill of his life. His enthusiasm, wild grin and occasional yelps of joy got to me, and it was the best ferris wheel ride of my life. Later I rode on the whirly plane (little cars on chains that spun quickly around a central "maypole") with Shiva as the protective deity prominently displayed.

Ben and I stood in front of a tent where a man was interviewing on stage a rather coy and cute young lady. They laughed and told jokes in Hindi, with obvious sexual intimation. "You know what?" said Ben. "That's a man! That's not a woman!"

200

I looked at the attractive woman on stage. "No, I don't believe it!" I said. "I mean, it couldn't be!"

"Really, that's a female impersonator. In Rajastan, it's illegal for a woman to perform on stage, so they have young boys do it! " He was right.

We watched the sunset from the park over the lake, by the Tourist Bungalow. Then we sat in restaurants full of hippies, where ganja was being passed around in a chillum. Later, we took photographs of the sunset near the camels.

Pushkar has the only temple in India dedicated to Brahman, the first of the Hindu Trinity, and this is apparently the reason why the annual Pushkar Fair is held here. At the end of the fair was the great highlight all the Rajputs had come for: the camel races.

First we saw a camel getting rings put in his nose, and he made the most terrible fuss, snorting and blubbering like nothing I'd ever heard before. But then, again, as Ben noted, "You'd probably snort like that if someone put rings in your nose." The camel races started, eight gallant steeds tearing it up around an oval track and actually running over some poor kid that wandered onto the race course. An ambulance took him away.

Utterly stunned and in shock from four days at the fair and its intense sensory bombardment, Ben and I escaped Pushkar just as a full moon was rising over the city. At the train station at Ajmer, he boarded a train heading south, and I one going north to the last of the Rajastan cities I would be visiting: Jaipur.

I arrived in Jaipur in a matter of a few hours. Known as the Pink City because of its many red sandstone buildings, it is the capital of Rajastan and a popular tourist destination. I checked into the Tourist Bungalow. They always have a nice dormitory for a dollar and are a chain of hotels found all over India.

Like all Rajastani cities, Jaipur has its red fort, plus a few palaces, and plenty of camels for us camel afficianados. It is especially known for its shopping, being a good place to buy jewelry, enamel ware, printed cotton cloth, and muslin.

I was sitting in a tea shop one night in Jaipur, watching a camel cart meander by, sipping tea and eyeing the moon between two rose-colored towers. I thought back on the trip so far: the crazy ashram in Poona with its egotistical guru, the kid in the tea shop at Mount Abu, the firewalkers and the terribly-burned German in Jaiselmer, plus the teeming multitudes in Pushkar. It had been, as usual, a strange journey. Inside my head, a voice spoke: "Be aware of your thoughts. Be positive." I still had many lessons to learn about life and many questions to ask. I looked at the moon, hoping she had the answers. But she, like the desert, was silent.

§§§

It's nice to be important
But it's more important to be nice.
-Indira Gandhi

After leaving Jaipur, and taking a train north, I found myself at the American Express Office in New Delhi. Standing before me, also waiting in line to get her mail, was a young lady in a pair of baggy, white silk pants that tied at the ankle, reminding me of harem pants. She had on a blue cotton jerkin with a padded money pouch over one shoulder. Her hair was long and brown, her small cute nose liberally speckled with freckles. I could just see the outline of her underwear when she stood to catch the light just right... "I just have to get to know this woman," I said under my breath.
"Pardon me, what did you say?" she said, suddenly turning.
"Uh, oh, I think it might snow this morning," I said, thinking fast, my face turning red. I pinched myself at this answer. What a stupid thing to say!
"Snow? In New Delhi? This morning?" she smiled at me.
"Well, it's a long shot, I admit...."
"You can say that again. It must be ninety-eight degrees outside!"
"Yeah, well, I like to think positively. Sort of a mental exercise."
As it turned out, she was a school teacher who lived in London, was born in Rhodesia, had lived in Capetown, and was here in India to travel around for a few months. We went out and had some mango ice cream at *Nirula's Ice Cream Parlor* just a block or two from the American Express Office. She was going down to the ex-Portugese Colony of Goa, the most popular beach spot in India for Europeans. In fact, she was leaving that afternoon.
I already had a reservation to Lucknow, on my way back to Kathmandu to see if some of the climbing equipment I had left there almost three years ago was still there. I thought seriously of changing my ticket and taking off for the western coast of India. This girl had such dark eyes, and her silk pyjamas were driving me wild. Before I knew it, though, she was on her train, and I was standing on the platform, waving goodbye.
My train was leaving the next morning. I went to the luggage room just to see about the policy of checking luggage overnight, when I noticed that on a chalkboard

202

behind the first-class reservations, it said that my train had been cancelled!

I went right up to the clerk and asked him what was going on.

"Oh, you mean the Assam Mail. The track's been blown up. It's those nasty Assam separatists again! Just blew those tracks right up. Ah-cha. They do that every now and then. Train will probably be running in a few days..."

"Ah-cha," I said, imitating this Indian expression meaning "Uh-huh." Assam is the extreme northeastern part of India, east of Bangladesh, and next to Burma. The people there aren't really Aryans, but more Burmese, although they are Hindus of a sort. They have been giving the central government a hard time for the last few years. Compounding the whole political focus on this area is the fact that this part of India has many of India's oilwells, producing most of India's domestic oil, although India still imports oil from the Arabian Gulf.

"Soooo...." I thought. "This is an odd turn of luck. What should I do now?" The answer, I found, was very simple: get the next train to Goa!

I went back to my hotel and checked out. I headed back to the station, only a few blocks away, got a refund on my ticket and caught the late-night express to Bombay. I didn't have a reservation, but I was pretty savvy dealing with the train system by now, and ten rupees, just over a dollar, can work miracles on an Indian train.

I bribed the conductor, and he found me a third-class berth in the very back of the train. It may well have been his. I was pretty tired from running around the day before, and the heat can get to you on the hot dusty plains of the north.

Lying in my bunk, I read the paper. There was an odd article with the headline, "Coke Bottle Dug Up With Ancient Bones." According to the article, a certain Dr. Ramar Kashim was leading an archaeological dig north of Delhi and discovered among ancient bones what turned out to be a modern Coca Cola bottle. The bottle was encrusted with ages of dirt, and "It was obvious the area had not been touched for thousands of years," Dr. Kashim was quoted as saying. One speculation in the article was that the bottle was left by some time travelers. Said Dr. Kashim, "If the bottle was left by ancient astronauts or time travelers, we know they liked something about our culture." I rolled my eyes at this story, discrimination was certainly called for here. I was soon dropping off to sleep. The last thing I remembered was the clickety-clack of the wheels beneath me.

I woke up late the next morning. We were still chugging

along southward through India. This was a special Mail Express which made very few stops, so we would be in Bombay in no time. I had a cup of tea and some potato samosas (pastries) for breakfast, and read the latest issue of the *Illustrated Weekly of India*, a pleasant magazine in English that is India's version of *Life magazine*.

There was a good story in there abaut Sir Thomas Metcalfe, British resident in the court of Bahadur Shah Zafar, Delhi's last emperor. Sir Metcalfe's mode of meting out punishment was rather interesting and humorous: when a native offender was brought before him, he wielded no whip and ordered no thrashing. He merely raised his eyebrow at a waiting attendant who produced a silver salver holding a pair of white kid gloves. As he gently advanced upon the waiting offender, he delicately put on the gloves. Reaching close to the man's face he raised his hands and gently pinched the offender's earlobes! (Many hardened criminals were known to faint after this!)

By late evening, we were in Bombay. Without leaving the station, I bought a third class unreserved ticket to Margao, one of the railheads in the State of Goa. Once again, I was on the train, and soon began looking for a possible berth. It would be a miracle if I could find one myself on the train. I'd learned, however, to ask a conductor to help, and have him try to find one.

I ran out of luck on this train, and, although the conductor made every effort to find me a berth, there was not one on the whole train. I shared one with a friendly Afghan refugee, a grisly but kind old man, with a long gray beard and a turban. We spoke Arabic together, and he befriended me like his long-lost son, whom I gathered had been killed by Soviet troops in Afghanistan in the invasion the year before. Sleeping end to end, we shared the berth. Each of us got some sleep, at least. In the morning, just before noon, we pulled into Margao. I popped into the tourist office, got a map of Goa, and then caught a bus to Colva Beach. Actually, the main tourist attraction is Calangute Beach, or I should say "Freak Beach," across the river from the main city of Goa, Panaji, the capital.

Travelers have been coming to Goa and hanging out on the beach at Calangute since the mid-sixties, and it is a circus, to put it mildly. It can really be a gas, and at different times of the year, especially at Christmas, it is one big party! "Christmas in Goa" is a famous saying among the many travelers in Asia, and just about every available hippy bus in India and Nepal heads down to Goa around Christmas.

There are literally hundreds of places to stay. Many people just rent beach huts or bungalows along the coast, plus there are plenty of guest houses and hostels. There is the oddest assortment of people in Calangute as well: travelers from all over the world plus people without any money who have been living on the beach for years. They get by using various methods, most of them not totally honest. Many people sleep on the beach. Restaurants abound, serving all kinds of tasty, cheap and exotic dishes. The latest in Indian music can be heard from the stereos of the many restaurants up and down the beach. Drugs of all kinds are plentiful, even alcohol. Goa is the cheapest place for beer in India, and it even produces its own wine, which is especially rare in the sub-continent.

However, I wasn't going to Calagute Beach this time around. Ms. Silk Pyjamas was going to Colva, a smaller, more isolated, and much quieter beach further south. That's where I was headed, too. Calangute is the place for people who are into circuses and human spectacles, but Colva is more the speed for people who like nice beaches, palm trees, good food, a cheap vacation, and some privacy, with the chance of walking nude down a beach without a lot of people following you. Nudity is permitted, at least unofficially, in Goa, and is common at both Calangute and Colva.

The best thing about Goa in general is that it is a truly relaxing place, something quite rare in India. India is so intense, and just the everyday hassles like train travel and shopping can be such a drain, that travelers need a vacation from India! Colva is one such oasis where you can rest your weary feet before returning to the real world; some travelers never do go back.

I stepped out onto the beach from where the bus had let me off. There were some semi-fancy beachfront restaurants, some souvenir shops, plenty of palm trees, and miles of beautiful white, sandy beach. I walked a little to the north along the beach to the *Sunset Resturant*, where I rented a room in one of their bungalows for a dollar a night, took off my clothes, put on my swimming trunks and went down to the beach.

I had a dip, then went back to the restaurant for a plate of french fries, poached eggs and a Kingfisher beer. Afterwards I took a stroll along the beach. I hadn't gone too far when I spotted Ms. Silk Pyjamas, minus her pyjamas, and in fact, minus everything else. There were really very few people in Colva at the time. Looking up and down the whole stretch of beach there were only about ten people, as far as I could see.

Rather impolitely, I suppose, I looked through my sunglasses at her very nice, very tanned body. She was lying on the beach, sleeping I suppose. I was just about to head on up the beach when she opened her eyes and

looked at me. "Oh, hello!" she said, apparently glad to see
me. "What a nice surprise! I thought you were off to
Kathmandu!"

"Oh, yes, well, my train got bombed..."

"Oh, how nice," she said, sitting up. I just stared at her.
She was beautiful. We went for a swim, then had a quiet
conversation over a romantic dinner.

And so began our south Indian love affair. It was full of
bottles of wine, empty beaches, seagulls flying overhead,
walks along the beach in the hot midday sun, baked beans,
eggs, fish, Spanish potatoes and beer at sunset, romantic
evening walks along the beach with the sea breeze through
the palms. Thank God for those Assam separatists and
their bombs, I thought one night after Ms. Silk Pyjamas had
fallen asleep in my arms.

But all things must pass. Lost cities and ancient
mysteries beckoned. I went with her to the bus station and
once again waved goodbye, having a distinct feeling of
deja-vu. I headed further south. There was a yearly Jain
festival of Bahubali just getting underway in the rather
remote part of Karnataka state. I would take a train to
Hampi, a "lost city," and then catch a bus down to
Sravanabelagola, where the Jain festival was being held.

I took the night train to Hospet, the town just outside of
Hampi, a deserted city now popular among hippies in
India. I stored my pack in a locker just by the railroad
station and then tripped into Hampi, hitchhiking with a
small day pack and a sleeping bag. Hampi is set along a
river, and is a series of ancient, ruined stone temples and
other buildings.

Hampi, originally called Vijayanagara, ("City of Victory"
in Sanskrit) once the flourishing capital of the Vijayanagar
Empire in the fifteenth century, now lies amid a wilderness.
The city sits among rugged granite outcrops weathered
into gigantic boulders. There are numerous temple
complexes and smaller shrines. The largest temple
complexes are from the sixteenth century and consist of
vast rectangular compounds defined by high granite walls,
the temples are entered through towered gateways. These
soaring pyramidical brick and plaster constructions were
the "skyscrapers" of their day, often more than 150 feet (52
meters) in height.

I was particularly interested in the high granite walls
that surrounded the temple complexes. It seemed older
than the rest of the city and was built out of cut granite
blocks that were fitted together with remarkable fineness
and joined without any mortar. Furthermore the blocks,
rather than regularly cut and placed as one would expect,
are fitted together in a polygonal fasion, with blocks

perfectly fitted together like a jigsaw puzzle.

This form of construction is highly unusual, and the most sophisticated technique for fitting stones. Walls fitted together in this fasion are earthquake proof, among other things. Futhermore, walls, identical to this, though generally built out of larger blocks of stone, can be found high in the Andes of Peru at Machu Picchu, Sacsayhuaman, Cuzco and other sites. Once inhabited by the mysterious Incas, most Peruvian archaeologists now believe that these gigantic walls were built before the Incas, possibly thousands of years before, and later utilized by the Inca Empire.

Was there a connection between Vijayanagara and Peru? I was suddenly reminded of the tunnel systems said to exist in both countries. Walls around Vijayanagara also had fish, snakes and other animals on them raised out of the stone, just like ancient walls in Cuzco! One theory of the ancient structures in Peru is that they were built by a mysterious group called "The Atlantean League." After the sinking of Atlantis, these seafarers theoretically journeyed all over the world, and, incredibly, on reed boats! Was the ancient wall at Vijayanagara built by the Atlantean League? In this theory, the city here, like in Peru, was ancient to begin with, and then utilized by the Hindu Kingdoms of sixteenth century India when strong fortresses were needed in the many civil wars that India was going through.

In the past it was visited by travelers from Italy, Arabia, and Russia. It is now a lost city full of French, American, Japanese and Italian hippies, who fill the temples and courtyards with parties.

Just after entering the city, where the bus route stops, there are a few restaurants, mere palm shacks with one or more walls open, where you can get a hot meal, tea, or yogurt. There are fruit vendors as well, and grapes are quite plentiful. Most people just sleep in the many empty temples or on the big sandy beach that is a short walk from the river. After an afternoon of hanging about by the river, talking with a gal and a guy from the Netherlands, I headed down to the big beach at sunset, where a little party was just getting going. Hampi has been turned into a city of freaks and hippies, travelers from all over the world hanging out in the deserted buildings on the beach, by the river, or at the few restaurants back by the bus station.

People played guitar, smoked chillums, drank wine, played guitars, sang and looked up at the stars. Everyone eventually crashed out in their sleeping bags or blankets. I was up with the sun, and wandererd back to the bus station for some tea. Hampi was really a social scene, one of the many places to hang out in India, and an especially out-of-the way spot, I thought. For the counter-culture freaks of the world, this was a spot where they could truly get lost, no matter who was after them. Many a draft-dodger from Europe could once be found in Hampi.

For the kids coming from the restrictive industrial societies, India was their opportunity to cut loose, dress outlandishly, wear their hair any way they pleased, do whatever they wanted, or just hang out smoking chillums all day. Generally speaking, this did not go down too well with many Indians, who have absolutely no respect for most of these people, although they were constantly trying to get the women into bed and often succeeded.

I took an overnight bus south. It was a long journey of twelve hours to Sravanabelagola, one of the most sacred spots for Jains. As Jainism arose in eastern India just prior to Buddhism in the sixth century B.C., it, like Buddhism, was a reform of Hinduism, protesting the caste system and rituals prevalent at the time. It is likely that Buddha himself may have met and studied with the slightly older Mahavira, the founder of Jainism, who taught the "three gems": right belief, consciousness, and conduct. Similarly, Buddha's "eight-fold path" included right thinking, action and belief. Mahavira was actually the last of a succession of twenty-four saints who are always depicted naked.

Jains today are mostly ascetics. Strict vegetarians, and something of health-food nuts, most modern Jains, some two million of them, do not believe in killing anything. This is not necessarily the original doctrine of Mahavira, as Jainism has undoubtedly become corrupted over the years. They have readapted the caste system and these days are hardly distinguishable from Hindus. Today, they are known as a sect of Hinduism and have even adopted a number of Hindu deities.

The largest free-standing statue in the world is in Sravanabelagola, that of Jain saint Lord Gomateshwar. I nearly gasped as I stepped off the bus in the small village of Sravanabelagola: there, at the top of the hil, was a solid granite statue of a naked man standing several hundred feet tall! I checked my pack at the tourists' office and walked up the hill.

There was scaffolding around the back and sides of the statue, so that colored water could be poured over his head for the festival. A naked Jain ascetic sat at the base of the statue, dwarfed by the gigantic statue of the perfect, immovable ascetic standing above him. I was very impressed. This was an incredible piece of art, no doubt about it. Built several thousand years ago, it was a tribute to the knowledge of Jain engineers, artists and architects. I was reminded of the Jain fortress Palitana in Gujerat, another Jain masterpiece of impressive architecture. The Jains liked to do things with a keen sense of grandeur. Even today most Jains are very prosperous, and are known as excellent and honest businessmen all over India.

I watched the sunset from the top of the hill, standing on one of the platforms built around the statue. Looking back at the statue, there was a full moon rising, and it was just at Lord Goma- teshwar's height. He seemed to be turning his head just slightly in order to kiss the moon with his full, perfectly-formed lips. He looked, truly, like a saint.

I spent the night in a small hotel, and took a bus the next morning to Mysore, the ancient capital of Karnataka state. Mysore is a fairly big city, well-planned, spacious and prosperous. When the reigning Maharaja of Mysore ceded Bangalore (Karnataka's other main city) to the British as an administrative capital for the state, he kept the city of Mysore as his dynastic capital. The splendid Mysore Palace which has tours during the day is one of the main tourist attractions of this pleasant city and is dramatically lit up at night. The bazaar in town is particularly interesting, and fun to stroll through.

Southern India is less traveled by tourists than the north, and also is less known. One of the oldest geological formations on earth, it was inhabited by an early, prehistoric people known as Dravidians. Dravidians are dark-skinned, Caucasian-featured people, with black hair. According to many anthropologists, the Dravidians were the earliest inhabitants of India, and were driven south by the invading Aryans around 3,000 B. C. Ancient Indian tradition, however, tells another tale. Dravidians inhabited the south at an early time, while the north was inhabited by a lighter-skinned people, the Nagas (Naacals) who came westward from Burma. (While a few Nagas still live in central India, others live in northeast India, Assam, just on the border of Burma. They have their own state and it is called Nagaland.) Apparently the Nagas got to India first, coming from the semi-mythical "Motherland Mu." Dravidians came from Malaysia, and many of their words are the same. Some Dravidians supposedly emigrated to Ethiopia,where people with identical racial features live today.

I checked into the *Palace Hotel* for a couple of rupees a night. I was enjoying the south of India. It seemed more relaxed than the north. It seemed like a virgin country to me, and I hoped it was full of lost cities. Was this area of India part of the Rama Empire? As I studied my literature, it seemed that the south has its share of lost cities too...

The step temple of Palenque (above) compared with the Madurai Temples (below) of southern India. Many historians believe they are of similar design.

Chapter Twelve

SOUTHERN INDIA NORTH TO ORISSA:

SHIVA DANCING TO THE JUGGERNAUT

Some places were not so good, but maybe we were not so good when we were in them.

—Ernest Hemingway

I caught a bus from Mysore up into the Nilgiri Hills to the "Queen of Hill Stations," Ootacamund, or Ooty for short. It was a half-day bus ride up through thick pine and eucalyptus forests, and even past a wildlife sanctuary, into the green, cool, and wet hills around Ooty.

Once a popular resort for the British in India, Ooty has some nice botanical gardens, a two-mile-long lake which is fine for bathing, and splendidly cool weather. I decided I could use a little of that before I went back down to the coast and hit the beaches of Kerala.

My first night I went out walking around the lake just at sunset, and then had dinner. The rain made the streets rather slippery, but everywhere was the fresh, clean smell of eucalyptus. I went back to the YMCA where a number of other travelers were sitting around the fires; I joined them, all of us swapping a few tales. Ooty was a refreshing and different break from the rest of India. It felt somewhat like being at a ski resort.

The next day as I was walking through the park, I came upon a movie crew filming a movie in the Tamil language. There was an absolutely ravishing Tamil girl in the finest silk sari cavorting around the park lip-syncing the words to some scratchy record. It was a park-frolic scene, the sort that seems to show up at least once in every Indian film. I noticed a rather overweight, greasy, heavily made-up gentleman with a thin black mustache who looked something like Snidley Whiplash.

"Is that the villain?" I asked the cameraman during a

211

break.

"The villain?" he sputtered. "Oh, no. That's the hero!"

Well, so much for that movie, I thought as I headed into town.

Ooty is indeed a pleasant place, I mused. Many rich Indians still come up here for holidays. I had some coco tea at one restaurant, bought a bag of cashews, and made a reservation on the train down to Cochin in Kerala.

The next afternoon I sat in my seat as the little toy-like train wound down through the mountains on the slimmest of narrow-gauge tracks. I went up to the engine to see what was going on, always having been something of a train aficianando. Three rather muscular Indian fellows were busy keeping the small steam engine running. One would open the boiler while the fireman would shove in a load of coal.

Meanwhile, the engineer stood with his hands firmly on the wheels to regulate the steam. "I am driver," he said in his best English, turning and smiling proudly to me. I grinned back at him and ducked a sudden shot of steam. Chugging through tunnels, and there were many of them, was a bummer as steam and cinders would fly everywhere. I pulled my shirt up to breathe through in the tunnels, though the engineer, a dark, cheery fellow, didn't seem to mind them. From the look of the instruments, I decided the engine must have been a hundred years old.

At Coimbator, I changed trains to a slightly more modern one, which took me down to the coast overnight. By early morning I was walking out of the Ernakulam train station, looking for a bus to take me across the water to the island just off the coast that was the ancient city of Cochin. I decided to make my reservation to Trivandrum right then as long as I was in the station, so I stood in line for a couple of hours and at one point noticed this sign on the wall which read:

1. Queues should not be formed before 7 A.M. for reservation on tickets.

2. Passengers are informed not to engage unauthorized persons or railway porters for getting reservations.

3. Only self, relatives, servants, or *peons* of the traveling party will be allowed to form queue.

I looked twice at this sign, and then checked out the room for peons. However, since I didn't know what a peon was, I wasn't really able to spot one. Looking it up in my dictionary, I discovered that in India, a peon meant a foot soldier, a messenger, or even a policeman! Hmmm, now that was interesting....

On another wall was a sign which stated, "TICKETLESS TRAVEL IS SOCIAL EVIL," and a few feet away was another sign, hung on a wall covered in the red juice of beetlenut, which advised: "SPITTING IS UNHEALTHY".

Soon I was sitting on a wharf at Fort Cochin drinking a Kingfisher Lager beer, eating cashews and reading, of all things, the want ads of the daily English paper in south India, *The Hindu*. I was captivated by the column headed, "Brides and Grooms". Some of the ads read as follows:

WANTED VERY intelligent, well-educated Brahmin match, in early twenties, for Kannada Brahmin boy, tall, good personality, well settled in USA. Please respond urgently with horoscopes. Box No. 5755 c/o *The Hindu*, Madras, 600002

Hmmm, I thought, taking a gulp of beer. This guy, or his family at least, sounded desperate. Perhaps his family was afraid that he was going to break down and marry an American girl. I read a couple more:

WANTED BROAD-minded, handsome, qualified, well-employed, affluent boy, good family, preferably USA for beautiful, slim, fair, 156 cms, double graduate, journalist, propertied, only daughter, 23. Subsect no bar. Horoscope optional. Box No. 58994....

MATRIMONIAL correspondence invited from parents/relatives of good looking, Nair community, male Doctors/ Engineers/Businessmen, aged below 35 years, employed/settled down in USA/UK/West Germany for well accomplished, pretty, Nair girl, aged 28, Doctor MBBS and DGO, presently employed in UK, willing to join husband. Other locally well-established Medical Graduates will also be considered. Reply to....

I finished my beer and leaned back in the chair. Very interesting. I considered applying for that last one myself, but they seemed to know what they wanted, and I doubted that I could fool them for too long. Besides, my horoscope wasn't too handy....

I had checked into the Tourist Bungalow in Fort Cochin, after taking the bus from Ernakulam. Fort Cochin is rather spread out, and lacks any real downtown or center. However, it has a great fishing beach, famous for its Chinese fishing nets that are just off the beach. They dip down into the water from a simple huge wooden hinge, and are then raised, hopefully with a net full of fish. It's the lazy man's way of fishing and quite ingenious. They were apparently brought from China to Cochin hundreds of years ago.

Cochin is a very old city, though not exactly ever "lost." Kerala was an active trade center in ancient times, known as the Malabar Coast in Marco Polo's age. There is a nice long bazaar to walk through. Land at the end of the bazaar is "Jew Town", and has a synagogue built in the mid-1500's.

The Jews of Cochin came to India in 72 A.D., driven from Jerusalem by Roman legions. At one time, the white Jews numbered tens of thousands along the Malabar (Kerala) coast. Now most of them have gone to Israel, leaving only about eight left in Cochin. All the other synagogues have been closed. This is the last one, and it has no rabbi. The Cochin synagogue, open for visitors, contains many historic treasures; among them copper plates given by the local ruler in A. D. 379 to the Jewish community, granting a large tract of land. 36

This little bit of history proves not only that the Jews and Romans knew about this part of the world, but that travel in large groups of people was possible, including mass emigration. Ancient trade was probably a great deal more extensive than is thought by mundane historians. There is considerable evidence that Phoenician galleys and Roman ships sailed to South and North America, and that Chinese traders sailed all over the world, as Chinese pottery has been found in Africa and South America 53 and ancient Chinese seals have even been discovered in Ireland. 7

According to Chinese records, a Buddhist named Fahien traveled fom India to China via Ceylon and Java in 400 A.D. His ship carried more than two hundred passengers and crew and was larger than the ships of the Portugese explorers who came to India for the first time one thousand years later. In 499 A. D., according to the ancient Chinese records known as "Fusang," the Chinese Buddhist priest Hoei-shin traveled by ship across the Pacific Ocean to a distant land thought to be Central America. 53

This is certainly possible, as within the last century a Chinese pirate junk reached California, and in 1815, a Japanese junk drifted across the Pacific to California. 9 Within the last couple years, a Roman galley was found off the coast of Brazil, and divers brought up such artifacts as amphorae (wine flasks of clay, about three feet high), a fibula, used to clasp the Roman toga, and more. In 1961, Dr. Garcia Payon of the University of Jalapa discovered a large hoard of Roman jewelry in six graves near Mexico City. Professors at the University of Vienna and the German Institute of Archeology identified it as Roman and dated it about 150 B.C.

In 1972, a shipwreck discovered off the coast of

Hondoras was found to contain a cargo of Carthaginian amphorae and other artifacts. Columbus and other map makers were known to possess ancient maps that showed areas of North and South America. Less than twenty years after Columbus discovered America, the famous Turkish admiral Piri Ries published a series of maps showing the entire coast of South America, including rivers that were not "discovered" until a hundred years later, and even sections of Antarctica. He claimed to have based his maps on ancient and secret maps, many of them from the Orient.
9, 53 ,11

Pulling out the most important map to me at the time, my map of India, I noticed that I was getting pretty far south. I wasn't far to the tip of India. I was sitting by the Chinese fishing nets, watching the sunset, when, looking over my shoulder, I saw a Jew. Not one of the Cochin Jews, though, this one was a psychiatrist from New York, traveling about India.

"What a nice place," he sighed, looking out over the water.

"Yeah, India is a fascinating place," I said. "I just can't get enough of it."

"Traveling is like sex," said the psychiatrist. "The more you get, the more you want."

I turned to look at him. That was a rather profound statement, I thought. In the distance, the sky was a deep red. The fishing nets were silhouetted in interesting polygons all along the shore. Afterwards, for something to do, we decided to go see a Bruce Lee movie playing at one of the local cinemas.

Kerala, a lush tropical state, gained prominence some fifteen years ago when it produced the first democratically-elected Communist government in the world. Many of the people are Syrian Catholics, or members of the Eastern Orthodox Church in Kerala, a church founded by very early Christian missionaries, even before the formation of the Roman Catholic Church. Kerala is often known as a Marxist-Catholic state, much to the chagrin of many Catholics and Marxists who traditionally maintain you cannot be both.

Kerala's capital, Trivandrum, is a day's train ride south of Fort Cochin. I stopped in Quillon on my way down to pick up some cashews. As Quillon is the cashew capital of Kerala and I was the biggest cashew nut in India, we made a great team. A few miles further south was the town of Varkala. There I met my old Australian friend John from Jaiselmer, the only other tourist I saw there. He introduced me to the watchman of a little guest house, and I got a room.

After talking about our travels over tea, we went behind

the guest house for a super sunset, and then to a Hindu temple where they were celebrating Krishna's birthday. They were playing music and dancing. Women in silk saris and gold jewelry danced to the sitars and tablas while the moon shone down into the temple. It was a magical birthday party!

It was a one-mile stroll into the small village where there were a couple of restaurants. We had some egg curry with parantha, a flat bread. The next morning it was down to the beach for a swim, and I found that many of the Hindus would go out in the morning for their ritual bath, going into the water with all their clothes on. John decided to hang out on the beach, and I hitched a ride into town on the back of some kid's bike. I had a shave by the local barber, who used a cut-throat razor to give me the closest shave I've ever had. He would turn my head from side to side as he shaved, which made me laugh nervously. I liked the thought of living dangerously, but this was ridiculous. After all, one slip and this guy might cut my throat....

Milk, tea, and bananas
for breakfast.
Catching a ride
to the beach
on the back of a bicycle.
A fingerless leper
stops to fill his bowl
with vegetable curry.
Sunset and palm trees
on Varkala Beach.

§§§

I enjoyed my stay in Varkalla a great deal. As my search for lost cities was not revealing much in the south, I decided that Varkalla could be my own private lost city, a little Shangri-la on the beach of the Kerala Coast. There are some real lost cities in the south, but they are difficult to get to, largely because most of them are underwater!

Off the west coast of India are the low-lying island groups of the Lacadive and Maldive Islands. The Lacadive islands are part of India but are separated by a deep channel from the Maldive Islands which are an independent Islamic Republic. According to some archeologists, most notably James Churchward, that old India-hand who wrote a great deal of interesting, though ques- tionable, material on lost cities and vanished civilizations, these islands were once part of a large oval-shaped island which was ancient Ceylon.

216

This land, now sunken, contained a number of cities that can still be seen, or so some say, submerged in the narrow channels between the islands. Water is quite shallow around the islands, and local fishermen tell stories of seeing man-made structures on the bottom on calm, clear days. Many Indian scientists are aware of these submerged lands, though no one can really account for their submergence, when it happened, or just what civilization existed here. Pilots flying over the islands have reported seeing what appeared to be foundations and walls of ancient cities.[8]

Quite possibly, this is the "Ancient Ceylon" that is spoken of in the Indian epic of the Ramayana, the land of an evil king who kidnaps Rama's lovely young bride. Rama's good buddy Hanuman, a monkey, goes to Ceylon to rescue her. Theoretically, when "Ancient Ceylon" was submerged, perhaps in a cataclysm that took place around 7000 B. C., according to some cataclysmic geologists, the present island of Ceylon, or Sri Lanka, was formed.

Tamil literature contains a flood myth which is also connected with atale of two lost cities: Tenmaturai and Kapatapuram. In a historical work at least a thousand years old by the Hindu historian Narkiren speaks of three literary academies, Tenmaturai, Kapatapuram and Maturai, the third of which exists to this day. The durations of the these academies belies the extreme age of civilization in India; 4440 years, 3700 years and 1850 years. The first two academies were destroyed in a cataclysm and are now under the water![80] Were these cities once part of the ancient Rama Empire?

One interesting "lost city" said to be in south India somewhere is the ancient Tamil capital of Dravida. The Tamils are the ancient inhabitants of southern India, know as Dravidians, and according to some ancient Indian sources (mostly mysterious tablets that few people have seen) existed in India at least twenty thousand years ago in an organized and civilized culture. Their ancient capital of Dravida was perhaps located somewhere in northwestern Tamil-Nadu State, though no one has ever found this city. In this way, it's much like the ancient city of Troy, dug up in the eighteenth century.[8]

The Tamils are a mysterious race, even to Churchward. Many historians say they came out of Central Asia, others say they came by ship from Malaysia. According to one Naacal record that Churchward claimed to have read, "A company of Tamils took ships and sailed in the direction of the setting sun. They came to a great land where they settled." This great land is believed to be in Africa, probably Ethiopia. Ethiopians are very similar to Tamils racially, as are many Malaysians. No race similar to Tamils has ever been found, to my knowledge, in Central Asia.

When searching for lost cities in India, one cannot help but return to the legends of the great Rama Empire and its Seven Rishi Cities. Generally speaking, it is thought that the Rama Empire coincided with Atlantis, and was the other world power at the time of this great civilization in the Atlantic Ocean. (This information comes from ancient Greek, Egyptian, Mexican, Indian and mystical writings.)

While Atlanteans were noted for their high practicality and inventive technology, the Rama-Indians were noted for their high spirituality and for their priest-kings of high mental development. The Rama Empire extended over much of northern India and Pakistan and included such cities as Mohenjo-Daro, Harappa, Lothal, Kalibanga, Nagpur, and perhaps such extant cities as Benares, Patna, and others. There are a number of stories about the Rama Empire, and a war they had with Atlantis, and while many of these stories seem so incredible as to hardly be possible, there is some evidence to back them up. I was deter- mined to find out about the Rama Empire, and visit some of these cities. So, I decided to eventually head back north to Pakistan, where the best of these cities are found. (Further discussion on the Rama Empire will wait until the next chapter.) In the meantime, I wanted to see as much of southern India as I could.

John and I took a train down to Trivandrum, and from there a small, motorized, three-wheeled taxi out to Kovalam Beach to the south of Trivandrum. We got a double room, and then had a beer at the major tourist hotel by the road, the Kovalam Ashok hotel. Kovalam is a lot like Goa, though not quite such a circus as Calangute Beach. It is one big, long bunch of bungalows: they are everywhere. The restaurants around Kovalam serve good, cheap, Indian and western food, and often play the latest pop music from Europe. It is quite a nice place to hang out, and there are other travelers here, not like Varkala.

I spent a few days hanging out on the beach, watching sunsets, drinking Burton's Export Lager beer, eating bananas and mangos, fruit drinks and yogurt, swimming and tanning, as if I wasn't tanned enough already. But I find that I can't just "lie around" on beaches forever like some people, and soon my feet were itching to get going. I left one afternoon for Madurai, and John was planning to leave shortly for Sri Lanka.

Madurai has one of the most incredible temple complexes in India, the Meenakshi Temple. Legend claims that there are more than thirty million idols in the temples, though more recent estimates put them at something more like a million. However, they could never really be counted. Madurai is an exceptionally pleasant and interesting town, especially because of its temples, but also because of the Maharaja's Palace where there is a sound and light show, and a nice market to wander in.

Madurai is the ancient city of Maturai, having the literary academy previously mentioned with the lost cities of Tenmaturai and Kapatapuram. It was the most recent of the academies, lasting a mere 1850 years, yet even this date is scoffed at by academic historians (but not Indian academics, who take this stuff seriously). Was this one of the Seven Rishi Cities of the Rama Empire I wondered as the train pulled into the station?

I came out of the train station, turned to my right, and walked up the street into the main market, near the temple complex. I settled on a small hotel called the Ruby Lodge. After a shower, I was out on the street, heading for the temples. They were four gigantic towers, set on each side of a square. Dravidian architecture is quite different from the Aryan-Hindu architecture of the north. The temples are square; fort-like enclosures with four pyramid-like towers centered at each wall. The pyramid-like towers, called "gopuras," are not really pyramids: they are more flattened on their two inner and outer sides, coming to a flattened and rounded top, rather than coming to a point.

I walked inside. There was an elephant, dressed up in some ceremonial outfit, by the entrance. Inside, hundreds of pilgrims swarmed around statues of various deities and in the art museum that takes up one great hall. In the center of this vast "temple city" was a large, square pool with steps leading down to it. Walking past the curio and gift stalls that sold incense, idols, beads and little souvenirs, I sudenly came to the hall of one thousand pillars, where I gasped in wonder.

There, at the end of the hall, back-lit with red light, was a fifteen-foot-tall Dancing Shiva—a statue of the god Shankar (as Shiva is also called) the destroyer, who is one of the Hindu Trinity. He was standing in a bronze circle with one leg lifted up in a dance, and his four arms making various gestures. It was beautiful and awesome. I walked slowly down the hall toward the god. He seemed to beckon me with his graceful movements. In fact, I'd have sworn I could almost see him move. I came up to him. It was a wonderful statue, exquisitely cast in a greenish bronze and, I imagined, thousands of years old.

A voice behind me suddenly said, "It's a dancing Shiva."

I turned to see an Indian man standing next to me. He was of meduim build and brown-skinned, balding, elderly and clean-shaven. He wore a white cotton *longi* with part of the fabric thrown over one shoulder like a Roman toga. "Why is he dancing?" I asked quietly.

He smiled gently. "It is the dance of life. Shiva is showing us how to dance. Unfortunately, many people just do not know how to do the 'Dance of Life,' if you understand my meaning."

"Hmm," I said, looking back at Shiva, the exquisite dancer. "Well, I think I may understand what you are saying. How does one dance properly?"

"The dance of life is one of care. Be watchful not to step on other people's toes, as then they would step on yours. Dancing itself is a good allegory for the art of getting along with other people. If you dance with a person, you should leave them and yourself with a pleasant feeling when you have finished your dance. This is the art of living. Try not to make too many waves, nor to step on too many feet. "

"That could take some practice," I said. "I could probably use some dancing lessons."

The elderly man laughed and said, "So could we all. Realizing the need for lessons and self-improvement is a good first step forward." I laughed this time, and Shiva nodded in approval.

Later, I was sitting in a cafe outside the temples in the market, having a cup of south Indian coffee. I looked at an ad in the paper, *The Hindu,* out of Madras, and shook my head in disbelief. It said, "For Men Only: Introducing CIG, the smoke for lion-hearted men." And then there was a photograph of a male lion with a great mane, smoking a cigarette!

"Whew, that's bad taste," I said under my breath, and took a sip of coffee. Tamil Nadu is a dry state in India; no beers to be had around here. A news story headline read, "Woman commits suicide." The story read, "A married woman allegedly committed suicide by burning herself yesterday. The cause is not known." "Hmmmm," I sighed. There was a sudden "Ahem!" I looked up, and son of a gun, if it wasn't an old buddy of mine from Africa, Patrick!

We had roomed at the youth hostel in Salisbury (now Harare), Zimbabwe. I had seen him once in Capetown when I was working in a sporting goods store. Wow, what a treat! We shook hands, and had lunch together there. He looked great, tanned and healthy, and he was going to Madras, just coming from Sri Lanka. He had been back to Australia since the last time I saw him, and was on another trip abroad. We talked, laughed, and talked some more about the old times.

We were sitting inside a small cafe, directly under a ceiling fan. The entire front was an open wall, and we had a good view onto the street. As we were preparing to leave, I noticed an old lady in a torn, worn cotton sari, her gray hair unwashed and tied up on her head. She must have been sixty or seventy years old. She was begging, holding out her palm to passers-by, but no one was paying much attention to her. Her face wore a grim, sour look. There are literally millions of beggars in India, many people making a real profession of it, but her sad aura touched me. How terrible that some poor old lady was left to wander the street begging. As Patrick and I left I put my hand on her shoulder. She turned to look at me, as I pressed a few coins in her hand, and gave her a smile.

It was the highlight of the day to see that woman smile. Her face brightened and she gave me a toothy grin. Our smiles said, "God bless you," to each other.

After watching a beautiful sunset, a huge red sun floating over the hills with the southern towers of the temple silhouetted in the sky, Patrick and I saw the sound-and-light show that night. It was in Tamil, which naturally neither of us spoke, but was still great fun, with good light effects on the Maharaja's Palace and good music. I "spaced out" for a while watching the pillars and halls turn green, red, blue, and cream while the sitar music floated through my head, accompanied by an occasional elephant trumpeting. We went to the Indo-Ceylonese hotel for some grape juice and ice cream afterwards, and then back to our hotels.

We decided to travel together on to Madras, but first we stopped in Tiruchirapalli and Thanjavur, two other Tamil-Nadu towns famous for their tourist sights. In Tirunchirapalli is the famous rock fort up a hill above the city, which is a nice hike past elephants in dress, temples, and markets to gain a superb view of the countryside. In Thanjavur is the Brahadeswara Temple, quite ancient and impressive, but the Meenakshi Temple in Madras is the most impressive.

It was overnight to Madras, where we got into the station just before dawn. We had breakfast at the railway restaurant and then took a motorized rickshaw to Broadlands, a popular travel hotel well-located in Madras. With nearly three-and-a-half million people, Madras is the fourth largest city in India. Founded by the British in 1639 and used as a trading outpost, it later grew into a great trade center, and capital of the British southern Indian colonies. It is a well-designed and laid-out city, with sea breezes, coconut trees, movie theaters and temples of all religions. It is an important industrial center, and the second-largest movie production center after Bombay.

It is fairly easy to find a cheap hotel in Madras. We chose

Broadlands, off Mount Road on Vallagha Agraharam Street, just near the Star Cinema. It has beds or rooms at anywhere from fifty cents to two dollars. It seemed like some huge mansion turned into a guest house; rooms and staircases just sprout all over the place.

Patrick and I spent a couple of days wandering around town, eating ice cream and shopping. I sold my Pentax camera to the "Cine Equipment Shop" as its sign out front announced itself. There are some things to do in Madras, though it doesn't have a wealth of museums. There's Fort St. George, which has everying that a good seventeenth-century fort should have: a mote, drawbridge, battlements, cannons, and an arsenal. There's a Marina, with a fine esplanade and a beach that allows swimming. But, the most interesting thing I found in Madras was the Cathedral of San Thome, a small Catholic church built by the Portugese about three miles down along the Marina to the south. Incredibly, it is reputed that the remains of Saint Thomas the Apostle are buried here.

Saint Thomas was also known as Didymus, a word meaning twin, although there is no mention of the other brother or sister who was his twin. In some early Christian legends, it was said that Thomas was the twin of Jesus. [28] It is also from Thomas that we get the phrase "doubting Thomas," as he was a healthy sceptic and found it hard to believe that Jesus had appeared to the other apostles after his crucifixion and asked to inspect Jesus's wounds upon meeting him. I had been told of this church and the supposed tomb of Thomas by an Indian gentleman in the United Arab Emirates some years before, and now was my chance to see it for myself.

Thomas had apparently gone to Babylon after Jesus had left the apostles for good, and then probably sailed to the Malabar Coast (Kerala) much as the Cochin Jews did a few years after him. He wandered about, possibly doing saintly miracles and what not, and came eventually to the Coromandel Coast, south of Madras, where he was "martyred" in 68 A.D., according to the 1968 edition of the *Columbia Encyclopedia.*. In some traditions, his bones are said to have been removed and sent back to the west where they were buried in Edessa. In others, the Portugese moved his body from another older tomb to this cathedral several hundred years ago. His tomb can be seen in the church, which is also quite interesting and historical.[36]

Thomas' efforts as a missionary were belatedly successful. His death came from the local king, Misdaeus, who was then stricken by guilt and converted to Saint Thomas' Christianity. Misdaeus' son, Vizan then spread what is known today as Nestorian Christianity throughout

India, Central Asia and China. Even today there are
Nestorian Christian sects, though they are mostly in
remote cities in China and Central Asia. Nestorian
Christians believe in reincarnation, karma and that Christ
was the archangel Melchizedek.[73]

Patrick and I had "dosas" baked at the Wheat Hotel. He
had a masala dosa and I, a special onion dosa. A dosa is a
thin fried crispy pancake, much like a crepe, with some
potato or other things folded inside. I went to the State
Bank of India where I thought I might buy some Indian
rupee traveler's cheques with the extra rupees I had from
selling my camera. When I found out that they could only
be refunded at the issuing bank, and that it would take at
least three months, I decided that they would be useless.
Unfortunately, I had already paid, and it created a great
bureaucratic hassle trying to get my money back after I
had decided that I did not want them.

I also happened to have a one-hundred rupee note that
was torn, taped up and not negotiable. Money that is torn,
especially if it has been taped together, is not legal
currency and will often not be accepted by merchants, in
fact banks won't even take it. You have to go to a Reserve
Bank to change it, of which there are only a few in the
country, and even then it can take all day. With a five, ten,
or one rupee note, I wouldn't have bothered. I'd have just
given it away as a tip, bribe, or baksheesh, but a one
hundred rupee note was worth the effort.

When I got inside the bank, it was a terrible mess. It
seemed as if every Tom, Dick, and Harry in India was in
there trying to change their worn and torn notes. I
wandered around in a daze, not knowing what to do, and
horrified at the thought of standing in line for a couple of
hours to change this note, probably just to be told that I
was in the wrong line. Fortunately, some hawker came up
to me and offered ninety piastres (cents) to the rupee for
whatever notes I wanted to turn in. I took it, giving him my
hundred-rupee note for ninety rupees. Both of us split fast,
each thinking we had gotten the better deal!

Patrick and I were soon on our way north, plowing our
way though Andhra Pradesh on the Madras-Howrah Mail.
We had gotten third-class sleepers to Bhubaneshwar, the
capital of the State of Orissa. It was a one-day, two-night
journey. We settled back and read books, drank tea, and
talked with other passengers.

"Ah, cha," said the Indian gentleman in the seat across
from us. He was from the south, a match salesman of all
things, and reclined in white muslin pyjamas on his seat.
When I asked him about marriage customs in India, he
said, "In the south we have some interesting marriage

customs, isn't it?" Many Indians continually use the phrase
"Isn't it?" when they speak English. "What are those?"
asked an elderly Bengali on his way back to Calcutta, who
was also in our compartment.

"I've read the marriage ads in the paper," I chipped in,
taking a sip of tea from a disposable clay cup.

"Well, among the Brahmins of southern India," said the
match salesman, pausing for effect, "a younger brother
may not marry before an older one. When there is no bride
available for the senior brother, he is sometimes married to
a tree! This leaves the younger brother free to take a wife.
Often the tree marriage takes place at the same time as the
regular marriage, in the belief that some evil influence that
might otherwise attach itself to the newlyweds will be
diverted to the tree, instead!"

"My, what a ghastly custom!" said the elderly Bengali.

"Yes," said Patrick, looking up from his book, "I've heard
of people marrying trees before. I suppose it's better than
nothing."

At sunset the second night, I stood in the doorway of the
train while the fiery orb hung suspended over the palm
trees. As we passed a villa, a boy saw me and I nodded at
him. He then waved to me and I waved back. Then a young
girl spotted me hanging out the door as she walked home
with a basket on her head. She pointed me out to some
other girls she was walking with, and then I waved to her
and smiled. She broke into a big grin, a huge white smile
enveloping her beautiful brown face. It made me grin ever
the more, and I turned my smile to the setting sun. It was
great to be alive!

Directly to our west in the eastern end of Maharashtra
State was Nagpur, a modern industrial city and once the
capital of the state. In remote antiquity, it was apparently
known as Deccan, and was the capital of the Nagas
(Naacals). Having moved into India from Burma, this
white, Caucasian-type race founded an empire that would
stretch across the Deccan Plateau and northern India,
becoming the semi-mythical Rama Empire. I mused
silently about the Nagas as I watched the sunset from the
train. The Rama Empire had come to a sudden and violent
end, and Deccan (Nagpur), was apparently its ancient
capital. Now there was little left of the once-great Nagas.
Some, generally thought of as untouchables and
aborigines, lived around Nagpur. In Nagaland, northeast of
Calcutta in Assam, Nagas were animalistic-head hunters
until recently. It would be interesting to see the archaeological remains of Deccan, lost city that it was. However, I
was informed that the modern city of Nagpur is directly on
top of it, so there is little to be found. Most people have

never even heard of Deccan, or the Rama Empire for that matter.[4]

One day later, I was watching the sunset from the beach on Puri, an ocean resort on the Bay of Bengal. Oddly, the sun both rises and sets over the Bay of Bengal at this point. One of India's most ancient temples lies here, the Jaganath, "Lord of the World," Temple. Jaganath is one of the titles of Krishna, who is himself the eighth Avatar of Vishnu (one of the Hindu trinity). Every year is the "Juggernaut" festival during the rainy season, in which an effigy of Lord Jaganath is drawn in a gigantic forty-five foot cart before hundreds of thousands of ecstatic pilgrims. In times gone by, spectators were occasionally crushed by the gigantic wheels of this great cart being drawn throughout the streets of Puri, hence the European legend of pilgrims throwing themselves in front of the cart to be crushed.

The temple itself is maintained by no less than six thousand priests, and is for Hindus only, being one of the most sacred Hindu temples in India. According to Eklal Kueshana in *The Ultimate Frontier,* Jesus studied in Orissa for many years, and in that case, would surely have visited the temple, and may have even studied there. Buddha, Mahavira, even the Chinese sages of Meng Tzu and possibly Lao Tzu have visited the temple, the "Lord of the World" being one of the great centers of learning in the first millenium B.C.

There are a number of places to stay in Puri, and plenty of hitchhikers, hippies, and travelers. It is fast becoming the Goa of the east coast. Nearby is Konarak, a magnificent temple dedicated to the sun and built in the mid-thirteenth century A. D. Built to resemble a huge chariot of colossal proportions which was to symbolically draw the sun, much of it has vanished throughout the years. It is still regarded as one of the great sights of India, and is on Indian rupee notes. It is built with great skill, and the small niches about the wheels of the chariot and other parts display amorous figures of voluptous proportions.

I had a banana burger for breakfast, an egg burger for lunch, and was now having a fish burger for dinner (Decisions, decisions!) Patrick, I, and a couple of guys from New Zealand sat around the Amigos Restaurant after dinner. We had been tanning on the beach, using coconut oil as a lotion, playing frisbee, and hanging out. The days, as at the other beaches, melted into one another. Time was passing at an alarming rate, I suddenly discovered.

I took a walk along the beach. The moon, a pale creamy disc over the silvery shimmering sea, was just coming up. Walking along the ruined and deserted beach palaces, left-over from when the British would come down here from Calcutta, I saw that the sands of the beach were slowly reclaiming their own.   I thought of the Nagas, the Dravidians and the ancient Rama Empire. I smelled the sweet scent of coconut oil from my own body.   In the distance I heard a grinding crunching noise: the Juggernaut was lumbering down the road. On the water, I seemed to see Shiva, dancing to the light of the moon...

The ruins of Kot Diji.

A so-called Priest-King from Mohenjo Daro. Is it possible that
he was one of the adepts who ruled the Rama Empire?

The excavation of the Great Bath at Mohenjo Daro, built out of high quality kiln fired brick. It and hundreds of other cities flourished many thousands of years ago in the Indian sub-continent.

An inscribed stamp seal found the ruins of Mohenjo Daro. depicts an extinct animal, so sort of bull. Possibly a relati of the auroch and the mode brahma bull, it was probably result of thousands of years breeding by the "Indus Val Culture" otherwise known as Rama Empire. The inscripti remains undeciphered.

Portion of the ancient port of Lothal, now several miles from the coast.

KALIBANGAN : RAJASTHAN
HARAPPAN TOWN

0   50   100   150 M

DRY BED OF R.GHAGGAR

KLB-1

KLB-2

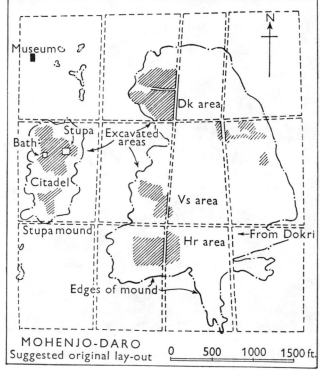

Museum

Dk area

Stupa
Bath   Excavated areas
Citadel
Vs area

Stupa mound
Hr area   ←From Dokri

Edges of mound

MOHENJO-DARO
Suggested original lay-out

0   500   1000   1500 ft.

When Mohenjo Daro was first excavated, people were just lying dead in the streets, often holding hands, just like the ancient Indian epics had indicated.

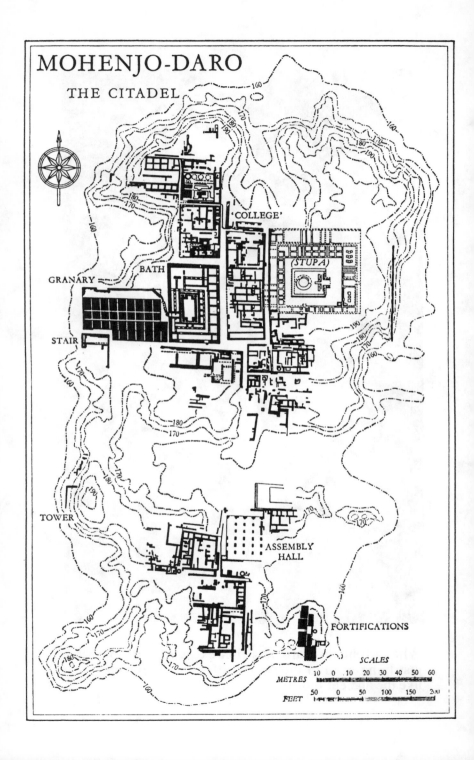

MOHENJO-DARO
THE CITADEL

'COLLEGE'

(STUPA)

GRANARY

BATH

STAIR

TOWER

ASSEMBLY HALL

FORTIFICATIONS

SCALES

METRES 10 0 10 20 30 40 50 60

FEET 50 0 50 100 150 200

Chapter Thirteen

CENTRAL PAKISTAN: THE SEVEN RISHI CITIES OF THE RAMA EMPIRE

" ...(a weapon) so powerful that it could destroy
The earth in an instant—
A great soaring sound in smoke and flames,
And on it sits Death....."
—*The Ramayana*

I felt I was hot on the trail of the Rama Empire, and I was tired of the endless sleepy beaches of the coasts. I bade farewell to Patrick, shot up to Calcutta, and took an express train across northern India to Delhi and then on to Amritsar, where I had been on my previous trip to India, intending to enter Pakistan. I sensed, as I stepped off the train in Amritsar, that I was headed for adventure!

In many ways, Amritsar was my favorite place in India. One reason, I mused as I finished off my third bowl of cornflakes at the Railway Restaurant in the Amritsar train station, was that this was one of the few places in India where you could get cold, fresh milk! I always carried a bag of Mohan Mekin's "Golden Corn Flakes" in my pack just in case I chanced on the luxury of finding a place with fresh whole milk for sale. While milk is plentiful in India, a land of sacred cows, it is generally to be found warm, not cold.

Amritsar has other things to offer, and is the center of the Sikh religion with its most holy shrine, the Golden Temple. Sikhism itself was founded by the mystic teacher, known as Guru Nanak. Guru Nanak lived from the mid-fifteenth century to the mid-sixteenth, and his religion filled an important gap. It became the bridge between the Muslim religion and the Hindu religion.

Sikhism is based on monotheism, and meditation, and the universality of all religions. It opposes idolatry and the Indian caste system. It became popular in the Punjab region of India and Pakistan, and eventually developed into quite a military power under other Sikh gurus that followed Guru Nanak. The tenth and last guru, Govind Singh, in the early eighteenth century, finally created a warrior

233

fraternity of Sikhs who introduced the practices of wearing turbans, and never cutting their hair.

This warrior fraternity began to openly oppose the Islamic rulers because of the general Muslim intolerance of other religions, and a series of bloody wars was fought. Amritsar was founded in 1577 by the fourth guru, Ram Das, and has been a center for pilgrimage ever since. *Amrit* means the "elixir of life", and the waters around the sacred pool, in which the Golden Temple sits on a central island, are thought to be "life enhancing". Singh is the word for "lion" in Punjabi, symbolizing bravery, and most Sikhs have taken the word Singh for their last name. Virtually any person you meet in India or elsewhere with the name Singh will be a Sikh.

Bravery is what the Sikh religion demanded, as its history has been one long bloody struggle. Souvenir shops around the Golden Temple are full of posters that depict scenes of horrible fighting with the Muslims in days of yore; another favorite artistic subject is the disembodied head of one of their beloved Gurus. Amritsar was the scene of the April 1919 massacre, when thousands of Indians, mostly Sikhs, were killed fighting the British. During the Partition of India in 1947, the Sikhs sided with India, fought a holy war with the newly-born Muslim state of Pakistan, and 2.5 million Sikhs moved from the Punjab in Pakistan into the Punjab in India.

More recently, a Sikh uprising in the summer of 1984 against the Indian government of Indira Gandhi led to the destruction of much of the Golden Temple and to the death of hundreds of fanatical Sikhs. Sikh militants turned the temple into an armed fortress, having secretly stored arms there for years. When the Indian army, which is composed mostly of Sikh (the most militaristic of India's many cultural groups) officers, took the temple, the rebel Sikh leader, Saint Jarnail Singh Bhindranwale, was dead. The Golden Temple was somewhat destroyed, although the government troops had orders to spare the most holy shrine on the central island in the lake. As a result, a twenty-four hour curfew was placed on Punjab, the most prosperous state in India, and much of India seemed on the brink of civil war. Indira Gandhi, who had ordered the attack on the temple, was herself assassinated by Sikhs in her own army some weeks later.

Fortunately for me, these things were yet to happen, and I merrily finished my cornflakes, booked myself a ticket to Lahore, across the border in Pakistan, and then took a cycle rickshaw into town. About half-way between the railway station and the Golden Temple is the Tourist Guest House, located on the Grand Trunk Road by the Hide

Market and Bhandari Bridge. I debated whether to stay here for the night for a dollar or so, or go on to the Golden Temple where I could stay for free at the gargantuan guest house there. It is part of the Sikh religion to provide free accomodation and food for travelers, and the guest house at Amritsar is the world's largest.

I decided on the free *Sikh Guest House*. Arriving there, I was told to sleep in one of the three rooms that were kept for the foreign travelers that were constantly stopping in at Amritsar. Indian families may be given an entire room with beds, out of the many hundreds of rooms here, but since the early hippy days, foreign travelers are required to sleep on the floor in one of these three rooms reserved for them. I didn't mind too much, as the rooms weren't crowded owing to the takeover of Iran by Khomeini, and the virtual cessation of travelers through Iran and Pakistan to India. I locked my pack in a rough plywood cabinet in one of the rooms and went to have a shower in the center shower-washrooms.

The guest house is shaped like a four-story, square donut. It has a large courtyard in the center, with a tiled shower building in the center of it. People can do their laundry in buckets, or shower inside. As I stripped down, and started to take off my underwear to shower, an older man (not a Sikh, I surmised by the lack of a beard) shook his finger at me, saying "Nahi, nahi." It sounded rather like "Naughty, naughty," but meant "No, no," in Hindi. I then noticed that he was wearing some bathing trunks while he showered. One should not strip entirely when at a public bathhouse, I gathered.

After my shower, I met a few of the people who were also staying here in the three foreigner rooms. One was a young, bearded Dutch fellow who someone said had just come from Pakistan by way of Quetta in Baluchistan. I went up to ask him what it was like in Quetta, and instead of an answer, I got a lecture on how rude Americans were, and how they didn't care about the local people, but clomped around in big boots making a nuisance of themselves. I felt rather taken aback by his snap-judgments. I looked down at my feet. I wasn't wearing big boots at all, but he, in fact, was! I turned away, thinking that he might have been infected by the Central Asian sun, and perhaps by Iran's newly-inspired hatred of Americans.

As I stood there, feeling somewhat dazed and still wondering what it was like in Quetta, a young French woman, with smeared eye make-up and a yellow, Sanskrit-printed shawl on her shoulders, came up to me and asked if I would buy her a tea. I looked at her for a moment, and then she said in English with a heavy French accent, "If you buy me a tea, I will tell you a story."

"Well, okay," I said. "As long as it's not a lecture on the rudeness of Americans. I've had one of those already today."

"Oh, no, no, " she said, as we walked out of the Sikh Guest House and into the streets. "Americans are very polite, and generous!" We sat at a small tea stand, at a table on the street, and drank sweet milk "chai." She began by telling me that she was the daughter of a French mother and an English father, and grew up in France. She had come to India, like so many Europeans, for an extended vacation some four years ago. Now she was out of money, and she wanted to get back to France. She stayed here at the Sikh Guest House. It was free, and they fed you two times a day. For some reason or another, she couldn't have her parents send her the money to get home.

I was somewhat suspicious of her. I had my doubts that she was even French to start with—her accent was extremely heavy—but she wasn't Indian, nor did she seem European....."Oh, *mon Dieu*," she sighed finishing her tea. I braced myself, thinking she was about to hit me up for the money to get back to France (if she was really leaving) or wherever she was really going. "Life in India is so miserable. Ah, to be back in Paris..." She batted her eyelashes. She was pretty in a tired way, but somewhat shopworn. "If you need some femm-male companionship, gener- ous American traveler, I would be pleased to accommodate you...."

I thanked her politely, and paid the bill. "My wife back at the Guest House probably wouldn't like that very much. But thank you anyway," I told her, and with that, we parted. I went down to the market and bought a tomato and a small onion, and went back to the Golden Temple, where dinner was just beginning to be served.

They feed literally thousands of people a day there, and it is quite fascinating to watch. You are swept in turns to a large hall, seated, and are passed a brass plate. Men come along and pass out whole-wheat chapatis, and then someone else comes by with a large pot and ladles some thick lentil stew into your dish. I was sitting next to a Japanese guy I had met in line who had just finished bicycling across India. He now planned to bicycle across Pakistan, and perhaps Iran, if they would let him in. He too, had cleverly brought an onion and tomato, and using our pocket knives, we cut these vegetables up into our stew, and made what I considered quite a good meal out of their free dinner.

After dinner, I wandered about the Golden Temple. It is spectacularly beautiful. The central island temple is covered with heavy gold leaf that glows in the light, even on a cloudy day. I took a drink of the Amrit water, known for its curative powers, and stood there watching a young Indian man, with a club foot, gazing into the artificial pool of the temple, across which was the small island on which the inner holy Golden Temple lay. The young man would look at the temple, and then down at his foot.

I realized once again how lucky I was, not just to be a whole, healthy person, but also to be an American (rude and insensitive as they may be). I wanted to go over to him and place a com- forting hand on his shoulder, but I didn't, out of shyness. Instead, I went back to the guest house and unrolled my sleeping bag to catch some sleep before leaving the next morning for Pakistan.

I was awakened by such a racket at six thirty in the morning, made by the stirrings of hundreds of Indian families, that I couldn't have slept later if I had wanted to. I packed up my stuff, and took a rickshaw to the train station where I enjoyed the last of my cornflakes with some whole milk. While waiting for my train, I changed some of my Indian rupees into Pakistani rupees and was advised by the same man to take some beetle leaf into Pakistan and sell it, as I would double my money. I was wary at first, but several other people told me the same thing, so I purchased a large bundle and boarded the train for Pakistan.

It takes a couple of hours to cross by train into Lahore. It can also be done by bus, and takes about the same amount of time. Lahore has a bad reputation among travelers. Hotels there seem to be mostly in the business of ripping off folks on the overland trail to India by sneaking into their rooms to steal valuables; most travelers merely stop for the night in Lahore and leave the next day for India.

One interesting legend concerning Lahore is that there is a secret tunnel connecting the Red Fort in Lahore with the Red Fort in Delhi, more than two hundred miles away. Several times in Delhi I was told about this tunnel, which must run under a number of rivers, connecting the two Mogul forts. Apparently, it was constructed about a thousand years ago, when the forts were first engineered by the invaders. Were they older than that? Did they have some connection with other rumoured tunnels in Central Asia? Did this tunnel even exist?

I was more interested in my quest for ancient cities and mysteries than in hanging around Lahore. I booked a train to Sahiwal, just south of Lahore, where I would go by bus to Harappa. I met a young American traveler in the station just after I had sold the beetle leaf for exactly double what I had paid in India. The traveler, named Rick, told me that the Shia Muslim observance of Mahran was happening, and he urged me to go out into the streets with him to check it out.

Mahran is the observance of the death of Hussein, the son of Ali, who was in turn the son-in-law of Mohammed. Hussein was the fifth Imam, descended from Mohammed, and was killed in battle in 680 A.D. while facing a superior army. Shia Muslims see Hussein as the ultimate martyr and observe that day with great emotional grief.

Rick and I walked out into the street to find huge crowds chanting and mourning on the street. We pressed in closer to have a good look at what was hapening, and found that men in the center of the crowd were whipping themselves with some sort of cat-o-nine-tails whip. These whips however, were made of five to nine chains and at the end of each was an S-curved knife blade! These men, to the chanting of the crowd whipped themselves on the back in an increasing frenzy, and the men's backs were bleeding profusely.

Rick and I were amazed and shocked at this display of martyrdom and self-torture. In all my years in North Africa and Arabia, I had never witnessed anything like this. It is a peculiarly Shia Muslim observance and therefore happens only in Iran and parts of Pakistan, Afghanistan and the Persian gulf. Rick was trying to get photos of it and there was so much blood flying around, he got blood on his camera. Many of these men were so cut up from their self-inflicted wounds that their backs were a solid flow of blood; a few got so carried away in the frenzy that a relative would dive in and tackle the penitant to keep him from harming himself more, as the person would not stop. The man would often then collapse, and be carried to a small medical tent.

Looking around on our way back to the train station, we saw hundreds of riot police with flack jackets and helmets watching from the sidelines in case things "got out of hand." Among some groups there were young boys who were whipping themselves with little curved-knife whips, preparing themselves, I supposed, for later years when they could mourn the death of Hussein with a little more vigor.

Rick headed north, and I was soon on a train to Sahiwal, which is near Harappa, one of the Seven Rishi Cities of the Rama Empire.

Once called Brahminadad, it was brought to light by two brothers, John and William Brunton, who were engineers for the East Indian Railway. In 1856, they were looking for ballast on which to lay the railway tracks; locals told them that not far away was an ancient ruined city. They looted the ancient city and obtained ninety-three miles of good kiln-fired brick ballast at little expense from the ancient city. Eventually, the Director-General of the Indian Archaeological Survey became aware of the site, and began to excavate it.

India's own records of their history claim that their culture has been around for literally tens of thousands of years. Yet, until 1920, all the "experts" agreed that the origins of the Indian civilization should be placed within a few hundred years of Alexander the Great's expedition to the sub-continent in 327 B. C. However that was before another similar city, Mohenjo-Daro (Mound of the Dead), was discovered 350 miles south, and eventually other cities with the same plan were found and excavated, including Kot Diji, near Mohenjo-Daro, Kalibanga, and Lothal, the port in Gujerat, Lothal being discovered just in the past twenty years. [22]

The discoveries of these cities forced archeologists to push the dates for the origin of Indian civilization back thousands of years, just as Indians themselves insisted. A wonder to modern-day researchers, the cities are highly developed and advanced. The way that each city is laid out in regular blocks, with streets crossing each other at right angles, and the entire city laid out in sections, causes archaeologists to believe that the cities were conceived as a whole before they were built: a remarkable early example of city planning. Even more remarkable is that the plumbing-sewage system throughout the large city is so sophis- ticated, it is superior to that found in Pakistan, India, and most Asian countries today. Sewers were covered, and most homes had private toilets and running water. Furthermore, the water and sewage systems were kept well separated. [22, 51, 43]

This advanced culture had its own writting, never deciphered, and used personalized clay seals, much as the Chinese still do today, to officialize documents and letters. Some of the seals found contain figures of animals that are unknown to us today.

As I walked through the dusty, deserted city streets of Harappa, a city once possibly containing forty thousand people, I thought of its origins. Archaeologists really have no idea who its builders were, but attempts to date the ruins, which they ascribe to the "Indus Valley Civilization," an admittedly pre-Aryan culture, have come up with something like 2500 B.C., and maybe older. According to ancient Indian epics and esoteric doctrine, Harappa and Mohenjo-Daro were two of the Seven Rishi Cities of the Rama Empire.

The Rama Empire was supposedly contemporary with the great culture of Atlantis and Osiris in the west. Atlantis, well-known from Plato's writings and ancient Egyptian records, apparently existed in the mid-Atlantic and was a very highly technological and patriarchal civilization. The Osirian civilization existed in the Mediterranean basin and North Africa, according to esoteric doctrine, and archeological evidence. The Osirian civilization is generally known as pre-dynastic Egypt, and was flooded when Atlantis sank, and the Mediterranean began to fill up with water (there are over 250 known sunken cities in the Mediterrean). The sinking of Atlantis had been dated at 8,500 B.C. by Plato, and the civilization existed for thousands of years before that.

The Rama Empire flourished during the same period, according to esoteric tradition, fading out in the millenium after the destruction of the Atlantean continent. Ancient Indian epics des- cribe a war betwen Rama and Atlantis, in which Atlantis attempted to invade the Rama Empire, which stretched from the Indus Valley across northern India. The Mahabharata and the Drona Parva, two ancient Indian epics, speak of the war and of the weapons used: great fireballs that could destroy a whole city, "Kapilla's Glance" which could burn fifty thousand men to ashes in seconds, and flying spears that could ruin whole "cities full of forts." [9, 43, 13]

The Rama Empire was started by the Nagas (Naacals) who had come into India from Burma and ultimately from "the Motherland to the east" if the tablets that James Churchward claims to have read are correct. After settling in the Deccan Plateau in northern India, they made their capital in the ancient city of Deccan, where today the modern city of Nagpur stands.

The empire of the Nagas apparently began to extend all over northern India to include such cities as Harappa, Mohenjo-Daro, and Kot Diji, now in Pakistan, and Lothal, Kalibanga, Mathura, and possibly other cities such as Benares and Pataliputra. Just exactly which were the seven cities of the Rama Empire is anyone's guess, though it seems fairly certain that Deccan (Nagpur) was the capital, and that Mohenjo-Daro, Harappa, and Lothal were important centers, if not one of the Rishi cities. Probably there were many thriving cities in the Rama Empire and there were seven capitals, which became known as the "Rishi Cities." *Rishi* is a Sanskrit term meaning "Master" or "Great Teacher."

It was these "Great Teachers, "or "Masters" that were the benevolent aristocracy of the Rama civilization. Today, they are generally called "Priest-Kings" of the Indus Valley civilization, and a number of statues of these so-called "Gods" have been discovered. In reality, apparently their mental-psychic powers were of a degree that seems incredible to most people of today. It was at the height of power for both the Rama Empire and Atlantis that the war broke out, seemingly because of Atlantis' attempt to subjugate Rama.

We know of this horrific war from several sources. First of all, there are the many and profuse Indian epics which talk in great detail about the war, possibly referring to Atlanteans as "Asvins." There is also the archaeological evidence, which we will deal with shortly, and there are certain esoteric sources, which cannot be confirmed, such as the Lemurian Fellowship, whose headquarters are in Ramona, California.

Atlanteans, according to the ancient Indian epics, and other esoteric sources, had airships similar in appearance to zeppelins which were called vimanas by the ancient Indians and vailixi (plural) by the Atlanteans. The ancient Mahabharata speaks of "an aerial chariot with the sides of iron and clad with wings". [27]

The Ramayana describes a vimana as a double-deck, circular (cylindrical) aircraft with portholes and a dome. It flew with the "speed of the wind" and gave forth a "melodious sound" (a humming noise?). Ancient Indian texts on vimanas are so numerous it would take at least one entire book to relate what they have to say. The ancient Indians themselves wrote entire flight manuals on the control of various types of vimanas, of which there were four. The Samara Sutradhara is a scientific treaty dealing with every possible angle of air travel in a vimana. There are 230 stanzas dealing with construction, take-off, cruising for thousands of miles, normal and forced landings, and even possible collisions with birds. [9, 43] Would these texts exist (they do) without there being something to actually write about? Traditional historians and archaeologists simply ignore such writings as the imaginative ramblings of a bunch of stoned, ancient writers. After all, where are these vimanas that they write about? (Perhaps they are seen everyday around the world and are called UFOs!)

In 1875, the *Vaimanika Sastra,* a fourth century B. C. text written by Bharadvajy the Wise, was rediscovered in a temple in India. The book (presumably taken from older texts) dealt with the operation of ancient vimanas and included information on steering, precautions for long flights, protection of the airships from storms and lightning, and how to switch the drive to solar energy, or some other "free energy" source, possibly some sort of

241

"gravity drive." Vimanas were said to take off vertically, and were capable of hovering in the sky, like a modern helicopter or dirigible. Bharadvajy the Wise refers to no less than seventy authorities and ten experts of air travel in antiquity. These sources are now lost. [48]

Vimanas were kept in a Vimana Griha, or hanger, were said to be propelled by a yellowish-white liquid, and were used for warfare, travel, or sport. Airships were present all over the world, if we are to believe these seemingly wild stories and look at archeological evidence accordingly. Besides being used for travel, airships unfortunately came to be used as warships by the persons of Rama and Atlantis.

The plain of Nazca in Peru is very famous for appearing from high altitude as a rather elaborate, if confusing, airfield. Some researchers have theorized that this was some sort of Atlantean outpost. It is also worth noting that the Rama Empire had its outposts: Easter Island, almost diametrically opposite Mohenjo- Daro on the globe, astonishingly developed its own written language, an obscure script lost to the the present inhabitants, but found on tablets and other carvings. This odd script is found in only one other place in the world: Mohenjo-Daro! Could it be that a trade network, operating even across the Pacific Ocean, was used by the Rama Empire and the Atlanteans? It seems incredible. However, it's interesting that pottery found at Nazca has drawings of zeppelin-like airships, much as described in Indian epics. [52, 31]

According to the Lemurian Fellowship, the non-citizenry of Mu (Lemuria) had evenually split into two opposing factions: those who prized practicality and those who prized spirituality. The citizenry of Mu, themselves, were balanced equally of these two qualities. The citizenry then encouraged both groups to emmigrate to uninhabited lands. Those that prized practicality emmigrated to the Poseid Island Group (Atlantis) and those that prized spirituality eventually ended up in India. The Atlanteans, a patriarchal civilization with an extremely materialistic technology-oriented culture deemed themselves the "Masters of the World" and eventually sent a well-equipped army to India in order to subjugate the empire and bring it under the suzeranty of Atlantis. One account of the battle related by the Lemurian Fellowship in their lessons tells how the Rama Empire's Priest-Kings defeated the Atlanteans.

Equipped with a formidable force and a "fantastic array of weapons," the Atlanteans landed in their vailixi outside of one of the Rama cities, got their troops in order and sent a message to the ruling Priest-King of the city that they should surrender. The Priest-King sent word back to the Atlantean general: "We of India have no quarrel with you of Atlantis. We ask only that we be permitted to follow our own way of life."

Regarding the ruler's mild request as a confession of weakess, and expecting an easy victory, as the Rama Empire did not possess the technology of war nor the aggresiveness of the Atlanteans, the Atlantean general sent another message: "We shall not destroy your land with the mighty weapons at our command provided you pay sufficient tribute and accept the rulership of Atlantis."

The priest-king of the city responded humbly again, seeking to avert war: "We of India do not believe in war and strife, peace being our ideal. Neither would we destroy you or your soldiers who but follow orders. However, if you persist in your determination to attack us without cause and merely for the purpose of conquest, you will leave us no recourse but to destroy you and all of your leaders. Depart, and leave us in peace."

Arrogantly, the Atlanteans did not believe that the Indians had the power to stop them, certainly not by technical means. At dawn, the Atlantean army began to march on the city. Sadly, the Priest-King watched the army advance from a high viewpoint, then he raised his arms heavenward, and using a mental technique, perhaps known today by certain very knowledgeable persons, he caused the General, and then each officer in order of rank to drop dead in their tracks, probably of some sort of heart failure. In a panic, and without leaders, the remaining Atlantean force fled to the waiting vailixi and retreated in terror to Atlantis! Of the sieged Rama city, not one man was lost.

While this maybe nothing but fanciful conjecture, the Indian epics go on to tell the rest of the horrible story, and things do not turn out well for Rama. Atlantis, assuming the above story is true, was not pleased at the humiliating defeat, and therefore used its most powerful and destructive weapon, probably an atomic weapon! These are verses from the ancient Mahabharata:

> "...(it was) a single projectile
> Charged with all the power of the Universe.
> An incandescent column of smoke and flame
> As bright as the thousand suns
> Rose in all its splendor.....
>
> ...it was an unknown weapon,
> An iron thunderbolt,
> A gigantic messenger of death,

243

Which reduced to ashes
The entire race of the
Vrishnis and the Andhakas.

...The corpses were so burned
As to be unrecognizable.
The hair and nails fell out;
Pottery broke without apparent cause,
And the birds turned white."

"After a few hours
All foodstuffs were infected...
...to escape from this fire
The soldiers threw themselves in streams

To wash themselves and their equipment." [27]

§§§

In view of the way we traditionally view ancient history, it seems absolutely incredible that there was an atomic war approximately ten thousand years ago. And yet, what else could the Mahabharata be speaking of? Perhaps this is just a poetic way to speak about cavemen clubbing each other to death, the way we are told the ancient past was like. Until the bombing of Hiroshima and Nagasaki (ironically the two Christian centers of Japan), modern mankind could not imagine any weapon as horrible and devastating as those described in the ancient Indian texts. Yet they very accurately described the effects of an atomic explosion. Radioactive poisoning will make hair and nails fall out. Immersing yourself in water is the only respite.

Interestingly, Dr. Oppenheimer, the "Father of the H-Bomb" is known to be familiar with ancient Sanskrit literature. A familiar quote of his after watching the first atomic test is from the Bhagavad Gita; "Now I've become death—the Destroyer of Worlds. I suppose we all felt that way." When asked in an interview at Rochester University seven years after the Alamogordo nuclear test whether that was the first atomic bomb ever to be detonated, his reply was, "Well, yes, in modern history." [9]

Incredible as it may seem, archaeologists have found evidence in India indicating that some cities were destroyed in atomic explosions. When excavations of Mohenjo-Daro and Harappa reached the street level, they discovered scattered skeletons about the city, many holding hands and sprawling in the streets, as if some horrible doom had taken place. I mean, people are just lying in the streets of the city, and these skeletons are thousands of years old, even by traditional archaeological standards! What could cause such a thing? Why did they not decay or be eaten by wild animals? Furthermore, there is no apparent cause of a violent death (heads hacked off, bashed in, etc.).

These skeletons are among the most radioactive ever found, on a par with those at Nagasaki and Hiroshima. Soviet scholars have found a skeleton at one site that had a radioactive level fifty times more than normal. [9, 45, 43, 53, 13]

Thousands of fused lumps, christened "black stones," have been found at Mohenjo-Daro. These appear to be fragments of clay vessels that melted together in extreme heat. Other cities have been found in northern India that show indications of explosions of great magnitude; one such city was found between the Ganges and the mountains of Rajmahal, seems to have been subjected to intense heat. Huge masses of walls and foundations of the ancient city are fused together, literally vitrified! Since there is no indication of a volcanic eruption at Mohenjo-Daro, or at the other cities, the intense heat to melt clay vessels can only be explained by an atomic blast or some other unknown weapon. [53, 45, 43]

The cities were wiped out entirely. If we accept these stories as fact, then Atlantis (the Asvins?) wanted to waste no more time with the Priest-Kings of Rama and their mental tricks. In terri- fying revenge, they utterly destroyed the Rama Empire, leaving no country to even pay tribute to them. The area around the cities of Harappa and Mohenjo-Daro are desolate deserts, though agriculture takes place to a limited extent today in the vicinity.

Similarly, it is said in esoteric literature, that Atlantis at the same time, or shortly afterwards, also attempted to subjugate a civilization extant in the area of the Gobi Desert, which was then a fertile plain. By using so-called "Scalar Wave Weaponry" and firing through the center of the earth, they wiped out their adversaries, and, possibly at the same time, did themselves in! Much speculation naturally exists in connection with remote history, we may never actually know the complete truth, though ancient texts are certainly a good start!

I looked over the empty streets of Harappa. The kiln-fired brick of the city is still copied today by the locals, and it is excellent building material, especially in an area where forests are extremely rare. The Rama Empire lives on today, helping in its own way to build the railway line between Lahore and Karachi by providing the ballast for the tracks. I, myself, would shortly be riding over the bricks of the cities on my way north.

Atlantis met its own doom, according to Plato, by sinking

into the ocean in a mighty cataclysm; not too long after the
war with the Rama Empire, I imagine. As my bus pulled
away from the dusty, empty streets to take me to the
railway station at Sahiwal, I looked back from my seat.
This area was an incredible adventure of the intellect, and
a lost city definitely worth visiting. To the west the sun was
sinking. For the Seven Rishi Cities of the Rama Empire, it
had set long, long ago.

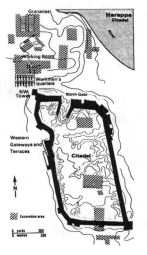

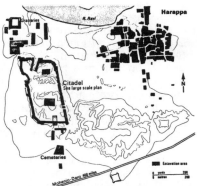

Map of Harappa, Pakistan.

The face on the Shroud of Turin. Did this man travel through India, Nepal, Tibet and Persia two thousand years ago?

The tomb of Yuz Asaf in Srinagar, Kashmir. Many locals believe that this is the tomb of the Jesus, buried here after he was crucified. (photos courtesy of Andreas Faber-Kaiser)

Chapter Fourteen

NORTHERN PAKISTAN:

CARAVANS THROUGH THE KARAKORAM TO HUNZA

Never utter these words:
'I do not know this, therefore it is false.'
One must study to know;
Know to understand;
Understand to judge.
　　　　　–Apothegim of Narada

Late the next evening, I stepped off the train in Rawalpindi, the colonial city of northern Pakistan. Just nearby is the newly designed and built captial of Pakistan, Islamabad, a spacious, modern, but rather empty planned city that closely rivals Harappa or Mohenjo-Daro.

I discovered a whole new perspective during my train trip up from Harappa: travel in the luggage rack. Not surprisingly, the train had been full, and I stood around by the door for a while, watching the villages go by, then was suddenly seized by inspiration, and climbed up into an empty luggage rack. In the next luggage rack were a bunch of Afghan *mujaheddin* on their way to the Afghan border to join the fight against the Soviets who had invaded their country the year before.

They seemed pleased to see me up the luggage rack above everyone else, just as they were, and even more pleased to discover that I was American. "Journalist?" they asked, no doubt having met lots of journalists on the border wanting information on the war. I thought they looked like a wild and crazy bunch in their baggy pants, long shirt-tailed shirts, ragged turbans and bushy beards. They were just coming from India. They did a lot of praying, taking turns prostrating themselves on the rack next to me. I leaned back on my pack and read for most of the trip. Luggage racks, I decided, were not such a bad way to go; it was too bad that trains in India didn't have them.

I had a hell of a time trying to find a hotel room in

249

Rawalpindi that night. I walked down the street, asking at the many hotels I saw about getting a room. They were all full. I finally ended up sleeping in what was a virtual cave in the recesses of one hotel. The price was rather steep at a dollar and a quarter, considering what I got for it. The "room" was musty and damp with no window, and the bed was small, rickety, old and wooden. From the wall hung a naked light bulb. I couldn't have imagined a more depressing place to spend the night.

In the morning I split, went to the train station for breakfast, and then got a room at the Al Shams Hotel, just down the street, that was clean, semi-modern and decent. I wanted to hitchhike up the Karakoram Highway to Hunza, and had to apply for permission in Islamabad, a few miles away. I was told that it would take four days to process, and then would be valid for two weeks. I decided to head for Peshawar and perhaps Chitral in the Hindu Kush while my application for the Karakoram Highway was being processed and before I knew it I was off on a mini-bus, headed for Peshawar.

Peshawar is just near the border of Afghanistan, a few miles from the famous Khyber Pass. Peshawar literally means *frontier town*, and has commanded the traditional gateway to India for thousands of years. Even today, it borders on the tribal territories of the Pathans and Pushtos, who are hardy mountain warriors who tote automatic weapons and don't pay much attention to the central Pakistani government in Islamabad.

I went to the *Pakistan International Airways* (PIA) office downtown to book a ticket to Chitral, a place nestled nicely in the Hindu Kush mountains far to the north. I found that internal flights around Pakistan were amazingly cheap, about ten dollars a flight, and that to go by four-wheel-drive jeep for two days over the mountains to get to the same place would cost the same. I decided to fly. After I had purchased my ticket, I began chatting with a tanned, rugged-looking Australian who was also at the office. He was in his late thirties and wore a jaunty Australian bush hat on his wiry red hair. His name was John, but he liked me to call him "Man from Oz" (*Aus*—tralia).

"This here's wild country," the Man from Oz said, as we sat in a tea shop later that afternoon. "A real man's country. Peshawar's pretty civilized," he went on as he looked down the narrow streets and untidy jumble of low, mud-brick houses, "but out there in the country, it's 'anything goes.' And now with the war in Afghan- istan, it's open season on foreigners, not just Russians, either."

"Why? Why would they want to just shoot somebody?" I asked.

"Why not! Of course, it's not really that bad. You can safely go to Dera, just to the south, but there are road blocks after that, to stop foreigners from going any farther to the south. It's just not safe. The government has no control over that area."

"What is in Dera?" I asked. I recalled my trip to Landi Kotal years before.

"Dera?" he laughed, finishing his tea. His face was scarred and tough, and he appeared to have led an adventurous life. I found out he had been a mercenary in Malaysia when he was younger, smuggled all kinds of things into all kinds of places, broken out of jail once in Laos, and stuff like that. I took it with a grain of salt, but didn't really see why it couldn't all be true. You meet all kinds of characters on the road. In fact, in a place like Peshawar most of the people you meet are likely to be interesting characters.

"Dera is the arms market of Asia!" he continued. "It's a great place: you can buy any gun, explosive or whatever grabs your fancy. They make a lot of it right there, and other stuff gets smuggled in. The Pakistan government knows about it, but there's nothing they can do. Dera is tribal country. Hell, if you like, I'll take you to Dera tomorrow! Love going there myself! It's a great place!" And with that, we had a date to go to Dera. I went back to my hotel, the Khyber Hotel, and he went off to his.

The Man from Oz came by my hotel the next morning after breakfast and we took a taxi out to Dera which was an hour or so away. On the way, we passed a police check; the officer looked briefly in the taxi, a beat-up old Ford, and waved us on. We continued on to Dera, a snug little smuggler's town about two blocks long, with a number of small shops along the main street. I bought some dried apricots and looked through the shops, maybe some forty in all.

Four out of every five shops sold guns; Dera must have the highest concentration of gun shops per square foot in the world. John, the Man from Oz, went on ahead. I looked in the shops. They had shotguns, stenguns (a type of early British machine gun, now made in Pakistan around Dera), and all kinds of pistols. They even had Soviet AK-47s, Pakistan-made G-3s, which are a standard NATO-issue automatic rifle, 20 mm cannons, and a few hand-held rocket launchers. Often, the back wall of a shop was piled high with one-kilogram blocks of hashish brick, plus other interesting odds and ends.

I was told by one friendly old shopkeeper who spoke English that the local Pathans bought all the nice rifles, usually the automatic rifles like the G-3s or the shot guns, for shooting at night, or hunting. The less desirable bolt-action rifles, stenguns (which are automatic, but cheap unreliable copies made here in the hills of Pakistan) and the 20 mm cannons were for the Iranians, Afghanis, and tribesmen that came up from Baluchistan. I asked if these guns were used at all by the Afghan *mujaheddin,* and he said no, not much; they get their weapons from Egypt, China and America.

He suddenly leaned over his counter, put down his cup of green tea, and wiped his bushy gray beard with his hand. "Is it possible for you to buy a silencer in America?" he asked me. I wasn't sure, and told him that. "If you could, you should bring one here, because we would like to copy it. We can manufacture any gun or part here." He snapped his fingers. "If we could only get one of those silencers to copy..."

I went on down the street to the other end of town. There, I found the Man from Oz haggling with a dealer over the price of a Pakistani-made 44 magnum pistol. They had trouble agreeing. The proprietor said he would throw in a brick of hashish, too, and plopped one onto the table. The Man from Oz put some bullets in the gun, and then fired a shot out the back door. Meanwhile the proprietor rolled a large cigarette of tobacco and hash, and began smoking it. He offered me some but I declined. But the Man from Oz stuck it in his mouth and began puffing on it. Then he strapped on a holster, took out his wallet, and started counting out bills for the owner.

We suddenly heard several loud blasts coming from the street. I looked out the door, and saw a wide-eyed, turbaned fellow, carrying a bolt-action rifle, staggering about in the street, firing it every now and then more or less into the air. I described the scene to the Man from Oz and told him that he was coming our way.

The Man from Oz, like a sheriff in some Wild West town, stepped to the doorway and squinted at the turbaned outlaw. He then took the hash cigarette out of his mouth, like Clint Eastwood in a spaghetti-western. "A couple of hot slugs in the chest ought to slow him down," he said calmly, reaching for his holster.

I grabbed his wrist with my right hand. "Are you crazy?" I cried. "He might have friends here! You'll get us both killed!"

He gave me a hard macho stare: who was I to tell him what to do? Then his eyes shifted slightly. "Yeah, I guess you're right, kid. Shooting that nut would be a rather impulsive thing to do...." Just then one of the shopkeepers ran out and tackled the renegade, one last shot going off into the air. I turned away, and exhaled in relief. This Dera

252

was some wild town all right. I glanced at some of the other weapons on the wall. If the Man from Oz wanted to have a shoot-out at the OK Corral, then maybe I should be armed, too. Suddenly, our taxi driver was at the front of the shop, his taxi idling, and his face red. He was from the city, and wasn't used to these kind of shenanigans, either.

"Let's go," he said in Urdu. Then, in fair English, "Time to split." The Man from Oz tossed his brick of hash into the trunk, but kept his pistol up front. I got in the back seat, and we were off, the Wild West town of Dera receding in the rearview mirror.

Shortly, we came to a checkpost. The police didn't see the pistol, which was hidden underneath the seat. They asked the driver to open the trunk. I thought we were sunk, but when they looked inside and stared straight at the brick of hash, they didn't say a thing! An hour later, we were pulling into Peshawar. The taxi driver and I were really glad to be back.

§§§

Two days later, I was crouching behind the pilot of a PIA Fokker Friendship plane that was winging its way over the Hindu Kush into the remote mountain center of Chitral. I had to gasp at the beauty of the mountains. At the head of the valley was the icy giant, Trichmir Peak, a good 25,000 feet high. We were floating below the peaks. Even the lower ones were covered with snow. Beyond was Afghanistan and the struggle against the Soviets. The pilot, who had been educated in Texas, said to me, "The difference between a freedom fighter and a terrorist is which side you're on."

We were soon on the ground in Chitral, a village and small wooded valley in the Hindu Kush mountains. The main street winds around for a couple of blocks with some low, wooden buildings around it. There is a tourist office down by the airport, and several small hotels, including one which is government-run and modern, meaning that you have sheets on your bed, and a toilet down the hall that might actually flush. Modernity is expensive, though. I was content to pay a dollar and get a small private bed with a woven-wood frame and cotton mattress that I could throw my sleeping bag onto. I wandered about the small town, the district capital, and the next day, took a jeep up north to the Garam Chasma Hot Springs.

The hot springs, an hour by jeep towards the Darah Pass into Afghanistan, were supposed to be a nice place, and many Afghan refugees came over the mountains into Pakistan from here. As it was autumn, and apricot, apple, and other deciduous trees were turning bright reds and oranges, it was rather crisp riding in the back of the American Willy's Jeep. I hung onto the back, looking up at the mountains and fall colors.

At the Government Rest House in Garam Chasma, I got a room, one of only two there. The caretaker asked me if I had permission to stay there. I thought for a moment. No, actually I didn't, but it didn't seem like a good idea to tell him that. "Yes," I said. He nodded. It probably didn't make much difference to him. He seemed like a nice guy, a small grey-haired old man, dressed in the baggy pants and matching long-tailed shirt of the Pakistanis. He wore, as did all men in Chitral, the peculiar hat of the region, a sort of flat wool hat with the sides rolled up. He unlocked the guest house, a nice place, with a big, four-posted bed, and showed me the hot springs, which were a large communal bathhouse in the next room, between the two bedrooms. Immediately, I had the water going, and took a hot bath. Heavenly.

It was just dusk when I tripped out into the tiny village of Garam Chasma to find a tea house and have dinner. Garam Chasma was a picturesque village nestled against the towering mountains, in a heavily wooded area. I walked past the few buildings in town. I came to a small general store and next to it a tea house, with an open fire. I sat inside and ordered tea. The tea shop was full of Afghan *mujaheddin* and refugees, some fifteen or sixteen of them, and a few Chitralis. Like most Afghanis, these looked like a rugged bunch, with bushy beards, and wild stares. They were heavily armed, and some of them had on bandages. I said good evening in Urdu, and looked out the window. To the west was a mighty peak, heavily glaciated, catching the last golden rays of the sun. Across the river was a small hydroelectric station, one of the few in the remote mountains.

It got a bit chilly, so I got up and stood by the fire. Every eye turned to me, a strange young American here on the border of the remote hinterland of the Hindu Kush, in a tea shop full of Afghan rebels. The eyes were not unfriendly, though. Everyone returned to eating their meals, plates of rice with some mutton, and tea as a beverage. There was a certain warm camaraderie, and I felt that I was being included in the group. Of course, there was not a woman to be seen.

I managed a conversation with some of the *mujaheddin*, in bits of Urdu, English and Arabic. Some had been injured crossing over the passes, as the Soviets had scattered food and small items on the passes that were booby-trapped. Picking them up would make them explode in your hand, sometimes blowing your hand off, and perhaps causing you to bleed to death.

One Afghan came up to me and gave me a piece of lapis lazuli, a blue uncut stone with some gold-colored, iron pyrite flecks in it, as a gesture of good will. I was touched and offered to buy a round of tea. I looked hard into the Afghani eyes; they were distant and confused. A people virtually straight out of the Middle Ages, assaulted by a superpower, and now facing a long and difficult struggle to regain a country which, for all practical purposes, would never exist again.

I recalled my own experiences in Afghanistan a few years before, prior to the Soviet invasion. It would never, could never, be like that again. Iran, too, was not the same, seeking to turn back to those simpler days of the past when change was not like a rocket to the moon; what would happen instead in both Afghanistan and Iran were years of death and violence. Was the rest of the world to follow?

Sad and a little depresssed, I left the tea house and walked back through the crisp night to the guest house. There was a full moon in the sky. It shone brightly on the passes into Afghanistan. It had been a busy day; I would sleep well that night. The next day, I rode hanging onto the back of a jeep into the town of Chitral. I spent another night in town, at the Garden Hotel, and had dinner with another foreigner I met, a female American journalist, who was at the PTDC Motel on a brief holiday from Islamabad. Afterwards, we drank some Chitral wine and mulberry spirits, something best done rather surreptitiously, as alcohol is illegal in Pakistan.

My destination the next morning was the Kailash Valley, home of the mysterious Kafir Kailash, a tribe living high up in the mountains who have not yet totally converted to the Islamic religion. Instead they remain faithful to their ancient religion, a form of nature and ancestor worship, and live in a somewhat matriarchal society. *Kafir* is the Arabic word for infidel or unbeliever, and this region of Pakistan, including Nuristan on the Afghan side, was known as Kafirstan. The Nuristanis were converted to Islam just at the beginning of this century, while the Kafir Kailash are just now starting to feel the pressure to become Muslims.

By mid-afternon, I was hanging onto the back of a Willy's Jeep with decidedly unreliable brakes, a passenger door which constantly swung open, and a dashboard with not one working instrument. We were switchbacking up the sides of a steep mountain road from Ayun on the way to Bumberet in the Kailash Valley. The road was absolutely incredible. There were no less than twenty switchbacks up the nearly vertical face of a mountain on a dirt road originally meant for mule trains. I felt better hanging onto the back, so that I could leap off if the jeep should careen over the road, since it would fall thousands of feet to the bottom before it would stop. When we reached the top, the road suddenly turned into the heavily-wooded valley of the Kailash known as Bumberet. There wasn't a town here, but a number of homes were scattered up the valley, and a dusty dirt road stretched west up the valley toward a white, glaciated peak at the end. They let me off at the Bainazir Hotel, only a small wooded cottage, where I was the only guest, and I took a walk up the valley. It was cloudy, cool and windy and the trees were all orange and yellow. The fields had already been harvested for the winter.

Just before dark, I met a young kid who spoke some English. He took me to his family's house where they offered me some local grape wine, and I sat with his mother and sisters. The women all wore black wool gowns with lots of red and white beads around their necks. Their hair was braided and long, and they wore pieces of wool covered with beads and shells for hats. It was fun to sit there with the women. They teased me, and played with my Swiss Army knife. They were so forward and fun, I could hardly believe I was in Pakistan. Normally, you never even see a woman in this country, much less flirtatious ones!

I reflected on the origins of the Kailash. It is thought that they are the descendants of Alexander the Great's Greek army when he invaded India in the third century B. C. They decided to stay behind in this little pocket of paradise, make their wine, tend their goats and live their lives in secluded peace far away from the rest of the world in their little alpine valleys.

Until recently, they had an interesting custom: at the final harvest, a young man was selected from among the shepherds of the mountains and given the privelege of having intercourse with all that he could of the women in Bumberet in one wild, orgiastic night to celebrate the final harvest! Everyone would drink wine and eat their fill, and the chosen young man, usually the first to bring the goat herds in from the mountains, would have his night, as it were. It was considered quite an honor to become pregnant on this night, and a child born of this coupling was considered charmed.

Kafirs generally worship an effigy of a goat, now in the secret, dark halls of worship called Jahstakhans, and bury their dead in carved wooden coffins covered with stones and laid above the ground.

The next day, I walked about the valley. It was a magical wonderland; the women walked about in the green flowery fields with little streams meandering through them, wearing their beads and black dresses, playing flutes and watching the sheep. The whole place was one giant peaceful park, with none of the disturbances of civilization, except for the recent encroachment of the jeep, of which there are maybe two a day from Chitral. It struck me that these women, wholesome and beautiful, had never even been down to Chitral, much less to the teeming cities of Peshawar, Rawalpindi, or Karachi! On my second day, after some stewed apricots for breakfast, I felt sad that I had to leave Bumberet. Would that I could stay in this Shangri-la of the Hindu Kush forever!

But, alas, I soon found myself hanging onto the back of a jeep, switchbacking down the road to Chitral. Several times I almost jumped off, thinking we would go off the road and down the mountain at any moment. Fortunately, it never happened, and by evening I was having dinner at the Mountain View Hotel in beautiful downtown Chitral. And early the next morning, I was on a Fokker Friendship plane flying back to Peshawar. The Kafir Kailash was one lost tribe I would never forget.

§§§

No sooner had I arrived back in Peshawar than I took a mini-bus to Rawalpindi. Travel by bus in Pakistan is probably the best way to go for day trips. There are more buses in Pakistan than Fiats in Italy! Everyone wants a bus, and there are a million different bus companies. As a Pakistani friend of mine who was working in Dubai once told me, "When I get back to Pakistan, with all the money I've earned here, I'm going to buy a bus!" Well, I suppose there is always room for one more bus in Pakistan.

In Islamabad I got my permission to travel the Karakoran Highway up to Hunza. I decided to fly to Skardu, however, in far eastern Baltistan, near the second-highest mountain in the world (now supposedly the highest mountain, because or recent surveys), K2 (or Godwin-Austin) just above Indian-controlled Kashmir. It was another PIA Fokker Friendship flight for ten dollars into Skardu, and worth it just for the scenery from the air on the way. One passes the famous and spectacular peak Nanga Parbat, and K2 can be seen in the distance.

K2 is an amazing peak, but quite remote, much more so than Everest. Just to get to the base of it requires two weeks traveling on foot or pony over a glacier, carrying all your food and supplies, plus an armed escort (which the Pakistani goverment insists on, supposedly because of wild tribesmen and bandits). Such a trip must be booked in advance with the Pakistani authorities in Islamabad. All the hassle is probably more trouble than it's worth, unless you're a real mountain nut, I decided.

Skardu is a small dusty frontier town, a sprawling scattered bunch of one-story, mud-brick houses. It is geographically part of Tibet, although most of the people are Kashmiri Muslims. However, you may meet some Tibetan Buddhists in Skardu or other parts of Baltistan. There are a couple of hotels in the downtown crossroads, an area of a dozen or so low mud-brick buildings. That just about sums Skardu up.

I went to Satpara Lake one day, and hung around Skardu, but there just wasn't very much to do. Skardu, situated on the upper end of the Indus River, is undoubtedly an area full of ancient history, but here it seems irretrievably "lost." There is little to see and do except go hiking or climbing, which requires a permit.

I was itching for some hitching, and took off one morning down the road, heading west for Gilgit, and ultimately Hunza. There is a daily bus to Gilgit from Skardu for six or seven dollars, but I wanted to hitch, riding on top of some trucks, and taking my time. I would enjoy walking down some mountain roads, and taking in the scenery. I soon got a lift in a huge Ford truck that kept stalling, and the four other passengers and I kept having to get out and push-start it. It was a big cattle-cage type truck and after the fourth time it stalled, and we had to push this big truck to start it, I beginning to get a little tired of that ride. Eventually the truck let everyone off in a small roadside village called Kachura, and we all had lunch in a small tea stand.

The road was being worked on by road crews in many places and wan't too bad, considering it wound around the Indus Valley for hundreds of miles, and was often a straight drop of five hundred feet down to the raging river below. I began walking out of Kachura with my pack on my back, enjoying the sunshine and spectacular mountain views of the Karakoram. I soon saw a truck coming toward me from around a curve.

I took off my pack and began to wave both hands over my head. Hitching in Central Asia in not done as in America or Europe, by merely holding out one's thumb. A hitchhiker must use sweeping, exaggerated motions, usually waving and even jumping up and down wildly. As the truck got closer, I pointed down the road in the direction he was going and then made a sweeping pointing motion toward my feet, indicating that I wanted him to stop. All of this was quite exaggerated, and perhaps even kind of silly, but the truck driver saw me from a distance, and was perfectly aware that I wanted a ride. Naturally, he stopped, and I climbed up on top of the cab, to get a nice view, even though he beckoned me to sit inside with him and his mechanic.

It was a big, caged lory, similar to a cattle truck. Like all the big trucks one sees in India, Pakistan, Nepal and Afghanistan, it was painted like a rainbow, with little tassels, lights, and doodads everywhere, a few pictures of some Muslim saints and Mecca at various places inside the cab, and extra little lights scattered here and there around the truck. It looked like a kind of funny space-ship-cum-Christmas-tree that Flash Gordon would have flown around in back in the thirties.

After driving all afternoon, it started to get dark, and I got inside the cab. The driver was a clean-shaven Punjabi in his thirties, and his mechanic was a greasy, friendly kid in his late teens. They were a cheery pair, but didn't speak any English. We talked intermittently in Urdu. With the headlights on, we shot around the hairpin corners, the lights shining off into the abyss to our left. It was kind of scary. Somewhere down there was the Indus, a straight drop of hundreds of feet from the narrow road, a road with no guard rails or anything, not that that could stop this truck from going over the edge anyway. I suddenly remembered the DON'Ts in the tourist brochure on Baltistan: DON'T take photography of bridges and military installations, and DON'T drive on the mountain roads at night. I got a bit nervous, to tell the truth, and started holding my breath as we turned corners.

Finally we came to Sangus, where I got off and slept outside in my sleeping bag on a rope-strung bed at a roadside tea stall. The truck went on, driving through the night. The next morning I was on the road again, hoping to make it to Gilgit that day. No sooner had I started walking down the road than a truck stopped, heading for a petrol station called Sasi down the road. Unfortunately, they hadn't gone too far before they ran out of diesel and ground to a halt. I waited for a while, and when no truck came, decided to walk on down the road. It was a pleasant day, and I enjoy a good hike.

The sun was shining, and light glistened off snow-covered peaks that were a good twenty to twenty-three thousand feet high. Across the valley I could see some Baltistani walking parallel to me on a trail on the other side of the river. My truck came along shortly, having gotten some fuel from another vehicle, and picked me up. I rode in my favorite spot above the cab. We twisted, bounced, and turned our way to Sasi, where I ate a box of banana cream cookies and drank tea for lunch while they gassed up. Soon we were on our way to the crossroads of the Karakoram Highway and Gilgit, crossing the Indus River at a place called Bunji. My truck was going south down the Indus to Rawalpindi, and I began hitching north up to Gilgit. After being invited for tea with an army road crew that I stumbled onto, I caught a lift in a jeep to Gilgit.

After a night in Gilgit, I was itching to get to Hunza, that magical land of healthy octagenarians who play soccer all afternoon. Hunza is well-known for its healthy, long-lived, and good-natured people. Until recently, their diet consisted chiefly of unleavened bread, fresh vegetables, apricots and goat's milk. Because they are so high up at the most northern part of Pakistan, surrounded by twenty-thousand-foot peaks, they would often exhaust their winter food supplies by spring, and then fast for a couple of months, living on a handful of dried apricots and walnuts a day.

Hunza was also part of the ancient silk route that came up the Indus and went to the fabled cities of Kashgar and Yarkand in China, crossing a high pass just beyond Hunza and meeting the other caravan trail through the Wahkan Valley in Afghanistan, just to the north of Hunza. Today, the Chinese have built an excellent paved highway through this pass, and down through Hunza. This is a great way to travel across Central Asia, into the Takla Makan region of China and the ancient city of Kashgar.

Just outside the Tourist Cottage, I caught a little Japanese van into the Hunza valley, only a few miles away. It was like a magic carpet ride through the valleys sweeping along the newly-paved road past the autumn trees, the river beneath us, the mountains towering above us. I went to the end of the valley to Ganesh and then walked up the hill to Karimabad, the main village in Hunza, a valley approximately twelve miles long and five miles wide. The view was fantastic: snow-capped peaks surrounding us, and trees in their autumnal foliage.

There are two small hotels in Karmiabad, the Hunza Inn and the Hunza Tourist Hotel, both offering rooms for a dollar or so a night. I met two adventurous Danish ladies at my hotel and had afternoon tea with them. They told me that the next day they were going on a trip across the valley to the Kingdom of Nagar, which was on the opposite side of the river (the Kingdom of Hunza being on the north side) and invited me along. As the sun set over the mountains toward Gilgit, I looked at Baltit castle, home of the old king. It was perched high on a hill looking over the town, with a glacier coming down from the mountains just behind it. It looked really fantastic and romantic, straight out of some storybook fairy tale. Such was the formerly lost, but now found, kingdom of Hunza.

The tiny principalities of Hunza and Nagar, ruled by two brothers, existed peacefully lost to much of the world for 1,700 years. The people appear to be leftovers of the Greek migration to India with Alexander the Great and subsequent waves afterward, much like the Kafir Kailash in Chitral. However, the Hunzas speak a very peculiar language called Brusheski, which is related only to Basque, nestled in the Pyrenees mountains of Spain and France!

Perhaps, I surmised, if we assume that esoteric tradition is somewhat correct in that the Basques are something of "leftovers" from Atlantis themselves, and that the Aryans were part of a massive airlift into Central Asia just prior to the cataclysm, then the Hunzas and their peculiar "Basque" or Aryan language are the last vestiges of the original Atantean-Aryans of Central Asia.

No one really knows where the Hunzas actually came from, but they are different, that is for sure, and their language is related to Basque. They are also known to be especially healthy and live a long time. Renee Tayor, in her book *Hunza Health Secrets,* reported that Hunzakuts typically live to be 110 and 125 years old, and remain active all their lives. She was astonished to see a 140-year-old man playing volleyball! One eighty-year-old man told her that the secret of their longevity lay in growing old rather than aging. Aging, he felt, was not due so much to deterioration of the body, but to a person's attitude about life—man's enthusiasm about life, will to live, and faith in himself. No one in Hunza, he assured her, ever talked of age or of being too old to do things.

Still, life was not always so idyllic. Food was often scarce in the spring, which has actually aided the Hunzakuts' health, by forcing them to fast every year. And the rivalry between Hunza and Nagar sometimes took on scary proportions. The Great Gun of Hunza was built a few hundred years ago by an itinerant Chinese gunsmith out of bronze and copper pots. The ruler of Hunza then promptly decapitated the poor Chinaman so he would not be able to make a similar weapon for the Mir of Nagar!

The Danish ladies, a mother and daughter team, and I were off trekking over the hills and rivers to Nagar the next day. We brought our sleeping bags and a few things to spend the night in the rest house there. It was several hours' walk up past the peaceful and unspoiled apricot and apple orchards into the small village of Nagar, where we had tea at the police station. The Danish ladies had been there the week before, and were familiar with the police captain. In fact, I gathered they had stayed in the police station the time before and the captain had made a pass at the mother, who had gray hair and was in her forties. Her daughter was in her twenties and powerfully built. It was she who had slapped the policeman for her mother, and that was that. He was friendly enough, and we played cards until dark, and went to bed early after a dinner of flat bread, mutton, and vegetables.

The next morning, we found that we had been invited to have breakfast with the king of Nagar! I was thrilled, never having had breakfast with a king before. We walked down by the "palace," a large, western-style home of sorts near the small, primitive telegraph-phone building. We were supposed to meet the operator of the exchange at eight o'clock, but he didn't seem to be around. Suddenly, a small, old man asked us in English whom we wanted to call. I looked at him. He was quite short, wore a wool Karakul cap, baggy Pakistani pants, and a cheap nylon ski jacket.

"No one," I told him. "We were supposed to meet the operator." Then, suspecting that he might be the king, I said, ""Perhaps you, sir, are the Mir (king) of Nagar?"

"Perhaps," he smiled, and invited us in for tea. He was a bit crazy, but seemed to like foreigners, especially Americans. He took us into his study, full of trophies, carpets, shields, swords, photographs, postcards, and other souvenirs. We looked around his simple "palace" which was very nice for Nagar or Hunza, but it was not on a par with magnificent Baltit Castle, though more modern. We had tea and some yak meat pies, with an apple for desert. Afterwards, he showed us around his yard.

I asked him about his jacket, and he proudly showed me a J. C. Penney's tag, and told me that a friend of his had gotten it for him in America. In the end, the Danish ladies had a polaroid photo taken of us all, and gave one to the King. He seemed a nice-enough fellow, cheerful and chubby, apparently bored with the role of king. He told me he'd rather be in a shopping mall in America. We waved goodbye and went for a walk up the valley to the glacier of Hoppar, 30 miles of boulder-strewn ice, pressing down on the valley of Nagar.

Every twist and turn of the road in Hunza and Nagar is a spectacle to behold: a ridge of snow-capped peaks above you or across the valley, a solid wall of glacial ice crashing practically on top of you, great rock pinnacles stabbing upward like the spires of temples, a river raging through canyons below you, massive rock formations like ancient stone carvings of gods. It has been said that Hunza is a mixture of Arizona and Switzerland, and dwarfs them both. The high desert gives way to the terraced green fields and orchards of the peaceful farmers. It is, indeed, a magical kingdom.

We spent another night in Nagar and went back to

Karimabad the next day. We had dinner with the headmaster of the school, who, like all Hunza people, was absolutely friendly and wonderful. He told us that the women here were quite protected from the outside world, having never even been to Gilgit, and had no conception of a train, ship, or the big city. Now with the road through Hunza, things were starting to change, and the effects of civilization, good and bad, were starting to creep in.

The school teacher explained to us that when the women hear of crimes committed in the big cities to the south, they are astonished and exclaim, "But are they not good Muslims?" Most people in Hunza are members of the Ismaili sect of Islam, which recognizes the Aga Khan, a person who is theoretically the direct descendant of Mohammed over the last thousand years or so, lives in London and Bombay and divides his time between charitable pursuits such as building hospitals and other positive activities.

My last day in Hunza, I walked about town, around Baltit Castle, and down to Altit Castle, at a good nine hundred years old, the oldest castle in Hunza, and now abandoned. An old man, the caretaker of Altit, gave me a gift of some apples, and let me walk around the castle. At the very top, on top of a tower was an effigy of an ibex in wood, probably the ancient object of worship for the Hunzas. This struck me as similar to the Kailash in Chitral and the Minaro in Ladakh who also worship the goat, domestic and wild. The Minaro are a tribe in a remote valley who are believed to be the ancient descendants of the Aryans, as well.

On the way back to the Hunza Inn, I met a young lady, about sixteen, who was utterly beautiful. I talked with her briefly in Urdu. She did not seem at all shy. It is quite a rarity to have any interaction with a Pakistani woman. I asked her if I could take a photo of her, but she declined.

Soon, I had hitched back to Gilgit, and after a day of wandering the market there, decided to hitch back down the Karakoram Highway to Rawalpindi. My time in Pakistan was coming to an end. I only had a month-long visa, and my time was just about up. It had been fun. I caught several rides south down the Indus Valley, usually riding on top of the cab.

A petrol truck stopped and picked me up, and I had to ride inside the cab. The driver, a young, clean-shaven man in his late twenties, was puffing away at a hashish cigarette. I took a few puffs, and leaned back in the seat. Pakistan! What a wild country, what a history, from the days of the Rama Empire, thousands and thousands of years ago, to the bloody tribal and political wars of Central Asia and the Hindu Kush! Now, Islamic law was being installed in the country, and the military was busy entrenching itself in the government; it had already declared martial law. The question of Kashmir had never been settled between India and Pakistan, and many Pakis felt that they should go to war with both India and the Soviets in Afghanistan. Many would tell me to go back to America and tell the government to send weapons to Pakistan so they could attack the Soviets. I am totally against arming the destructive wars of the Third World (or the First World, for that matter) but it seemed as if I didn't need to tell the American government to send arms, as they would do it anyway.

My petrol tanker stopped at a small roadside restaurant for a dinner of chicken curry, and then dropped me off a few miles farther down the road where I slept on a rope-strung bed outside under a chilly starry sky in my sleeping bag. The next day, I hitched into Abbottabad, one of the hill stations around Rawalpindi, and from there caught a bus into the city. I went straight to the train station, and caught a night train for Lahore and eventually India. After bribing the conductor to get me a berth, I was able to lie back and listen to a thunderstorm outside the train, and the clickety-clack of the wheels.

I had learned a lot on this trip through the rugged lands of the Hindu Kush and Karakoran. In many ways, Pakistan was a real political hotbed. Would the nuclear disasters of the Rama Empire be repeated in this country again? The Pakistanis were busy creating their own atomic bomb—hailed by many Muslims as an Islamic bomb. What country would it be used against—India, Russia, Iran or Israel? I closed my eyes. Well, at least I'd had breakfast with the king.

Ruins of the Temple of Parhaspur in Kashmir. A destroyed megalithic city, portions of which are said to be radioactive. Was one of the battle of the Mahabharata fought here?

Two views of Parhaspur in the Valley of Kashmir. This massive stone complex is completely destroyed. Was it one of the cities of the Rama Empire that was devastated in the horrific war spoken of in Indian Epics?

Chapter Fifteen

KASHMIR AND WESTERN TIBET:

AT THE LOST TOMB OF JESUS

And they killed him not,
nor did they cause
his is death on the cross.
    —The Quran 4:157

I had heard an interesting rumor in many places (Africa, Taiwan, Kathmandu, and Israel) that Jesus had not died on the cross and had returned to India, where he had studied for many years. After living to a ripe old age, he died and his tomb could be found in Kashmir! This was quite an allegation, and one that I intended to investigate. If the Tomb of Jesus could be found in Kashmir, I would like to see it. I had already visited the supposed Tomb of the Apostle Thomas, the Twin, down in Madras. I mused about the thought of Jesus being buried in Kashmir. After all, anything is possible. Right?

I thought about all this, and read an interesting publication on the subject, called "Christ in Kashmir" by Aziz Kashmiri. I was on the bus from Jammu through the mountains to the vale of Kashmir. I had entered India again from Pakistan at Amritsar, and gone straight to the train station. I was able to get an overnight train right up through Pathankot, and on to Jammu, an industrial city at the foot of the mountains before the vale of Kashmir.

The buses for Srinagar, the historical and present capital of the Indian states of Jammu and Kashmir, leave very early in the morning, as it takes all day, so I just spent the night at the train station, sleeping on the floor in the waiting room with what seemed like a hundred Indian families.

It was quite early in the morning when they started selling tickets for the buses. A whole fleet of them were ready to take off for a destination which many people consider the "Garden of Eden." I bought a ticket, put my luggage on the bus, and then went inside the station again to have breakfast. When I came out, fifteen minutes later, my bus was gone! On the verge of panicking, I looked around for my bus with all my worldly goods on board, and in desperation, showed my ticket to another conductor who pointed down the road and said my bus was gone, and was at a checkpoint down the road. Frantically, I tore down the road, running as fast as I could.

I could see the bus in the distance, about a quarter of a mile away. Out of breath, I jumped on, just as the checkpost lifted the railing that was blocking the road. Almost immediately we were winding our way up into the Pir Panjal mountains. By noon, we were high in the hills of the Pir Panjal, with snowcapped peaks all around us. I could see tiny vehicles winding through steep valleys far below.

According to the *Lost Books of the Bible,* ancient Indian Texts, *The Aquarian Gospel of Jesus the Christ,* Gnostic writings, and countless other esoteric metaphysical doctrines passed down through "secret societies" such as the Essenes,Rosicrucians, Hermetics and Masons: Jesus traveled through India and Central Asia for many years, basically during those 'missing years' between the ages of twelve and twenty-five, prior to his ministry. He, too, must have looked on these hills and forests of Kashmir, I thought, looking out the window.

According to most records, he left on a caravan out of Jerusalem with Prince Ravanna from Orissa, after Prince Ravanna had inquired with the Rabbi Hillel. Jesus studied for four years in the Jaganath Temple in what is present-day Puri. He was taught by a secret group of 'Great Sages;' but found the doctrines of castes and transmigration of souls (humans incarnating as animals) which were taught by the local Brahmin priests offensive to his under-standing of life, and would often preach his word of love and universal brotherhood to the oppressed lower classes.

At seventeen he theoretically left Orissa and journeyed to Benares on the Ganges, literally escaping with his life, as the priests in Orissa had him hunted as a seditionary. Jesus was not safe in Benares either, and finally made it to the birth place of Buddha, Kapilavastu in Nepal (now Lumbini) where he was eagerly greeted and protected by the Buddhist priests there. Jesus studied at Kapilavastu for some months and arrangements were made for him to travel on to Lhasa in Tibet. He passed through Kathmandu, and on into Tibet where he could study at the vast archives secreted near there by a mysterious group called the "Great White Brotherhood."

Tradition relates that he met the Chinese sage Meng-tse, usually known in the West as Mencius, and famous for his classic commentary on the analects of Confucius, *The*

Book of Mencius. After studying in Tibet for five years, Jesus turned homeward, traveling across Tibet, Kashmir, Persia, Assyria and eventually to Athens. After studying and teaching in Greece for some time, he sailed to Egypt and visited his cousin, John (the Baptist) in Zoan, today a suburb of Cairo. Jesus was twenty-five years old at the time. He then studied in Heliopolis for five more years, before beginning his ministry. The rest is history, according to the New Testament. [3, 1, 21, 28, 46]

We were just coming to a three-mile long tunnel at the top of the mountains, on the amazing road built over years by the Indian Army Corps of Engineers. On the other side of the tunnel would be the vale of Kashmir.

The crucifixion of Jesus was a curious event. When in some ways it seems evident that it had been planned hundreds of years beforehand by Jesus himself or the "Masters" for whom in was in supposed contact with, a case can be made that he was not meant to die on the cross. It was customary in Roman times to break the legs and arms of persons who had died on the cross (usually by starvation or by suffocation, from the rib cage pressing down on the lungs). It was also customary for all criminals to be taken down from their crosses just prior to the Sabbath, which starts on Friday at dusk. Jesus was nailed to his cross in the early afternoon of a Friday, and taken down just before dusk, being crucified for as little as four or five hours, during which time he "gave up the ghost."

It is rather remarkable that a person as healthy and knowledgeable as Jesus would die within a matter of a few hours on a cross, when most criminals take several days to die. Persons are crucified every year on Easter in such diverse places as the Philipines and Mexico in commemoration of the event, all of them coming through it quite safely. Crucifixion does not kill a person in four hours!

It seems more possible that Jesus, who had undoubtedly studied certain forms of yoga, was able to go into an altered state of consciousness: a deep mental state, where he would appear dead to any person, including a doctor.

Such states are not uncommon, and are known generally as catalepsy. Even today, yogis in the Himalayas and elsewhere are still performing such feats. I recalled how an Indian gentleman on the train to Mount Abu had told me of one team of French scientists in the sixties who hooked up the latest medical gear for determining clinical death to yogis near the city of Rishikesh. Clinical death is defined as the stopping of the heart, the stopping of the breath, and the brain ceasing to function according to an enceph-alograph test.

Yogis were able to stop all of these functions while in a meditative trance, and would be pronounced dead by these scientists. They were able to stay in the state for days or hours, and return "from the dead," as it were, to function perfectly normally. Indeed, there are many cases in hospitals around the world where someone is pronounced dead by doctors and wakes up in the morgue, or on some occasions, in tombs! [55]

The crucifixion of Jesus is a remarkable event fraught with interesting contradictions and interpretations. It is worth noting that when Jesus said on the cross, "My God, my God, why hast thou forsaken me?" he was drawing attention to the 22nd Psalm. At that time, it was common for scholars to refer to a whole verse by quoting the first line, as everyone knew the Old Testament by heart. The 22nd Psalm, written by King David, goes on to say, in the sixteenth verse, " ...a company of evildoers encircles me; they have pierced my hands and feet—I can count all my bones—they stare and gloat over me; they divide my garments among them, and for my raiment they cast lots. But thou, Lord, be not far off!..."

Therefore, it would appear that Jesus was not in despair, but was instead drawing attention to the 22nd Psalm as a prophesy of the terrible wrong that was being committed against him. Taken down from the cross at dusk, Jesus appeared to be dead. His mother, Mary, and Joseph of Arimathea, a tin merchant who spent a lot of time in Britain, stood by to claim the body, which was not "pulverized" (i.e., had its bones broken) as was the Roman tradition. Instead, they wrapped the body in a shroud after they had covered it with aloe sap, known for its natural healing qualities. Jesus had been pierced in the side by a spear, and was bleeding, which is rather suspicious, since a dead person does not normally bleed after his heart has stopped.

The possibility that Jesus survived the crucifixion seems a credible one. In fact, what is incredible is that someone with the vitality and personal power of Jesus would have died on the cross in such a short time. More likely, he could have lasted many days, probably outliving the common criminals. But what happened to Jesus after his crucifixion? While the New Testament claims that he rose into Heaven in a shower of light, the same ancient records that speak of his journeys to India, the so-called "lost" books of the New Testament, say that when he last appeared to his disciples, they simply saw his astral body, a mental projection. Jesus asked them not to touch this body (which, although real, was a physical illusion) and then he appeared to float into the sky, dissolving the projection in an explosion of light, which greatly impressed the Apostles.

What to do now? According to the records, Jesus journeyed to England and Europe with Joseph of Arimathea, the tin trader. Other legends say that he traveled back to India and Tibet, and especially to his beloved Kashmir, where he had supposedly lingered for some time on his return journey. Some legends even suggest that Jesus sailed across the Pacific to South America and walked through the Americas. American Indian legends from all over both continents speak of a bearded white man who did miracles and preached brotherly love. This person is usually called Quetzalcoatl or Viracocha, but had many names. Whether he is the same person as Jesus (these stories arise at about the same time period) there is no way of knowing, although on a technical level, ships certainly had the capability of making the journey in those times.

Yet what interested me (since I was on my way there) was the legend that Jesus had returned to Kashmir; a paradise in many ways, with an ideal climate, plenty of water and resources, and tremendous scenery. According to this tradition, Jesus was known locally as the Saint Yuz Asaf, and lived in the vale of Kashmir about two thousand years ago, in the first century A.D.

Yuz Asaf was known as a prophet and performed many miracles for the people, coming to them from a foreign land. There is a distinct similarity between Jesus' Hebrew name, Yazu and the name Yuz Asaf. Interestingly, in Arabic and in the Koran, Jesus is known as Isa. It is truly the opinion of many Muslims, and especially Kashmiris, that Yuz Asaf was, in fact, Jesus. There is significant evidence that the Kashmiris are one of the "ten lost tribes of Israel," as they have Semitic rather than Aryan features, and a vocabulary that is remarkably similar to Hebrew. Kashmiris say that the Tomb of Yuz Asaf is located in the suburb of Srinagar known as Khanyar.

Some researchers point out that there is some evidence of a strong connection between Kashmir and ancient Israel, indicating that it was Kashmir that was the "Promised Land" rather than Palestine. Today in Kashmir, there are ancient places with names like, "The Tomb of Moses," the "Throne of Solomon" (which is a mountain), the last resting place of Mother Mary, just near Rawalpindi a few miles away in Pakistan, and the "Garden of Solomon." Most Kashmiris genuinely believe that Moses is buried in Kashmir, and that the forty years of wandering and hostile tribes were not in the Sinai, but across Asia to Kashmir. After all, forty years is a long time to wander around the

Sinai Peninsula, which could be walked across in a few days, and is virtually uninhabited, with no hostile tribes to be found, then or today. [56]

One of the most interesting features, I felt after reading about this, concerns the mountain known as the "Throne of Solomon." There is at least one other "Throne of Solomon" mountain in Central Asia and it is in Iran. Why should a mountain be called "The Throne of Solomon?" According to an ancient Ethiopian text, the *Kebra Nagast*, Solomon had some kind of airship with which he would fly great distances, probably landing on top of mountains. The ancient kingdom of Ethiopia was founded by the son of Solomon, born to him and the Queen of Sheba. The *Kebra Nagast* says that Solomon had a "heavenly car" which he inherited from his forefather (King David, I suppose) and used frequently. "The King...and all who obeyed his word, flew on the wagon without pain and suffering, and without sweat or exhaustion, and traveled in one day a distance which took three months to traverse (on foot)," says the Kebra Nagast. [34]

Could it be, I wondered, that Solomon possessed a vimana airship, left over from the days of the Rama Empire and Atlantis, some several thousand years before? Did he use his "heavenly car" to fly to "Solomon's Throne" in Iran and Kashmir? According to Nicholas Roerich, other "Thrones of Solomon" can be found elsewhere in Tibet and Central Asia. That Solomon flew there in his airship is a popular belief throughout Central Asia. [69] Perhaps the mountain in Iran, which, like the one in Kashmir, is flat-topped, was a landing pad between Israel and Kashmir. If so, are some of these airships still around today, and is someone operating them from a secret base in some remote hinterland of Central Asia, South America, a remote Pacific Island, or somewhere else? Could they be responsible for some of the UFO sightings? The thought was mind-boggling!

Kashmir is also connected with the fantastic war in ancient times that destroyed the Rama Empire. The massive ruins of a temple called Parshaspur can be found just outside Srinagar. It is a seen of total destruction, huge blocks of stone are scattered about a wide area giving the impression of explosive destruction. The large dressed blocks of stone are reminscent of the massive stone slabs at Puma Punku, near Tiahuanaco on the Altiplano of Bolivia. [81]

Was Parshaspur destroyed by some fantastic weapon during one of the horrendous battles detailed in the Mahabharata? Or was tossed about in an earth shaking cataclysm? One things seems for certain, the ruins are ancient and weren't just left to decay in peace.

History is certainly very subjective, and the past, like the present, is often distorted by historians and the like. One can only read as much on a subject as possible and then make up his or her own mind on what seems reasonable. At the very least, searching for the lost tomb of Jesus would be a grand adventure, a stalking of the truth, of a man, of a God; the stalking of the self.

The thought was a pleasant one, I mused, looking out on the green jewel of a valley spreading out in front of us as we came over the mountain and into Kashmir. Suddenly, I looked up in horror! Our bus driver, an unshaven Kashmiri with a white Muslim cap on and a rather greasy shirt, had just passed a big truck, and then a small truck and was busy passing another big truck on the windy, steep mountain road down into the valley. I was sitting right up front, just opposite him, and as he was passsing the last big truck, another prepossesing truck was coming from the opposite direction, heading directly toward us!

I braced myself, and tensed my whole body for what seemed the ultimate collision, when the driver swerved back into his lane, just in time, and there was a big 'whoomp" in the back of the bus. People who were standing by the side of the road looked anxiously behind us. We had apparently hit the truck with the back of our bus. We kept going, and I let out a long sigh of relief. Under my breath, I muttered, "Insane, simply insane," and the driver threw me a quick glance.

My heart was beating normally by the time I had checked into a houseboat on Lake Dahl later that evening. Srinigar is famous for its textiles, especially carpets. The city sprawls with low wooden buildings forming the south shore of the lake. Scores of canals intersect the lake and twist about the town. Many of the people live on house boats on one of the canals or lakes, and they can be quite inexpensive—or luxurious. Boys will come down to the bus station and pitch the virtues of the houseboat they are working for to you and often offer incentives to stay with them.

At the bus station, I encountered an American medical student named Peter and we decided to get a room together. A young boy in a wool jacket and baggy pants offered us a bed each for a dollar in a completely furnished and very comfortable houseboat named the Zaffaron, so we took it. We spent the next few days exploring exciting Sringar; one can take a shikara taxi about town, a small gondola-type craft that will get you around the canals and lakes. They will come right up to your houseboat as little floating grocery stores selling everything from radishes to carpets.

One of the main tourist sights are the many Moghul Gardens, created in the seventeenth century by the Muslim emperor, Jahangir, for the love of his queen Nur Jahan. This idyllic romance, reminiscent of Shah Jehan and his wife Mumtaz, is the subject of a sound-and-light show at the Shalimar Mughal Garden.

One day Peter and I rode bicycles around Dahl Lake and stopped in at the Moghul Gardens. I found out that the tomb of Yuz Asaf was not one of the major tourist attractions in Srinagar, and in fact most people, including the tourist office, had never heard of it. It took some detective work to find out if such a tomb even really existed, and if so, where it was. Finally in a book store on the main street of Srinagar, I found an elderly gentleman who knew what I was talking about.

He was gray-haired, and wore thick, ancient spectacles. He brushed his shock of hair back from his forehead and said in English, "Ah, yes, the Tomb of Yuz Asaf!" He peered at me, then out the window of the shop and into the street. "You'll find the tomb of Yuz Asaf in the area of Srinigar known as Khanyar. You must find Rauzibal Khanyar. This is where the tomb is located!" It felt as if I were getting a secret map to a great treasure. The old man was familiar with the theory that Yuz Asaf was in actuality Jesus. He gave me a knowing wink, and said, "One never knows. Truth is often stranger than fiction!" I agreed with him on that one.

After having ridden around the lake, we arrived in the suburb of Srinagar known as Khanyar. We got lost a couple of times, got some bad directions from a few people, a few blank stares from others, but eventually, one grisly unshaven Kashmiri in baggy pants and pointed shoes pointed down the street toward an alley and said very clearly, "Rauzibal Khanyar!"

We rode our rented bikes down a narrow, winding alley until we came to an old, wooden mausoleum in a state of tremendous disrepair. Obviously very old, it had a fence that had long since become useless. On the wall of the mausoleum were the words, scratched in English, "Rauzibal Khanyar" and "Take your shoes off here." There were some other words, too, but they were in Arabic characters.

We parked our bikes, and walked inside the yard which was totally overgrown by weeds. Walking up to the door of the mausoleum, we took off our sandals, then tested the door. It was open, so we stretched the cobwebs back, and entered. The room was dark and dusty, and just inside was a small entryway, beyond which was the tomb itself. Most of the room was taken up by an inner building-within-a-building that protected the stone tomb. The inner shelter, centuries old, was made of wood, with carved wooden grates and windows through which you looked at the low stone tomb itself.

I stared for a long time at the tomb: plain and elongated, with a smooth, curved top. The whole thing was so low, it was practically flush with the ground. It was unadorned and, I supposed, was nineteen hundred years old, it if was the original tomb of Yuz Asaf. The room was incredibly dusty and the atmosphere was musty with an air of antiquity.

I discovered a small box at the end of the protecting building that said in English "Donation Box for the upkeep of the tomb of Yuz Asaf." This was the only indication anywhere in the mausoleum that the tomb was actually that of Yuz Asaf. I was suddenly filled with wonder. If this was really the tomb of Jesus, under the name Yuz Asaf, as many Islamic scholars believe, it was incredible! Here was the tomb of Jesus, a man over whom whole nations have warred, in whose name churches have conquered whole continents and put hundreds of people to death, either for believing in or not believing in him. Even today people are killing themselves and others over him. And here possibly, lay the tomb of the amazing man who started it all! Could this rundown, barren and forgotten tomb be the burial place of such a man?

Tradition relates that Yuz Asaf, at a ripe old age, lay down one day in 109 A. D., stretched out, and died quite peacefully, and the people built a tomb around him. He was always considered a saint. In fact, when the Muslims converted Kashmir to Islam, old Yuz became a Muslim saint. It's unusual for Muslims to take on other religion's saints; usually they desecrate the tombs and temples of "heathens" when they conquered an area. Kashmir was Hindu prior to the Muslim invasion. [56]

Looking about the room a bit, I noticed a small platform with some books in Arabic, probably Korans, which were very old. In one corner of the inner sanctum, there was an old, black wooden cross standing up. Peter wanted to leave, and kept looking nervously out a small window at our bikes, and a group of kids that were hanging around them.

Back in the sunlight, after I had dropped a fifty-piastre coin in the box for the caretaker of good ol' Yuz (even though I suspected that the caretaker was as dead as Yuz). I reflected on this extraordinary experience. I didn't know if that really was the tomb of Jesus, and probably I never would, unless some new evidence came to light. It was still an inspirational and historical experience, an adventure of the intellect and the physical—a lost mystery to tackle and devour. I was grateful to have stalked one of the world's great teachers and travelers of the world. In fact, Jesus is known in the Koran and to Islamic scholars as the "Great Traveler" and the "Chief of Travelers"!

§§§

Kashmir is fun and quite touristy, not just with foreign tourists, but with Indian travelers as well. Kashmir is India's playground, with everything from water and snow skiing to horseback riding, golfing, and suntanning on top of your houseboat. If they can afford it, honeymooners of India like to come to Kashmir, and with nearly a billion people in India, it can get kind of crowded in the wondrous vale of Kashmir.

More than half of the state of Jammu and Kashmir is arid wasteland, however, as the entire eastern portion of the state is geographically and ethnically part of Tibet: Ladakh. Ladakh, historically the most western part of Tibet, is currently controlled by India, while the rest of Tibet is controlled by China. I was planning to head for Tibet, but first wanted to see a little more of Kashmir. Peter and I went up to Gulmarg, known as the "king of the hill stations," for a couple of days. It is a green alpine resort that is picturesque, refreshing and well-developed for tourism. When the plains of India are suffocatingly hot, it is brisk and cool in Gulmarg. Here you can hobnob with India's famous movie stars and take a ride on an authentic Indian chairlift, even if there isn't any snow.

Soon, Peter and I were sitting on top of a bus, heading east for another hill station on the way to Lakakh, a place called Sonamarg. We climbed aboard a bus in Srinagar one afternoon, after checking out of our houseboat, Zaffaron. The bus, as usual, was crowded, so we cheerfully climbed up on top, sandwiching ourselves between the luggage. I leaned back on my back, happy to be on top, as it was the most comfortable, I felt, and afforded the best view.

Shortly afterwards, a blond, shaggy-haired and bearded German, aptly named Harry, swung his pack up next to us, sat down on top of it, and introduced himself. He was on his way to Sonamarg too, and then on to Leh, the capital of the Tibetan province of Ladakh. It was always nice to have another traveling companion. With a sudden lurch, we were off to the east, stopping occasionally at the various small villages along the way, and reached Sonamarg in the mid-afternoon.

Sonamarg immediately reminded me of the Swiss Alps; pine trees and alpine meadows everywhere against the backdrop of spectacular ice-covered peaks. We walked around the pastures, and up to a glacier nearby. There were young girls herding sheep and goats, and men riding their trusty steeds around the main street of Sonamarg, which was a Wild-West-type town with wooden shacks and a truck stop.

Harry, Peter, and I sat down on the rock by the glacier to enjoy the view, while a group of children came up to us and watched Peter eat a mango with wide, hopeful eyes. They were beautiful children, curious, strong, and healthy, with brown hair, wonder- fully dressed in colorful, embroidered wool clothing. Harry remarked that it was a joy to see such fine-looking children, after seeing so many diseased and ragged children in the plains of India.

We spent that night at the Tourist Hut in Sonomarg. The next morning we started looking for a truck to take us over the mountains and into Ladakh. There is a daily bus that makes the two-day trip from Srinigar to Leh, stopping overnight in Kargil, but it doesn't run all year, and often needs to be booked a week or more in advance. We were content to hitch on a truck, as there are plenty. We would have to pay for our ride, but it would be inex- pensive, plus we could ride on top, over the cab!

We rode all day, Harry occasionally emptying out a bidi, one of those funny little cone-shaped leaf cigarettes that he filled with ganja. We had to duck when we went through small towns with the traditional weeping willow and poplar trees growing by the road, as they would whip our face. We headed up over Zoji Pass, a low pass at only 11,500 feet, and then we were in Ladakh, known as the Moonland!

The scenery suddenly changed as we went from green alpine forest and meadow to harsh, rocky, barren hills and snowy, rocky mountains of the high-altitude desert. Hardly a tree or meadow could be seen anywhere. We drove past several military checkpoints where they glanced curiously at our truck, to the town of Dras, which, according to Harry's guide, was the second coldest place in the world, the first being the Siberian city of Yakutsk. We then went over another pass, this one more than 18,000 feet high, the highest motorable pass in the world! After the pass we were in Kargil, the second largest town in Ladakh, the Moonland, with a whopping population of 2,300.

The population is more Muslim-Kashmiri-Pakistani types than Tibetan, although the odd Tibetan person could be seen on the muddy, winding streets. The town winds along the side of a hill with two- and three-story wooden buildings stacked next to each other in a haphazard fashion. We had a dinner of mutton curry, and went to bed. We were to get up at four A.M. to continue our trip to Leh.

Four in the morning came pretty fast, and sleepy-eyed,

we made our way to the truck, a large, Tata-Mercedes caged cattle-type truck that was painted in wild colors, and, like most other trucks in India, Afghanistan and Pakistan, had all kinds of lights, streamers, and slogans painted all over it, as well as pictures of whatever local deities resided in the area, with a few gods from the Hindu pantheon thrown in for good measure. Our driver was a Sikh, wearing a red turban, with his long beard wrapped in a black net. He was friendly enough, spoke no English, and I guessed him to be about thirty. He cheerily told us to climb in, as he started the truck and warmed it up. His faithful mechanic, a ragged Punjabi teenager, with a toothy smile and greasy turban, accompanied us too. Harry and I huddled up on top of the cab in a box that is there for bedding material and tools, while Peter rode inside where it was warmer, on the chilly Ladakhi morning.

Soon we were dodging willow trees, and watching the sun rise over the high plateau of the Moonland. Around us were gray-brown peaks, high with tops of snow, but not as steep as the main range of the Himalayas which were now behind us. Everywhere were the brown mountains and jagged peaks, plus the occasional rock spire and steep ravine. I could see why this was called the Moonland. It was truly like another planet!

We drove all day, stopping at a few army camps, and noticing the occasional Tibetan villages that were nestled in the valleys. After cruising through a village, we would climb onto a plateau, barren and dry, cross it, and descend to another valley to do it over again. We crossed another high pass, this one over 13,000 feet, and stopped at the top where there was an army post.

I spoke English to the Sikh officer in charge. He was tall, muscular, and handsome and dressed in warm military clothes. He told me that the road had been started in 1947 in a race to get a road to Leh, which the British had brought under their British Indian Empire in the eighteen-hundreds. They were afraid that the Chinese would take over Tibet (which they did) and might get to Leh before them. The first jeep reached Leh in 1955 over what was the world's highest road (and still is). They have been improving the road ever since. It was just opened to foreigners a few years ago. As it happened, the Chinese did eventually take over quite a chunk of Ladakh, that area directly east of Leh. In fact, the Chinese road comes within 90 kilometers (35 miles) of Leh!

It actually rained for a while when we were on the pass, a phenomenon that is very rare in Tibet. We ground our way down the pass and wound through more valleys until our truck, as all Indian trucks frequently do, broke down.

278

Luckily, a local bus just happened to be coming along, and to our surprise, it was quite empty. We got our stuff, thanked our driver, who gave us a friendly nod of his head, jumped on the rusty, beat-up old bus, and headed for Leh, which was about two hours away. It was about 7:30 when we rolled into the capital, after passing a huge, seemingly endless military facility on the outskirts of town. Most of Ladakh and Kashmir is a military area as it is India's frontline with China and Pakistan. As we checked into a hotel in downtown Leh, the sun was casting a last few red and orange streaks in the sky, and we were terribly tired from the long journey of two full days' traveling. After tea and biscuits in our hotel room, a spacious, pleasant room with four beds, we crashed for a much-needed long rest.

Ladakh, called the Moonland because of its high, dry and moutainous landscape, means The Land of Many High Passes (*La* means "a high pass" and *dakh* means "many"). It remained hidden and unknown from the outside world for centuries even though it is twice the size of Switzerland. It wasn't until 463 A.D. that Buddhism officially came to Tibet. Prior to that, the predominant religion was the mysterious Bon religion, a shamanist-magical religion, now virtually extinct. Approximately six hundred years later, Tibet was divided up between three brothers, and western Tibet, mostly Ladakh along with some other territories such as Zanskar and part of Spiti, were given to Detsun Gon, who never even lived in Ladakh. Rather, he sent his son Songde to rule. Thus, Ladakh came into existence.

Ladakh has always, since the rise of Islam, been on the far edge of the Muslim invasion, and something of a buffer state for the rest of Tibet. It was invaded in the late sixteenth century by the Muslim chieftain Mirza from Kashmir, but the "many high passes" kept the Muslims back, and Mirza failed twice in two invasions ten years apart. In Hemis Gompa, the most famous monastery in Ladakh, a statue of an evil demon named Mirza can be found, commem- orating the invasions.

Meanwhile, the great palaces of Leh were built, the first begun in 1533. They are like miniature Potala Palaces, modeled after the Dalai Lama's in the Lhasa, and are quite impressive. The Tibetans kept fighting with the Muslims of Kashmir. Skardu to the north, now held by Pakistan, and today almost entirely Muslim, kept changing hands between the Buddhists and Muslims. Finally, in 1645, the King of Ladakh, one Delek Namgyal, probably tired of the wars, accepted Islam and changed his name to Agabat Mohammad Kahn. The rest of Tibet could not have one of their states turning Muslim, so a huge army was raised and marched to Ladakh. The Muslims were again defeated, and the Muslim-convert King was forced to flee to Kashmir.

A period of enlightened and flourishing art came to Ladakh for a time and then followed a period of weak kings and a "dark age" for Ladakh. Then in 1833, Zorawar Singh, a Sikh, commanding the armies of Maharaja Singh of Kashmir, dethroned the king of Ladakh, banished him, and annexed Ladakh to the Kingdom of Jammu and Kashmir, permanently ending the autonomous status of the Moonland forever. When the Kingdom of Jammu and Kashmir was absorbed into the British Indian Empire, so was Ladakh, though the people continued to look to central Tibet and Lhasa for their culture, inspiration, and the bulk of their trade. The once-flourishing trade between Tibet and Ladakh came to an end when the Chinese invaded Ladakh and came within firing distance of the capital, Leh.

Leh is situated in a wide, cultivated and irrigated valley in what is esssentially the center of Ladakh. As I stood on the roof of our hotel, looking over the brown, low city of two- and three-story adobe homes packed tightly together, the first thing that struck me was the lack of vegetation on the surrounding mountains, and the brightly colorful bursts of saffron, rust and gray that painted the hills, as if the rocks themselves felt that they had to make up for the lack of flowers and add color to the hills. The sky was a beautiful deep blue, and the passes nearby all seemed to have some monastery or chorten (Buddhist tower-marker) or even a palace on them.

To the north of town the great palace of Leh dominated the scene; a great adobe skyscraper rising an awesome fourteen or fifteen stories above the city like a man-made cliff built into a hill. For several days I wandered the back streets of Leh, down to "Chang Ghali" or "Beer (chang) Alley" behind the main street, where there are numerous souvenir shops and other places to buy trinkets, to have a cup of tea, or even a glass of chang. The streets form an endless labyrinth, winding up into the brown hills toward the palace, through archways, up staircases, into dead-ends where the smell of human excrement becomes all too powerful, turning you back before you even make it to the dead end of the alley.

I heard a curious story while I was in Leh. It concerned Nicholas Notavich, a Russian traveler, who in 1887 reached India through Afghanistan. He came to Ladakh, and spent some time at the monastery of Hemis Gompa because of a broken leg. While at the monastery, the Head Lama claimed told him of a document that was kept there. It was about the life of Saint Issa and his wanderings in India and Tibet. Notovich was given this manuscript, supposedly, which he took off to Russia. He escaped Russia and went to Paris, where he published his book *Life of Saint Issa,* (or *The Unknown Life of Christ* as it is now titled)which details Jesus' many travels through India and Nepal, much as we have discussed earlier. The Head Lama told him that the manuscript was a copy from the great library in Lhasa, and it was aparently written in the Pali tongue originally, but then translated into Tibetan. Notvitch's copy was in Tibetan.[61]

Harry and I decided to go out to Hemis Gompa and check the place out. Could Jesus actually have stayed here, perhaps upon his return to Kashmir? It was a half-day, bumpy, but not-too- crowded bus trip out past Shey Gompa and Thickse Palace to the south of Leh. We got off at Karu, and from there walked the several miles up the hill to Hemis Gompa, which cannot be seen from the road. We walked toward a grove of trees that we could see up the hill, and from there, came to a narrow valley with a prayer wall, and many Buddhist Stupas. There were women working in the fields, harvesting barley and millet, dressed in black dresses, with their funny Ladakhi hats, like stove pipe hats with pointed front corners turned up.

Around a rocky spot was Hemis Gompa, the largest and second-oldest monastery in Ladakh. We met with the "manager" of the gompa, as the head Lama was in Darjeeling for a conference. We were given a small room in a building in front of the monastery after we had made a small donation. A young boy then showed us around the monastery, which was virtually empty at the moment, as most monks were gone to help with the harvests.

Hemis Gompa is quite impressive, with several stories, a virtual "monks' fortress" holding five hundred monks and sixty Lamas (teachers). Inside are a number of huge copper images of Buddha, each about twenty feet tall, waiting quietly, cross-legged, in nirvana-bliss-consciousness. At lunch we emptied a jar of peanut butter that Peter had brought from America and I gave the empty jar to a young boy who had just shown us around.

In my whole life, I have never seen such a look of sheer delight as that young ragamuffin in black yak's wool had on his face when he got that jar! I thought he might die of pleasure. He was so charming, so beautiful. Children all over the world, in every country, should be to us like that peanut butter jar was to the boy: a wondrous treasure of infinite value!

We spent the night on the lawn outside the monastery. The night was clear and starry. We lay in our sleeping bags and gazed up at the mountains and galaxies. The next day I wandered about the monastery and once, while walking behind it, was suddenly attacked by a big Tibetan mastiff, who confronted me from behind a rock, and barked viciously. I held my ground for a moment, not wanting to show any fear, when an even bigger, more vicious mastiff came up and threatened to lunge at me from a rock above the trail.

Terrified, I screamed, "Help!" and ran like hell, scrambling down the hill, and groping for rocks to throw, as I thought this dog was really going to go for my throat! The dog missed his chance, but some other dogs joined the chase until it seemed that every dog in the area was barking and and chasing me around the gompa. In the end, I jumped inside a window of the monastery, safe at last!

In some books on Jesus in India (notably Christ In Kashmir) it is claimed that Jesus actually studied and lived at Hemis Gompa and that his portrait can be found there. In an effort to check out this story about Jesus, I looked around the monastery for the portrait of a bearded white man, supposedly Jesus, but could find none. In actuality, the monastery at Hemis was not built, according to history, until the tenth century A.D. Much of Tibet was not inhabited in those days, and even today much of the highland desert of Tibet is still uninhabited. The Tibetan saint Naropa, sometime around the tenth century A. D., built a small hut near where Lamayuru monastery is today, and Hemis was built sometime just after the building of the first monastery in Ladakh, which was Lamayuru, designed by Rinchen Sangpo, a famous scribe sent from Lhasa.

It is difficult to believe, given this, that Jesus could have lived in Hemis Gompa at any time, but certainly not around the time following the crucifixion, as the monastery simply did not exist then. To Notovich's credit, he does not claim that Jesus ever lived at Hemis, but merely that the manuscript had been obtained there, and it a copy from Lhasa. It is likely that this story is largely fabricated by those who wish Jesus to be a born, bred and buried Kashmiri. As for Yuz Asaf, he supposedly died in 109 A.D. and whether he was Jesus or not, at least he did use many of the same parables that Jesus used, from what little we actually know about Yuz.

Later that night back in Leh, I stood on the roof of the Antelope Guest House and gazed up at the stars. What really hapened to Jesus? Had he really traveled in India, Persia and Tibet during the missing years? This, I decided probably was true. Many modern yogis speak of it as historical fact, at least as far as they are concerned.[77] Was Jesus Yuz Azaf? Possibly. Was he buried at Rauzibal Khanyar in Srinagar? Somehow, I didn't think so, but that too was possible.

I thought of some of the other legends about Jesus. Some say that he is still alive, and the body is kept in suspended animation, through mental means, at the Essene headquarters in the Pyrenees mountains between France and Spain. The biblical Ark of the Covenant is also said to be kept here in this secret mountain retreat.

Other traditions say that he is now a "Master" and lives in the headquarters of the Great White Brotherhood somewhere in Tibet, and appears at a special gathering somewhere in the Himalayas at summer solstice. Nicholas Notovich himself would be envious of a party of eleven American mystics who journeyed to India and Tibet in 1894. In the fascinating and inspirational book, *The Life and Teaching of the Masters of the Far East* (five volumes) the author Baird T. Spalding relates some incredible experiences that the group had with Masters in the Himalayas, and even meets Jesus, Buddha and other famous sages from times gone by.[80]

Jesus gives them practical as well as spiritual advice and other Masters perform certain miracles. In the reality structure advanced in this book, and most groups that believe in "Master- ship," Jesus became a Master, and was now above aging, dying and the limits of the physical plane. This is theoretically the goal for every person.

It is also worth mentioning that in Nestorian Christianity, an eastern church founded by the Apostle Thomas (whose tomb is in Madras) doctrine has it that Jesus was a person, specifically incarnated to create a physical vehicle for the Archangel Melchizedek, who was Christ. Melchizedek took over Jesus' body when John the Baptist was emersing Jesus in the Jordon River. What rose from the river was then Melchizedek, the Christ, a literal "God" on earth. When Jesus appeared after the cruxifiction, it was he, rather than Melchizedek.

This rather heretical version of Jesus' life is the same told in The Aquarian Gospel of Jesus the Christ as well as in the Edgar Cayce readings. Nestorian Christians are a real and ancient sect who believe in the divinity of Christ and reincarnation.

Perhaps, I thought from my balcony in Leh, that it is all true, but then again, it may all be like a yak pie; burnt in the fire, and smoke up the chimney. Probably I would never know, I thought, as I gazed at the evening stars. But then, perhaps I may yet find out. I turned my thoughts therefore to the Great White Brotherhood, the mysterious organization that supposedly trained Jesus. Who were they and where did they come from? I looked up at the stars. What was life without mystery, without a quest?

Principal geographical features of China

The well-known Russian artist, mystic, and Central Asian explorer Nicholas Roerich. Here Roerich holds a chest containing the Chintamani Stone, a powerful talisman which was sent to the League of Nations in the late 1920s. Roerich traveled across Asia to return the stone to an unknown destination.

In his travel diary of 1926 Nicholas Roerich, a well-known artist and explorer, told of a strange sighting in northern China:

> On August 5th—something remarkable! We were in our camp in the Kukunor district not far from the Humboldt Chain. In the morning about half-past nine some of our caravaneers noticed a remarkably big black eagle flying above us. Seven of us began to watch this unusual bird. At this same moment another of our caravaneers remarked, "There is something far above the bird." And he shouted in his astonishment. We all saw, in a direction from north to south, something big and shiny reflecting the sun, like a huge oval moving at great speed. Crossing our camp this thing changed in its direction from south to southwest. And we saw how it disappeared in the intense blue sky. We even had time to take our field glasses and saw quite distinctly an oval form with shiny surface, one side of which was brilliant from the sun. [Nicholas Roerich, *Altai-Himalaya: A Travel Diary*, pp.361–62]

Nicholas Roerich was a Russian landscape painter and archeologist who traveled widely in India and Asia from 1923 until 1928. New York City's Roerich Museum houses several hundred of his paintings.

1942, Tientsien, Hopeh Province, North China. A Chinese street photographer captured this photograph of a cone-shaped structured craft of considerable size flying down the street of the city. A witness in the picture points to the object as the picture is taken.

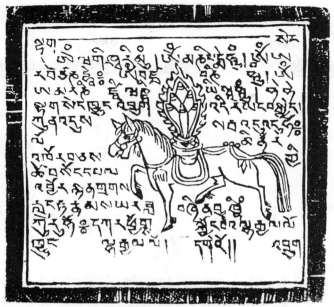

This Mongolian prayer flag with Tibetan script, shows the horse *Hi-mori* carrying the Chintamani stone. From *Men & Gods In Mongolia,* by Henning Haslund, 1935.

The 13th Dalai Lama.

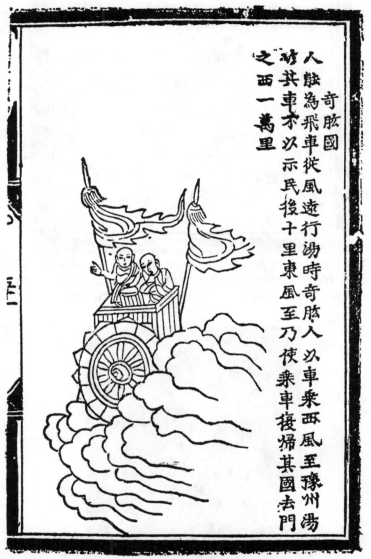

之西一萬里

奇肱國人骷為飛車從風遠行湯時奇肱入以車乘西風至豫州湯放其車术以示民後十里東風至乃使乘車復歸其國去門

A woodblock print from a Chinese encyclopedia from the year 1430 AD showing the legendary Chi-Kung people and their aerial carriages, called *vimanas* in Indian texts.

Chapter Sixteen

ZANSKAR AND CENTRAL TIBET:

IN SEARCH OF THE GREAT WHITE BROTHERHOOD

Sanjay are the enlightened beings;
their wisdom may see everything without obstruction.
One must be conscious that the enlightened ones
are everywhere and know our every action.
We must always keep in mind the enlightened ones.
By remembering the enlightened ones
we can stop all non-virtuous action.
—Tibetan Lama
at the Tibetan Educational Institute
Dharmsala, India

I stepped off the bus in Kargil and looked around. It had been one long day's trip from Leh back to the second city of Ladakh, and I was seeing it in a new light—daylight! (The last time, we had arrived at night, and left early in the morning.) Peter and Harry would stay another day in Leh, and take the bus back to Srinigar. So, as all traveling companions must eventually do, we parted. Now I would have a day or so here in Kargil before I could catch a truck for Padum, the capital of the small, formerly Tibetan kingdom of Zanskar, nestled in a remote valley in the southern portion of Ladakh. I was in the mood for a good trek through the Himalayas and some Tibetan country before I left India for good and went to China. I also wanted to contemplate what I had learned thus far on my search of the lost cities and ancient mysteries of Central Asia, especially the things about the Great White Brotherhood, where my search had now led me. What was the Great White Brotherhood?—a name bandied about by a number of different metaphysical organizations, and about which information was often quite contradictory. What was its connection with Jesus and Tibet?

Zanskar, where I was heading, was once an autonomous

Tibetan kingdom, but was subjugated by the Maharaja of Kashmir in 1839—the same year that Ladakh was annexed—although Zanskar still retained its king. Situated between the Himalayan range and the Indus valley, Zanskar is higher than most of the rest of Ladakh, and the climate is harsh and dry. During the winter, it is completely cut off from the rest of the world, but the people of Zanskar find this the ideal time to visit Leh, as they can just walk down the frozen Zanskar river which runs through a very narrow and steep gorge.

The people are Tibetan, and there are many Buddhist monasteries in Zanskar, but virtually no roads, although the Indian government has just finished a dirt road from Kargil to the capital of Zanskar, Padum. The road is very rough: it takes two days to travel one hundred miles by truck on it. Padum itself is but a tiny village with a few shops and rest houses. The ex-ruler and his wife still live there.

To me, it was a perfect place for a contemplative trek: quite undisturbed, wild, and very Tibetan. I planned to trek from Padum up the Zanskar river to Shingo La, a pass more than 18,000 feet high, and then down into the ex-Tibetan kingdoms of Lahaul and Spiti on the other side of the Himalayas. But first, I needed to find a hotel in Kargil for the night.

Kargil is at a much lower altitude than the rest of Ladahk, and enjoys a comparatively nice climate. Apricots are the big cash crop, and the growers do well. Kargil has electricity for three hours, give or take a couple of hours, every night, depending on how things are going that day. The inhabitants are called Yurik-Pas and are composed of Muslims of both the Shia and the Sunni sects. They are ethnically Kashmiris, and one sees very few actual Tibetans in town.

In the Kargil area they practice a curious custom, which may betray a certain pre-Islamic matriarchal tendency; that of the "mutah" marriage. A mutah marriage is a short-term marriage, a trial marriage of sorts, in which a matrimonial alliance may last a few short weeks with no subsequent obligations or negative ramifications on either side. This is highly unusual in the Muslim world, and perhaps unique. Still, just nearby, in the Buddhist areas of Ladahk, polyandry, the practice of a woman having more than one husband—usually brothers—is practiced.

Kargil has a number of shops, and is a good place to stock up on goods before heading into Zanskar, where shops are virtually non-existent. The RTDC (Regional Transport District Commissioner) told me that there wouldn't be another truck into Zanskar until the day after tomorrow, so I checked into the Hotel Lylo and spent a couple of days looking around Kargil, a pleasant, wild, frontier-type town, where the shop keepers lounge on their bolts of cotton cloth and gaze with glazed eyes at the passers-by on the street. I washed my clothes and bought supplies, relaxed in the hotel, and prepared myself for the big trip. I bought a ticket for the truck to Padum, and on the way back from the market, noticed a sign on a shopkeeper's store. I took a closer look. It was in English. The shopkeeper, a thin, friendly man in his thirties, stepped aside so I could get a better look, and gave me a cheerful, toothy grin. It said:

"Who brought the deposed Shah to power by a coup engineered by the CIA in 1953?

"Who has been giving support to a man who has killed 70,000 and disabled 100,000 during his rule in Iran?

"Who was plotting against the Islamic Republic of Iran and their people in their so-called 'Embassy'?

"Who was violating International Law and Vienna Convention by turning an Embassy to a den of Espionage?"

Well, in case you don't know the answer to this riddle, it is "THE AMERICAN IMPERIALISM." Above the poster was a death's head with an American-flag top hat being choked by a revolutionary fist, all in full color. I discovered posters like that all over Kargil, some in English, some in Urdu. A large portion of the population of Kargil is Shiite Muslim, the sect that is predominate in Iran, and of which Khomeini was the spiritual leader. I stared at the poster for a bit—it was commemorating the second anniversary of the Revolution in Iran—and then the shopkeeper asked me what country I was from. I looked at him and then at the rather grisly poster. I was tempted to say, " Canada," but with courage told him, " America."

He shrugged his shoulders and nodded, as if to say, "What the hell: we're all people; it doesn't matter." I nodded to him and smiled, he smiled back, and I tripped off down the street. Khomeini's hatred of America hadn't conquered Kargil yet, anyway.

I got up the next morning at four fifteen and headed straight for the RTDC lot where the truck for Zanskar was going to leave at five o'clock. When I got there, the truck was absolutely packed with people, including a few other travelers. Fortunately, I was squeezed in just above the cab, and before dawn we were shooting through the valleys and dodging the willow trees as we headed up the Karcha River Valley.

It was a great trip. We bounced along the rough dirt road as if there were no tomorrow. There were six of us sitting in the box above the cab while four sat up front inside the cab, and another thirty people were packed in the caged back like sardines. All day we could see the spectacular peaks of Nun and Kun to the end of the valley.

At one point, the truck caught fire in the back and we literally blazed down the road until the screaming of the crammed-in hoards brought the truck to a stop. Some burlap bags in the back had caught on fire and had smouldered for a long time before setting some boxes alight. Fortunately, nobody was hurt. We stopped for a picnic lunch, and then wound our way up toward the top of Pensi La Pass. We stopped for the night at Ringdom Gompa just before the top of the pass, and we slept in some large tents, as a nice little halfway-house had been set up there.

The next morning, we were off again, slowly making our way to the very top of the pass in a slight drizzle. There was a large glacier coming down onto the pass at the top. It was green, and good summer pasturing for sheep and goats. We had to fix up a bridge before we could cross it, and then we were in the legendary, remote, lost kingdom of Zanskar!

A chill shot up my spine. How I loved the road! The thrill of traveling and discovering new worlds! How I loved the excitement of day-to-day living! With a terrific grin, I stared back at the curious children who came out to watch the truck pass by. Green wheat and barley waved in the wind, while brown mares with their colts stopped to look up from their pastures. Marmots whistled at us from the rocks. So, this was Zanskar!

I had a bit of a problem getting a room in Padum when I got there, as it turned out there wasn't much in the way of hotels or even inns. There are some people who put up guests in their houses, and one can always camp in Padum, for the town is largely a grassy-green valley with a few houses. There is one special tea-shop/hotel, but it was closed when I was there.

I was fortunate to find a nice room in someone's home on the south edge of town for fifteen rupees a night, which was about a dollar-fifty, practically a king's ransom in Zanskar! But I gladly paid it, as I would be camping out in my tent for several weeks on my trek through Zanskar.

I spent a couple of days looking around the valley; it was green and beautiful, a wide silt plain with the Himalayas towering high above it to the southwest. There are a number of small temples, and a gompa (monastery) on a hill above the town. It was fun in Padum. People were friendly and uncomplicated, and this was the big city of Zanskar! I bought a few more supplies, sardines, peanut brittle and coconut cookies, at one of the few small stores in town, and then set out one morning on what would be a ten-day trek through Zanskar.

The first day, I went as far as Raru, a small village on the west side of the river. Tired, I pitched my tent in the middle of the village, while all the children came out to see the new stranger in town. I was taken to someone's house, where I had some Tibetan (salty butter) tea and flat bread while sitting by the fire. As I returned to my tent just at dusk, I found ten or so old men sitting in a circle on the ground near my tent, drinking chang (beer) which is quite popular in Ladahk. They invited me to join them, so I got my cup, and sat with them; soon the whole village was drinking chang and eating cracked barley.

It turned out that someone had just died in the village, and this was the wake. I suppose they naturally had their wake in the center of the village, where my tent was pitched. People laughed and told jokes, and were quite friendly to me, although I didn't know what they were saying.

In the west, the evening star was sitting on top of one of the icy mountains. As it was dusk, the sky was a kind of luminescent blue, while the jagged line of peaks was quite dark. It was like a crack between two worlds. A half moon was rising on the east side of the sky, lighting up the barley and wheat fields. We sat there for quite a while, drinking chang. I talked in English with a couple of young boys who had learned the language at school in Padum. Several hours and cups of chang later, I crawled into bed, a bit tired and tipsy after my first day on the trail.

The next day was a long, hot day. I was headed for the village of Purna, which was on the other side of the river, near the famous Phuktal Gompa, the most important tourist site on the trek. I nearly collapsed from the hard day of trekking, carrying a fifty-pound pack up and down the trails. On several occasions when I passed a man on the trail, he would say in his best English, "You, horse?" —meaning, did I have a horse?

I would look at him and reply, "No horse."

The man would nod, and say, "Ah, cha," an Indian expression like, "Oh, I see," with the implication, " Oh, I see, you're a crazy foreign tourist!"

There were some Germans camped there at Purna, so I had some tea with them before going to bed. The next day I left my tent and luggage at the field where I was camping, and walked up the valley toward Phuktal Gompa. Up this narrow tributary canyon was a bridge built for the Dalai Lama for his trip to Phuktal Gompa in 1980. He never came, though, staying in Padum the whole time. I hesitated to cross the bridge, as it was a large arch of woven branches spanning a raging river, and didn't seem to have much substance to it. Then I saw that there were two steel cables beneath the sticks and branches and deciced to brave it.

Just around a corner was Phuktal Gompa, a fortress monastery in a wide section of the valley. It was built on a cliff, under an overhang, by Gangsen Sherap, a Tibetan saint of sorts who built a number of gompas in the Zanskar region. This was the most impressive one, rising ten stories above the river, made with sheer adobe-mud walls, and with a"miraculous spring of healing water" inside it. As soon as I stepped inside, a monk whisked me off into his room to have some pea soup and tsampa, a barley porridge with salt and butter that was the best I'd ever tasted. I took a sip of pea soup and glanced at the monk. He was forty or so, I guessed; in good health, and of a cheery disposition. He spoke excellent English. "What are you doing in Zanskar?" he asked me.

"Well, I'm on a trek, and I'm looking for the Great White Brotherhood," I told him.

"The Great White Brotherhood?"   he said. "How do you know about them?"

"Oh, I've read a few things about them. Do you know about the *Great White Brotherhood?*" I asked him.

"Well," he hesitated, "I know some things. I have read some of our books which speak of them."

"Really!" I said, my eyes lighting up. I took another sip of pea soup and tried to hold back my eager anticipation of the information that the monk might have. I had been interested in the *Great White Brotherhood* for years, and had dug up bits of information here and there.

The *Great White Brotherhood* is indeed an elusive and confusing organization. It has been made all the more confusing by the use of its name by all kinds of diverse groups. Anyone can claim to be a representative of the *Great White Brotherhood,* or a member in good standing, or what not; separating the fact (if there are any facts in this case) from the fiction is a job that will probably not be completed in this century. From the wealth of material to be found on the *Great White Brotherhood,* however, I had surmised that the mystical organization did exist, and that it is the organization at the very pinnacle of "white" or good occult groups at work in the world today.

"Why do they call themselves the Great *WHITE* Brotherhood?" I asked the monk.

"They are called 'white'," he said, " to symbolize 'good' as opposed to 'black' which is symbolic of evil. The Brotherhood has been said to be a collection of the 'higher egos' of humanity, or to be a small elitist group containing only a handful of 'Masters': human beings who have totally mastered everything to do with the first four planes of existence. While the members of this exalted Brotherhood may or may not be incarnate, they do have a physical headquarters, a secret retreat, which is located in Tibet somewhere."

"How did they originate?" I asked.

"The Great White Brotherhood was started," he said, "tens of thousands of years ago in what was called by the ancients 'Rutas,' 'Mu,' or the Motherland, which was defined by what I believe your geologists call the 'Ring of Fire'—the great volcanic earthquake belt that rings the Pacific Basin.

"The first civilization of Rutas, or Mu, began in a certain area, and eventually became a highly developed civilization. The elders of this country formed schools to educate the common people. There were twelve of these schools, and then a *Thirteenth School* that was composed of the Elders, the wisest men of this first civilization. Eventually, the civilization achieved great heights, though not the degree of technology found in Atlantis in the days following Rutas (Mu)," he went on. "The twelve schools taught people the basics of life—the natural sciences, plus all forms of psychology—and the mental development of the self.

"The *Thirteenth School*, as it came to be known, was composed only of those persons of exceptional quality who possessed great mental power and capabilities: 'Masters,' as they are known. I should tell you that a balanced, and wholly positive, loving, unselfish, and giving disposition with a net positive karmic balance was needed as well. It is possible for persons of a negative, greedy, evil disposition to gain great mental powers too, unfortunately. Such persons are said to practice black magic, or the like.

"As has happened to quite a few ancient civilizations," he continued, sipping his tea, "a great cataclysm, a geological shifting of the continents, destroyed Rutas (Mu). Many of the people escaped to other lands. In fact, they had been doing so for thousands of years, and many other civilizations had appeared toward the end of the Rutas civilization. The twelve schools were dissolved, but the *Thirteenth School*, with its Masters, realized that the world needed Its help and relocated itself in Tibet, becoming the Great White Brotherhood, the first of other Brotherhoods that were to be created. Seven Masters were the head of it, and they are known as the *Council of Seven*."

"Why did they move to Tibet?" I asked.

"In the awesome cataclysms that have occasionally devastated all of mankind, like the great flood of your Bible, and others described in nearly all mythologies in the world, whole continents have sunken beneath the oceans, the oceans themselves have spilled out of their basins and washed over other continents as two-hundred-foot tidal waves, while other lands, former ocean beds, have risen thousands of feet to create new continents. Tibet is a high plateau in the center of the earth's largest land mass and is one of the safest areas on earth during such catastrophes.

"The *Thirteenth School* relocated itself somewhere here on the unpopulated and desolate plateau of Tibet. Just exactly where is not known by me. It established a library and school in the vicinity of what is today Lhasa. The actual headquarters of the group are in another location. I have heard that it is possibly in north-western Tibet.

"In more recent times, other Brotherhoods were established in different areas around the world, and the city of Lhasa was built up around the ancient school, while the population of Tibet began to slowly increase." With that, the monk finished his incredible story and his salt-butter tea.

I, too, had finished my pea soup and tsampa, and was staring into my empty bowl during the last part of the story. The monk stood up and put a hand warmly on my shoulder. "I suppose it is a strange story to you," he said in his accented English, "but that is how I understand the story myself. May I show you the rest of the monastery and the wonderful spring?"

We walked to the top of the monastery where a dark pool of water, known for its healing powers, was kept. Afterwards I thanked him for our talk, and left, returning to Purna, where I packed up and was on the road again.

I pondered the possible location of the *Great White Brotherhood* on my map of Tibet, while I stopped for a snack on the way south through Zanskar. There is some indication that it is in the Kun Lun mountains, which are in Western Tibet, as the monk said. If the retreat was in the Kun Lun mountains, then it wasn't really far away, hardly two hundred miles as the crow flies. I even pondered trying to trek there, crossing the border illegally into China, and making my way overland in search of the *Great White Brotherhood*. As I finished a packet of coconut cookies, reason told me that neither my sardines or my inspiration were likely to hold up on the trek!

§§§

I made it that night to Kuru, where I pitched my tent. Kuru is a pleasant village, on a shelf of good soil above the river, and it was full of flowers. As I came through town, wondering in awe at the galaxies of snapdragons, geraniums, buttercups, peas, and other flowers in bloom, all the kids in town came running out to meet me. Unfortunately, they all wanted candy, something that I had not brought with me. Apparently, a few other trekkers before me had give them, some and therefore they expected it of me. I offered them a playful smile instead, and pitched my tent.

Walking around the town, I discovered two handsome monks, young, healthy youths in their early twenties, who were busy working in a makeshift tent chiseling out Mani stones, flat stones with the prayer, "Om mani padme Om," which may be translated as "the jewel inside the lotus," the lotus being the mind, and the jewel being "cosmic consciousness," so-to-speak. There were hundreds of stones around them and they were going gangbusters, chiseling away while an old Tibetan lady kept pouring them glasses of chang.

One of these fine, cheerful young men was a deaf-mute, I discovered, and for some reason, perhaps his infectious smile, I was very attracted to him and liked him immediately. I had some chang with them, watched them chisel their stones and then watched the sunset, which curiously took place at both ends of the valley at once. After some re-constituted dehydrated tomato soup and a can of sardines, I went to bed.

I was off early the next morning, past the mani-stone chislers, to whom I waved goodbye. I supposed that they were monks at one of the nearby gompas, perhaps even Phuktal Gompa. It is customary among Tibetan Buddhists to have youngest sons enter monasteries at an early age and become monks. I crossed the river and, after wading a stream, came to the last permanent settlement in Zanskar, Kargyag. After lunch with a family of barley flat-bread and salt-butter tea, I looked around the village.

Some Tibetan traders had come over Shingo La with various and sundry household items. They were a wandering dime store, it seemed, and from a look at their stuff, it must have been quite a load for their ponies to carry. The ladies of Kargyag were shopping in their finest clothes, decked out in black wool dresses and heavy wool hats that lay flat on their heads with pounds of turquiose stone, orange coral, and silver attached.

I headed out that day, but it began to rain, so I pitched my tent by a boulder near the river, with the help of two young Tibetan cowboys on horses, who were tending sheep farther up the valley. The next morning, on my way up to the shepherd's hut just before the pass (a spot known as Lakong, which is Tibetan-Ladakhi for "hut"), I stopped at the camp of these cowboy-herders, had some yogurt with them, and watched the father of this nomadic clan of eight or nine sheer a sheep with his dagger. I was rather shocked to see that it had hundreds of ticks on it, but that didn't seem to bother the shepherd (I don't know about the sheep).

I met the two young Tibetan cowboys once more. Complete with nylon cowboy hats, red bandanas, and wool boots, they smiled golden to see me again. I gave them some postcards of Montana as a souvenir, though they seemed to think they were of Kashmir, as the countryside and mountains looked so familiar.

At the end of the valley, I had to wade a stream, a hundred feet wide and rushing with great force down a steep gully out of the Himalayas. I took my pants off and held my pack over my head as I waded into the icy stream. It was fortunately not so deep at this point, reaching up to my waist in the middle of the torrent. I leaned into the stream to keep from being washed over, gritting my teeth against the cold. From there it was a steep uphill climb toward the pass, and the hut, Lakong.

The hut was a small cave, with part of its opening closed up with stones. I suppose four or five people could have slept inside it. It was late by the time I got there. I tried to build a fire out of yak and sheep dung, but could not get it to more than smoulder. In the end, I used my stove, and retired with the dusk, so as to get up early the next morning for my assault on the pass, which was nearly 18,000 feet high.

I was up at dawn, and on the trail within a matter of minutes. It was a cloudy, overcast day, and it had rained the night before. The trail wound steeply up the glacial valley, with a great, icy peak just south of me, though that morning it was all shrouded in clouds. Soon, the trail disappeared, and I was scrambling up glacial scree toward the top of the pass. There was a narrow gully, with snow bridges covering a stream, and rocky scree coming down steeply from the soaring Himalayan peaks on either side. This was the main range of the mightiest mountain range of the world! A chill of exitement shot up my spine, and I pressed on.

As I neared the top of the pass, it started to drizzle a bit. I could see a large burgshrund, a fifteen-foot wall of vertical ice and snow that completely encircled the entire pass. If I could surmount it, I would be on the summit of Shingo La pass. There was no more trail—it had disappeared long ago. I tried to figure out how to get over the burgshrund. I didn't have an ice ax, and it was high. I was probably a bit to the west of the actual route, but could see no other way to the top of the pass.

I looked around for a rock that I could use to cut steps in the fifteen-foot snow wall. I found a flat, pointed rock about the size of my head, and began chopping steps with it, creating a crude staircase up the wall of snow and ice. Once I had breached the top, pulling myself up over the lip, I could see some prayer flags and a large cairn (pile of stones) to my east. This was the top of the pass, and it was all glacier, covered by occasional rocky scree. At the prayer flags, and large Buddhist cairn marking the top of the pass, I stopped for a moment and put on my rain coat because of the drizzle. At 18,000 feet, I was lucky it wasn't snowing!

No sooner had the thought entered my mind than it did start to snow, and I was enveloped in a total white-out on the pass. Nothing could be seen in any direction except white, swirling snow and mist. I attempted to descend the other side, but couldn't find the trail anywhere, and just kept running into glaciers that were fanning out from the mountain tops. It is quite dangerous to be walking around on glaciers alone, un-roped, and in a snowstorm, especially if you don't know where you are going! I searched in vain for a trail, or more chortens, cairns, or other trail markers, but with no luck. Meanwhile, the snow got worse, and the white-out closed in on me. I huddled beside a particularly large boulder just near the summit for a while, hoping things would clear, and then when the snow and wind picked up, decided to pitch my tent right there on the top of the pass.

It took nearly an hour to secure my tent on the north side of the boulder, piling up rocks to literally create a rock wall around it, to shelter it from the fierce Himalayan winds. That was my main worry: that during the middle of the night in a fierce storm, my tent would be blown away into the mountains! I crawled inside my tent. It was fairly dark, even though it was only the middle of the afternoon. I felt terribly alone, stranded in the desolate highlands of the Tibetan plateau... then my thoughts turned to *Sanjay* and the *Great White Brotherhood*....

While what the monk at Phuktal Gompa had told me was pretty far-out, to say the least, there is, surprisingly, some evidence to support the theory of a great continent once existing in the Pacific Ocean. It is often called Mu, sometimes Lemuria (Leumria can also refer to a land bridge in the Indian Ocean between Africa and India, called Lemuria in reference to the mysterious presence of lemurs in both Madagascar and India), and very occasionally, Rutas.

In the late eighteen hundreds, there was a French traveler and writer by the name of Louis Jacolliot (1837-1890) who collected a great many Sanskrit myths on his travels to India. According to him, the Hindu classics told of a former continent in the Pacific which they called

Rutas. This continent was where civilization had begun, and it had sunken into the ocean in remote antiquity, leaving only a bunch of small islands.[57]

Jacolliot's tales are remarkably similar to Churchward's, and he is one of the few sources that back up Churchward's tales of stone tablets which say pretty much the same things about ancient Indian sources and a lost continent in the Pacific. The Ring of Fire is certainly the most active earthquake zone in the world, and there is some archeological evidence of an advanced civilization in the Pacific, such as the gigantic megalithic stone city of Metalanim (Nan Madol) on small, sparsely populated Pohnpei Island, the 11,000 year-old cement cylinders in New Caledonia, or other evidence on mysterious Easter Island and other islands scattered throughout the Pacific.

But even if such a lost continent did exist, what of the *Great White Brotherhood*, and all this *Thirteenth School* stuff?

The great Chinese philosopher, Lao Tzu, often talked of the "Ancient Ones" in his writings, much as Confucius did. They were wise and knowledgeable, human beings that were as Gods— powerful, good, loving, and all-knowing. Born around 604 B.C., Lao Tzu wrote the book which is still perhaps the most famous Chinese classic of all time, the *Tao Te Ching.*. When he finally left China, at the close of his very long life, he journeyed to the west, to the legendary land of Hsi Wang Mu, which may have been the headquarters of the "Ancient Ones," the Great White Brotherhood. It was as he was leaving at one of the border posts of China that a guard persuaded him to write down the *Tao Te Ching* , so that Lao Tzu's wisdom would not be lost. No one ever heard of Lao Tzu again, though it is presumed that he made it to the Land of Hsi Wang Mu.

> The Ancient Masters were subtle,
> mysterious, profound, responsive.
> The depth of their knowledge is unfathomable.
> Because it is unfathomable,
> all we can do it so describe their appearance.
> Watchful, like men crossing a winter stream.
> Alert, like men aware of danger.
> Courteous, like visiting guests.
> Yielding, like ice about to melt.
> Simple, like uncarved blocks of wood.
> —Lao Tzu, *Tao te Ching (Chapter 15)*

Hsi Wang Mu is also another name for the popular Chinese Goddess Kuan Yin, the "Merciful Guardian" and

"Queen Mother of the West." Therefore, this land, traditionally located in the Kun Lun mountains, was known as the "Abode of the Immortals" and "The Western Paradise."

In the Chin Dynasty (265-420 AD) the Emperor Wu-ti ordered the scholar Hsu to re-edit the "bamboo books" found in the tomb of an ancient king named Ling-wang, the son of Hui-che'ng-wang, ruler of Wei State, c. 245 BC. The records the travels of the Chou-dynasty emperor "Mu" (1001-946 BC) who journeyed to the Kun Lun mountains to "pay a visit the Royal Mother of the West.". The emperor met with Hsi Wang Mu on the auspicious day *chia-tzu"* (The ancient chinese counted days and years in a special way, similar to the ancient Mayans of Central America. There are ten characters known as the ten stems of heaven and another twelve characters known as the twelve branches of earth. The combinations of these two sets of characters give names to the sixty years of of the Chinese cycle. The and named and counted the same way, in a cyclical fasion.). Emperor Mu had an audience with Hsi Wang Mu on the bank of Jasper Lake in the Kun Lun range. She blessed and sang for him and emperor promised to return in three years after bringing peace and prosperity to his millions of subjects. He then had rocks engraved as a record of his visit and departed eastward across the desert back to his kingdom.[146]

Over the years of Chinese history, expeditions were sent out to the Kun Lun mountains, the "Mount Olympus" of ancient China, in their many efforts to contact the "Ancient Ones."[38, 114,146]

In *Myths and Legends of China,* [114] published in 1922, Hsi Wang Mu (Kuan Yin) is connected to a lost continent: "Hsi Wang Mu was formed of the pure quintessence of the Western Air, in the legendary continent of Shen Chou....As Mu Kung, formed of the Eastern Air, is the active principle of the mlae air and sovereign of the Eastern Air, so His WAng Mu, born of the Western Air, is the passive or female principle (yin) and sovereign of the Western Air. These two principles, co-operating, engender Heaven and earth and all the beings of the universe, and thus become the two principles of life and of the subsistence of all that exists. She is the head of the trooop of genii dwelling on the K'un-lun Mountains (the Taoist equivalent of the Buddhist Sumeru), and from time to time holds intercourse with favoured imperial votaries.

"Hsi Wang Mu's palace is situated in the high mountains of the snowy K'un-lun. It is 100 *li* (about 333 miles) in circuit; a repart of massive gold surrounds its battlements of precious stones. Its right wing rises on the edge of the

Kingfishers' River. It is the usual abode of the *Immortals*, who are divided into seven special categories according to the colour of their garments—red, blue, black, violet, yellow, green, and 'nature colour.' There is a marvellous fountain built of precious stones, where the periodical banquet of the Immortals is held This feast is called P'an-t'ao Hui, 'the feast of the Peaches.' It takes place on the borders of Yao Ch'ih, Lake of Gems, and is attended by both male and female immortals."[114]

In Taoist legends there is the strong tradition of the Eight Immortals, eight Masters who reside at the secret headquarters in the Kun Lun mountains. The first and oldest of the Immortals, Li T'ieh-kuai (also known as K'ung-mu and Li Yuan) journeyed to the Kun Lun mountains where Hsi Wang Mu cured him of an ulcer on the leg and taught him the art of becoming immortal. He was said to have a commanding stature and devoted his life to studying Taoist lore. Hsi Wang Mu then sent him east to the Chinese capital. [114]

The strong similarity between legends of Shambala and the secret land of Hsi Wang Mu are easily noticed. Note the marvellous fountain built of precious stones and that the land is surrounded by a magical ring of mountains. Although with Shambala the leader is always a man (King of the World, typically) which seems to underscore the patriarchal system of Tibetan Lamaism, while in Chinese tradition the apparent leader is a woman. And undoubtedly there are more than eight people, men and women, who reside or have access to this fortress near the Kingfishers' River. Was the legendary continent of *Shen Chou*. the same as the lost continent in the Pacific from whence the *Thirteenth School* had come?

I cast a glance outside my tent and saw that it was still snowing. In the distance, high above me, I heard the rumble of an avalanche. I tensed slightly, and then thought about the *Great White Brotherhood* again, and their supposed library in Lhasa.

It was possibly underground, and it has been said by many to be near Lhasa, possibly connected to the underground tunnels beneath the Potala, the Dalai Lama's fabulous skyscraper. The tunnels, however, being reportedly quite extensive, would be very difficult to explore, and certainly such a library would be ingeniously hidden. The prolific occult writer T. Lobsang Rampa tells an interesting story of the exploration of these underground tunnels beneath the Potala in his fascinating book, *The Third Eye*. While the story is somewhat dubious, it does at least indicate that there is a great deal of myth about the existence of such tunnels. Rampa reports them as very extensive, and including a large underground lake. Nicholas Roerich also mentions tales of the tunnels and lake beneath the Potala, perhaps it is from here that Rampa learned of such things, if not from actual experience.[69]

Just north of the Kun Lun mountains, in Sinkiang, the famous Russian artist, explorer and mystic, Nicholas Roerich heard of the "Valley of the Immortals" just over the mountains. "Behind that mountain live holy men who are saving humanity through wisdom; many tried to see them but failed–somehow as soon as they go over the ridge, they lose their way," he was told. A native guide told him of huge vaults inside the mountains where treasures had been stored from the beginning of history. He also indicated that tall white people had been disappearing into those rock galleries.[93]

Nicholas Roerich at one time was in the possession of a fragment of "a magical stone from another world," called in sanskrit the Chintamani Stone. Alleged to come from the star system of Sirius, ancient Asian chronicles claim that a divine messenger from the heavens gave a fragment of the stone to Emperor Tazlavoo of Atlantis. [94] According to legend the stone was sent to Tibet to King Solomon in Jerusalem (also said to have a vimana airship) who split the stone and made a ring out of one piece.

A fragment of the stone was supposedly sent to Europe to help aid in the establishment of the League of Nations. With the failure of the League of Nations, Nicholas Roerich then had the stone in his possession. On one of his expeditions in the 1920's he returned the fragment of the stone to its rightful owners, whoever they were. Probably the Thirteenth Dalai Lama. The stone has been described as being the size of a small finger in the shape of a fruit or heart, shiny grey in color with four unknown hieroglyphs inscribed on it. It has certain magical properties, and can be used for divination. [94]

The stone is believed by some people to be Moldavite, a magnetic stone sold in crystal shops said to have fallen to earth in a meteor shower 14.8 million years ago. Moldavite is said to be a spiritual accellerator and has achieved a certain popularity in recent years. It is entirely possible that the chinimani stone is a special piece of Moldavite. It is worth noting here, too, that the sacred black stone kept in the Kabah of Mecca in Saudi Arabia, to which all Muslims pray, is also a piece of meteorite.

Roerich may have taken the stone to the "Valley of the Immortals" in the Kun Lun Range, or possibly to Lhasa, where it is also said that the Thirteenth Dalai Lama was also in possession of a fragment of the stone (perhaps this was the one sent to Europe). The Thirteenth Dalai Lama was a man of certain mystery. Tibetan tradition had it that would be but one more Dalai Lama after him. This is the Dalai Lama of today.

One legend of the Thirteenth Dalai Lama was that he never actually died, but essentially faked his own death. He was born in Tibet in 1876 and died (officially) in 1933. He was a mere 57 years old, a very young age for initiates to Tantric Yoga and other disciplines.

According to the rare and unusual book Prophesies of Melchi-Zedek In the Great Pyramid & the Seven Temples [98] by Brown Landone, published in 1940, the Thirteenth Dalai Lama left Tibet in 1922 for the Andes mountains of South America. Says Landone (pages 76-77) "...on February 22, 1922, the last great conclave of the holiest of the holy was held in the Temple of Temples in Lhasa. On March 6, the Thirteenth Dalai Lama left Thibet; a subordinate took his place and name, so that the remaining lower orders of priests did not even know the great holy man had gone. These two dates are indicated in the Pyramid by circles determined by the cubic space of the Temple, finished 4802 years before the two events took place."

Landone, in his esoteric decoding of the Great Pyramid (a popular pastime in the 30s and 40s) claims that teleois circles (geometric relationships within the passages of the Great Pyramid) reveal "to those who know, the events of the journey of the Dalai Lama and his holy men, who left Thibet with him. April 27, 1922—glorification of shrine of the Son of Heaven in Japan; July 27, 1922—Temple of the Northern Light; January 12, 1923—Mountain Temple of the North; October 23, 1924—sanctification of four masters in Europe; November 5, 1924—New Temple in Russia; December 13, 1925—in Jerusalem; August 17, 1926—hidden Holy of Holies in Ethiopia; February 2, 1927—Coptic Temple; May 4, 1927—leaving Africa for South America; June 25, 1927—arrival in the eastern Andes; July 16, 1927—consecration of the first stone of New Temple.

"This change—from Thibet back to the eastern Andes, after many thousand years' absence—is a symbol of the reglorification of the Western World, the active participation of supremely great powers of good, activated to work with man to BUILD UP a new era, to let brutal power destroy brutal power, and to establish peace forever on earth."

Though Landone Brown may have what is merely an active imagination, it is a fascinating thought, and one expounded by a number of different people, that a shift has taken place from Tibet to the high Andes. That the Thirteenth Dalai Lama, with the help of trusted aids, faked his own death, traveled the world for five years and eventually ended up consecrating his new headquarters at some secret spot in the Andes is an astonishing thought! According to this belief, he can still be found at this "Temple" which is probably underground and well hidden, much as the secret fortress in the Kun Lun Mountains is said to exist. It is an interesting notion that the chintimani stone may have been taken around the world and ultimately to South America by the Thirteenth Dalai Lama. More on secret cities and strange legends in the Andes can be found in my book *Lost Cities & Ancient Mysteries of South America.*

However, this scenario creates one problem, Dalai Lamas are supposedly successive reincarnations of the same ego. Who then is the Fourteenth Dalai Lama? Landone would probably say that the present Dalai Lama is an ego who has stepped in for the previous Dalai Lama with his permission, in order to keep stability within the orthodox Tibetan church. The Thirteenth Dalai Lama was therefore well aware of the political problems Tibet would face, including the Chinese invasion, and like any person who sees beyond Nationalism to the planetary whole, act to preserve wisdom and the plans of the Masters, rather than remain the political head of his country (which was soon to cease as an independent entity).

While the thought may be unthinkable to devout Tibetan Buddhists, it does not indicate that the present Dalai Lama is an imposture, but is merely acting on authority given him. Without a doubt, the present Dalai Lama of Tibet, currently in exile in India, is a man of great spirituality, integrity and a world class leader in the most positive sense.

§§§

The Potala Palace is a fairly recent structure, built by the fifth Dalai Lama, Ngwang Lobsang Gyatso who was born in 1617. It was he who persuaded the Mongol king and the Chinese emperor to recognize his suzerainty over Tibet. The Potala, the most famous building in Tibet, is a tall, massive, imposing mud-and-brick skyscraper, now turned into a museum by the Chinese.

Recently, Sanskrit documents discovered by the Chinese in Lhasa were sent to India to be studied by experts there. Dr Ruth Reyna of the University of Chandigarth said that the manuscripts contain directions for building interplanetary spaceships!

Perhaps this document is from the *Great White Brotherhood's* ancient library near Lhasa. In any case, Dr. Reynal explained that the document stated that the method of propulsion was "anti-gravitational." On board these machines, which were called "astras," the builders of these crafts could have sent a detachment of men to any planet. The manuscripts do not say that any interplanetary communication was achieved, but do mention a trip from the earth to the moon, though it is not clear whether the trip was just planned or actually carried out.

Indian scientists were at first extremely reserved about the value of these documents, but became less so when the Chinese announced that certain parts of the data were being studied for inclusion in their space program![14, 97]

Certainly, this is the type of manuscript that would have been theoretically stored in the Thirteenth Schoool's library in Lhasa. It is also interesting to note that the *Great White Brotherhood* is said to be in possession of a number of such airships, similar to these "astras" or the vimanas and vailxi of the Rama Empire and Atlantis. These airships, powered by "anti-gravity," as the document found by the Chinese suggests, are theoretically kept in secret bases within the Tibetan plateau and Mongolia.

Nicholas Roerich himself saw what was possibly a vimana from the land of Hsi Wang Mu in the Kun Lun. In his travel diary of August 5th, 1926 while in the Kukunor district, he noted that their caravan saw "something big and shiny reflecting the sun, like a huge oval moving at great speed.Crossing our camp this thing changed in tis direction from south to southwest. And we saw hos it disappeared in the intense blue sky. We even had time to take our fild glasses and saw quite distinctly an oval form with shiny surface, one side of which was brilliant from the sun."[134] (For more information on the fascinating subject of vimanas in Central Asia, see my book *Vimana Aircraft of Ancient India & Atlantis*[97])

Incredible at it may seem, a hollow mountain with ancient technology in the Kun Lun range of north-western Tibet is quite possible. Just as the NORAD defense command at Cheyenne Mountain in Colorado Springs is a hollow mountain with an entire city inside it, certain mountains elsewhere in the world may be similarly hollow. I might also add that for the normal citizen to walk inside Cheyenne Mountain, he would be absolutely astonished at the technology within the facility. Should these airships actually exist within secret areas of Tibet, they would be virtual UFO's, and the possible cause of some UFO sightings, especially those in Central Asia. Interestingly, the Kun Lun mountains and the Lop Nor desert nearby are the center for Central Asia's main UFO mystery![97]

§§§

To let understanding stop
at what cannot be understood,
is a high attainment.
Those who cannot do it
will be destroyed on the lathe of heaven.
—Chuang Tzu

Travel in Tibet has always been difficult. Until recently there were no roads, and the trails through the mountains were so fraught with bandits and other dangers that even monks went on trips armed. Travel was generally by foot for the lower class, and by yak or pony caravan for the more wealthy, and higher lamas. The Chinese have built a few roads which cross the country, generally east to west plus there is a road to Kathmandu and one to Gangtok. The Chinese opened the road to Kathmandu for tourists a few years ago, and this is easier than trying to go by road from Kunming or Chengdu in China proper.

Even though there are roads linking Tibet with a number of cities in China, the Chinese generally perfer that tourists fly into Lhasa from Lanchou, Peking, or Chengdu. There are no trains in Tibet, though there are some ferries and other primitive barges and yak-hide boats that ply certain parts of the Brahmaputra (Tsang-po) River.

Before the Chinese opened the road to Kathmandu, a few tourists had gotten special permission to travel overland into Tibet and then to Nepal. I know of a couple of people who managed to get permission to go overland from Sichuan to Tibet while in a remote town in Inner Mongolia where the local officials were more than hazy about the official line from Peking. Once in Lhasa, they looked around for a couple of days and were then smuggled out in a truck to a monastery in the country for several days, and before going back to Lhasa, the head lama asked one of the travelers, an Australian, if he would take a message to the Dalai Lama in India. He agreed.

Back in Lhasa, the Australian told the Chinese authorities that he was totally out of money and had to get to a bank in Nepal. After several days of repeating his story, he was allowed to go by truck to the Kodari border between Nepal and China. The trip normally takes four days, but took him nine days because of lack of transportation. He then became the first Westerner to cross the Chinese-Nepalese border.

Otherwise, if you want to visit Tibet, you merely have to get a visa to China, enter the country, and then fly into

Lhasa, paying one hundred dollars a day tourist fees as long as you are in the "Tibetan Autonomous Region." Hotel accomodation, even in Lhasa, is rather primitive, and costs tourists sixty dollars a night, though it's only three dollars a night for students. With a little inven- tiveness, perhaps, some of the exhorbitant fees can be avoided.

There is one other way to travel in Tibet: to dress up as a Tibetan and wander the countryside illegally. Some years ago at a motel in Zimbabwe, southern Africa, I met an old British ex-patriot, Mr. Searle, who told me of his journeys through Tibet, Chinese Central Asia and Mongolia in 1970. He hopped a camel-yak caravan out of Kashmir with the teenage king of Bhutan and traveled around for a year. He said that passports were important in these remote areas, even though no one could read them, so they just had to have your photo and look official. He carried bars of gold, a hack saw and scale, and Maria Teresa silver dollars, an old but popular Austrian mintage.

Most Central Asians, he said, didn't use paper money and he would pay them in gold, hacking off a piece and weighing it on his scale, or paying with a silver dollar. Things have changed somewhat in the fifteen or twenty years since, but it is still possible to travel throughout Central Asia in such a manner, though not in a huge caravan. The thing to do would be to stay out of the main towns and have a Tibetan or Mongolian guide, as well as remaining disguised as a native.

Most of Tibet is a vast, unpopulated unexplored plateau, and rugged as hell. The Chinese have a couple of roads through the country and they can only be traversed, basically, by a four-wheel-drive vehicle. Tibet is almost inconceivably vast, and that is how such places as the Great White Brotherhood's headquarters can remain hidden, even today.

If anyone desired to move around Tibet illegally on their own, they might try hitchhiking. Outside of the roads, they'd be best off to travel in a caravan, probably of yaks, making their way to some remote village or gompa. Trekking would also be possible, but one should be prepared and carry food and a tent, as it might be several days, even weeks, between inhabited areas. No doubt, it would be quite an adventure!

I awoke that morning bright and early, and leaped out of my sleeping bag—having slept with all my clothes on in case I had to rescue my tent in a midnight blizzard—and tripped outside into the sunshine. It was a beautiful day. All around me the sky was clear, and the panorama of icy, white peaks was spectacular! Just to the north was a massive icefall tumbling down a 20,000 foot peak towering right over my tent, and I hadn't seen it at all the day before. All around me were icy peaks with glaciers carving out valleys. During the night I had heard several avalanches, and there was an inch of fresh snow everywhere. I could now see clearly the way down. Packing up the tent, I started downhill.

Soon I was zipping along down the hill, the way to go being obvious in the light. I crossed an ice bridge over a stream, and found a trail which I followed for several hours downhill. I came to some Tibetans who were herding sheep in a pasture, and then, by mid-afternoon, came to the Barai Kade River, which I had to cross by wading waist-deep through the icy water. I camped my last night on the banks of the river at a place called Dakbajan, and the next day walked down to the Leh-Kyelong road, where I caught a daily bus from Darcha to Manali, a pleasant, pine-forested town in the cool Kulu Valley above Delhi and the hot plains.

I sat back in a restaurant, had my first beer in quite awhile, a "Mohan's Goldwater Lager," and waited for the large dinner of chicken curry I had ordered. What a strange odyssey it had been. I seemed no closer to the Great White Brotherhood now than I had been before. Did it even exist? I took a sip of beer—somehow, I thought it did. Was it really from the lost continent of Mu? I had no idea. I finished my beer and flipped though the *Illustrated Weekly News of India.*

Looking out the window of the restaurant, I saw a great orange sunset had set the Kulu valley alight with its yellows and reds. Life was good, I sighed. The quest for Sanjay and the Great White Brotherhood—one and the same, I figured—was doubtless neverending, and in that I found some comfort and inspiration.

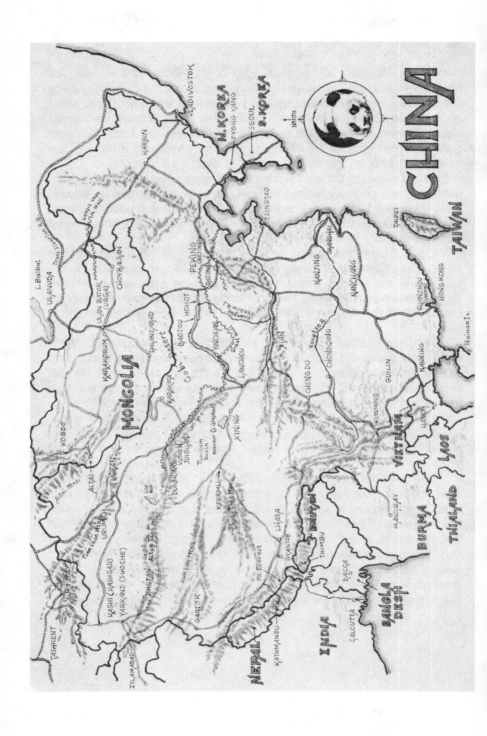

Chinese	*Khitan*	*Jürched*	*Hsi Hsia*		*'Phags-pa*	*Syriac*	*Uighur*	*Mongolian*	*Manchu*

Scripts used or created by Central Asian peoples.

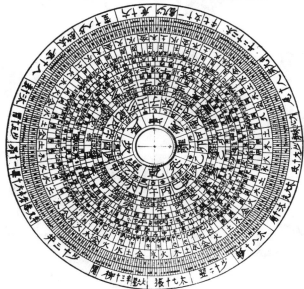

A Chinese Geomancer's compass. With this compass, a geomancer can plot the earth's telluric currents, power spots, gravity vortex areas, and ley lines.

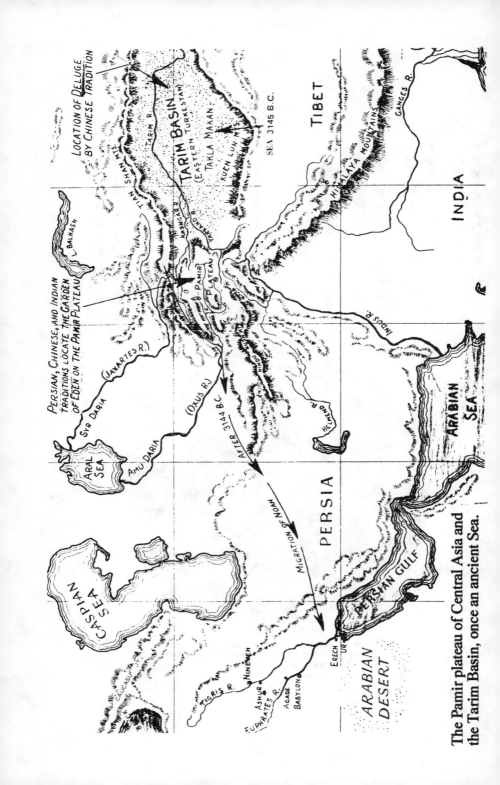

The Pamir plateau of Central Asia and the Tarim Basin, once an ancient Sea.

LOCATION OF DELUGE BY CHINESE TRADITION

TIBET

INDIA

TARIM BASIN (EASTERN TURKESTAN)

TIAN SHAN MTS.

TARIM R.

KASHGAR

YARKAND R.

TAKLA MAKAN

KUEN LUN MTS.

SEA 3145 B.C.

GANGES R.

PERSIAN, CHINESE, AND INDIAN TRADITIONS LOCATE THE GARDEN OF EDEN ON THE PAMIR PLATEAU

L. BALKASH

PAMIR PLATEAU

(JAXARTES R.)

SYR DARIA

AMU DARIA

(OXUS R.)

ARAL SEA

AFTER 3144 B.C.

HELMOND R.

HIMALAYA MOUNTAINS

INDUS R.

ARABIAN SEA

MIGRATION OF NOAH

PERSIA

CASPIAN SEA

CAUCASUS

PERSIAN GULF

ARABIAN DESERT

TIGRIS R.

NINEVEH

ASHUR

EUPHRATES R.

AGADE

BABYLON

ERECH

UR

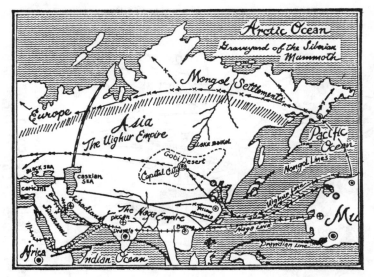

Churchward's map of the Uiger Empire prior to the pole shift which drained the inland sea of Central Asia and created the Gobi Desert. The capital city in the center of the map is Karakota.

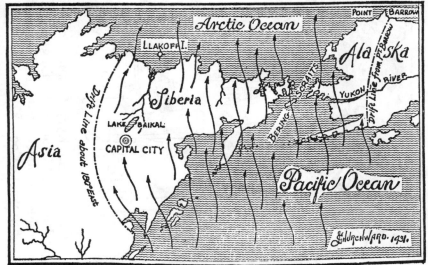

Churchward's map of the tremendous tidal wave that washed over eastern Asia destroying the civilizations of China and Central Asia. Areas like the Pamir Plateau, the Kun Lun Mountains and the Tibetan plateau were safe areas.

At the ancient Kyzyl temples near Turfan is this fresco of by the German archaeologist Grunwedel of a group of visitors in a fashion that could have been considered modern in the 1960s. (From *Buried Treasures of Chinese Turkestan* by Albert von Le Coq, 1928).

Chapter Seventeen

CHINESE CENTRAL ASIA:

SILK ROAD ACROSS THE GOBI DESERT

Yea, even unto China journey,
for knowledge is the most excellent of all things.
-Mohammed

China has always fascinated me. It is almost exactly the same size as the United States, and within its borders can be found the most varying climactic zones and geology of anywhere in the world. With a civilization dating back at least seven thousand years, I figured that there must be plenty of lost cities and ancient mysteries around.

China has been closed to the West and to virtually all foreigners for the last thirty years or so, and it is just recently that travelers have been allowed to wander China more or less as they pleased. In fact, most Chinese, and most foreigners, are not yet aware that this can be done. China would just as soon have all the tourists come in on some expensive package tour, whip around China for two weeks, and whip right back out as soon as possible. But you don't have to see China that way. In fact, you can get an individual visa for China and travel around on trains and buses pretty much as you would in any other country, though you generally need to have a better idea of what you are doing in China, and it's a good idea to take a Chinese phrase book with you.

China's main link with the outside world was the ancient Silk Road, leading westward from Han China along the northern edge of the Tibetan Plateau, through the Gobi desert to Dunhuang— where the Great Wall ends—and into the Sinkiang-Uiger province in the far west. The Silk Road branched, leading to Kashgar (which was part of Turkestan, called Uigeristan back in Marco Polo's day) both by a north route through Turfan, and by a south route, skirting the Lop Nor salt marshes and the Taklamakan

315

desert. Stops along the southern route, on the edge of the Taklamakan, were Qiemo (known as Qarqan hundreds of years ago), and Khotan, on the banks of the Hotan He River which cuts through the desolate Taklamakan desert. From here the route was generally through the Wakhan Valley (now in Afghanistan) and into Bactria and Persia where the caravans from Jerusalem, Damascus and Asia Minor met to head east.

Many Chinese goods were carried across the silk route, but silk made up the bulk of the trade. Because only the Chinese had the techniques for getting silk from silk worms, the fabric was rare and in very high demand. China, in return, imported very little, mostly jade from Central Asia and pearls from Arabia. The journey could be quite hazardous, and therefore, it was necessary to always travel in a caravan; the bigger, the better. Even today in some parts of Chinese Central Asia and Mongolia, it is better to travel in a caravan, as bandits (called "Campas" in Tibet), will occasionally raid travelers or villages.

Within China itself, the main highways were the many rivers and canals, down which countless sampans piled their cargo. In order to protect their precious trade routes and provinces, the government built special roads for moving armies and their supplies. While government officials were allowed to use these special highways, peasants had to use other, more crude, roads.

The Great Wall was built largely to keep the Mongols to the north out, but also to create a series of linked forts that stretched out to the west, along the *silk road* and out into the desert and mountains of Central Asia. As caravans left the last fort, at Jiayuguan, and headed for Dunhuang and Turfan in Uigeristan, they were, in a sense, leaving civilization behind, and heading into the great, wild unknown.

Danger in those days, however, was relative. In 1610, when tea was quite the rage in Europe, and China was the major source, it was deemed safer to bring it over the Silk Road—though the vast deserts, wild forests and high mountain passes—than through the seas, swarming with pirates and cutthroats, using straits that had hardly been charted, and were unsafe for ships!

The great Swedish explorer, Sven Hedin, who explored much of Central Asia and traveled the Silk Road around the turn of the century, called the journey "an unforgettable experience." Hedin was amazed at the varied cultures that were extant along the Silk Road. Most people just naturally assumed that the Silk Road was populated by the nomadic Turkomen tribes that dominated the Central Asian steppes, but, according to Hedin: "Instead of a Turkish-speaking country, the investigators discovered Indo-Germanic people along the Silk Road till the eighth century: Iranians and even Europeans. Many manuscripts contained their idioms but some were unknown. These were translated and scientifically examined at London, Paris, and Berlin. The Indo-Germanic and Turkish scholars found they had to deal with seventeen different languages and twenty-four varieties of writing."

Hedin was quite an authority on Central Aisa, and on March 28th, 1900, he discovered near the Lop Nor marshes the ruins of a city called Lou-Lan, a civilization that had flourished in ancient times. According to the manuscripts, which were written in clear, excellent Chinese, this culture was later wiped out by a large seismic occurance which drastically changed the climate of the area and turned it into a desert. Later, corpses from the cematary at Lou-Lan were exhumed and found to be perfectly preserved: both the bodies and their clothing. It is not known how this odd preservation occured. Some of the bodies were said to be of an unknown race that had never been seen before![31] Still, preser- vation of bodies can be remarkable in especially dry climates. Eleven thousand-year-old mummies were discovered in 1982 in the Atacama desert in Chile. They were perfectly preserved, and most were actually reburied because they would rapidly decay if left in a museum or the University of Arica!

At the far western end of the Chinese side of the Silk Road is Kashgar, called Kashi today by the Chinese. It is an oasis on the edge of the Taklamakan desert. There are many odd legends that center around Kashgar. Both Marco Polo and Gengis Khan stayed here for a time. The famous first century A.D. Chinese warrior Pan Chao is buried here. Possibly, the legendary hero, the "man of jade," who could "walk in the sky" and "let loose green thunderbolts" is buried here as well. For more than two hundred days a year, Kashgar is enveloped in a huge cloud of sand, raised by the winds of the Takla Makan desert. One legend says that "men from the sky" set up house here as "they could not be seen by human beings."[31]

The Silk Road is indeed an unusual highway, ancient as China herself. It is said to have been started by the emperor Shun in the second millenium before Christ as a trade route, not just for silk, but to send many other goods to the west. It appears that it was well known even in remote antiquity, thousands of years before and many Mediterranean peoples and even Europeans journeyed along the trail, perhaps looking for adventure, riches, or lost cities.

I felt that Sinkiang-Uiger was a good place to start my

journey through China, and from what I had heard, this area of Central Asia was perfect for the adventurer in search of lost cities. From Delhi, I had flown a roundabout way to get to Urumchi. While it was a mere 1,500 miles or so to the north of Delhi, politics and flight schedules would not allow me to make the journey, although I seriously considered going overland through Tibet, though it might be awkward to be caught in China without the visa or travel permit that everyone must have (or at least, so the authorities believe). Today, the Karakoram Highway between Pakistan and Kashgar is open, making such a trip overland legal and fairly easy.

I flew to Bangkok, and on to Hong Kong, where I met my old friend from Kathmandu and Rajastan—the one who'd seen the firewalkers—Bill, an electrical engineer from Ohio. He was tall and athletic, with a blond beard and rugged good looks. Bill was a seasoned traveler, and prepared for several months of adventure in the remote areas of China. He seemed a perfect companion. We got visas at the hostel in Chungking Mansion in Kowloon, and were off to Canton (Guang-zou), where we bought a train ticket that took us straight to Urumchi, a journey which took several days by train.

It had been a long and exiting train ride, full of wonderful sights and sounds, people and adventures. We were somewhat in shock the whole time. We could hardly believe that we were in China! How fantastic it was! What a wonderful, ancient, exotic country! In the mornings on the train, a three-day ride in the second-class berths, I would awaken and not know where I was. Looking around at the friendly and curious Chinese faces, I would realize that I was indeed, fortunate to be traveling in China!

Now that we were sitting comfortably in a shish-kebab stand in a square in Urumchi, the most inland city in the world (the nearest ocean is the Bay of Bengal), eating mutton and flat bread, I could still hardly believe that we were in China!

It is not all that easy, but if you follow the right steps, you can go almost anywhere in the country, and stay for quite a while. It is necessary to get a visa to enter China. If the nearest Chinese Embassy will not give you one, then you can get one in Hong Kong at the official Chinese Travel Service, although they would prefer that you signed up in a group—or even as a group of one, which has been known to happen. It is also possible to join a group to Canton on a short trip and then get your visa extended by a month and travel around China on you own from there. This whole process will get easier and easier as time goes on, and more and more people travel in China on their own.

Most tourist visas are valid for a month and are renewable twice, for a month each, thereby making the typical "long stay" (a short time really) about three months, after which one would probably have to leave the country. Visas are extended at the Public Security Bureaus (the Police), and the more remote and out-of-the-way the town you are in, the better your chances of getting an extension. Avoid getting your visa extended in one of the big tourist cities such as Peking or Shanghai, as the authorities are notably stricter about red tape and bureaucratic rules.

Until recently, every foreigner in China needed to have an Aliens' Travel permit issued by the Public Security Bureau. It listed all the places that you were allowed to visit, but as it was in Chinese, you weren't really too sure where you were allowed to go. When we got ours in Canton, we just had the officer write down every city that we were allowed to go to, as we wanted to go everywhere. These days, in the late-eighties, there are at least twenty-eight selected cities that can be visited without a permit. If you are going to go anywhere out of the way in China, however, you will need a Travel Permit, which is free and easy to get. Ask for any place you want to visit; the worst that can happen is that you'll be denied permission.

Travel in China is comfortable but relatively expensive, compared to other Central Asian countries. Train travel is preferred: it is fast, comfortable, and railways go to every major city except Lhasa. Long-distance trains come in three different classes: soft sleeper (deluxe tourist class; ordinary Chinese citizens are not permitted to travel this class unless they are on government business), hard sleeper, and hard seats. Hard sleepers are not hard at all, but quite comfortable, sleeping six people in an open compartment, compared to four in a closed compartment with frilly curtains for the soft sleeper. For the adventurer in search of lost cities and dusty roads to hitch down, the hard sleeper is more than adequate.

Third class, the cheapest fare, is a padded seat in the back of the train, and it is quite crowded. Seats may be reserved, but most people just pile in and sit on the floor or whatever. A night, or at least a day, in the hard seats at the end of the train, where most Chinese ride, can be one of the most memorable experiences in China, and certainly brings you into very close contact with the down-to-earth locals!

Train tickets are sold at stations, and there are special prices for foreigners—more expensive, of course—unless you are a student, and then you can go for the same price as the Chinese. Keep your ticket when you get off the train, as you will need it to get out of the station. Meals are served on the train, but you must buy a voucher first. You can eat in the meal car, or have a meal served to you in your compartment.

Hitchhiking is also possible in certain areas of China, particularly remote areas in the west and north. As long as you know where you are going, just start walking down the road and flag down a truck in typical Central Asian manner: waving your arms wildly and jumping up and down. All over the Gobi desert hitchhiking is quite good. In more remote spots, such as Tibet, you might have to pay for your ride, depending on how long it is.

Buses or electric trolleys are the best way to get around the big cities, and bus-route maps are usually available at bookshops and railway stations. Boats are another form of transportation that is possible. While there are regular services along all the major rivers and along the coast, foreigners are generally restricted as to their use. Flying around China on CAAC is also possible, and an airline ticket is generally only a little bit more than the cost of a soft sleeper on a train to the same place. Flying is about the only way, aside from hitchhiking, to get to a few remote cities, notably those in Tibet.

China has plenty of hotels, all run by the government. The budget-conscious adventurer should stay in the "Overseas Chinese Hotels" which are generally a lot cheaper than the normal tourist hotels—those cost twenty-five to fifty dollars a night. Most Chinese cities have a hotel (usually the Overseas Chinese Hotel) with a dormitory in it. A dormitory can be had for one dollar or less, and a double room in an Overseas Chinese Hotel costs two to four dollars a night, or more, depending on the hotel. I found the hotels generally clean, with clean sheets, and usually a bathroom down the hall, if not in the room.

§§§

Bill and I were staying at the Ba Lou Binguan (Eight Story Hotel) in the northern part of Urumchi, which was apparently the only hotel for foreigners. We got dormitory beds, but as we seemed to be the only people in the hotel, we had a large, comfortable room with four beds all to ourselves for two dollars each. Urumchi is a city of eight hundred thousand and is not the most scenic or fascinating city in China, but it is interesting. It has such a Turko-Uiger-Central Asian flavor that it seems more like Afghanistan than China, although three-quarters of the city is Han Chinese. It is an industrial center, with oil refineries belching out smoke constantly, but it can still be enjoyed. Bill and I walked down to the "ethnic" section, where there were shish-kebab stands, dried-fruit sellers, a carpet market, and even some old mosques. Uigers are not Mongols but Caucasians, often having blue eyes and brown hair and seeming a bit out of place in China.

I traded a down vest for a heavy-duty sheepskin-lined blue Mao jacket, and then we tripped on down to a shish-kebab stand. I was happily munching away on some charcoal-broiled mutton, sandwiched in some flat wheat bread ("nan"), when a young Chinese man sat next to us, and asked us in English where we were from.

"We're from America," Bill said. The man was Han Chinese, rather than Uiger, about five-foot-six, without any facial hair (like most Chinese) and quite friendly. He also spoke pretty good English, which is rare in China. "Where are you from?" asked Bill.

"I am from U-ru-mu-chi (Urumchi)!" he said.

"What do you do here in U-ru-mu-chi?" I asked him as I finished my kebabs.

"I am study at Xinjiang College. I live in apartment near here. Do you want to come and see it?" he asked eagerly.

"Sure!" chorused Bill and I simultaneously. This was great: we were already making our first friend here in China.

We followed him a few blocks away to some cement apartments that were four stories high and formed their own city block. Climbing the stairs to the third story, we entered his apartment. It was neat, though rather drab. Buildings, like the clothing adults wear, is typically gray, and rather depresssing. His apartment was fairly large, three and a half rooms, all made of cement—floors, walls, and ceiling—and all gray. He had some furniture and a few pictures torn out of magazines on the wall for decoration.

"Would you like some tea, please?" he said. He seemed absolutely delighted that we were there and very proud of his apartment, which was probably fairly large by Chinese standards. He was a cheerful, eager person, with a lot of energy. I thought him very likable.

"You are the first foreigners to meet me here in U-ru-mu-chi!" he said after we had our cups of jasmine tea. "I am so pleased to show my apartment to you!"

"It is a very nice apartment," I said.

"Oh, thank you, thank you," he said, his head nodding. We talked about America. He wated to know everything about America; it was his favorite country, and he read everything about it in the papers or magazines. He told about his college life; he was not married. He did occasionally date a fellow student, though it was nothing serious. In the end, we finished our tea, had a second tour of his apartment, and then took our leave.

"Good night, good night!" he cried as we left. I thought he would literally burst with the excitement of having met a couple of real live Americans and entertained them in his home! We shook his hand warmly and thanked him for his hospitality. He seemed a wonderful person, and his enthusiam was contagious!

Back out on the sreet, Bill and I decided to go to a movie that was just nearby. It was in a lot, near the square where all the kebab and nan stands were clustered on the sidewalk.

Chinese films are sort of like drive-ins, only they are walk-ins! We walked through a gate and sat outside on benches to see the movie, which was a story about young people fighting some nameless enemy on the borders of China somewhere. It was well done, and even though we could not understand what was being said, the plot was obvious, and so was the message of the film. It stressed such positive attributes as devotion, self-sacrifice, patriotism and virtuous chastity. At one point toward the end of the film, a young, pretty nurse ran through a hail of falling shells to save a friend who had been hit by a bullet. In the end her friend lived, but the rescuer died.

At another point in the film, during a climactic battle on the frontier complete with exploding bombs and shells, there was a sudden, loud bang beneath our seat, and then small missles were arcing across the screen and falling in the audience, exploding! People in the audience, it turned out, were lighting firecrackers and pop-bottle rockets, participating in the movie in a way rarely done in Western countries, except perhaps at a midnight showing of the *Rocky Horror Picture Show*. Bill and I were at first a little shaken, wondering if there was a sudden raid on the theater, but then got right into it as soon as we realised what was happening. It was really quite fun and added a certain comic realism to the scene.

The next day we headed out to Tianchi Lake (Heavenly Lake), the main excursion and tourist attraction around Urumchi. It is an hour and a half away by bus to the northeast in the mountains, and is well worth the trip. Bill and I left early in the morning, and soon were staying in the alpine forests and beautiful mountain scenery of Tianchi, a spot that looks a great deal like Switzerland. There is a nice guest house just by the lake, and also some yurts nearby where travelers can stay.

Hiking around the lake and into the mountains is the thing to do in Tianchi. It is possible to take a ferry across the lake for the start of a trip. Mount Bodga (Bodga Feng—Peak of the God) sits at the end of the valley to the south of the lake, all white and grandiose with 21,000 feet of icy splendor. It's a popular peak for Japanese and Chinese climbing expeditions.

Bill and I spent the night, walked around the lake, and had lunch at the People's Restaurant at one end of the lake. We went by a house on the northeastern part of the lake, where we saw an old man sitting on the grass near the lake, holding his grandson in his lap. Standing behind him was a pet fawn, just starting to grow horns. It was a romantic picture I shall always remember: Heavenly Lake, the mountain backdrop, pet deer, and the idyllic old man and child. It struck me that it seemed to symbolise the Chinese ideals of the union of man and nature, and the regeneration of life.

Bill and I had planned to go camping around Mount Bodga for a night or two, but the weather got bad, so we decided to go back to Urumchi. We hitchhiked back to Urumchi, catching rides on local trucks, stopping to take photos of local Uiger nomads with their camels and yurts. Bill sold his watch to a guy in one truck, and as we caught a last bus that was going into Urumchi, I leafed through a Chinese UFO magazine that the driver had.

Another nice thing to do in Urumchi is to watch the sunset from the park on top of the hill overlooking the city. There are a couple of cement tower-pagodas at the top, and it has a tremendous view of the city and of the Tienshan mountain range, including Mount Bodga. On several nights we watched the pagodas silhouetted against the orange sky and the burnt brown hills to the west.

Before we left Urumchi for Turfan, we hitchhiked out to the south of Urumchi, heading for the Nan Shan pastures, a few hours away. We took the #1 bus to the end of the line, and then took another country bus to the end of its line, and hitched from there. After several truck rides (cars are rarely seen in China, except in big cities) we reached the Nan Shan range: snowy, fir-covered moutains stretching out across a yellow-brown plain. A truck, driven by a youthful, clean-shaven Han Chinese man, and a faded blue Mao jacket, gave us a lift. The driver wore a perplexed smile as if to say, "What are these two Americans doing here in the chilly plains of Central Asia?"

After he dropped us off at a crossroads, we walked to a small village and aggravated a few dogs with our presence. Eventually, some of the villagers came out to see what all the ruckus was about, and soon every kid for miles was peeking behind some fence or doorway to have a bashful look at us. We took pictures of a few Uiger cowboys. They were wearing cowoy hats, chaps, denim shirts, and bandanas, and they sat tall in the saddle. They had a herd of sheep and the picturesque mountains rising behind them made everything seem larger than life.

We got a lift back to Urumchi in the back of a truck carrying a hundred sacks of potatoes. I sat in the back, marveling at the awesome, panoramic scope of this big country—it was sort of like my Montana home—but I couldn't keep from thinking that those were mighty cold potatoes!

§§§

It was snowing when we left Urumchi the next day. The sky was dark and vast. Wet snowflakes fell softly by the millions. We warmed ourselves by a pot-bellied stove in the station, then boarded the train in the inevitable mad dash that always occurs when the train pulls in. It was quite a scene, people running to and fro on the platform, lugging big crates and bags on their shoulders, while the snow came down more heavily. I went to get Bill and myself seats in the hard seat section, as we would only be going a short distance, and was literally carried along in a sea of people.

Soon we were on our way to the east, through the mountains, and into the Turfan Depression. As I sipped some jasmine tea from the cup I'd bought for the train ride (hot water was at the end of the car), I couldn't help thinking about the Uigers, and their ancient empire.

Traditionally, the Uigers are said to be of Turkish stock, and certainly today they speak a language largely derived from Turkish in Sinkiang-Uiger. The oldest Turkic writting known can be found in grave markers in Mongolia dating from the sixth century. In this same century says a *Newsweek* magazine article (March 5, 1990): "Turkic speaking tribes swept out of northern China in the sixth century and long dominated much of Eurasia."

Their capital was at Karakorum in Central Mongolia, just south of Lake Baikal and near today's Ulan Bator, capital of Mongolia. This empire lasted only a short time—a hundred years or so—until their capital Karakorum was overrun by the Mongols. The Uigers moved west to where they are today, re-established their empire, and then were overrun again by the Mongols in the thirteenth century. They have been controlled or governed by the Mongols or Chinese in some way or another ever since.

Even more interesting than the recent history of the Uigers is the strange story of this "white, European race" of China. One of the cities also credited to the Uigers lies south of Karakorum, in the sands of the Gobi desert, near the shores of Lake Gashunhu near the town of Ejin. This area is the Inner Mongolian Autonomous Region of China— and the ancient, mysterious city is called *Karakota.*

Karakota was once the ancient capital of the "old " Uiger Empire, according to some historians, such as Churchward. Karakota is in one of the most desolate parts of the Gobi, although just near it is an oasis, and one of the few inhabited towns in the "true" Gobi desert. Curiously, while its ruins can be found on a good map (such as National Geographic) no mention of the city is ever made in books on the Mongols or the Turkic-Uigers. Even the name of the city is a mystery. The ruins were known to local Mongolian nomads as "Kharo-Khoto" or the "Black City."

In 1907, the Russian archaeologist Professor Kosloff became the first modern European to discover the ruins of the ancient city. On his first expedition he unearthed an ancient library written in the now extinct and untranslated Tangut script. Later, in 1909 on his way back from Amdo in Tibet to report to the Russian Academy of Sciences, he discovered another ancient library with artifacts, countless scrolls and artifacts, together with some three hundred Buddhist graven images, and a number of statues.

Within the library were a number of Mongolia letters and folios, including one that mentioned one of Ghengiz Khan's most faithful companions, the Bugurchi noyan. This clearly gave evidence that Karakhota had been occupied in the 14th century. The ruins of an Islamic mosque outside the crumbling walls of the city also proves a fairly recent occupation.

Yet, it is believed that Karakhota is a city that has existed for thousands of years, and which goes back to the early Tangut empire, at the very least. Churchward believed that the city went back to the time of the lost continent in the Pacific, which is probably an imaginative claim, at best.

In 1923, Kosloff unearthed a tomb fifty feet below the surface of the present-day ruins of Karakota, after uncovering nearly fifty feet of stratum consisting of boulders, gravel and sand to expose the more ancient, original city underneath.

Because of ancient records indicating that the ancient capital of the Uigers was beneath the newer city, they were able to find the original capital.

Kosloff apparently found many "wonderful" articles in the tomb, and took photographs of the items, many of which later appeared in the journal, *American Weekly*. One of the photographs showed a woman, apparently a "queen" painted on silk, with a "Mu Sundisk" on her head, or so Churchward called it. In addition, there were photos of various scepters, finely wrought in gold and other metals. Kosloff was not allowed to disturb or take anything from the tomb, and it was sealed again after they left.[31, 8, 145]

One thing is certain, there is currently no water nearby to Karakhota, indicating that there has been a climatic change in the area since the city was originally created. It is quite possible that Karakhota was once a major city in the legendary fertile Gobi that managed to hang on much longer than other cities after the climatic change which created the Gobi. Possibly some sort of cataclysmic flood/tidal wave (in the middle of the Gobi desert!) destroyed the city, and covered it with sand and boulders, which was then rebuilt. This is not really unusual—several cities in Mexico have been found like this.

A Mongolian legend that has sprung up around Karakhota is that the last ruler of the city, a man known as Hara-Tzyan-Tzyun, attempted to take control of China, and therefore the Chinese army sieged the city and ultimately diverted the Etsingol River so that the inhabitants would have no water. Hara-Tzyan-Tzyun then buried the treasure of the city including eighty carloads of silver, plus gold and jewels, in a waterless well. Then the inhabitants left forever. In one version of the legend, they sneak out into the desert, and in another, they go out to do battle with the Chinese and are defeated.[145,151] Apparently, however, there are no Chinese texts to support the legend.

Kosloff felt that the city was extremely ancient, and shared much of the information he had gotten with his friend, James Churchward. Esoteric tradition maintains that the Takla Makan was an inland sea, much like Lake Baikal and the Gobi desert was once a very fertile area, a large plain with many cities and great industry and agriculture, from which a great civilization sprang: the Uiger Empire!

The Uiger Empire existed, apparently, at least some sixteen to eighteen thousand years ago. They spread out all over Asia, from the Pacific, across Mongolia and northern China, into Central Asia, and even into Europe. Perhaps their capital was ancient Karakota! For instance, the ancient Hindu text, the *Book of Manu* says, "The Uigers had settlements on the northern and eastern shores of the Caspian Sea." The distiguished German anthropologist Max Mueller once wrote, "The first Caucasians were a small company from the mountains of Central Asia." It has been suggested that the Caucasians have their origins in the ancient Uigers.[8]

Then, of course, there are the frozen mammoths in Siberia which seem to have been flash-frozen there during some sort of crustal slippage, perhaps a slight rotation of the poles, though the date when this may have happened is in doubt. Churchward suggested that it happened about

16,000 years ago. This is about the same dating given to the mammoth and mastadon bone graveyards found in Alaska and Siberia.

Was it some sort of global cataclysm about 14,000 BC that turned the Gobi into a desert, flash-froze mammoths with food in their stomachs, and destroyed a large portion of civilization? Atlantis was said to sink in stages, the first occuring in 14,000 BC or so, unsettling the island continent, and the next in 8,500 B.C., when the continental arch collapsed and Atlantis sank beneath the ocean. Churchward thought that during the first cataclysm, the entire eastern portion of the Uiger Empire was totally wiped out, leaving only persons in the west alive.[8]

There are many legends of lost cities in the sands of the Gobi desert. Soviet aviators flying over the Gobi desert have photographed the ruins of quite large cities, recognizable from their foundations. The psychic Edgar Cayce occasionally talked about cities existing in the forgotten sands of the Gobi, some with "elevators" (to my knowledge, no one has ever found an elevator in the Gobi desert). It is true that local people, Uigers and Mongols, told stories of such lost cities emerging after fierce sandstorms, and even knew where many of them were located.[31]

The Russian traveler and mystic, Gurdjieff, describes in his book, *Meetings with Remarkable Men*, an expedition that he and some friends made in 1898 in search of one of these ancient Uiger cities. It was in a particularly remote part of the Gobi, in what is today the area around the border of China and Mongolia. While standing in a village on the border of the Gobi, they learned of an area where it seemed rather certain that a great city lay buried beneath the sands, and many artifacts could be found. No one would tell them the exact location—generally, such knowledge was kept secret—and the information about the whereabouts of such cities and riches was passed down from father to son under strict vows of secrecy. A violation of these vows entailed a punishment that depended upon the importance of the secret betrayed, and the punishments could be quite severe.

After a great deal of preparation, Gurdjieff's party set off with a herd of sheep for food. They had several ingenious inventions, such as a sixty-foot ladder for seeing over sand storms, and stilts to walk on, plus plenty of luggage, and camels to carry it all. For weeks they traveled into the heart of the desert, traveling mostly at night, and guiding themselves by the stars. They weathered two horrendous sandstorms—the stilts and ladders coming in rather handy, he reports—and just as they neared their destination, spotted a herd of wild camels on a sand dune.

One of the members, one Soloviev, was a good hunter, and he ran off to shoot one of the camels. When he did not return after some time, the party went to look for him, and found that his throat had been bitten in two by a wild camel. There was no indication, apparently, that he had actually shot one of the camels. Stricken by grief at the death of their good friend, the party abandoned their expedition, buried Soloviev right there in the heart of the desert, and headed for civilization. The area of these occurances, and supposedly of the lost city, is the Keriyan Oasis, according to Gurdjieff.

Ancient Chinese legends, according to Churchward, say that the Uiger Empire was at its height about 15,000 B.C., just prior to its devastation. Churchward believes that the tomb dug up at Karakota is from this period. Churchward, an English colonel who lived a great deal of his life in India around the turn of the century, and traveled around the world looking for evidence of prehistoric civilizations, said he got much of his knowledge from ancient "Naacal" writings. These were preserved in certain monasteries in India and Tibet (though they do not appear to be from the libraries of the Great White Brotherhood—these seem to be something different).[24]

These records, he says, stated that the Uigers had reached a high state of civilization by the time of their demise. They knew architecture, medicine, mathematics, writing, astrology, mining, textile production, agriculture, and more, and practiced them all with great proficiency. In short, they were an amazing bunch, and make for fascinating adventure stories. Even if the legends of the Uiger Empire are only partly true, it does give one something to think about.

And just where did the Uigers come from? Apparently they emigrated from that intrepid lost continent to the east, the Pacific continent named Mu (and apparently Rutas) by the ancient Chinese, Dravidians, and Naacals. Today it is largely known as Lemuria, but that is another story. Oddly, there is a great deal of material to substantiate Churchward's theories. Ancient Indian and Tibetan sources say that the Uigers came from Mu, making the Uiger territory appear to have been something of a colony of Lemuria's until it sank about twenty-four thousand years ago.

It was all a wild notion, I had to admit, as Bill and I stepped out of the train at Turfan Railway Station. Bill took it all in stride. "Who knows what is going on in this crazy world?" he'd say. Civilization, as Bill liked to point out, was likely to go back a lot farther than just the couple of thousand years many historians would have us believe. Any adventurer on the trail of lost cities and ancient mysteries could tell you that!

Turfan is a genuine "Uiger" city, and one of the most interesting cities in Sinkiang. Once the capital of the last Uiger Kingdom, overrun by Ghengis Khan in the thirteenth century, it is in the Turfan depression, 504 feet below sea level, and the hottest place in China. For two thousand years it was an important stop on the northern Silk Road, and it often changed hands between the Chinese and the Turks. There is a nice guest house in Turfan, which is in fact the only hotel. It is called, aptly, The Turfan Guest House. Bill and I, however, stayed our first night at a small hostel by the railway station, which is forty kilometers from the actual town of Turfan.

At dusk, we walked around the small, dusty village at the railroad station. A blood-red sun set silently over the brown, flat buildings. The last few vendors were packing up their sunflower seeds, watermelons, sunglasses, and pocket knives as we walked down the almost-empty streets. We had dinner in the cafeteria of our hostel, which was the ground floor of an old, two-story, concrete drab building. The restaurant consisted of a few old tables set out on the concrete floor, and a primitive kitchen at the back.

We both happily ate a humungous bowl of noodles each, a plate of green peppers (capiscum), and a plate of eggplant, both fried up with tomatoes. The atmosphere was great: dusty, tired workers, perhaps railroad employees, coming in out of the streets, all of them Han Chinese. Their eyes were intent on their food, and they hardly cast us a glance. They'd sit down, dust off their gray workers' jackets, and dig into the soup. I sighed. We were really in Central Asia; we were really among the working people!

One grizzled old man sat opposite us at our table, indulging in the free tea the cafeteria gave out and eating some steamed wheat buns he had brought in himself, apparently being too poor to buy food at the kitchen. We watched him for awhile, and he us. Later we gave him some of our fried capsicum and he took it silently, getting up for some chopsticks after a few minutes, and then hungrily digging in. This was really the hinterland of China, and for most Han Chinese, something of an exile spot. For us, it was a great adventure in humanity in one of the world's most remote areas.

We retired upstairs to the bunks, made of steel and strung with rope. Fortunately we had our sleeping bags, as there was no bedding. In the morning we woke up early to catch a bus into Turfan at eight o'clock. It was still dark outside, and a wind was blowing fiercely through the town. We lay in our snug sleeping bags listening to the raging, dry, dust-blowing wind howling down the streets of that lonely railroad town. If only we could have stayed in bed all morning savoring that feeling of being there in that forgotten village! But we swung out of bed, had some hot water to drink, put on our packs, and hit the street. The wind bit and stung! I had a bandana over my face, but it didn't keep out the sand and grit that flew down the dusty, dark corridors and alleys. We fought our way up the street to the bus station. To the east was the sun, rising out of the black sandy wind. With a mighty grunt, we swung off our packs and made it into the shelter of the bus!

Not long after, we were safely ensconsed in the Turfan Guest House, a pleasant and colorful hotel for tourists. There is live folk dancing and music in the evenings and the staff is very helpful to tourists. Bill and I generally ate at the market down the street, where they sold hami melons, mutton kebabs, nan or rice pilau; you might be anywhere in the middle east. There is all kinds of produce, and Turfan is especially famous for its grapes.

Turfan is good for several days of sightseeing, and is a quiet, small, picturesque place that seemed ideal in many ways for the tourist. There were donkey carts to ride in, for those who didn't want to walk. One good excursion was a walk to the Imin Mosque with its Suliman's Minaret just on the eastern edge of town. It was built in 1776, and its central minaret is a large, tall, mud-brick tower that commands quite a good view, and is rather impressive. It was fun to walk along the streets, and peek into the courtyard of people's homes. Often, the kids or the whole family would come out and have a look at the foreign visitors.

There are several ancient cities to visit around Turfan, now ghost towns, but not quite "lost." One is Jiaohe (confluence of rivers) about ten miles to the southwest. It was an ancient Chinese garrison, and was destroyed by the advancing armies of Genghis Khan. Deserted for seven hundred years, not a great deal of it is still intact. In better shape is Gaochang, which is to the west, near Flaming Mountain, a famous place from classical Chinese mythology. Gaochang was a staging post along the Silk Road reached through a pass in the Flaming Mountains (so named because of their bright red sandy soil). It was also destroyed by the Mongols, but was left in better condition.

Bill and I hitched out toward Flaming Mountain, after a bowl of fried greenbeans, onions, capiscum and mutton with a piece of nan at a small restaurant in the market. Hitching was slow, mainly because there weren't any vehicles around. We got a lift in a donkey cart for a while, but then eventually flagged down a truck, which took us to Flaming Mountain.

We checked out Gaochang, a two-mile walk from the crossroads of the Gaochang-Thousand Buddha Caves. Back at the crossroads, we hung out at at small tea house cum truck stop. We caught another truck up into the Flaming Mountain. Nearby, at the foot of the mountain, is the Turfan Cemetary, where hundreds of Chinese officials were buried, including some from the Tang dynasty (618-907 A.D.) and Jin Dynasty (265-420 A.D.). Some of the corpses are on display and a few are mum- mified. We hitchhiked back into Turfan, first getting a ride on a tractor, and then a ride in a truck back into town.

We enjoyed one last night in Turfan, sitting out on the street, eating the flat bread (nan) with mutton and vegetables, and watching the people in donkey carts go by. The moon was rising, and from the Guest House nearby, the music of the folk dancing could be heard. Sinkiang indeed had its own flavor, a blend of Chinese and Persian, and it was thoroughly enjoyable. The great days of the ancient Uiger empire had long since past. Things are a lot different now, but it is still a great place.

By noon the next day, we were on the train heading east across the Gobi desert, on our way to Dunhuang. The scenery was vast and expansive. I grinned like a fool with the joy of being on the road, traveling east across the Gobi. I thought hard as I looked out the window at the bleak, mountainous scenery before us. To the south was the Tibetan Plateau, and the Kun Lun Mountains, although they could not as yet be seen through the desert. How mysterious and mystical it all seemed. Lost cities in the sands of the Gobi, tunnels and cave communities in Tibet, and somewhere to our south, in the wasteland of the Kun Lun, was supposed to be the Great White Brotherhood, if it existed.

I was suddenly struck by another unusual story I had heard. Only about a hundred and fifty miles to the south of us was the Lop Nor desert and salt marshes, a depression where the occasional waters of the River Kongqi empty. There were once a number of oases and cities along one of the major routes for the old Silk Road. Though today is virtually uninhabitable desert, in the past it must have been a rich, and fertile area. Climatic changes both recently and in ancient times seem to have drastically changed the landscape.

In *Ruins of Desert Cathay*, Sir Aurel Stein crosses the desert on his way to some ruins first discovered by the explorer Sven Hedin a few years before him. Stein's caravan moves across a waterless salt desert for days, where "remains of flint implements and coarse pottery, manifestly neolithic, continued to crop up in plenty at frequent intervals. There could be no doubt that we were still passing over ground which had seen human occupation during prehistoric times. These finds presented an increased interest, since we were now well within the area where Hedin had been led to located his earlier Lop Nor lake depression." [88]

Stein was finding piles of pottery which was many thousands of years old, according to him. Furthermore, this pottery was in an area that Sven Hedin believed to be the ancient lake bed. This posed a mystery for Stein. What had caused the climatic change? Could a cataclysm have been responsible for both the climate change and the piles of "washed-up" pottery?

In 1949, Lop Nor became China's principal nuclear and missile testing site. Lop Nor has always been shrouded in mystery; it is just north of the desolate Kun Lun range where the Valley of the Immortals (Great White Brotherhood) was said to be. Lop Nor is totally uninhabited, and persons are known to see mysterious things and occasionally appear or disappear here.

It became even more mysterious, when, in 1979, the prominent Chinese scientist Peng Jiamu, who was a well-known biochemist, was with several other scientists in a jeep while they were off in the sand dunes doing some tests. His friends left him in the jeep while they went off to do some testing, and when they returned, after several hours, he had utterly vanished! It was a complete mystery; huge numbers of troops and aircraft were mobilized to search for him, but no clue was ever found. One theory was that he had been kidnapped and taken over the border (thousands of miles away) to the Soviet Union. The official press published a report saying, rather shakily, the "investi- gations prove the theory that he lost his way while looking for water and that his body was buried in the shifting sands."

This didn't convince me, but who knows what happened to Peng? Was he taken to the "Valley of the Immortals?" Somehow, I doubted it. Perhaps he fell into some underground tomb, or discovered some lost city, or something even more incredible— what could it be? Why was Lop Nor such a mysterious place filled with legends?

It has been suggested that certain areas of the world have what are termed "gravity vortexes" which cause certain anomalies. The Bermuda Triangle is one such area. Advocates of the "World Grid" theory of power points, ley lines, and vortex areas claim that most atomic testing and space programs are purposely done at such spots. [89,90] Was this part of the secret of Lop Nor? I would not find out the answers to these things on this trip as Lop Nor is a highly sensitive and restricted area. It is doubtful that foriegners will be allowed into the region for some time to come.

Oddly, too, I reflected, Sinkiang, the Lop Nor Region espec- ially, is the center of a UFO mystery, according to many Ufologists. Though it is difficult to ascertain whether there are an enormous amount of UFO sightings in this area—largely due to the Chinese government's slience on the subject—this part of China is usually considered a very active UFO area. Is it possible that some of these UFOs are airships of the Great White Brotherhood, left over from the vimanas and vailixi of Rama and Atlantis?

Nicholas Roerich reported in his travel diary in 1926 that his party had seen a huge, shiny oval disc speeding across the sky in this very area. A left over vimana on it's way to the Valley of the Immortals? King Solomon's famous flying disc? Mass hallucination?

Another odd report is the rather bizarre suggestion of an enigmatic "mystery satellite," dubbed the "Black Knight" that has been supposedly orbiting the earth since at least 1957 (when it was first discovered, I suppose). It has been suggested that the Lop Nor desert is its base or tracking station.[33] The idea of a satellite such as this seemed rather doubtful to me, and even assuming that it existed, it would indicate a man-made, rather than alien-made, craft, and what purpose it might serve is difficult to imagine. Still, here in the Lop Nor, the Bermuda Triangle of Central Asia, anything was possible!

I looked out the window; behind the train a dark, shadowed sun was setting into the Gobi desert. The whole horizon was hazy with dust. The light cast an orange hue on Bill's face as he gazed outside. Life, I had always felt, was rather strange, even though it was fun. Out here in the Gobi desert, it seemed to get a little stranger, as if life was being intensified by the Central Asian sun. What new wonders and adventures awaited at the next turn of the bend? What great spectacle would we behold? Life was strange—and superbly wonderful!

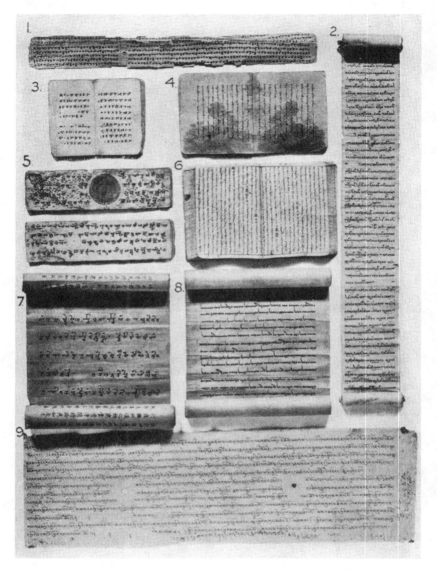

ANCIENT MANUSCRIPTS IN SANSKRIT, CENTRAL - ASIAN BRAHMI, SOGDIAN, MANICHAEAN - TURKISH, RUNIC TURKI, UIGUR, TIBETAN, FROM WALLED-UP TEMPLE LIBRARY, 'THOUSAND BUDDHAS,' TUN-HUANG.

Scale, one-seventh.

1. Sanskrit Prajna-paramita text on palm leaves. 2. Roll with Manichaean 'Confession of Sins' in early Turkish. 3. Book in Runic Turki. 4, 6. Uigur texts in book form. 5. Pothi in Central-Asian Brahmi script. 7. Text in cursive Central-Asian Brahmi written on reverse of Chinese MS. roll. 8. Roll with Sogdian text. 9. Leaf of Tibetan Buddhist Pothi.

From Sir Aurel Stein's *Ruins of Desert Cathay* (1912).

One of the scrolls written in an unknown language, found in
the secret library in a cave in Dunhuang, China in 1910 by
Sir Aurel Stein. They are now in the British Museum.

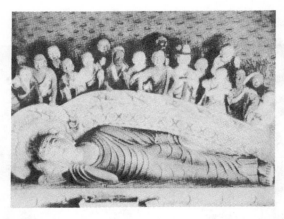

The "sleeping Buddha" in grotto 58 at Dunhuang. Among the various figures behind the figure are what appear to be American Indians.

Two Bodhisatvas from the manuscripts found in the secret library discovered at Dunhuang by a Taoist monk.

Colonel James Churchward

An Uighur queen and her consort.

Two Bodhisatvas from excavations at Karakota by the Russian archaeologist Paul Kosloff. Churchward believed that these figures were ancient Uiger royalty from a time when the Gobi Desert was fertile.

Courtesy of P. K. Kosloff

This photo was taken by the Russian archaeologist Paul Kosloff and was published Kosloff's friend Colonel James Churchward in his book *The Sacred Symbols of Mu* (1933). Kosloff discovered it in the mysterious ruins of Karakota in the Gobi Desert. Churchward believed it showed the Dual Principle of the first man. He claimed it that Karakota was the capital of a Uiger Empire that existed from 20,000 BC to aproximately 3,000 BC. While Karakota was inhabited briefly by Muslims it has apparently been in decline for thousands of years.

Chapter Eighteen

MONGOLIA AND NORTHERN CHINA:

SOJOURN TO THE TOMB
OF GENGHIS KHAN

Achieve results, but through violence?
Force is followed by loss of strength.
That is not the way of the Tao.
That which goes against the Tao comes to an early end.
—Lao Tzu, *Tao Te Ching*

By early morning we were in Liuyan, a small station on the Urumchi to Lanchou line, from which we could get a bus to Dunhuang. I recalled how I had gotten out to look for a snack on the platform the night before, when we had stopped at a small, dusty station somewhere in the Gobi. Instead, I found an old Han Chinese man, wrinkled and gray, with a bag slung over his shoulder, trying to get onto the train at the dining car.

I stopped for a moment, at first curious, but became more involved when the controller told him to go farther down the train. Becoming more and more involved, I went with the old man down to the next open door, but the people standing around it wouldn't let him in. I tried to help, but they jabbered away at me, shaking their heads, and even though I understand some Chinese, I could not understand what they were saying. It seemed safe to assume that this old codger, who seemed seventy or eighty years old, did not have a ticket, and was looking for a free ride.

I looked at him with a tear in my eye, as he glanced at me, his lower lip slightly extruded and a glazed, sorrowful look on his wrinkled, pained face. I thought, "What does it matter whether this guy, so old and wizened, has a ticket. Let him on!" Well, if it were my train, I'd have let him on. But then, if every old man in China were allowed to ride the trains for free, what might happen next?

I took him down to one more door, giving him some encouragement, but a car attendant, a young girl, started to yell at me, so I left the old man there, the girl shouting at him, and I never found out what happened after that. It was chilly on the train that night, and the attendant woke us at dawn to tell us that we were in Liuyuan. We jumped off the train in that chill early morning light, and another adventure began!

It is about one hundred miles to Dunhuang (or Tun-huang) from Liuyan, the closest railway station, and there are normally two buses that make the trip daily; one early in the morning, and the other around noon. Bill grabbed a seat up front. The bus wasn't too crowded, and I took a seat in back, where a bunch of traveling Chinese guys happily practiced their English with me. We talked of China and America—a typical conversation. They were a gay bunch, on their way to Dunhuang, and tourists themselves as well. They came from some nearby town on the railway line between Urumchi and Lanchou.

Bill and I stayed at the cheaper hotel in Dunhuang: the Overseas Chinese Hotel, near the bus station. It cost about a dollar fifty a night. The town is very small, and nothing is more than one or two blocks away from anything else.

Dunhuang is something of a lost city in its own right. It was the last stop on the Silk Road for caravans heading out of China and into the vast lands of Central Asia on their way to the Middle East and Europe. Fifteen miles to the southeast of town is the "Cave of a Thousand Buddhas," a sanctuary of several hundred caves and grottos cut into sandstone cliffs and elaborately decorated with paintings and statues of Buddha. In the fourth and fifth centuries B.C., Dunhuang flourished as a center of Buddhist culture, as did so many other oases and towns along the Silk Road. Much of Central Asia was Buddhist just prior to the rise of Islam, which swept well into China and India, as well as conquering most of Central Asa.

Dunhuang has also been the center of an archaeological controversy for the last seventy years or so. A hoard of Buddhist manuscripts, paintings, books, and other writings were found in one of the caves in 1900. A Taoist monk named Wang Tao-Shih found this hidden library in one of the caves. A room had been walled up with bricks sometime in the eleventh century in order to keep the treasures from falling into the hands of invading barbarians. For eight hundred years they laid there, preserved by the dry desert air, remaining in excellent condition. Then the famous British/Hungarian explorer and archaeologist Sir Aurel Stein passed through Dunhuang in 1907, and convinced the monk to allow him to view the treasure, still kept in the secret cave. Stein's books *On Ancient Central Asian Tracks* and *Ruins of Desert Cathay* describe his findings in the secret library, which proved to be an archaeological gold mine.

There were Buddhist texts in many languages: Chinese, Tibetan, Sanskrit, Runic Turki, Uiger, Central Asian Brahmi and in the most ancient known languages in Central Asia; Khotanese, Saka, Kuchean and Tocharish.[88,147] Some texts are in languages that are completely unknown. Just how old some of these manuscripts are is impossible to tell. Many ancient Central Asian libraries were reputed to contain texts that were literally thousands of years old, diligently copied over and over and the originals could easily have come from the ancient Uiger Empire, the Rama Empire, or other unknown civilizations of the Gobi. One manuscript had fragments of an ancient map showing parts of a continent in the Pacific Ocean! [31, 59, 88]

The oldest known printed book was found here, a Buddhist text printed in the year 868 A.D. Stein was able to purchase a portion of the library and made off with twenty-four packing cases of manuscripts and five of art relics, all of which ended up in the British Museum. Today, a bitter debate exists over the ownership of these documents. The rest finally made their way to the Imperial Court in Peking, and many Chinese feel that the rest of the library should be returned to China.[59, 88]

There are a number of odd legends connected with the caves at Dunhuang. One is that the first caverns were not built by Buddhist monks but by someone who had preceded them by thousands of years. The structures were later built to hide labyrinths stretching under vast areas of Central Asia. These tunnels—part of the legends of the Shamballists and the Agarthi—presumably would lead to cave communities, or hidden monasteries. Or, assuming the tunnels exist, they may be relics of some other culture (that of the Atlanteans or even of the Uigers) which had its own purposes for them.[31]

Mildred Cable, in her book *The Gobi Desert* [147] tells the curious tale of a Chinese priest who was travelling back toward Tunwang from a lake two days walk away when a great sandstorm came up in the desert just as darkness fell. As he peered about, seeking shelter, he thought he saw a light, as if from a double lantern. Walking toward the strange light, he found himself at a place where there were three small monuments. According to the priest, the light still moved on, and he followed it through an opening in a cliff, and down a steep path which led him toward a river. Just there the river flowed in a very deep bed, and the path he took was so difficult to descend, even by day, that it is difficult to imagine how he got down in the dark, and in such rough weather. "However, he safely reached a ledge on the bank and felt his way to an opening like the mouth of a cave, which was a welcome shelter from the wind. There he lay down and slept. When he awoke it was daylight, and from the walls of the cave he saw paintings of holy men looking down on him. He tells us that he got up, explored farther and found various other small opeings leading into caves hollowed from the cliff. He pushed on to Tunhwang and immediately reported the matter. Some of us went out to see the place, and found that it was as he said, and that a quantity of loose gravel, recently washed from the bank, had left these caves exposed."[147] Mildred Cable and companions visited the spot, known as Nan-hu.

How many other desert caves and secret libraries are waiting to be discovered in the Gobi Desert? It takes a certain amount of courage and faith to follow a supernatural light through a sand storm among cliffs and ravines to find ancient dwellings, to say the least.

§§§

Bill and I took the local bus out to the caves early the next morning. The bus left daily at eight o'clock. It went past many fields, out into the sand dunes, and then suddenly, there were sandstone cliffs! There was a small admission to pay, and then we wandered around the caves for a couple of hours. Of the five hundred or so caves, only about forty are open to the public, and photographs are forbidden. Many of the caves contain wooden statues of the Buddha covered with plaster. At the southern end of the caves are two huge sitting Buddhas, with a nice pagoda entrance to the largest, and a gigantic sleeping Buddha.

Interestingly, in grotto No. 58, there is an altar with a sleeping Buddha, behind whom is a crowd of faithful people (statues), from all over the world, including some figures which show by their clothes and facial features that they are like American Indians! And these are supposedly from the fourth Century A.D.!

We climbed to the top of the cliffs; a vast sand dune plateau, with a few markers for incoming caravans. The caves closed around noon, and the public bus heads back for the town of Dunhuang, so we had to go back. There is a small snack bar at the caves, so lunch could be had there.

Back in Dunhuang, Bill and I decided to rent bicycles and ride out to the vast dunes to the south of town. The Dunhuang Guesthouse rented bikes to tourists, and soon we were off through the streets, past the farms and occasional camel carts to the edge of the desert.

The dunes looked like huge Chinese dinosaurs sleeping silently in the sun, waiting for their time to arise. We climbed up the backbone of one, several hundred feet up through the reddish-tan sand to the top, where we had a great view of the setting sun and the vast humped dunes stretching away to the Altun Shan mountains to the south, and the Tibetan plateau beyond. We were watching the scenery from on the top of the sand dunes as the sun set, when suddenly we noticed that a troop of Chinese soldiers was coming up our sand dune after us!

There were about eight of them, dressed as Red Guards and carrying the Chinese version of an AK-47 assault rifle. They were coming right for us, their rifles ready, having presumably spotted us on patrol. Like condemned men, we waited to be arrested. But they had just come up for the sunset as well, and sat about ten feet away to catch the view while Bill and I took photos of them. Some gave us friendly nods and smiled, but mostly they just ignored us.

It was dusk as we rode our bikes back the few miles to Dunhuang. There was still an orange glow on the dunes and a silvery sliver of a moon was rising in the east over the dunes. We had to stop to take in that breathtaking scene: cornfields, trees, sand dunes looking like mountains, and a new moon! Back at the town, we returned our bikes, and went out to one of the local restaurants to have some momos (Chinese dumplings with meat or vegetables inside), some corn bread, and a bottle of Chinese sparkling apple wine, which was good and refreshing.

§§§

That next morning we were off again to Liuyuan so we could catch the train to Lanzhou. The train was three hours late, and Bill and I decided to ride this trip in the hard seats, for the experience and to save some money. We were given two seats that were reserved for us. We fought our way through the car to our seats. There are four to a side, facing each other. We had to ask two Chinese guys in blue to get up, as they were in our seats, and they reluctantly collected their bags and moved to the back of the crowded car.

The hard seats are filled with all sorts of characters, the flotsam and jetsam of Chinese travelers, including young men in their Red Guard uniforms—green shirts, green slacks, a green Mao cap with a red star in the front and red lapels on the collars. There were lots of wizened, white-haired old men, with wisps of hair on their wrinkled faces and chins. Some were so cool that nothing could faze them, while others looked tired and nervous, holding their tea cups on the way to the hot water boiler at the end of each car, where they would fill up their mugs of tea.

One old man had on the most padded grey cotton suit that I had ever seen. He looked like a Himalayan mountaineer in full down clothing. He leaned against the window, putting his head against a corner of the sill, and fell immediately asleep. He had a number of big bumps on his head, and I wondered if they were from the occasional jolts of the train.

Another old character came aboard at a windy, dust-ridden station in the desert, hauling a huge bag of grain. Confidently, he plopped it down in the aisle right next to our seat and sat down on it. He looked around with a calm, slight smile, adjusted his little blue Mao cap and leaned back to enjoy the journey. His sack of grain looked as comfortable as one of our beanbag chairs. A Chinese family across from us immediately attacked him with a barrage of Mandarin chatter. Why does he have to sit here? Why doesn't he move his bag down to the end of the car? Can't he see he's blocking the aisle?

He just grinned back at them and looked down the car. Nothing could bother this old fellow, I thought. He acted as if he were thinking, "You lucky people, I'm going to sit next to you."

There were also women, usually mothers with young children sitting on their laps eating some fried bread. Without the slightest bit of warning, mothers will swing the children onto the floor, have them squat, and the children poop or pee right there in the aisle. The children's pants are already split up the bottom for just such emergencies. Later, an attendant comes along and mops the floor.

The Chinese have the bad habit of constantly spitting on the floor at their feet, or at your feet, for that matter. It is something they do quite often, no matter where they are. They would never spit out the window even if they were right next to an open one, yet spitting on the floor is considered appropriate.

During dinner, an attendant came through the car, selling meal tickets. Bill and I bought one, and an hour later, a big cart was wheeled through with little square tins of rice, pork, and veggies. We ate ours up, and settled back in our seats—padded at least, but not very comfortable for sleeping. Sitting opposite each other next to the window, we took our shoes off, and put our legs up on the opposite seat. Using some of our extra clothing for pillows, we dozed through the night. In the morning we awoke to find people sleeping beneath our seats. In fact, there was someone sleeping beneath every seat.

At breakfast, while I was sitting there having a steamed bun, a round-faced, cute little girl about five, in reed shoes and a blue jumper, came over to sit with us and pass a few minutes. She gazed at Bill and me in turn, and then, satisfied that we were for real, moved back to rejoin her parents.

People amused themselves on the train with Chinese chess (similar to our chess), or played cards, and others played with a small live tortoise on a table between seats. Some spent their time fighting their way through the carriage to get to the water boiler at the end of the car, where there was always a long line for a cup of tea.

We arrived in Lanzhou later that afternoon. In past history, it was the main garrison post linking the Silk Road with the interior of China, and so a strategically important city. When the Chinese built the railway from Lanzhou to the northwest, the city suddenly became an important industrial center as well. Today it has a population of over two million, and is thought by many to be the most heavily polluted city in China. It is a rather drab, gray industrial town with little to offer the tourist. White Pagoda Mountain offers a view of the city for those who want to see all the factories. From Lanzhou, you can fly to Lhasa; or you might go by train to Koko Nor, also known as Qinghai Lake, in Qinghai Province just near Lanzhou.

Qinghai is actually part of Tibet, and in fact, the present Dalai Lama of Tibet was born in Qinghai. Qinghai is closed to foreigners at present, but may be opened soon. It is a vast, unpopulated area, with a reputation for being China's prison-labor state, where undesirables were sent to help develop the area. Koko Nor is a beautiful inland salt sea which supports a healthy fishing industry. It also has its own monster, something similar to the Loch Ness monster in Scotland.

Tibetan herdsmen have reported seeing a huge animal surface on hot days, and a news story reported that some fishermen near an island in the middle of the lake saw a huge animal rise out of the water nearby. It was black and yellow, about thirteen or fourteen meters long, and the shape of an overturned boat. How such an aquatic animal—similar to those reported in North America, Scotland and Africa, as well as those occasionally found in the ocean—got into a lake in the middle of Central Asia is quite a mystery. If indeed it is true, this animal's existence would tend to support the theory that much of Central Asia, and in particular the Gobi, was once an inland sea of sorts. Many Central Asian and Indian legends say just that.

Bill and I walked about Lanzhou, watching people, and

being watched in return ourselves. We booked berths on a train into Inner Mongolia for that evening, and decided not to spend the night in Lanzhou. This time we had an overnight hard berth (three-tier berth) to Yinchuan in Ningxia province. Ningxia Province is also closed to foreigners, like Qinghai, but what the heck, we were on our way to Baotou in Inner Mongolia and had to pass through the state.

It is known as an especially poor and backward province, mostly desert, with a mixed population of Muslims—about one-third of the four million people—the rest being typically Confucian-Buddhist-ancestor worshipping Han Chinese. We slept soundly, and woke early the next morning, just before arriving in Yinchuan.

We didn't have much time before we had to catch the train to Baotou in Inner Mongolia. We sat in the hard seats for awhile, enjoying the view of sand dunes and mountains across the Huanghe River. The trip took only a day and we arrived in Baotou in the late afternoon. Suddenly, a conductor came up to us and took us back to the berths, giving us a seat. I looked at him, a thin, nervous-looking man in his forties, clean-shaven and Han Chinese, in a blue conductor's uniform with a blue hat and the railroad insignia, a red rail.

I told him that we had only paid for a hard seat, not a berth, but he said that didn't matter. He did not speak English, and we conversed in Mandarin and used our phrase books, pointing to the phrase in Chinese that we wanted to say. The train chugged on, and I got off at one station to take a photograph, but the same conductor, who was watching us like a hawk, told me that I shouldn't take any photos. Politely, I put away my camera.

Later, at another station, I was buying some candy on the platform when a young schoolgirl in a white shirt and blue cotton pants came up to me and told me in English that she was an English student.

"That's nice," I said, meaning it.

"Yes, I've been studying English for many years now, but you are the first English person that I have ever gotten to talk to!" she told me, beaming.

"Really?" I said. "Well, it is a pleasure to talk to you. Where are you going?"

"I am traveling to..." she began, when suddenly the conductor, the same man I had dealt with earlier, came up to us on the platform, rather gruffly asked the girl where she worked and then told her that she shouldn't be talking to me. He left, without saying a word to me. I gave him a dirty look after the girl told me what he had said, and then reluctantly said, "I'd better go."

"Bye!" I said, heading back to the car to tell Bill what had happened. Then at the very next station, somewhere in Inner Mongolia, a young man in a gray worker's suit came to us in our car. He apparently worked at the station. We had a basic English conversation that went something like this:

"Hello, what is your name?" he asked. He had a thin mustache, and looked to be in his mid-twenties. I thought he must be fairly well-educated to speak English as well as he did.

"My name is David," I said.

"My name is Bill," said Bill.

"What is your name?" I asked the young man.

"My name is Liu. Where are you going?" he asked us.

"We are going to Batou," I told him, enunciating clearly.

"Where are you from?" he asked, trying to remember his phrases. He was obviously delighted to see us here, in this backwater of northern China.

"We are from America," we started to say, when suddenly, like some ghoul in hiding, the aforementioned conductor swooped out of nowhere and began asking the young man in an angry voice why he was talking to us, and what we were talking about. His thin, mousey face was distorted with suspicion as he questioned the hapless youth.

The kid suddenly turned to us. "I must go," he said, and left with the conductor.

A moment later Bill looked out the window and said, "Wow, that conductor is hitting that kid!" I looked out the window onto the platform of the tiny little desert village to see the conductor pushing the boy and yelling at him loudly. I just couldn't take it anymore. I'm normally a very tolerant person, but the old guy had pushed me beyond my limits. Fortunately, Bill had not witnessed the earlier run-ins with this man, whom I realized was a throwback to the famous Cultural Revolution of the sixties and early seventies when everyone was encouraged to spy on everyone else and foreigners were held in deep suspicion. I rushed out onto the platform where the old man was hitting the kid, determined to do what I could.

A crowd had formed, and as I strode quite forcefully down the platform, people turned their attention to me instead of the fight. The conductor stopped hitting the kid and turned to look at me just as I reached them. The kid was red in the face and stuttering. About the only thing that I could do, I realized, was to try and appear a lot more important than I really was, and swing some non-existent weight around in an effort to lessen the kid's burden and

347

punishment.

I stood there in front of them silently for a moment while everyone looked at me, wondering what I would do. I put my hand on the kid's shoulder to comfort him and then took out my notebook and pen that I always carried with me, and began very slowly and deliberately to take down the conductor's badge number that was embroidered just above his breast pocket.

"Yes, take down his number and report him!" said the kid in excellent English.

Slowly I wrote down the number and made it very clear that I strongly disapproved of the conductor's actions and intended to report him (which I had no intention of doing, as I didn't know who to report him to anyway). I stood there for a moment glaring at the conductor, while everyone calmed down, then we went back to our car just before the train pulled out. Bill remarked that it was odd that this English-speaking kid was sweeping up some dusty backwater train station. He was probably there as a disciplinary measure, anyway.

Shortly after, the conductor came to our compartment, this time with an armed Red Guard, and asked us in Chinese who we were and what we were doing in China. He also asked why I had taken down his number and what we intended to do with it. We told him that we were guests of the China National Travel Service, and that we intended to report him to that organization. Satisfied, and maybe carrying a bit more caution into his future dealings with foreigners, he left us.

§§§

As the sun was setting later that afternoon, and we were nearly to Baotou, I thought about Inner and Outer Mongolia. Centuries ago, even before that larger-than-life Mongol Genghis Khan created the world's largest empire, the Chinese had some control over Mongolia. They called the area just beyond the Great Wall "Inner Mongolia" and the more distant part "Outer Mongolia." The Gobi desert, or at least the bulk of it, lay between "Inner" and "Outer" Mongolia.

The history of Mongolia is one of the least-known and strangest in the world. Even today, most of Mongolia remains unsurveyed and "wild." The government exercises as much control as it can over the more remote areas, though it is minimal, as roads are scarce. Mongolia is about one-third the size of the United States, with the population the same, approximately, as Michigan. As a country, it is quite similar to the great plains of the United States, and the non-desert areas can easily remind one of eastern Wyoming. Most people in Inner and Outer Mongolia are nomadic herders who move with their herds seeking pastures. Today, however, the Chinese government has resettled a lot of Han Chinese in Inner Mongolia, making the Mongolians a minority in their own "autonomous region."

"Gobi" is the Mongolian word for any broad expanse of semi-barren country, and the area now known as the Gobi desert is a true desert area thinly covered with gravel and sand. There is a scant covering of grass and scrub brush, but very little water. The Gobi does, however, support quite a few wild animals. The desert is known for its fierce sand storms, cold nights, and blistering days. What created the sands of the Gobi is something of a mystery. Perhaps it was a great flood/cataclysm, or perhaps most of the Gobi was an inland sea at one time. Both theories are supported by various sources, although it seems fairly certain that the Gobi, much like the Sahara, was fertile and inhabited at a time in the not-so-distant past.

The Gobi is known for its "Singing Sands"—wind blowing over the sand dunes, causing a constant sound that varies from a roll of drums to a deep chant. There is a hill with a similar phenomenon in the Ordos Desert to the west, located today in China, called the Ongon Obo: a hill that when walked upon produces "the sound of music!" I suppose that a hollow depression in the hill—part of a cavern or tunnel—could cause such a sound.

Archaeologist Roy Chapman Andrews, on his famous expeditions into the Gobi in the nineteen-twenties, found relics of what he called the "mysterious dune dwellers." These people, according to Dr. Andrews, "inhabited the Gobi desert in the many millions—more than there ever have been in historical or traditional times." Sven Hedin, another great explorer, traced the culture as far west as Sinkiang, and there is evidence that these people used agriculture, as well-made mortars and pestles were found in the desert.[30]

Dr. Andrews felt these people migrated elsewhere because the Gobi was drying up. Mongolia shows signs of being the oldest known dry-land area in the world, never having been submerged for the last one hundred fifty million years, or so Andrews thought. This allows for a great wealth of fossil evidence; for instance, fossils of the largest known land mammal ever to have been found, a shovel-tusked mastodon called a *Baluchitherium*, were found by Dr. Andrews' team. While it is possible that

Mongolia may have been "high and dry" for the last one hundred fifty million years, it is also possible, and in my opinion, likely, that huge tidal waves have washed over the area—witness the mammoth-bone graveyards in Siberia. Much of the ivory used in billiard balls and piano keys in the 1800s came from huge mountains of bones and ivory found in Siberia, Alaska and Arctic islands. These giant piles of ivory were apparently created when huge mammoth herds were suddenly picked up by tidal waves, pulverized and washed up into various piles thoughout the arctic. This occuring during a poleshift circa 10,000 BC according to most cataclysmic geologists, including James Churchward, who wrote the popular "Mu" books and was keenly interested in the Gobi area, deeming it a key piece of the puzzle in unraveling earth's mysterious past.

While Andrews felt that the past inhabitants were fairly primitive "dune dwellers," living in sand dunes beside now dried-up lakes, could it be that these were the remains of the highly sophisticated Uigers, their artifacts washed up onto sand dunes during a tidal wave?

Even stranger is a report from the Soviet journal Smena (no. 8, 1961) about a joint Russian-Chinese paleontological expedition under the direction of Dr. Chow Ming Chen, which discovered in the Gobi Desert a fossilized print of shoe with ribbed sole. Members of the who carefully examined the shoe-print were quick to recognize that it was not the footmark of any animal, for the ribbing was too straight and regular to be of natural origin. While the fossilized footprint of a shoe that is fifteen to thousand thousand years old may not seem completely out of the realm of possibility, the team had a completely different date! The fossil was found in a sandstone formation of a type in which Roy Chapman Andrews had found dinosaur fossils pronounced to be fifteen million years old!

There are a large number of odd artifacts and fossils similar to the Gobi footprint which defy normal geological dating and time scale. Considering that the fossil is genuine, I would venture to say that it is probably not fifteen million years old, but rather of a much more recent geological period, say hundreds of thousands of years ago. This would mean that geological change happens in a much more rapid and violent way, and that many fossils are much older than said by most paleontologists, and much of our geological dating is wildly off.

A popular legend in Central Asia is that the Tarim Basin was a fresh water sea before 3145 BC. Around this inland sea was the last surviving remnants of the golden age of Ancient Civilization still survived. The Gobi desert was fertile and on the shores of large body of water. The Kun Lun mountains were along the southern edge of this sea.

The Pamir Plateau, on the western side of the lake is said by some Biblical historians to have been the original garden of Eden. In Genesis 4:10 we read "...A lake also sprang up in Eden to supply the Garden with waters, and from there it divided and became four rivers." The four rivers were named: Pison, Gihen, Hiddekel and Euphrates. Because the Euphrates is mentioned, it has been assumed that Eden was in Mesopotamia. However, E. Raymond Capt and F. Haberman assert that this is because the Hebrew Eden story is coming from the Sumerian Gilgamesh epic who would favor their own rivers (the Tigris joins the Euphrates).

The original Eurphrates, according to them, is the river Syr Daria whose original name was the Jaxartes River which now flows to the Aral Sea. The Indus River is the Pison and Tarim River is believed to the Hiddekel. According to Haberman & Capt, "The Oxus is still called by the natives the Dgihun or Gihon. The Pamir plateau of today is, of course, a different place from what it was six thousand years ago. At that time the whole of Asia was lower than it is today. A large inland sea covered the steppes of southern Siberia of which the Caspian and Aral Seas are remnants. Over the now frozen steppes of Northern Siberia roamed the mammoth and sabre-toothed tiger. All the indications are that northern Siberia then had a semi-tropical climate, and ideal conditions prevailed on the Pamir Plateau. The group of Alpine lakes, which now constitute the headwaters of the four rives, may once have been one lake."

Interestingly, Haberman and Capt believe that the early Hebrews originaly migrated from the Pamir Plateau to UR in Sumeria around 3100 BC. Later the Biblical progenator Abraham migrated with his wife Sarah and their clan into the Arabian Peninsula about . They eventually settled along the Red Sea in what is now Saudi Arabia aroun 1800 BC. Later they sold themselves into captivity to Egypt because of a drought. Around 1200 BC Moses led his people out of Egypt in the celebrated Exodus to the Jerusalem area.

A few generations later the Hebrews had built a magnificent capital, were extremely wealthy and influential, and King Solomon allegedly flew back into the Pamir region in an airship, according to Central Asian legend related by Roerich and others.

Central Asia has often been the focus historians. Many things, including the "Caucasian Race" and most European dilects stem from Central Asia. Esoteric schools like The Lemurian Fellowship and The Stelle Group maintain that a large number of citizens were airlifted out of Atlantis into Central Asia before Atlantis destroyed itself circa 9,000 BC. It has also been said that Atlantis ultimately destroyed itself with a radio-type weapon that it was using to shoot through the earth, backfired and destroyed themselves.

Should a scenario like this actually be the case, then perhaps the Tarim Basin civilizations continued until 3145 BC when another change in the earth's crust turned the area into a desert. The Pamir plateau was still habitable, though it did not have the same climate as before. In this theory, civilization did not resume in the Tarim Basin until about the second century BC. Most of the Buddhist caves, pyramids and abandoned cities in the Gobi can be traced to that period.

It was on the edge of the Gobi that the Uigers had their first alleged capital city, Karakota. That the "Caucasian" Uigers inhabited this area before the Mongols is quite certain. The Mongols apparently came from farther north in Siberia. How long the Uigers lived there, the level of their culture, and what exactly caused their decline, are still mysteries. As I said in the previous chapter, there are many stories, some of them substantiated, of lost cities in the deserts of Inner and Outer Mongolia, plus other areas of Central Asia.

Of far more recent history is the strange story of Genghis Khan and his magic ring. He was called "Genghis Kha Khan" by his people, meaning "Emperor of All Men." His real name was Temujin, "the finest steel." After melding together the feuding Mongol tribes into an army, he turned this army against the Tartars to the east and conquered them. With the Tartars added to his army, he turned against the collapsing Chin Dynasty, and took Peking in 1214. Soon, nearly all of China was under his control—except for a small portion in the south—and he turned his armies to the west, to march against peoples who had never even heard about the Mongols.

He swept over Turkestan, Persia, the Middle East, and Eastern Europe. The entire population of Herat, in Afghanistan, over one million people, were slaughtered at his command. When a Chinese historian visitied Balk, where Zoroaster had preached his cosmic battle between good and evil, it was immediately after Genghis Khan had leveled the city, and the scribe was astonished to find even one living thing in the smouldering ruins: a cat!

Good ol' Genghis is credited with saying, when asked

what would best bring great happiness, "To crush your enemies, to see them fall at your feet, to take their horses and goods, to hear the crying and see the tears of their women: that is best."

The Mongols, after Genghis' death, continued their bloody campaigns, and the one good thing they did do was to destroy the power of the Order of Assassins in Persia. The Mongols ruled over all of Persia, most of Russia, and many countries in Eastern Europe. The Kublai Khan, for whom Marco Polo was court minister, succeeded the other Mongol rulers, but was in turn overthrown by the Chinese, finishing off the Yuan, or Mongol, Dynasty. The Chinese then marched on Karakorum, the capital of the Mongols (which they in turn had taken over from the Uigers), and razed it to the ground.

All that is left now of Karakorum is a single stone tortoise, staring blindly out over the empty grassland. Also left from the exploits of Genghis Khan and his successors was the *Genghis Khan Wall* (similar to the Great Wall, which was originally meant to keep guys like Genghis out) which stretched for several hundred miles across northeast Mongolia.

Mongolia feuded and raided with other nations continuously for three hundred years. One Mongol chieftan almost took Peking again, until the Manchus, having toppled the Ming dynasty, invaded Mongolia, bringing it under the control of China. The Mongol Revolution of 1911 then sought to recreate the independent Mongol country. Sun Yat Sen was busy overthowing the Manchus in China, so it was an excellent time for the Mongolians to have their own revolution. The new capital was Urga, now Ulan Bator, and was just near the ancient, destroyed capital of Karakorum.

The chosen ruler of the new Independent Monarchy was the Khutuku or Kut-humi, eighth "Living Buddha" of the Mongols; the Bodgo Gegen. Their dreams of independence lasted a short time, as both the Russians and Chinese began grabbing bits of territory, and the Chinese captured Urga in a war that began in 1919.

The Bodgo Gegen, known as the "Master of the World" by his people, was the spiritual ruler of a hundred thousand lamas and a million subjects. He is a living Buddha in the same way as the Dalai Lama of Tibet is a successive incarnation of the same person, according to his followers. In the past, the Bodgo Gegen resided in the Bodgo Ol, a palace in Urga (Ulan Bator) that was started by his predecessors (he being the eighth Bodgo Gegen). Supernatural powers are ascribed to the Bodgo Gegen; he is said to possess a "magic" ring—basically a large ruby set in a ring—which is said to have been worn constantly by Genghis Khan and his successor, Kublai Khan, on the right index finger.[20,33]

The Bodgo Gegen, it is said, in one of his past incarnations, aided the Czar Alexander I against Napoleon, as records in the Kremlin supposedly indicate. Another popular legend in Russia is that the Czar wandered Russia under the name of Feodor Kusmich for years after his official death, which was faked, in 1825, and may eventually have ended up in Mongolia with the Bodgo Gegen.[20]

The Polish scholar, Ferdinat Ossendowski, once said that he was given a magic ring by the Bodgo Gegen which allowed him to escape from "grave dangers." The last Bodgo Gegen, it is claimed, aided V. M. Molotov, Stalin's former right-hand man, who was the Soviet Ambassador to Mongolia from 1957 to 1960 (this was something of a banishment by the new First Secretary, Nikita Khrushchev). Molotov was Khruschev's main adversary, and the Bodgo Gegen supposedly helped Molotov to escape the deadly purge aimed at him by Khrushechev.[20]

All of this is mere hearsay and legend, but what legend is not based somewhat on fact? The Bodgo Gegen seems to be somewhat concerned with the two mysterious occult groups, the Agarthi and Shamballists. In 1947, a man showed up in Paris, claiming to be the Maha Chohan, "Master of the World," and ruler of Agartha. He called himself Kut-humi and he claimed he wore the ring of Genghis Khan—all these are titles and artifacts of the Bodgo Gegen![33]

It is interesting to note here that the term Kuthumi or Kut-humi is a title, not a person's name. Sort of like Great King. Specifically, it relates to the ruler of Mongolia. It makes one wonder about metaphysical groups, channelers and churches in the west that claim to recieve information from "an ascended Master" named Kut-humi. Are they channeling the living Buddha from Ulan Bator? Probably not! This is a vague *nom de plume* at best. Probably one to be used by someone wanting to conceal their true identity.

Information on Shambala and Agartha is widely varied and contradictory. In some texts, Agartha and Shambala are said to be underground cities, or kingdoms, somewhere in Central Asia where occults live and study. Shambala is said to be north of Lhasa, possibly in the Gobi Desert, perhaps in Mongolia. Shambala and Agartha are some- times said to be at odds. In some traditions Agartha is the right-hand path, the "white occult" group, while Shambala is the left-hand path, or "black occult" group. Also, it is conversely said that Agartha is occupied by dark forces and Shambala is the abode of the "Masters of the World" and a place of goodness. [38, 33, 29]

Sometimes Shambala is associated with The Great White Brotherhood, and the "Valley of the Immortals" or Land of Hsi Wang Mu. The Bön religion of ancient Tibet has a legend of a similar secret kingdom named Olmolungring. According to tradition, the creator of the first systemic doctrinal structure of the Bön religion was gShen-rabmibo, who came from Olmolungring and returned there. [119, 148] Olmolungring may well be the secret land in the Kun Lun or another name for the cave communities which are apparently the anti-thesis of the Land of Hsi Wang Mu.

There are other stories of sinister "black occult" groups operating out of Central Asia, and they sometimes call themselves the Shambala or the Agarthi. Buddhists of Tibet were aware of some of these secret communities and outlawed them along with the Bön religion in Tibet. Yet reports indicate that they continued to operate underground and find students to work with them through gile, deception and the promise of power over others.

Theodore Illion, a German traveller who spoke Tibetan, travelled in disguise in Tibet in 1935 and 36. His first book, *In Secret Tibet,* [142] describes his early encounters while his second book, *Darkness Over Tibet,* [143] describes his entry to an underground city. Illion learns that the city, hidden underground and inhabited by hundreds of people, most of them monks, is an onclave of black yogis who seek to control the world through telepathy, astral projection to contact willing followers and deception of true spiritual seekers into the dark path of seeking to control others spiritually and religiously.

After discovering that he is being fed a gruel of human flesh, Illion escapes the city with an assassination squad after him. He wanders Tibet for several weeks being pursued, and eventually escapes, to warn the world. [143] While his book may be alarmist fiction disguised as a travelogue, there are many reports that such places do indeed exist.

The term "Shambala," like the term, "Great White Brotherhood," is quite ambiguous, and can be used by anyone. The Shambala and the Agartha seem to be in oppostition to some degree—though in fact, they may be the same group.

The Shambalists are strongly associated with the Grand Lodge of the Vril, an organization to which Adolf Hitler belonged. The Grand Lodge of the Vril was, at least one of the sources of a great deal of Nazi doctrine. Various other links have been found between the Shambala and the Nazis, and a number of books have been written on the subject. [20, 29]

Shambala and Agartha is also associated with the "Hollow Earth" theories of certain groups, including the Nazis. In these, the inside of the earth, which is thought to be hollow, contains the "sacred territory of Agartha." In Nazi occult doctrine, it is here that the Nazi "Supermen" lived. The Nazis hoped to contact these Supermen, who were a central part of their own "Hollow Earth—Eternal Ice" ideology. [29]

Nazis went so far as to make German scientists working for the Third Reich officially declare their belief in a hollow earth. Some Nazis even believed that our world was already inside a hollow sphere with the sun in the center. It is a recorded historical fact that the Nazi admiralty sent a naval expedition to the island of Ruegen in the Baltic in April 1942, with the purpose of taking pictures of the British fleet by aiming their cameras upward and shooting across the center of the hollow earth![49,29]

A number of authors, including Trevor Ravenscroft who wrote *The Spear of Destiny*,[60] believe that the Germans contacted black yogis of Central Asia who not only influenced the Nazis, but sent an entire school of monks back to Berlin!

According to ancient legends, familiar to the occult societies at the turn of the century, and related in the book *Le Roi du Monde* by Rene Guenon, there was a cataclysm in the Gobi desert, so the "Sons of Intelligences of Beyond" took up their abode in the vast underground emcampment under the Himalayas. There inside these caves, they split up into two groups; one, the Agarthi, supposedly following the "right-hand way" of meditation and goodness, and the other, the Shambalists, following the "left-hand way" of evil and violence.

Shambala, according to Guenon, was a city of black occults located underground whose forces commanded the elements and the masses of humanity through telepathic hypnosis, mediumship and other occult means, hastening the arrival of the human race to the "turning point in time," which might be construed to mean "Armaggedon."[20] Madame Blavatsky, founder of the Theosophical Society, decried the "black Bön" though she may have been fooled by them as well. Unfortunately, much of her "root race" material was used by the Occult Reich hierarchy in their "Eternal Ice" doctrine. That there had been earlier root races of man and that man was now entering a new, higher stage of evolution was twisted into doctrines of racial hatred against Jews, Gypsies and other minority groups.

Hitler sent several expeditions to Tibet in the late thirties (curiously, after Illion had returned to Germany and written his books on Tibet) to contact occult groups and apparently created quite strong ties with a group that Ravenscroft and others were to term "Shambalists." [29,60]

After the Nazis succeeded in contacting occult groups, a number of Tibetans were takent back to Germany to help the Nazis, or so some historians tell us. After Hitler's release from prison, one of his associates was a Tibetan monk, known only, it seems, as "The Tibetan." The monk and seer was said to have told Hitler that Germany could rule the entire world by conquering the Gobi Desert, which, he claimed, had been inhabited by the "Lords of Creation" who would direct Germany's future![50] When the Russians finally captured Berlin, they found a bunker full of Indian and Tibetan monks, who had committed mass suicide rather than be captured by the Russians. [29,74,149]

Even more incredible are the end-of-the-war myths surrounding the mysterious death of Adolf Hitler himself. Although he was supposedly cremated while a half-dozen of his various "doubles" were shot, his death was never proven to the satisfaction of many researchers, including Dwight D. Eisenhower and Josef Stalin, who both voiced the opinion that Hitler might still be alive. Some tales told of Hitler flying out of Berlin as the Russians took the city, landing in Denmark and embarking on a U-boat to Argentina or to a "secret base in the Antarctic."[15]

One story, related in May, 1950, by the openly pro-Nazi West German magazine *Tempo Der Welt*, claimed that Hitler escaped Germany and went to Tibet where he was hiddden by the forces who'd brought him into power. The periodical's publisher, Karl Heinz Kaerner, claimed he had spoken with Hitler's former secretary, Martin Bormann, the summer before in Spanish Morocco. (Borman himself, theoretically killed in a tank explosion while trying to smash through Russian lines and get out of Berlin, is the "biggest unsolved Nazi mystery" according to famous Nazi hunter Simon Wiesenthal, who believes Bormann alive, as no remains were ever found.)

Bormann supposedly told Kaerner that "Hitler is alive in a Tibetan monastery" and that "one day we will be back" in power in Germany![15] Considering the enormous amount of "Hitler survival" mythology, this is likely to be utter hogwash, but it does support the concept that Hitler had some strong ties with Tibetans, notably the so-called Shambalists. What ever happened to Hitler's aide "The

Tibetan"?   Perhaps they both escaped—back to the underground city in Tibet!

Were the Nazis in touch with the ancient Bön of Tibet, whom both Roerich and Blavatsky were both abhorrent of? The symbol for the Bön religion is a swastika running to the left, just as the Nazis had their swastika run. The Buddhist swastika, however, runs to the right, symbolizing the "right-hand path" as opposed to the "left-hand path" of black occults. While Buddhism sought to exterminate the Bön religion, it was only outlawed in the 7th century.

It has long been well known among travelers in Tibet, that "black occults," linked to the ancient Bön religion still wandered Central Asia. The famous mystic Alexandra David-Neel describes one such man she met in her book *Initiations and Initiates in Tibet*, who could hypnotise and kill from a distance. This is not the sort of thing that good Buddhists go around doing, and such powers are generally attributed to black sorcerers and Bön adepts.

Nicholas Roerich also mentions that "Bön Occults" were still at war with the Buddhists of Tibet. He, like most Tibetan Buddhists, does not associate Shambala with the Bön, but with the Ancients residing at the "Valley of the Immortals."[69] Certainly Bön adepts are clever and fiendishly deceptive.

Out of curiosity, I wondered where the location of Shambala might be. A story is told of a Polish nobleman who was studying in Tibet entering a smoking cavern and penetrating it into Shambala. Upon his return to the monastery where he was staying, he began to disclose the location of the cave community, but the lamas immediately cut out his tongue to prevent him from telling the secret of Shambala. [38]

Tradition places Shambala to the north of Lhasa, possibly in the Gobi Desert.   Aparently, the Buddhists of Lhasa and the Bön had an uneasy truce. The Dalai Lama used to go every year to Mongolia, and at one point their caravan stopped as the animals all began trembling for no apparent reason. The reason, the Dalai Lama explained, was that they were passing through the forbidden territory of Shambala.[38]

The Hungarian philologist, Csoma de Koros, who spent four years in a Buddhist monastery in Tibet from 1827 to 1830, gave the location of Shambala as 45 to 50 degrees latitude, beyond the river Syr Daria, which would place Shambala in southern Mongolia. The Panchen Lama, head of the Tashi Lhunpo monastic citadel near Shigatse, was said to be able to issue passports to Shambala, though he would never disclose its location. According to tradition, both Shambala and Agartha were connected to all the major monasteries of Tibet by a system of underground tunnels, and the monastery of Shigastse is either near, or at the actual entrance to Agartha.[38]

§§§

It is confusing—all this stuff about the Agarthi and the Shambalists. How does one separate the fact from the fiction? Perhaps it's all just "yeti piss in the wind." What, I wondered, is the truth of these occult cave communities, and how dangerous and extensive were they?

Ultimately, I decided that they were really crude, dirty hovels in some remote area, probably underground in extensive caves, quite possibly beneath Kunchenjunga or the Shigatse Monastery for the Agarthi, and in other caves to the north for the Shambalists. The occultists who lived there, so legend goes, had the ability to create, in the minds of their visitors, visions of a magnificent city by use of a kind of telepathic hypnosis.

Shambala draws strong similarities to the Land of the Immortals (Hsi Wang Mu) in that it is said to be a wonderful, lush valley in the high mountains with a tall, ornate solid jade tower from which a brilliant light shines. Like in the Kun Lun mountains, Agartha and Shambala have a cache of fantastic inventions and artifacts from distant civilizations of the past.[38]

In contrast with the "Valley of the Immortals" in the Kun Lun Mountains, the cave communities with their incredible sights were part illusion. At the "Valley of the Immortals, perhaps there really were ancient artifacts of a time gone by watched over by "Ancient Masters." Yet, it is unlikely that any person not chosen specifically by those who are the caretakers of this repository, would be allowed inside. Nor would those who had entered (such as possibly Nicholas Roerich) ever reveal the location or what they had seen there.

Shambala and Agartha traditionally had tunnels linking them with the major monasteries in Tibet in a vast network of underground passages. While this probably is not entirely true, it is true that monasteries in Tibet often did have secret tunnels and caves beneath them, which were forbidden to outsiders, though it is doubtful that many extended any great distances. Beneath the Potala Palace in Lhasa it is believed that there is a system of tunnels, though they are not necessarily connected with the Shambalists or Agarthi.

According to some sources, Shambala and Agartha got what was coming to them. Trevor Ravenscroft, in his fascinating book, *The Spear of Destiny*, [60] makes a good case for the Nazis working closely with the Shambalists. He says that when the Chinese invaded Tibet in the late fifties and early sixties, they genuinely believed that they were there to liberate the Tibetan people from a feudal religious autocracy that was keeping them in the middle ages. Indeed, most schools in Tibet still taught that the world was flat and that the sun revolved around the earth. [41] Reportedly, many of the women of Tibet were tired of most of the men going off to live in the monasteries and helped the Chinese take over the country.

Forcefully and violently, the Chinese reformed the country, destroying many monasteries and killing many monks in the process. Ravenscroft believes that the Chinese were aware of the Shambalists and Agarthi and actively sought them out in order to destroy them. They also accomplished the dual task of taking over Tibet and exiling the theocratic government of the Dalai Lama. The Chinese fought their way to the monastic citadels, which were in fact well-fortified fortresses, and savagely exterminated the monks in their fanatical revolutionary fervor (violence is never a solution to any problem, according to Buddha, Christ and Lao Tzu).

At the Tashi Lumpo monastic citadel in Shigatse, which once housed three thousand monks, the Chinese slaughtered many monks and forced their way to the forbidden tunnels beneath the monastery, as they did at many monasteries before it. Perhaps they actually entered the "Sacred Realm of Agartha" at this point, and destroyed the communities, as hypnotism and magic cannot stop a bullet!

According to Michael Edwardes in his book *The Dark Side of History*, [150] certain Tibetan Orders used magic rituals that included human flesh and blood to enforce an army of demons to combat the invading Chinese forces. It failed to work. The Tibetans had similarly failed against the British invasion in 1904 when the state oracle in Lhasa had predicted that the British would penetrate deeply into Tibet but would be defeated by Tibetan forces who would be magically protected. The British, however, defeated the Tibetans by using a newly developed magical weapon unknown to the oracle in Lhasa: the Maxin machine gun.

In this way, these sinister groups of occultists were ultimately destroyed by the savage wars that they themselves had promulgated, just as the Russians eventually smashed the Nazis in Berlin. [60]

"As you sow, so shall you reap": this, like everything, is the natural outworkings of karma, I suppose. The black

360

occults mentioned by David-Neel, Illion, Roerich, Guenon, and others are in theory still active, carrying on their actitivies disguised as "good," under the auspices of "Masters of the World," Kut-Humis and the like. And, while the underground communities in Shigatse may have been destroyed, Agartha, or whatever it is, may still exist somewhere in the remote Gobi Desert.

A certain legendary evil aura hangs over the Gobi. The Gobi is called the "Shamo" by Mongolians (Gobi being the word for desert) and this word may be related to the name of the god Shamos, who was worshipped in the Middle East as a "black star." Shamos is also the "evil luminary" of the Arabs, probably based upon Saturn, or perhaps some other heavenly body.[20] The Gobi has a reputation for magic that surpasses even that of Tibet, and certain areas of the Gobi are literally taboo to the Mongols. Could parts of the Gobi be the realm of these black occults? Could these black occults have brought Genghis Khan into power, giving him some "magic ring," causing him to terrorize the world and depopulate whole countries? Without a doubt, Genghis Khan was one of the world's most cruel, heartless, and evil despots that ever lived!

"And how are we to explain without magic," writes historian Charles Correga, "the fact that Genghis Khan, an untutored herdsman aided by a handful of nomads, was able to subjugate a succession of peoples and empires a thousand times more advanced than he was?"

§§§

One such forbidden area of the Gobi is the "Black Gobi" located in southwestern Mongolia. One story about the "Black Gobi" illustrates well, I feel, the passions and emotional background of the Mongolians. The story goes like this: The *Tushe Gun Lama*, born Dambin Jansang in the Altai mountains of western Mongolia in the eighteen seventies, was said to possess a hypnotic power and gigantic force of will. His early years were spent studying occult sciences in Tibetan lamaseries, as well as studying with fakirs in India and with Chinese mystics in Peking. As he traveled around Mongolia, the conviction spread that he was the reincarnation of *Amursana*, hero of the western Mongols who fought against the Manchus in the mid-seventeen hundreds.

Worshipped as a divine warrior, in a time when Mongolia was looking for heros, Dambin became the leader of the 1911 revolution against the Chinese. His horde captured and sacked the Chinese garrison at the western Mongolian

361

city of Kobdo. The story says that Dambin was unharmed, but his clothes were in shreds from bullet holes. The new ruler of the newly- independent Mongolia, the Bodgo Gegen himself, appointed Dambin governor of the west, with his provincial capital in Kobdo.

Meanwhile the Russians and Chinese were plotting to put an end to free Mongolia, and in 1914 when some Czarist Russian Cossacks attacked Kobdo by surprise, they found Dambin sitting on a throne covered with the human hides of Chinese that he had flayed alive. He was then imprisoned in Russia until the civil war broke out there, when he escaped and returned to Mongolia to raise ten thousand men to help the "Mad Baron." (This was Baron Ungern Von Sternberg, the leader of a "White" Russian army that was taking refuge in Mongolia and helping the Mongols fight the Chinese general "Little Hsu.")

Dambin was once again the "Mongol Messiah." He helped the "Mad Baron" defeat the Chinese and then fought against the invading Red Russian Army. The Red Russians, however, won, and Dambin escaped to the dreaded "Black Gobi" where he built a fortress in an oasis called Bayang Bulak. He commanded his own personal army, and was quite a threat to the new Communist power in Urga.

Late in 1922, a force of six hundred Russians and Mongols set out for the "Black Gobi" with orders to assassinate Dambin at all costs. The leader of the attackers, Baldan Dorje, had his men stop some miles outside the oasis, and then he and another went in alone, disguised as high lamas.

Baldan Dorje told Dambin that he was there on a mission from the Bodgo Gegen in Urga, who requested Dambin's aid in a revolt against the Russians. For several days they discussed how to free Mongolia. Then Baldan Dorje pretended to fall sick. He lay in bed for two days and said he was dying. He wanted a blessing from the Tushe Gun Lama (Dambin) before he died. As Dambin leaned over the man to give him his blessing, Baldan drew a revolver from beneath his lama's robe, put it to Dambin's chest and fired!

Grabbing a knife nearby, he cut off Dambin's head and before the guards could reach the door, flung it out into the courtyard! Baldan then ripped out Dambin's heart, and stepped outside to face Dambin's warriors with the heart high in the air. Then, as the terrified, panic-stricken warriors watched, Baldan Dorje swallowed the bloody heart of Dambin Jansang, the *Avenging (Tushe Gun)* Lama!

All the men were convinced that by swallowing the heart of Dambin, Baldan was now invincible, as had been their

362

leader, and fled into the desert. Baldan escaped with his life and took Dambin's head back to Urga where it was placed on a lance and paraded all around Mongolia to show the people that the revolution was dead. No one goes back to the oasis of Bayan Bulak, as it is thought to be haunted by the ghost of Dambin. Those that have gone, said that they have seen Dambin, with his head and mounted on his horse, followed by the fierce watchdogs that used to guard his tent. Many Mongolians sincerely believe that one day Dambin Jansang, the Tushe Gun-Avenging Lama, will ride out of the "Black Gobi" once again and old Mongolia will live once more!

As for the Bodgo Gegen, he died in 1924, and immediately afterward, the *People's Republic of Mongolia* was declared—the second communist government in the world, and the first Soviet satellite. But Bodgo Gegens don't die easily. Like the Dalai Lama of Tibet, he was reborn, and lives to this day in Mongolia. It is this new Bodgo Gegen that helped Molotov escape from Khrushchev. He still wears the ring of Genghis Khan, but no longer has his palace in Ulan Bator (Urga), for the palace has been nationalized by the Communist government. He now wanders the steppes, followed by an impressive court of lamas and shamans, with enormous trunks guarded by the Shabinari monks in his service. In them are the sacred books: the two hundred and twenty-six volumes of the Panjur and the one hundred and eight volumes of the Ganjur, plus other ancient religious objects, which are not identified.[2, 20]

§§§

The thought of Genghis Khan, the bloody battles, the Nazis and the evil powers behind it all, made me shudder. In my quest for lost cities, caravan trails and mysteries, I have come across many strange stories and places, but few I would call stranger than the riddles of the Gobi desert. I looked out the window at the sun-washed sand and parched desert. This was the Gobi, not much to look at, and a hell of a strange place!

I would vagabond around Mongolia for awhile, still one of the most remote and difficult places to travel freely in the world. It is possible to take the train from Peking to Moscow, which passes right through Mongolia, and stops for a few hours in Ulan Bator, at the very least. As long as you have a ticket, the Mongolians will give you a transit visa. It is more difficult to spend time in the country.

Some people explore the remote areas of Mongolia in the

guise a big game hunter, in search of Marco Polo sheep (a wild ram-horned sheep that lives in the Altai Mountains in western Mongolia). The cost is about one hundred dollars a day. It is quite possible that things will get easier for tourists in Mongolia in the next few years. Until then, it will still be "The Forbidden Land," like Tibet.

Another fascinating mystery is the Mongolian version of the Yeti (also known as the North American Sasquatch or Big Foot, and as the Yowie in Australia), called the *Almas,* the *wild man* of the steppes. This wild, hairy man is short, covered with fur, and quite shy. In other ways, he is the catch-all for unexplainable events or glimpses of strange animals in the desert, as are Yetis. However, lately, wild hairy men have been the subject of several scientific articles in China.[2]

We pulled into Baotou, the main industrial city of Inner Mongolia, quite late in the evening. It was after midnight. Bill and I slept on tables in the waiting room of the station, until some of the railway staff woke us up and asked us what we were doing. We told them we were sleeping there in the station until morning, and they insisted that we store our luggage in the cloakroom until morning, so that it wouldn't be stolen. We did as they said, a young lady helping us, and then went back to sleep.

In the morning, we were awakened by the staff, who gave us our luggage and called a taxi for us. With the taxi was a young English-speaking escort, a woman about twenty-five years old, with fifties-style horn-rimmed glasses. She escorted us to the hotel, which was in another section of town, where they seemed to be expecting us. Apparently, Baotou didn't get too many independent travelers just showing up in the railway station to spend the night!

We had a snack at the hotel, and then went down to the bus station to try and get a bus out to the beautiful Wudang Zhao monastery, a lamaist monastery that is open to tourists, is quite large, and well worth a visit. It's about two hours by bus from Baotou; however, the bus had already left, and we were faced with the idea of possibly hitchhiking out there. We decided against it, since there is virtually no traffic, and our chances for a ride were slim. It is better to try and get the seven o'clock bus, and it is even possible to spend the night at the monastery, which is a Tibetan-style building, built about two hundred years ago.

Instead, we walked about town, and met a young English student who was on holiday from the University of Inner Mongolia and wanted to hang out with us for the day. His name was Chiang. He was twenty-three, had a pleasant smile, spoke great English and was a fun guy to be with. We all walked around Baotou, a dusty, windy city, with lots of industry and low, brown, flat-roofed drab buildings.

Everywhere we went, huge crowds followed. Most of them had never seen a westerner before, as Baotou is far off the beaten track, and has little to offer the tourist. People would suddenly stop, drop their jaws and gape in a rather silly fashion. It was quite amusing at times, but occasionally annoying. We would often have thirty to fifty people following us down the street. One woman called in Chinese, as Chiang told us, "Come out and see the foreigners!" Once a policeman had to ask us to move on down the street, because the crowd that was following us was causing a traffic jam! In all my travels, in Central Asia or anywhere, I have never been to a place where people stared at us so.

Chiang took us to his family's house, a two-room apartment in a gray concrete building with half a kitchen—a sink and a counter. His father was a doctor, and apparently pretty well off; they were just packing up to move south.

"Water comes only in the evenings," said Chiang, sitting on one of the boxes in the kitchen. "Would you like some tea?" We had a couple of teas, and Chiang told us about the University, while his parents, in their fifties, gazed at us intently, obviously proud that their son had such important friends.

"I had an American friend at the *University of Inner Mongolia*," he told us. "His name was Steve, and he was from Seattle. I got reprimanded though, because I was caught in his dormitory room one night talking with him and another American. In China, they do not want the students spending much time with foreigners. Once," he said, winking, "Steve gave me a *Playboy* magazine from America! In China, we don't have anyting like that!"

"Why is it that almost everyone in China thinks that all foreigners are from America?" I asked Chiang, as, from my observations, that seemed to be the case.

"Because they think that all Americans are very rich," he said, "and can travel all over the world and do anything they want. Therefore, they think all tourists must be Americans."

"Well, that was fairly logical," I thought.

We had lunch in a small noodle shop. Noodles are popular in northern China, as rice is popular in the south. The lady who ran the place had to keep beating back people from the door as they crowded around her small restaurant and pushed inside to see us. In the end, out of desperation, she began throwing water on the kids who were crowding the streets.

Later, on our way back to the *People's Hotel*, I got separated from Bill and Chiang when they went into a department store. When I came out of a different shop, I was looking for them, and spotted a huge crowd of a hundred and fifty people on the street. I assumed it must be Bill and Chiang, and followed it. The crowd was so thick, I couldn't get up front, so I jumped up on a cart to get a look over people's heads.

It turned out that it wasn't Bill, but a street magician! Suddenly, someone in the crowd saw me and yelled, "Look, everybody, an American!" in Chinese. The entire crowd turned to stare at me, leaving the magicain nonplussed. Having had plenty of attention that day already, I hurriedly left, with about fifty people following me.

I found Chiang and Bill and we walked back to the *People's Hotel*, where we thanked Chiang for a nice day, and his excellent companionship. It had been a long day, and several hard days of traveling before that. We took hot baths, and fell soundly asleep.

By noon the next day, we were off on a train heading east. We stopped briefly in Huhehot, the capital of Inner Mongoila—a pleasant, spacious city, almost completely reconstructed in the 1950's. It is the tourist center of Inner Mongolia, and people are more accustomed to seeing foreigners here. Huhehot has its own "Living Buddha," though his power has been curtailed greatly, as nearly all of Inner Mongolia's temples were closed during the Cultural Revolution. Only five remain open at this time, though restrictions on religion are being slackened. Huhehot also has an extensive system of air-raid tunnels, as the city is a first line of defense against the massive Soviet forces that are being gathered on the Mongolian-Chinese border only a few hundred miles away.

As the sun set over Mongolia, and we pulled out of Huhehot, I thought of the Tomb of Genghis Khan not too far away to our south, in the Ih Ju League. There the old tyrant was resting after his exhausting conquests, although his rest has been disturbed by Red Guards who ransacked his mausoleum in the late sixties during the Cultural Revolution. It has been fixed up and re-opened for tourists recently.

We passed fields and grasslands with rugged hills behind them. A horsecart with a load of watermelons was being driven down a country road alongside the tracks. A freight train with two great greasy black engines pulled up next to our train, and I waved at the engineer. He waved back. The sun reflected off pools of water and rivers as we passed, twinkling in glittery reds, yellows, and greens; at one moment, we crossed a section of the Great Wall. This was the life, I thought, grinning widely. I was enjoying the little nuances of the scenery and life of the farmland and pastures of Inner Mongolia.

We were heading for Datong, and then on to Beijing (Peking). I sighed deeply and leaned back in my seat. Central Asia and the Gobi was teeming with wild characters and history! As a salute, I waved out into the growing darkness and called to the ghost of Genghis Khan. May he find peace at last!

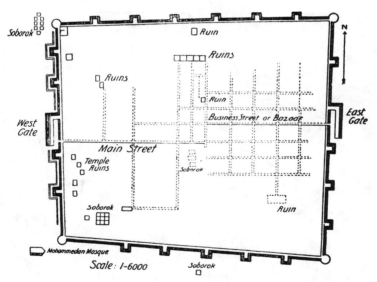

SCALE PLAN OF THE RUINS OF KHARA KHOTO.

367

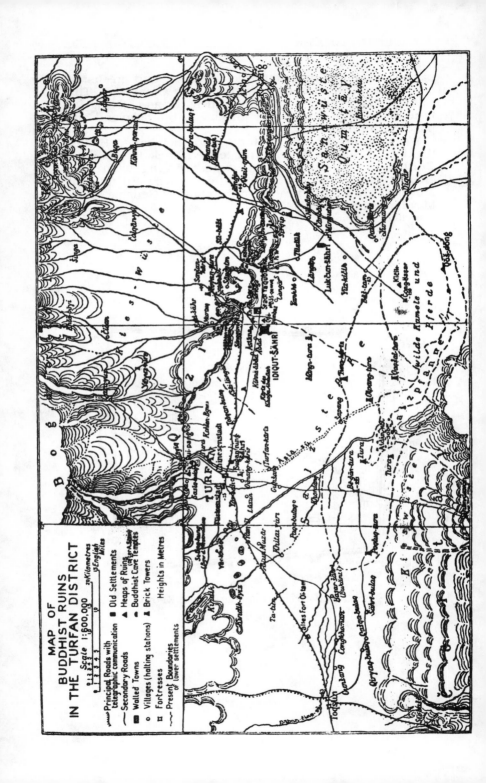

MAP OF
BUDDHIST RUINS
IN THE TURFAN DISTRICT

Scale 1:800,000

— — Principal Roads with
        telegraphic communication   ■ Old Settlements
——— Secondary Roads   ▲ Heaps of Ruins
■■ Walled Towns   ▲ Buddhist Cave Temples
○ Villages (halting stations)   ▲ Brick Towers
¤ Fortresses
— — Present Boundaries   Heights in Metres
        of lower settlements

Alexandra David-Neel (left) with her guide, traveled throughout Tibet in the 1920s and 30s. As one of the first woman travellers to visit Tibet she wrote *Magic and Mystery In Tibet* in 1929. In her book, *Initiations and Initiates In Tibet*, David-Neel claims that the man in the lower left (below) is capable of hypnotizing and killing at a distance. Such a person is generally thought to be linked to a black occult fraternity, often the Bön religion of Tibet.

An ancient Chinese inscription from an early Western Chou Dynasty vessel (1200-500 BC). Epigraphers have attempted to link this script with many ancient scripts, including ancient Mayan pictographs, ancient South American scripts, the Indus Valley script and others.

Stone rubbing of the Chinese script used just prior to the reform of Chinese script by the Emperor Chi' Huang Ti which created the Chinese characters of today.

A rare photo of the megalithic Dolmen of Chou-Chou in Manchuria. Note the finely cut and fitted slabs, weighing many tons each.

Chapter Nineteen

PEKING TO XIAN:

TALES FROM THE FORBIDDEN CITY

When we see men of worth,
We should think of equaling them.
When we see men of contrary character,
We should examine ourselves.
—Confucius (Kung-Fu-Tzu)

Bill and I arrived in Datong at about three o'clock in the morning on our way to Peking. The station was dead quiet. We settled down on some benches and slept. Unlike railway stations in India, in which whole villages of squatters may take up semi-permanent residence, Chinese railway stations are clean and generally uninhabited. In fact, persons without a ticket are not even allowed onto the platform. As Bill remarked, "What India could use is a little totalitarianism to straighten out some of its problems." It certainly cleaned up China, the most populous country in the world.

As people started to filter into the station in the morning, we woke up and went out for breakfast at a dim-sum place: steamed rolls, and dumplings filled with herbs and vegetables. Datong is famous for having what is probably the last steam locomotive train factory in the world. Based on a Soviet model of the fifties, it was opened in 1959 and procduces twenty-two or twenty-three locomotives per month. However, we were not in Datong to see the locomotive factory. Rather, we wanted to see the Yungang Caves, about ten miles to the west, which are considered to be the finest Buddhist rock carvings in China. The shrine consists of hundreds of carvings of Buddhas inside small caves, with a very impressive one at the western end which is fifty-five feet tall. We took the No. 1 bus from near the train station out to the end of the line, near the massive coal pits that are Datong's major industry, and then hitched the rest of the way to the caves.

A truck driver, a young, eager-looking man with a friendly, clean-shaven face, was heading back to pick up a load of coal. With wide eyes and a knowing smile, he stopped his dump truck when Bill and I waved at him from the side of the road. We jumped up in the cab with him, and told him we were off to the Yungang Grotto. He nodded, and the truck lurched into motion. It was a short distance and as we got off, he said something in Mandarin, which I couldn't fully understand, but took to mean, "I'd love to be out traveling the world like you guys." I smiled and shook his hand, thanking him for the ride, and winking. "Anything is possible," I said in my best Mandarin.

The caves, cut into the sandstone cliffs, are well worth the detour, with many fine statues and colorful murals and paintings inside. We sat for a while in front of the great Buddha, and then visited the temple which climbs vertically up the cliff face. The temple was built in the seventeenth century, while the Buddhas are from the late fifth, the heyday of Buddhist culture in Central Asia. The shrines are in varied condition, some quite poorly preserved as a result of being looted, and even flooded a few times.

Back in Datong, we had a few Chinese popsicles—pleasant in the hot sun—with a mild sugar-ginger flavor. They are quite popular in northern China, and a vendor can be found at nearly every street corner in the summer, it seems. We walked about town, and checked out the back streets of this dusty coal-mining city. At the Huayan Monastery in the center of town, not far from the station, we visited the hall of Buddhas, full of gigantic, wooden, seated Buddhas, some thirty feet tall and surrounded by other Chinese figures. Especially striking was a fifteen-foot warrior, tall and stout, fingering his rather long sword, and next to him a peaceful, female sitting Buddha. It seemed as if these gigantic but realistic figures would come alive at any moment.

We left in the early evening for the eight-hour train ride to Peking (Beijing). Happily, we met a British Chinese language student on the train, coming from Hohehot on his way back to the Beijing Language Institute where he was a student. As Bill and I sat in the hard seats of the train for the journey, we spotted him at the end of our car. We got to talking. His name was Ben, and he was twenty-three. He had almost shaved his head; his hair was very short, much like a typical Chinese male crew-cut. He was clean-shaven, had black hair, and was very friendly. He had been in China for almost a year, and his Mandarin was excellent. He invited us back to the Beijing Language Institute with him, where he said he could find us a place to stay.

We arrived just at dawn in Peking, and took a bus with Ben to the northwest outskirts of the city to the Institute, where we stashed our packs in his room. We then headed out by bus to the Forbidden City, the home of twenty-four emperors of the Ming and Manchu dynasties from the mid-fourteenth to the early twentieth centuries. Construction of the palace began in 1406 and more than one million laborers were used on the project. The citadel, literally a city unto itself, was completed in 1420.

As it was surrounded by a deep moat, no one could enter the royal Forbidden City unless they were invited. The main entrance is at Tiananmen Square, also known as "Red Square." It is the very heart of the city, and it was here that Mao Tse-Tung proclaimed the founding of the People's Republic on October 1, 1949. At Tiananmen Gate (a name meaning "the Gate of Heavenly Peace"), the main entrance to the Forbidden City, Mao looked over the crowd of several hundred thousand people standing in the square, and proclaimed, appropriately, "The Chinese people have stood up!"

A tour of the Forbidden City could conceivably take several days, as much of it has been turned into a musuem, and it is vast. No one lives inside it these days. Most people are satisfied with about half a day inside it, roaming the hallways, pavilians, photographing the many buildings and relics, and taking in the very heart of China.

On the other side of the Forbidden City is Coal Hill, with a pagoda on top of it—a good spot to get an overview of the city. It is a man-made mound, created to protect the city from the cold north winds and the "evil spirits" that came from the north. The Forbidden City contained the residences of all the court officials and government offices, and Imperial criminals were executed in front of Wumen Gate, just inside the Tiananmen Gate.

Peking, now renamed Beijing, "Northern Capital," has more to see than any other place in China, and deserves more time than any other place in the country. Bill and I stayed at the Language Institute for six days, wandering about the city and seeing the many sights it has to offer. Beijing was founded eight hundred years ago by the Mongols as the capital of their Chinese empire in 1261. The city was originally named "Khanbaligh" and made famous by Marco Polo. The capital was moved a couple of times to Nanking, once by the Ming emperors and once by Chiang Kai-Shek in 1928, but each time it was moved back to Beijing within a few years, perhaps because it is considered a strong "power spot" by the Chinese.

There is plenty to do in Peking. Aside from walking around town, or visiting Red Square, the Forbidden City, and the parks, there is the Great Hall of the People, the Museum of Chinese History and the Museum of the Chinese Revolution on the square. There is the Temple of Heaven at Tiantan Park in the south of the city. Here, at the main altar, the emperor during the Ming Dynasty conducted a solemn ceremony on the day of the winter solstice to insure a good harvest for the next year. It is a pleasant park with nice architecture; even the trash cans are beautiful porcelain containers, shaped like Pekinese dogs.

The Chinese love melons. Recently, melon rinds tossed in streets and parks during the melon season were blamed for a record 1,000 Shanghai accidents. In Peking, officials say 50,000 tons of rinds were left on the streets during a recent summer. Now that's a lot of melons!

We often wandered along Wangujing, the main shopping district, and drank in the beer halls: flat beer, good with various snacks, was twenty cents a pitcher. Life is fascinating to watch all over Peking. There are a number of department stores in Peking which are fun to shop at, including some that are for foreigners only. Wandering around the Beijing Friendship Store one day, I was amazed at some of the things for sale there. A partial list includes:

* Ginseng Gecko Extract—made with essence of gecko (a small lizard) and ginseng for "bodily weakness, lack of spirit, insomnia, insufficient saliva. A high-grade tonic." $4.00 for six oral ampules.

* Hilung (Seahorse) Pills—with "hippo-campu, sheep's penis, ginseng and Syngapus. A good tonic."

* Peking Royal Jelly—"fresh royal bee jelly and ginseng (oral)."

* Pantocrin-oral liquid, "from spotted deer antlers (25%) for general weakness, impotence."

* Rhinoceros Bezoar Pills, containing, "myrrh and mastix for all kinds of acute and chronic inflammations, swelling abscesses, carbuncle, arthritis and impotence. Improves the blood circulation."

Like many Chinese remedies, rhinoceros horn, as well as tiger's penis, and other phallic objects are taken to cure impotence and allow older men to satisfy women by having intercourse all night. In the Sui Dynasty (A.D. 581-618) sexual adequacy was considered very important, and a man was taught that sexual intercourse with as many women as possible each night was beneficial to his health and longevity. Moreover, sex should, it was thought, be ecstatically pleasurable for both man and woman. As it was a polygamous society, a man might have as many as thirty concubines, and was required by law to satisfy each of his concubines at least once every five days. No other society before or since has probably assigned as much importance to sexual intercourse, and many aids were developed, along with aphrodisiacs (usually for the man) and sex manuals.

There are lots of other things to buy in the Friendship Stores, which are located in all the major cities, from clothing to appliances to toiletries. There is a mini-Friendship Store at the Peking Hotel, just near the Tiananmen Square, the most prestigious of all the hotels in Beijing. Beijing has a dozen or more hotels for tourists, some of them quite luxurious and expensive, for the foreign dignitaries that come to the capital of the most populous country on earth. There is the Jianguo Hotel, jointly run by the Chinese and Americans, which is an exact copy of the Holiday Inn in Palo Alto, California, with a western-style coffee shop and live western music at the bar on weekends.

One night, at the Beijing Language Institute, some of the students, foreign and Chinese, decided to go to the old Summer Palace for the Moon Cake Festival, which happens every year in the early autumn. Ben, Bill and I rode bicycles out to it, and there was quite a little party going on with some of the students from the Institute. We danced to the tunes of a portable cassette stereo and drank Chinese wine while a huge crowd of other Chinese, not from the Institute, watched with fascination. It was fun to mingle with young Chinese students, under the full moon in the brisk autumn air, in the midst of the ruins of the palace. There wasn't much left; some walls, a few arches and the like. It had been destroyed by the British in the Opium War.

As the party warmed, I talked with some charming young Chinese girls who were English students at the Institute. They bombarded me with questions about America. I answered them as best I could, trying to make this mythical Utopia of the United States as real as possible. One particularly assertive young lady, whose English name was Nancy, talked with me for quite a while. I offered her a ride back to the Insititute on the back of my bicycle. She accepted, and we were off into the quiet, country streets beneath the moon.

Suddenly she asked me to stop, saying that she wanted to talk to me for a few minutes. We got off the bike, and sat behind a tree where we were hidden. It was nearly two o'clock in the morning. "What do young people do on a date in America?" she asked, her almond eyes opening very wide and looking seductively at me.

"Well, they sometimes go to a movie, or out to dinner, or just out for a walk on a nice evening like this," I told her. She was lovely; her short, straight jet-black hair was cut off at the shoulder. She was twenty-three years old and rather petite. She was incredibly smart, and her English was nearly perfect. Her knowledge of America was awesome.

"What else do they do on dates?" she asked, as a cool wind suddenly came up and she moved in closer to me.

"Well, they often hug, and put their arms around each other, like this," I said, putting my arms around her. We held each other for awhile and talked about dating in China, which was minimal. Women don't normally get married until they are in their later twenties, and premarital sex is not encouraged.

"Are you a Christian?" she asked suddenly.

I thought for a moment. Pictures of Jesus traveling in India and Tibet came to my mind, and his admonitions to love one another. "Well, America is generally a Christian country, so I suppose I might be thought of as a Christian."

"Oh, so you believe that Jesus is God?" she asked, her eyes wide, her hand on my knee. She obviously took a dim view of religion.

"No, I believe that Jesus was like Lao Tzu. God is like the Tao, a force, a life force behind the wonderful workings of nature. Don't you believe in the Tao?" I asked looking deep in her eyes.

"Oh, I don't know. What did Marx believe?" she asked, suddenly shivering.

"Well, I think that Marx was an atheist. He probably didn't believe in the Tao."

"Mmm," she said. "Well, then I don't believe in the Tao, either!"

"Well, that's okay," I said. "The Tao doesn't need to be believed in, it just is. You believe in love, though, I suppose?"

"Oh, yes, " she sighed, and suddenly it got rather chilly, or at least, it seemed to get rather chilly. She pulled closer to me and said softly, "Hold me closer." I could not refuse. As Lao Tzu said, one must flow with the Tao, and I was very much inclined to go with the flow on this occasion.....

Look, it cannot be seen—it is beyond form.
Listen, it cannot be heard—it is beyond sound.
Grasp, it cannot be held—it is intangible.

The form of the formless,
The image of the imageless,
It is called indefinable and beyond imagination.

Stand before it and there is no beginning.
Follow it and there is no end.
Stay with the ancient Tao,
Move with the present.

Knowing the ancient beginning
Is the essence of the Tao.
—Lao Tzu, *Tao Te Ching*

§§§

Early the next morning, Bill and I were on our way to the Great Wall. While it is possible to go on a bus tour to the Great Wall, Bill and I decided to take the train, which leaves from the Peking Station every morning at 7:40 a.m. We picked up the train at a station near the Institute, and within a short time we were piling off the train like two more of the hundreds of school children dressed in white uniforms who were on their way to see the "Great, Great Wall."

In a few moments, we bounded up onto the vast, gigantic wall, grabbing a "chishuai" (soda-pop) from a vendor, and then stared in awe at the stone dragon that wound through the hills north of Bejing. I wanted to get some photographs of the wall before it was too late in the afternoon, as the sky would be washed out.

Without a doubt, the Great Wall of China is one of the most stupendous structures ever built by man, rivaled only by the Great Pyramid of Egypt. If it were reassembled at the equator, it would girdle the globe with a wall eight feet high and three feet thick! Of all the man-made structures on the earth, the only one that might conceivably be visible from the moon is the Great Wall. A scientist in 1790 estimated that it contained more bricks and stones than all the buildings of England, Scotland, Ireland and Wales put together. The reported lengths of the Great Wall vary widely, from 1500 to 3500 miles. Generally, it is accepted that a straight line from one end to the other would measure 1,145 miles, while counting all the loops, arms, and spurs, it extends 2,500 miles from the Bohai Sea to the Tibetan Plateau.

§§§

"Fear not a tiger from the south,
but beware even a rooster from the north."

So goes the ancient Chinese proverb, warning people of the Barbarians of the north. Shortly after the new emperor Chin Shih-huang had been told by an oracle in 235 B.C. that his dynasty's downfall would come through "Hu" (which can mean "barbarian"), he conceived the Great Wall of China. Although parts of it were already built, it was Chin, son of an itinerant dancing girl and the last king of the Chou dynasty, who conceived it in its entirety. Chin consolidated a realm of disunited states with the aid of excellent ministers and generals in seven years, forming what today is modern "Chin-a."

Chin decided to erect a massive barrier that no Mongol

horseman could scale or ride around, and he was no small thinker! To execute the project, every able-bodied man in China was drafted, from scholars to the nation's criminals. Workers were driven to labor by the flail of overseers, and resisters were dragged to the Wall and buried alive. Workers who died, often from disease and overwork, were thrown into the Wall—which thus became the world's longest cemetary—in the belief that their spirits would help in protecting China.

Inch by tortured inch, the wall was laid. The first three hundred miles had hardly a level stretch in them. Superb workmanship was called for, and even when the wall stretched over remote peaks, rarely seen except by hawks, the blocks were cut and dressed as if they were for the Imperial Palace itself. Modern engineers have said that the wall could hardly be improved upon today. Behind each finished section, (which was about twenty-five feet high and nineteen feet wide) a huge permanent garrison was quartered. Detachments went on duty at blockhouses built at mile intervals. At projecting watchtowers archers stood ready. With one warrior every two hundred yards, nine would defend a mile. Chin's standing army numbered three million and was undoubtedly the most superior military power in Asia at the time.[37]

Emperor Chin died in 210 B. C. In the first great history of China, the "Shih Chi," it was said that the mausoleum of Emperor Chin, which he had designed himself, was "lined with bronze and surrounded by underground rivers of mercury." The constel-lations of heaven were depicted on the ceiling, and the floor depicted the extent of his empire. Crossbows were arranged so that they would kill anyone who broke into the tomb, which was disguised as an ordinary hill. A vast host of concubines and many of the laborers who worked on his tomb accompanied the king to his death and resting place in the tomb.[37]

And so, one of the most colossal works of man, the pet project of a fanatical emperor, came into existence. And indeed, it did hold back the northern barbarians for more than 1,400 years. It wasn't until the fourteenth century that that country boy from the steppes, Genghis Khan with his magic ring, was able to sweep over the wall and overrun China. An old saying about the wall goes, "It destroyed one generation and saved a hundred."

Standing at the last tower, I could hardly believe that I was on the Great Wall. I heard several other people saying the same thing. No one thing could symbolize China more than the Great Wall. Coming to China without seeing the Great Wall was unthinkable. What we see today is not wholly the work of Emperor Chin. Much of it was later repaired and added to by other emperors, the last of whom were the Ming emperors, who improved a great deal of the Wall from 1380 to 1644. Many of the portions are in excellent repair, particularly around Beijing. Other segments in the west have been reduced to mere mounds rising only a few feet above the shifting desert.

Staring out over the Wall, past the thousands of tourists — Chinese in funky Hong Kong sunglasses, Japanese (each with two or three cameras), Americans, Russians, soldiers, school girls—I became mesmerized by the lithe, twisting line of the wall. It was like a gigantic Chinese dragon, snaking over the rugged hills, lying lazily in wait for some unwary traveler who might venture too close. At certain parts, the Wall would split, and go off in two directions.

Generally, people combine their trip to the Great Wall with one to the Ming Tombs nearby, the burial place of thirteen Ming Dynasty emperors. The tombs begin with an impressive archway and road lined with statues of animals, but the tombs themselves are in very poor repair. It is a peaceful and pleasant place to get away from the hustle and bustle of the eight million people in Beijing, though.

The Summer Palace, built by the Manchu Emperors, is another spot to visit on an afternoon. It was largely destroyed by the British troops during the Opium War in 1860, but was rebuilt by the Dowager Empress in 1888, using funds meant for the Chinese Navy. This pretty well crippled China's military forces and opened the door for Japanese expansionism.

There is so much to see and do around Peking that it is good to buy a guide-book for the city. Transportation around town is relatively simple. The bus and electric trolley system is good, and taxis can be found at the major hotels and other popular tourist points. Most of the citizens ride bicycles, and it is delightful to see a major capital city that does not have traffic jams. Instead, hordes of bicycle riders pour into the streets like some massive *Tour de France*, especially in the late afternoon. Bicycles can be rented at many of the hotels. There is also a subway system in Peking that runs east-west from the railway station and it is the fastest way to get from one end of the city to the other, although naturally, you won't see much.

On our last evening in Beijing, after spending a week there, Bill and I went to our favorite beer hall, a nameless place in downtown Peking, and hung out for a while. We had pitchers of beer with peanuts and sausage for snacks and happily gawked around at the workers in their gray suits and caps. The beer halls of China are great places where you can meet and eat with the real working men of China in their own atmosphere, and they abound all over the country. Beer is cheap and food is served, and often there will be music in the background.

We went to a Peking Duck restaurant afterward. This particular dish is only served in restaurants that specialize in it. The duck was served with its special crispy covering and spring onions, sauce, soup, small flat bread and rice. We were able to order bottles of Peking Beer, brewed in Beijing, and available at many of the better restaurants, although *Tsing-Tao* beer, made at a German-built brewery, is said to be China's best brew. It was a great way to spend our last night in Beijing. We had loved every minute of our week, but it was time to go.

Early the next morning, we were off by train to Xian, the ancient capital of China. In fact, historically it has been the capital of China for a longer time than Beijing. It was a pleasant train trip, and we expected to arrive sometime the next morning. We met some Hong Kong Chinese on the train and had dinner with them in the dining car; some fried rice and a bottle of wine. As I settled into my bunk, I gazed out the window to see a waning moon hanging over an endless rice paddies that faded into the distance.

In the morning we were in Xian, known as the cradle of Chinese civilization. We immediately checked into the Liberation Hotel opposite the railway station, where we got a double room for a couple of dollars. There are several hotels in Xian for foreigners, as Xian is quite a popular spot for tourists these days, ever since the discovery of the Terracotta Warriors in the tomb of none other than Emperor Chin who built the Great Wall.

That crazy emperor Chin Shih Huang made headlines again in 1974 when part of his tomb was discovered by some peasants sinking a well. Excavation began, and is still being carried out. In subsequent excavations, an entire army of life-size clay warriors, some six thousand of them, were discovered in other vaults of the tombs, presumably to accompany the emperor into heaven, and protect him in the other world. They are arranged in battle formation, and carry real swords, spears and crossbows.

It reportedly took seven hundred thousand workers thirty-six years to construct the elaborate tomb of Chin, and it is an archeological find in the same category as the discovery of King Tutankhamen's in Egypt. The actual tomb of Chin, with its jewels, rivers of mercury (which were also said to have gold ducks floating on them), and a magnificent throne, has yet to be found and excavated. Its excavators will have to be careful, for, as in many Egyptian tombs, it was loaded with deadly traps to deter tomb robbers.

Also near the tombs are the Huaquing Hot Springs, a

place where many an emperor has bathed, and many palaces were built around them, starting in 747 A.D. It was here at these hot springs that Generalissimo Chiang Kaishek, the leader of the Guo Ming-Ton Nationalists, and president of Taiwan for years until his death in the mid-seventies, was captured by a local warlord who was secretly working with the Communists. In a dawn raid they captured the general and he was forced to negotiate with the Communists to form a united front against the Japanese. This was in 1936, when Chiang Kaishek was more interested in wiping out the Communists than in freeing his country from the invaders.

The Reds wanted to kill Chiang and have it done with, but it was Stalin himself who saved the general, saying that his death would cause chaos in China, and that he was needed for a united front against the Japanese. Chiang was later released on Christmas Day after intensive negotiations, and a plane full of banknotes was flown in for his ransom from Shanghai. The plane had so much cash in it that the pilot had to climb in the window of the cockpit.

There is also a museum in Xian, the Shanxi Provincial museum with an impressive display of ancient steles—engraved stone markers that recount some interesting facets of China's history. One stele recounts the story of how Christianity came to China in the seventh century when a Syrian named Raban came to the imperial court at Xian and presented the emperor with some of the early scriptures. He brought what is known as Nestorian Christianity which flourished along side Buddhism in China for several hundred years, with many of the towns along the Silk Road being essentially of the Nestorian Christian faith, until the advent of Islam.

Nestorian Christians, now virtually vanished, are a mysterious bunch, and little is actually known about them. They are named after the last patriarch of Constantinople, Saint Nestorus, who refused to sign the Nicene Creed in 431 AD when the Catholic Church was created. He was banished to the Libyan Desert, but his followers moved to Eastern Turkey and eventually Bagdad, India & China.

They are related to the Essenes, Gnostics and Coptics, as they believe that Jesus and Christ were not exactly the same person. Specifically, they believed that Jesus was a man, and Christ was the Archangel Melchizedek, who merely "borrowed" Jesus' body for a few years during the ministry. It was therefore Melchizedek (Christ) who performed the many miracles and was crucified, but Jesus who visited the Apostles afterward, and probably left for Europe, England, and other places he had not yet visited.

Another museum not to be missed is the Ban Po Museum

and Neolithic Site, an archeological dig with a number of pits and some murals of imagined prehistoric life in China, covered by a large barn-type building. This six-thousand-or-so-year-old village excavation is thought by some scholars to be the cradle of Chinese civilization, although most experts agree that Chinese civilization is certainly much older. Other excavations in the Golden triangle and Thailand, as well as ancient Chinese records, support this.

It is interesting to note that the term "cave man" originated from caves in northern China where bones of men and wild animals were found. This prehistoric man then became known as "Peking Man," and the expression and belief of cave men was popularized. Now, seemingly too late to change peoples minds about the past, it has been discovered that the caves were really the caves of wild animals, and that men had never lived in them. The reason the human bones were found there was because they had been dragged there by the wild animals!

Extant Chinese texts state that the first of the dynasties was that of the "Five Monarchs," in which there were, confusingly, nine rulers whose combined reigns lasted from 2,852 to 2,206 B.C., which is just after the time at which the archeologists date the Ban Po Neolithic Site. Confucius ascribed to one king, Yao, whose reign started around 2,357 B.C., ."..kindliness, wisdom, and sense of duty." He was succeeded by Shon, who built a vast network of roads, bridges, and passes through the enormous land, and many scholars attribute the building of the Silk Road to him.

All ancient Chinese texts, especially those of Lao Tzu and Confucius, as well as the *I Ching* , speak of the ancients and the glory of their civilization. They were presumbably speaking about the people living at least at the time of the "Five Monarchs" and probably before. Possibly, they are really referring to the people of the "Motherland, Mu."

Unfortunately, not much is known about the early part of Chinese history, from the first millennia B. C. and before. Just before he died, in 212 B.C., Emperor Chin Shih Huang ordered that all the books and literature relating to ancient China be destroyed. Vast amounts of ancient texts—virtually everything pertaining to history, astronomy, philosophy, and science—were seized and burnt. Whole libraries, including the royal library, were destroyed. Some of the works of Confucius and Mencius were included in this destruction of knowledge.

Fortunately, some books survived, as people hid them, and many works were hidden in Taoist temples where they are even now religiously kept and preserved. They are on no account shown to anyone, but kept hidden away as they have been for thousands of years. The recent persecution and closing of religious temples by the Communists indicated that the lamas still have cause to keep their ancient books hidden. It is known that the Soviets have supressed a great many religious texts that have been discovered in the Soviet Union, because they are afraid these would give the churches a boost.

Doubtless, there was a great deal of history relating to the early days of ancient China lost. What caused the emperor Chin to want to destroy any record of the past just prior to his death? Was he such a megalomaniac that he wanted history to start with him, or was he influenced by the same evil forces that inspired Genghis Khan and Hitler to the same sort of book burning?

> *We have heard that in the remote past*
> *kings had titles but no posthumous appelations.*
> *In recent times kings not only had titles*
> *but after their death were awarded names*
> *based on their conduct.*
> *That means sons passed judgment*
> *on their fathers, subjects on their sovereign.*
> *This cannot be allowed.*
> *Posthumous titles are herewith abolished.*
> *We are the First Emperor, and our successors*
> *shall be known as the Second Emperor,*
> *the Third Emperor, and so on,*
> *for endless generations.*
> –Chih Wang Ti

§§§

Xian is quite an ancient city, and therefore, an especially interesting one to wander about in. The entire town is enclosed in a wall, and the buildings are tiled, pagoda-like structures with a charm of their own. Walking the streets is fascinating in itself, and there is the Drum Tower and the Bell Tower to see, both in the middle of town. Another attraction is the Big Goose Pagoda built in 652 A.D. to house Buddhist scriptures brought from India by the Buddhist monk Xuan Zhuang, also known as Tripitaka. The pagoda is outside the city wall.

Bill and I met a young Australian gal on the street one day, and went out to dinner with her at a beer hall near the Liberation Hotel. We drank warm beer from bowls and ate kebabs, chicken, stir-fried vegetables, and other snacks. The Australian woman, a charming, blond-haired student from the University of Sydney, told us about a couple of her experiences in China.

"China is a pretty wild place for someone traveling by herself," she said, taking a piece of mutton with her chopsticks and popping it in her mouth. "Once at a banquet in Beijing, I was sitting next to a Chinese dignitary and we were talking about China. He suddenly turned to me and said, 'Tibet is a very difficult place to visit, unless, of course,' and he winked at me, 'you know the right people!' And then he put his hand on my knee!" We all laughed as she said this. Somehow, it just didn't seem in the Chinese character to be granting political favors for sexual ones.

We each got another bowl of beer and she continued. "Then, just the other day here in Xian, I was standing on a street corner just down the street, when this young Chinese guy, in a blue Mao jacket, plastic sunglasses and crew cut, comes riding a bicycle up to me, stops, and then nods to the back of his bike and says, 'Let's go!'"

"Great!" laughed Bill. It was a beautiful scene that she described, and in a way, we were sorry to hear that she hadn't jumped on and gone, as it were, into an adventure. China is certainly changing. The young people are getting more freedom, and the West is eating away at the closed society that seemed so mysterious only a decade ago. Today, in many cities of China, the Coca-Cola symbol can be seen everywhere.

As the guy on the bike had said, it was time to go, and Bill and I had to move on. Xian was fun, a great mixture of old and new. We were heading now for Sichan Province, the Yangtze Gorges, southern China and the honeymoon town of Guilin. We got our visas extended another month in Xian and were off to the the river town of Yichang the next day.

A rare photo of the largest pyramid in the world near Xian, China. This pyramid is approximately 500 feet high with a base width of 1,200 feet. Curiously, even though the pyramid would be a major tourist attraction in any country, the Chinese have denied its existence and declared the area off-limits to foreigners.

An Eastern Han Dynasty pictorial carving at Wu Lian tz'u, in Chia-hsiang, Shantung, showing (from right to left) the successsion of the Three Soveriegns and the Five Emperors in legendary history. (From Jung Keng, *Han Wu Liang tz'u hua hsiang lu*, 1936.)

A Han stone relief showing ching K'os attempt to assassinate the Emperor Chi Huang Ti, the builder of the Great Wall, the consolidator of modern China, and the Emperor who ordered all books destroyed in order to erase history. The blade is thrown with such force that it has pierced a palace column. Beside the pillar is a box containing the head of a general. The Emperor stands to the right of the pillar holding aloft a jade disc that is the symbol of his authority. Jade discs and scepters were also the symbol of authority to the Mayans of Central America.

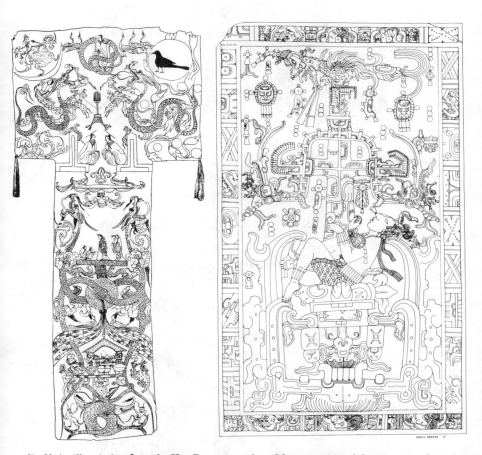

(Left) A silk painting from the Han Dynasty tomb at *Ma-wang-tuei* and the engraving from the Mayan sarcophagus from Palenque (Right) both depict the universe in three layers: the Upper World, the Middle World, and the Under World. Underlying both pictures is the idea of interwold penetration. Various devices were involved in both cases, for example, the animals, birds, the cosmic tree of life. Ancient Chinese culture has many similarities with the Mayans of America.

Foto: *Revue de l'Aluminium*, n.° 283, 1961

These aluminum belt buckles were found in ancient
Chinese Tombs by Chinese archaeologists in 1959.

Chapter 20

SOUTHERN CHINA TO HONG KONG:

TAOIST PILGRIM
IN THE JAWS OF THE DRAGON

The Way has more than one name.
There is more than one Sage.
Doctrines vary in different lands,
But their benefits reach all mankind.
—Tang Dynasty decree, 635 A.D.

Forty miles southwest of Xian is the largest pyramid in the world, known generally as the Great Pyramid of China. It is part of a group of sixteen ancient pyramids built by unknown engineers at an unknown time. Unfortuantely they are in a "forbidden zone" and tourists are not allowed to visit them. There may be a military base nearby and, as a consequence, very little information about the pyramid has been released. American aviators who have photographed the largest and believe it is at least twice as high as the Great Pyramid of Egypt (four hundred fifty feet) and have suggested a figure of one thousand feet. It seems to date from the Hsia Dynasty, about four thousand years ago, though other dates given are that it is one or more thousand years older than that.[27]

I mused about this little-known archaeological wonder as Bill and I took a train out of Xian to Xiangfan—about half-way between Xian and Yichang on the Yangtze River—where we would catch a steamer to go to Chungking. Bill and I sat back in the hard seats on a slow, amazingly uncrowded country train.

A Chinese worker in gray clothes was sitting next to me, staring hard at me and my clothing. "What place are you from?" he asked me in Mandarin. He seemed genuinely confused, and I surmised he'd never seen a foreigner in his life.

"I'm from America," I told him in my best Chinese.

He drew a blank. Perhaps it was my Chinese, or perhaps

he had just never heard of America. "Are you Chinese?" he asked me.

"No, I'm not," was all I could think to tell him.

The guy sitting next to him nudged him in the shoulder. "He's not Chinese; he's a foreigner!" he told him.

"Yes!" I said. "I'm a foreigner, and I can hardly speak Chinese!" They looked completely astounded and then gingerly touched my heavy denim blue jeans, continuing to stare open-mouthed at me. I felt like a visitor from another planet. I offered them some sesame cookies that I had in my pack. The encounter was as exciting for me as it was for them!

Looking out the window, I thought again about the Great Pyramid. Perhaps we were just passing it. It was out there somewhere, though I could not see it. No one knows who built it. One pyramid is in the vicinity of Xian and is believed to have been part of the tomb of Shih Hunag Ti, just east of Xian, and is about two thousand years old. Traces of the original coloring have been found on the Great Pyramid of China. It was black on the north, blue-gray on the east, red on the south, and white on the west. The apex was painted yellow.[27]

The significance of the colors apparently has to do with the Taoist (and pre-Taoist) system of five phases or five elements and everything may be catagorized under five elements (fire, water, earth, metal and wood). The directions of the compass, emotions and colors are included in this system. Black is for the north (water); green is for the east (wood); red to the south (fire); white to the west (metal); and yellow to the center (earth).

If the blue-gray color to the east is a faded green, then probably the pyramid was painted to the ancient Taoist elements. I should mention again that the pyramid is probably much older than Lao Tzu himself, though Taoist tradition is said to go back to the ancient continent of Shen Chou in the Pacific.

Archaeological excavations of the pyramid have discovered magnificent jade objects and "green stones." The purpose of the pyramid—tomb? astronomical observatory?—is not known. The pyramid is generally thought to have been built in the Hsia Dynasty, though very little is known about the Hsia Dynasty either. Its emperors are the first "authentic rulers" or recognized dynasty of China, following the semi-mythical "Five Monarchs" that ruled from 2852 to 2206 B.C. The Hsia Dynasty reigned from 2205 to 1767 B.C., though recorded Chinese history is not considered to have started until the Chou dynasty in 1122 B.C.

Bruce Cathie, an airline pilot and mathematician from

Auckland, New Zealand decided to calculate the "world grid harmonics" of the Great Pyramids of China several years ago and contacted the Chinese Embassy in Wellington, New Zealand about their exact location. To his astonishment, officials at the embassy denied their existence! Eventually the Chinese did acknowlege that there were some structures in the area, but they were not pyramids, but trapezoidal tombs from the Han Dynasty. Yet, they confessed that the "tombs" had not been excavated.[90]

In his book, *The Bridge To Infinity*, [90] Cathie suggests that the Great Pyramid of China is part of an ancient network of pyramids built at key places around the world to tap the earth's natural energies. Such a geometrical network could have been used in global communication, and Cathie believes that other pyramids, such as the Great Pyramid of Egypt were part of this network.

One of the few foriegners who has passed the pyramids was the American trader and gun-runner Fred Meyer Schroder who saw them in 1912. Schroder's guide, a garrulous old monk named Bogdo, told him they were not burial grounds, but "mountains as high as the sky." Bogdo told Schroder that the pyramids must be older than five thousand years, as texts five thousand years old mention the pyramids as old then.[90]

Schroder was awed by the largest man-made structure he had ever seen. He described the pyramids as having been encased in ordinary field stone about three feet square. "We rode around it looking for stairways or doors but saw none..."

Cathie also mentions the curious story of an American aviator named James Gaussman who was flying the "Burma Hump" taking supplies to Chungking from India during World War II. Gaussman was returning to an airbase in Assam from China, when he had trouble with one of his engines. Figuring that his fuel lines were icing up, he decided to descend to a lower altitude, hazardous in the many ranges of mountains (including the Himalayas) on the borders of China, Tibet and India. Banking to avoid a mountain, he came out in a wide flat valley. Directly below him was a gigantic white pyramid that shimmered as if it were made of metal. Limestone casing, as was once on the Great Pyramid of Egypt, would also shimmer. The most remarkable thing was that it had a capstone, a huge piece of jewel-like material that could have been crystal!

There was no way to land, so after circling the pyramid three times he continued his flight to Assam. He sighted the Brahma- putra River, and ascertaining his position, was able to safely reach his home base. In his intelligence report, quoted by Cathie, Gaussman says, "There was nothing around it, just a big pyramid sitting out in the wilderness. I figure it was extremely old. Who built it? Why was it built? What's on the inside?" [90]

Wouldn't we all like to know? Cathie suggests that perhaps the High Priests of ancient Lhasa (The Great White Brotherhood?) used the geometry of the World Grid to create a global communication system, and these pyramids were part of this network.

The Great Pyramid of China is without a doubt one of the most fascinating lost sites in China, and we can only hope that the Chinese will open this site to tourists in the near future. It is interesting to add China to the many far-flung areas of the world where pyramids were built—Egypt, Central America (where there are more pyramids than anywhere else in the world), ancient France, Soviet Central Asia, Polynesia, Peru, and the prehistoric Mississippi Valley.

After spending a comfortable night on the slow train through China, Bill and I arrived in Xiangfan in the late afternoon. We checked into the local hotel—there is only one in town, the Xiangfan Guest House. After checking in and being given a clean, double room for about a dollar fifty, we went out for a walk.

There is not really much to do in Xiangfan, except attract crowds, but it is an interesting town, completely off any tourist route, and therefore, especially virgin territory for the traveler. We had dinner in a local restaurant with the workers in their gray suits, and took a quick walk before going to bed. Yichang is a sprawling river-port town, with an active coal yard, if nothing else. The local free market was interesting; some entrepreneurs had a blanket spread out on the street, selling their wares. One guy was selling dead rats. Dead rats? I looked at Bill. Why would anyone want to buy dead rats? The seller winked. He knew.

Bill shrugged his shoulders. "Perhaps for medicinal purposes." I nodded. "Dead rats could probably cure anything," Bill mused.

The train left for Yichang at one o'clock, and was scheduled to arrive about five hours later. We got seats in third class (hard seats) but spent most of the time in the dining car with a policeman playing cards and drinking beer. In Yichang, we went straight to the port on the Yangtze and got our tickets for the trip to Chungking. We had a dinner of stir-fried mushrooms and rice at a restaurant near the port, with a famous Yichang beer.

We got our berth around eleven, and sometime during the night the steamer headed west up the Yangtze. At dawn, we awoke and noticed we were heading through the first of the

Yangtze Gorges.

The sight was spectacular. Sheer precipices rose steeply on either side of the river, this being the first and longest gorge, the Xiling Gorge. Leaning over the rail with the dawn breeze in our faces, we marveled at the rugged beauty of the scene. The sun cast yellow beams on the dark surging water, and the eastern sky was red and orange with the sunrise. An ancient poet once wrote of the gorges that they were like "a thousand seas pouring into one cup."

Next came the Wuxia Gorge, about twenty-five miles long with cliffs on either side rising over three thousand feet. We cruised slowly upstream all day; it was a nice day and the gorges were absolutely spectacular. We passed small junks with their tattered sails up, floating downstream, and people towing boats upstream by a rope from the bank. In the past, every boat making its way up the Yangtse had to be towed from the shore, and there are paths cut into the vertical rock cliffs that enabled the sometimes hundreds of laborers to haul a ship upstream through the rapid currents. Steam ships have pretty much put an end to the large-scale hauling, but small ships can still be seen being towed manually upstream.

The second day was misty and cold. Junks and sampans meandered along the bank. Our steamer's horn would blow occasionally, a mournful sound—loud, even and long—as we came round a bend. We drank tea and watched the scenery from the railing. On the shore was the Shi Bao Pagoda, a twelve-story temple built against a sheer granite cliff-block, jutting up from the banks of the river. We occasionally docked at small ports, where the locals would sell persimmons, oranges, and other fruits to the passengers. Life rolled on up the Yangzte River, or down, depend ing on which way you were going, of course.

China—
An endless cup of tea.
Misty soaring mountains
Flank the boatmen
Poling up the Yangtze.
Be a Marco Polo
Discover yourself.
—a 'pilgrim'

The last and most famous of the gorges is the Qutang Gorge. It is the shortest and most spectacular, with sheer precipices rising steeply in a narrow gorge less than one hundred yards apart. High on the cliff face above the raging rapids are coffins, placed there thousands of years ago by an unknown, vanished culture whose strange funeral rites included burial on the face of a cliff above the Yangtse....I gazed out at the banks and the stars from the railing of the ship that night, a bit tipsy on rice wine, marveling at the Yangtze, the life-line of China.

China—truly a land of lost cities and ancient mysteries, not to mention many important inventions which are a part of our lives. It was really the Chinese that invented moveable type; the inventor was a fellow named Bi Sheng in 1045 A.D., four hundred years before Gutenberg first printed the Bible. The Chinese are also credited with inventing writing paper, wrapping paper, paper napkins, playing cards and paper money! Toilet paper was another one of the spin-offs of their paper industry, about the time of Christ.

The Chinese were well aware of earthquakes and geological changes; they developed earthquake-resistant houses as long as seven thousand years ago. The world's first-known seismograph for detecting and recording far away earthquakes was invented by Zhang Heng in 132 A.D. This ingenious device stood about eight feet tall and featured eight bronze dragons holding balls between their jaws. When tilted by a distant earthquake, an internal pendulum opened the jaw of the dragon facing the source of the tremor and the ball dropped into the mouth of a bronze frog waiting below each dragon.

The first mechanical clock is attributed to two Chinese inventors around 725 A. D., and gunpowder was known in China at least as early as the ninth century, if not much earlier. Used only for fireworks and enjoyment, after it was first brought to Europe in the thirteenth century, the first cannons were made by the Dutch. The Chinese have always had great scope and vision regarding their projects; not only was the Great Wall a colossal endeavor, but the Grand Canal of China, which connects the Yellow River with the Yangtze, is twenty times longer than the Panama Canal—yet the Chinese con- structed it without modern equipment one thousand, three hundred years ago! There are other mammoth projects that still are largely unknown or waiting to be discovered, such as the largest pyramid in the world, previously mentioned. Even the Chinese version of the typewriter, called the Hoang typewriter, has 5,700 characters on a keyboard two feet wide and seventeen inches high!

The Chinese are even credited with the discovery of America! There are two ancient Chinese texts which tell of the exciting expeditions to a great land in the east. The text *Classic of Mountains and Seas,* is from 2250 BC and the text *Fu Sang* is from about 400 AD. Both are translated and discussed in detail in Henriette Mertz's book, *Pale Ink*.[91]

In *The Genius of China: 3,000 Years of Science, Discovery and Invention,* [95] the author Robert Temple (distilling the book from Joseph Needham's works at Cambridge University) says that the Chinese knew and used poison gas and tear gas, in the 4th Century BC, 2,300 years before the West got around to it! The Chinese were making cast iron in the 4th Century BC (1,700 years before the West), and they manufactured steel from cast iron in the 2nd Century BC (2,000 years before the West). The first suspension bridge was built in China in the 1st Century (at least 1,800 years before the West), and the Chinese invented matches in 577, a thousand years before the West.

Says Needham in the introduction of the book about the advanced level of civilization in China: "First, why should they have been so far in advance of other civilizations; and second, why aren't they now centuries ahead of the rest of the world?" Perhaps China, as Churchward and other historians suggest, inherited its knowlege from an older civilization. Its discoveries, like ours, are just the rediscovery of ancient technology from the roller-coaster ride of history.

§§§

The Yangtze steamers, generally run by the "East is Red" company, run from Shanghai to Chungking, a trip that takes a total of nine days upstream and seven days downstream. There are five classes on the steamers. Foreigners are allowed to travel on the first four, all of which include berths of some sort. First and second class are quite luxurious, third is a bunk in a room of ten beds, fourth is an open room of twenty or so bunks, and fifth class is deck passage. There are several restaurants and snack bars on board, and food can be bought at stops along the way. Most tourists go from Chungking to Wuhan or vice versa; going on to Shanghai by rail which is much faster. Bill and I bought fourth-class tickets for the three-to-five-day trip from Yichang to Chungking and it cost twenty-nine yen each, about fifteen dollars.

It was around noon the next day that we arrived in Chungking; another day, another city, another adventure! Chungking was the capital of China during the Second World War, with Generalissimo Chiang Kaishek as its leader. Even today, it has a distinct atmosphere of old China about it: narrow winding streets down steep hills to the river, small workshops, families hanging out on the staircased alleys. It is quite hilly (an ancient San Francisco).

Perhaps the most striking thing about Chungking is that

it has virtually no bicycles! The reason for this is the steep hills. It would be nearly impossible to ride a bike up or down one! Chungking was badly bombed by the Japanese during World War II, though it was never actually captured by them. As a result, many of the buildings are still in a state of disrepair, and Chungking has never really been totally reconstructed.

The city, and the entire state of Sichuan, fared rather poorly during the Cultural Revolution and was the scene of pitched fighting between Red Guards, as well as army units, and workers. Since the Communist take-over, agricultural production declined dramatically in Sichuan, the most populous state in China with over one hundred million people. Finally, it had to import rice, and rice ration coupons became so valuable there were rumours of families selling off their daughters to obtain them! With Mao's death in 1978 and the "Gang of Four," led by Mao's widow, arrested, Sichuan started on the road to economic recovery. It was Sichuan that pioneered the more radical "free enterprise" agricultural plots and free markets, all of which have apparently brought the province back to stability. In 1981 severe flooding, the worst in a hundred years, left one and a half million people homeless, and therefore, some land was given back to the peasants. They were told they could keep anything that they grew on the land in an effort to get agricultural production back together.

Chungking is an interesting town. Though there is not that much of special interest, there are the docks where the ferries come in, Pipa Shan Park with a nice tea garden and splendid view over the city, and the "US-Chiang Kaishek Criminal Acts Exhibition Hall" where instruments of torture used on captured Communist prisoners by the Nationalists are displayed. Chungking had a great many Americans in it before and after the war, and it was to Chungking that the "Flying Tigers" flew over the Burma Hump to bring supplies to China. Chungking also has many fine restaurants, serving spicy Sichuan food.

Bill and I took the overnight train to Chengdu, the capital of Sichuan, riding in the hard berths. Early the next morning, we were checking into the main hotel of the city, the Jinjiang Hotel. It has dormitories on the seventh floor and good hot showers, plus other rooms from five dollars a night.

There is a nice zoo in Chengdu, with a few of Sichuan's most famous animals: pandas! Bill and I went there one afternoon. It is a pleasant zoo with a nice park and a variety of animals. I dropped the lens cap of my camera inside the giant panda compound, a large open island surrounded by a deep trench. I leaped the railing and landed inside the pen with the pandas, who were casually munching away at some bamboo, and then Bill helped me out again before either the pandas or the animal keepers noticed.

Giant pandas, which can weigh up to three hundred pounds, are in reality related to raccoons, though they look like bears. There is also a lesser panda which lives in the mountains of Central Asia, and looks similar to a raccoon with red fur. Pandas have fur which covers their feet, including the bottoms, and this is one of the distinctions between pandas/raccoons and bears. Giant pandas live exclusively on tender bamboo shoots and inhabit the remote, heavily-forested areas of central China, especially Sichuan.

Although first mentioned by the Tang Emperors in 621 AD as the "black and white bears," they were not really discovered until 1869 when the French missionary Father Armand David obtained the fur of one from some hunters. Giant pandas were not heard of again for another half a century when none other than two sons of Teddy Roosevelt shot and stuffed one in 1929. Today they can be found in a number of zoos, but their exact number in the wild remains unknown, and they are considered to be an endangered species.

This illustrates the wildness and remoteness of the heavily forested mountain valleys in Sichuan, the most populated of Chinese provinces. It is also the home of the mysterious "Wild Hairy Men of China." Throughout Chinese history, poets and scholars have talked about "mountain ogres," bands of wild hairy men, and strange creatures in the mountains, "monkey like, yet not a monkey." Until recently, these stories, similar to those of Yetis and Sasquatches, have been treated in China and elsewhere with skepticism if not out-right disbelief. One famous story given to the Chinese Academy of Sciences in Peking in October, 1977 by Chinese commune leader Pang Gensheng is of how he met a "hairy man" in the woods on the slope of a lonely gully where he had gone to cut logs.[58]

"It came closer and closer. I got scared and kept retreating until my back was against a stone cliff and I couldn't go any further. The hairy man came up to about five feet from me. I raised my axe, ready to fight for my life. He was about seven feet tall, with shoulders wider than a man's, a sloping forehead, deepset eyes, and a bulbous nose with slightly upturned nostrils. He had sunken cheeks, ears like a man's but bigger, and round eyes, also bigger than a man's. His hair was dark brown, more than a foot long, and hung loosely over his shoulders. His whole face, except for the nose and ears, was covered with short hairs. His arms hung below his knees. He didn't have a tail and the hair on his body was short. He was a male. That much I saw clearly."

Pang Gensheng went on to describe how he escaped the curious, though terrifying, creature, "We stood, neither of us moving, for more than an hour. Then I groped for a stone and threw it at him. It hit him in the chest. He uttered several howls and rubbed the spot with his left hand, then he turned left and leaned against a tree, then walked away slowly toward the bottom of the gully. He kept making a mumbling sound."

There have been a number of other stories from communes and woodcutters in the remote forests of Sichuan, Hubei, Shaanxi, and Jiangxi provinces that confirm, to some scientists, the existence of "Wild Hairy Men." One interesting theory is that these may be sightings of a gigantic manlike ape called *Gigantopithecus* that inhabited the earth two million years ago and was thought to be extinct. Interestingly, giant pandas were known to live side by side with *Gigantopithecus* in prehistoric times. *Gigantopithecus* is described as being very similar to the "Wild, Hairy Men."

Noted archaeologist Myra Shackley suggests that the wild hairy men are the remnants of Neanderthal men, while according to other opinion, they may well be shy, giant hairy apes like *Gigantopithecus*. Reddish-brown hair taken from one site in China where a woman claimed to see a wild, hairy man scratching his back against a tree, proved when analyzed to come not from a black or brown bear but from an unknown creature with hair closely resembling that of primates.[58]

Until a creature is captured, it will remain a mystery.

§§§

Bill and I hung out in Chengdu for a few days, enjoyed the Sichuan food and beer halls, and spent one day visiting the Buddhist temple of Baoguang (Divine Light) in Sindu, an hour's bus drive north of the city. There are plenty of paintings here and a hoard of five hundred and fifty life sized statues of "Arhats," Buddhist deities of different sorts, some with the most bizarre expressions and grimaces imaginable—certainly impos- sible to describe.

We headed out of town the next day, intent on climbing one of the most sacred mountains in China, Emei Shan, in central Sichuan province. We left in the evening on a train heading south and stopped around 10:30 that night at

Leshan, the site of the largest rock-hewn Buddha in the world, carved into a cliff on the banks of the Min River. We spent the night in a small hotel opposite the train station and hitchhiked to the site of the giant Buddha, a most impressive statue.

A stone staircase is carved into the red stone cliff to the left of the four-hundred-foot tall image, and goes down to the river. Ferries from across the river will take you to the statue as well. It dates from the twelfth century and is similar, in some ways, to the gigantic statues in Bamian in central Afghanistan. The Buddha is sitting peacefully, superbly cut into the red cliffs around him. I gazed at a young Chinese boy in a blue suit and a fresh eager face standing at the foot of the statue; he was hardly as large as the big toe! There are a number of pagodas around the Buddha, and a large monstery on top of the cliff.

After hitching back to the railway station, catching a lift with a wrinkled old truck driver in a big green delivery truck, we took a train to Emei Da,the nearest train station to the mountain of Emei Shan. We spent a night in the small but pleasant Emei Da Guest House just outside the train station for fifty cents each in a double room. The next morning we hitchhiked to Baoguo Temple, the start of the three-day hike up sacred Emei Shan.

In the distance we could see the mountain, rising high like a great ship out of the mist. It is not especially high at nine thousand feet, but it is spectacular; its southern side a sheer cliff of several thousand feet. It is constantly in mist, and each view is a mystical, inspiring Chinese painting. There are seventy or more temples scattered up on the mountain, and a number of monasteries on the several different routes that one can take. It is one of the most sacred Buddhist mountains in China, and many Tibetans, living in western Sichuan, come on a pilgrimage to the mountain. One legend says that Buddha was flying by on his "magic elephant" and stopped at a pool on the mountain to give his elephant a wash. There is a monastery at this point today, called the "Elephant Bathing Pool Temple," and it has a statue of Buddha on an elephant.

We began hiking up the mist-shrouded mountain with our packs on our backs from Baoguo Temple, and passed several small temples each hour. At one pilgrimage resting spot, a bunch of Tibetan pilgrims who had never seen tourists before, ogled us for a while, felt our clothes, and said prayers. An old lady, pert and enterprising, was selling herbal medicine and convinced Bill to sell her a watch he was wearing. Then we were off again through the mist and forest, across beautiful, clear streams to Hong Jong Ping Monastery, where we got a double room and spent the night for a couple of dollars each.

In the evening, there was a ritual drumming and clanging of gongs by the monk in charge. It was a old, wooden building, with a dozen or so small rooms, and no electricity. After a big dinner of noodles and soup, we sat on the second-floor balcony and watched the mist move through the thick green forest. In the morning we were off again, this time intent on heading for the summit and staying that night at the monastery at the top.

It was misty again, we trudged up and up the hundreds of thousands of stone Ming Dynasty steps that wound their way up to the top of the mountain. After resting at a small pagoda, we were cutting across the mountain on a trail that would take us to the main trail leading up the summit ridge to the top. Suddenly, as we were hiking up a steep trail in a heavily forested gully, the mist cleared and we were attacked by four hairy, vicious bandits!

Terrified, I screamed, "It's the wild, hairy men! Run for your life, Bill!" It was too late. They were on us, snarling and intent on attacking us as they came out of hiding from the dense brush.

These "wild hairy men," greedy bandits on the run from the law, were actually a gang of monkeys, some of them deformed, who were notorious for attacking pilgrims on the mountain. I threw down a handful of soybean nuts, as I knew they were after food, and ran uphill screaming while three of them clung to my shirt, pants and backpack. Bill was following, and they attacked him after I had escaped, not content with the soy-nuts, but wanting whatever it was that we carried in our bags. These monkeys have been known to bite people who have nothing to give them, and have thrown people's cameras and shoulder bags down steep ravines. Security personnel have been scouring the moutain for the fugitives in the past few years, but they have, so far escaped capture and death at the hands of the law. Until this scourge is stopped, said one China Guidebook, no traveler will be safe on Emei Shan!

Bill and I made it safely (though we were somewhat out of breath), away from these small, "wild hairy men," and to a small temple where we were able to rest and have some tea. After lunch, we trudged on up the mountain, the mist coming in thicker and then suddenly clearing to give us a good view of the mountain and monasteries below us. As we neared the top, it was getting late. The thick fog settled in permanently for the night and it became freezing cold. We came to the summit just at sunset in the twilight world of the top, where there is a large monastery and cafeteria. Exhausted, we collapsed in front of the fire in the dining hall, where a half-dozen people sat drinking tea, and warmed themselves. We had dinner, and were shown to our rooms: small unheated, wooden cubicles with wooden beds and thick down comforters where, because of our crazy and exhausting adventures, we fell immediately asleep.

The next morning, we looked around the peak, we were on the edge of a precipice, though the fog was so thick, one could not see more than twenty feet in any direction. The view from the top is said to be magnificent; to the west are the snow-covered Daxue Shan mountains, many of them well over twenty thousand feet high. It is said that some people have been so moved by the awesome sunrise from the summit that they have thrown themselves over the top!

We headed down the mountain, past bamboo forests with a light covering of snow that had fallen the night before. We saw two pheasants on the way down, red and gold in their splendid autumn colors, flying across the trail. We carefully avoided the gully where the bandits had attacked us before, taking a different route down. The descent was quick. We reached the bottom of the mountain and the road to Emei Da by late afternoon. We hitched back along the muddy dirt road past flooded rice paddies. We got one ride with a handsome young Chinese guy who smiled enthusiastically when we told him we had climbed the mountain. "It's a great hike," he said in his best English, mixed with some Mandarin. "I am so glad that you have come and spent time in our area!" We were too, we told him. We spent another night at the Emei Da Guest House and then in the morning caught the train south on our way to Kunming.

By late morning, we had gone through a dozen or more tunnels. The line from Chengdu to Kunming in far southeastern China is approximately thirty-five per cent tunnels, including the longest tunnel in China—the line runs through some of the most mountainous country in the world.   It was an all-day train ride through Sichuan into Yunnan Province, the southern-most state in China.

It is in Yunnan that over half of China's minority races are found, mostly in the form of the various hill tribes along the borders with Burma, Thailand, Laos and Vietnam. The famous "Golden Triangle" comes together at the southern border of Yunnan, and it is here that a great deal of the heroin in the world is produced by tribal warlords that control the remote hills of northern Burma, Thailand and Laos.

During the civil war in the late forties, the Communists succeeded in driving part of the Nationalist army into these hills, where they hung on tenaciously. When I had lived in Taiwan years before, I boarded with the Secretary of the Treasury of the Republic of China (Taiwan); a general in the Nationalist Army who had commanded the Nationalist Army in Burma up to the sixties. He delighted in showing me his slides of Burma in those days, and in fact, a Nationalist Chinese Army still exists in northern Burma and the Golden Triangle, though in greatly reduced numbers. Today they are mostly engaged in heroin production and trafficking, but are a major part of Taiwan's rather fanciful plan to retake the mainland at some point. It is in this area today, most easily reached from northern Thailand, that the Fu Manchu-type warlords continue to do their dastardly deeds, commanding their private armies and mini-kingdoms. In the last few years, drug-taking and trafficking has picked up in Yunnan, and the local paper will occasionally editorialize on the subject.

We spent the evening looking out at the fantastic scenery (whenever we weren't in a tunnel), playing chess, and drinking beer with some Hong Kong Chinese in the dining car. We spent the night in the hard berths, and woke up the next morning as we were pulling into Kunming.

Kunming is known as the "city of eternal spring" because of its pleasant year-round climate with flowering parks and cool weather. Bill and I walked to the park from our hotel the first day, and were surprised to find that they were butchering a bear in back! He was half skinned, and the paws had been cut off, as bear paws are one of the delicacies of China. Another wild bear was in a cage nearby, waiting, I suppose, for the slaughter.

We walked around town. It had spacious streets, and many pre-World War II buildings, and also many sidewalk tea houses. We sat and had tea in one of the cafes, and met two young college girls who were studying English in a nearby college. We talked to the girls for a while, whose English names—which all English students seem to have—were Vivian and Rosey. Vivian had long black hair tied in a pony-tail, was very pretty, and wore a blue school uniform. Rosey was dressed the same, but she had shorter hair like most Chinese women and wore glasses, black-rimmed and thick. Bill and I found both girls very charming, and asked them what it was like at their college. Instead of answering, they invited us back to see their dormitory.

It was nice to meet some of their friends; they shared comfortable rooms with three other girls to a room, in double bunks. They showed us around town a bit and we then made a date to go the next day to the most famous tourist spot in Kunming: West Hill. It was a couple of miles by bus to the forests on the west bank of the Kinachi Lake, the sixth-largest fresh-water lake in China. Around the lake there are several famous temples, with the Golden

Temple and its five hundred Arhats and golden Buddhas standing in front of the door. We walked up the stone steps carved into a cliff above the lake by a Taoist monk and his assistants two hundred years ago to the Dragon's Gate, a cave-sanctuary in the cliff where one can enjoy a spectucular view of the lake.

Bill and I left one morning at 7:15 on a local bus for another must-see in Kunming, the Stone Forest, known as Shilin, about sixty miles from Kunming. It was a wild ride for three or more hours through the country to the Stone Forest, one of the most incredible natural sites in China—a veritable stone forest of fantastically shaped stones, like great menhirs sticking straight up out of the ground. Many of them are named, as they look like elephants, swans, arches, and people. There is a cultural show with some of the local hill tribe women, and a small hotel nearby.

Now Bill and I began to prepare for our journey out of Kunming. Our trip through China was coming to an end. China, Central Asia, and India were so jam-packed with interesting places to see, let alone mysteries and lost cities to explore, it hardly seemed that one lifetime was enough to do it all. I had been traveling now for five-and-a-half years, and admittedly, I had seen quite a bit, yet there was so much more to discover it seemed as if I had only scratched the surface.

One lost city worth mentioning in Yunnan is the site of Shih-Chai-Shan, only about thirty miles south of Kunming. In 329 B.C., a Chinese general was conquering the Tien kingdom of southern Yunnan—at that time not part of China—when his route home north was cut off by another, larger, hostile Chinese Army. The general decided to settle in Yunnan rather than battle this rival army, and created his own kingdom and culture. Nothing was known of this culture until 1955 when archeologists dug up a burial ground of these people in Shih-Chai-Shan. A large number of bronze objects were found, including bronze drum-shaped vessels which were used as containers for cowrie shells, apparently a form of currency at the time. On some of the larger bronze drum-vessels, a seated woman appears to be receiving offerings. On another, human sacrifice is depicted.

The culture vanished, and Yunnan was assimilated into China by the Kublai Khan at the end of the seventh century. Most interestingly, all over southeast Asia and even Polynesia, bronze drum-shaped vessels have been found, quite similar to those at Shin-Chai-Shan, and human sacrifice was known to have been practiced in these regions, especially in parts of Polynesia, for a long time. What are the connections? Some researchers suggest that these people settled throughout southeast Asia and even migrated to parts of Polynesia, though it has been pointed out that they did not have the maritime experience and came from a land-locked country. Were they escaping the Kublai Khan or are the ruins and bronze artifacts from an older culture that actually came from Polynesia and settled in southeast Asia? The use of shells as currency betrays some ties to the sea. The site remains a mysterious archeological puzzle. No sound dating techniques have been used yet, and it is not certain that the site is actually that of the Chinese general.[51]

Bill and I prepared to go by overnight train to Guilin, east towards Hong Kong. Vivian and Rosey showed us around the last day. We talked of life at college in America and China. They expressed the opinion that China and America were meant to be allies. At dinner I asked Vivian how she felt about Mao and the Gang of Four.

"Mao was our great leader, but he made mistakes," she said, fingering her ponytail. "As he got old, he became senile; that is why he made so many mistakes. The Gang of Four took his power and misused it for their own purposes, especially Mao's widow, Chiang Chinguo. She ruled China while Mao was old and senile. It was she who caused the terrible Cultural Revolution." Suddenly she stood up from the table, raised her fist and proclaimed, "Madame Mao is an enemy of the people!"

We finished our last meal together and they took us to the train station. "If only you could stay here with us," exclaimed Rosey, "perhaps you could become students at our college!" Vivian nodded in agreement. I looked at Bill. We both looked at the great, green diesel engine that would be taking us across the underbelly of China. These young gals were tempting, but we were too travel-happy to stay.

"We'd like to," said Bill, "but there are many lost cities yet to be discovered!" I nodded my approval. We shook hands with the girls, and said farewell. It can be difficult constantly saying farewell to new friends, but it is a way of life for the traveler. With a great screaming of the train whistle, we were off in the night on another adventure!

When the uneducated hears
the teachings of the Tao,
He laughs and says: "But that is simple!"
And yet, he does not apply them!
—Lao Tzu, *Tao Te Ching*

It was evening of the next day when we arived in Guilin, China's best-known tourist resort. It has been a favorite holiday spot for centuries and artists, poets and singers have composed many a masterpiece while wondering at the scenic marvels of the area. If you have ever seen a Chinese painting, then you know what Guilin is like; picturesque limestone hills, straight, narrow and towering, rise out of the rice paddies beside the meandering Li Jiang (Li River). There are literally thousands of these phallic hills—perhaps that is why it is such a popular honeymoon spot for the Chinese. One ancient Chinese poet wrote, "The river forms a green silk ribbon, the mountains are like blue jade hairpins."

There are many lovely sites to see around Guilin, a town of three hundred thousand. Bill and I went out to the Reed Flute Cave, which is lit to highlight the beautiful stalagtites and stalagmites inside. There are several hills in the northern part of town that have had steps cut into them and have been turned into temples: Folded Brocade Hill and Fubuo Shan, plus the Seven Star Crag on the eastern bank. There is also the famous Elephant Trunk Hill depicted on the label of the local Guilin beer.

The most popular thing to do in Guilin is to take a cruise on the Li River on one of the many tourist boats that make the thirty-mile trip south to the town of Yangshuo, where you then take a bus back to Guilin. The boat trip looked beautiful, but too expensive for us poor travelers at forty yuan, about twenty-three dollars or so. Bill and I decided to take the bus to Yangshuo and then try to get a ride back to Guilin on the empty boats heading home.

As the constant stream of boats, a score or more, disgorged their tourists in Yangshuo and left, all in a matter of only a few minutes, we jumped on board a boat, walked to the back, and didn't show ourselves until the boat was cruising back down the river. We paid a few yuan to the boatmen, and then settled down in deck chairs on the rooftop observation deck to watch the scenery in the late afternoon. It was an hour before the good views began—it was an overcast day, though bright enough, and there were lots of fishermen out on the river. The limestone hills shot straight out of the earth up into the sky like so many worn, crooked teeth of a mighty dragon.

In the distance more mountains, fading off into the white haze of the sky, seemed like a Chinese painting in 3-D. We had a few beers and a plate of fried rice on the boat, and then a bottle of orange sparkling wine at sunset as a new series of awesome mountains appeared around each bend in the twilight. Each was silhouetted against a dark, cloudy sky, fading away into nothingness. As the wind picked up, I was spell-bound by the timeless beauty of the moment, caught forever in the swirling mists of the Li River, like a Taoist pilgrim caught in the jaws of the mighty dragon, ready and willing to be engulfed with a great gulp into the bowels of Guilin.

I thought of the many adventures I'd had and the mysteries I'd explored over the years. I thought of the great civilizations that had come and gone, often through some great cataclysm. I thought of the great teachers that had come to enlighten the world, often just to be condemned. I thought of the black mentalists who created a web of evil and false information to lead seekers astray. The Dead Sea Scrolls, Essene texts found in a cave on the shores of the Dead Sea in 1947, spoke of a cosmic battle between the forces of good and evil. Who, I wondered, was winning this battle? What have we to learn from the great vanished civilizations of the Rama Empire, Atlantis, the Uigers, the Nagas, and the legendary land of Mu? Are we, too, destined to be wiped out by some geological upheaval or a devastating war? Perhaps both! As I gazed into the growing darkness, it didn't seem to matter at that moment, and in the next, it made all the difference in the world. At any rate, what could I do? What could any one man do?

§§§

It was dark when we reached the jetty at Yangti where the boat docked. We hitched back into Guilin, catching a lift in an army truck in the dark after walking for two hours.

The next evening, I was on a train to Hong Kong, with the last of my money in my pocket: about twenty dollars. Bill was going on to Shanghai in the east a day later.

By mid-afternoon the next day I was back in Guanzou (Canton) and I booked myself on a train to Hong Kong. I spent one night at the Liahua Hotel opposite the train station, and then was rolling into Kowloon by late the next afternoon. I looked at the lights across the harbor of fabulous twenty-first century Hong Kong, and fingered my last few dollars.

In a few hours I had traveled through several decades in time: from struggling China to the glittery modern world of Hong Kong. In a few years I had traveled through several thousand years of time: from the early history of Rama, Uiger, Atlantis and Mu; to the Middle Ages of Central Asia, and now back to the twenty-first century.

I leaned heavily against the rail of the ferry, gazing intently across Hong Kong harbor and looking at the setting sun. Where did I go from here?

両郭烟村白水環速
雜紅葉間蒼山恍闌谷
口清猥喉民巖秋光想
像間 御題

A typical Chinese painting of the famous mountains of Guilin.

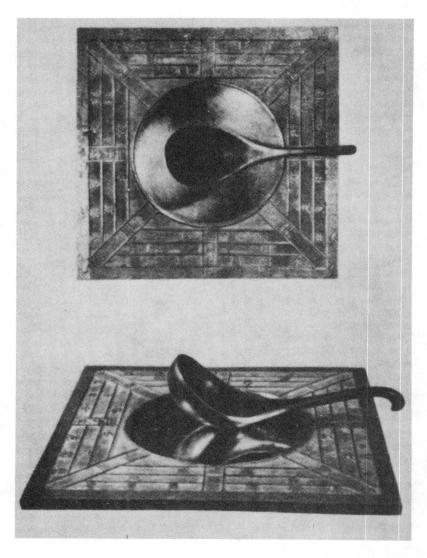

The earliest form of the magnetic compass; the diviner's board (*shih*) of Han times (first century B.C. or A.D.) with the lodestone spoon (*shao*) upon it. (Wang Chen-to)

Selected Bibliography and Footnotes

1. **A Pilgrim's Guide To Planet Earth**, 1981, Spiritual Community Publications, San Rafael, CA.
2. **The Adventurer's Guide**, Charles Jack Wheeler, 1976, David McKay Co., NYC.
3. **The Aquarian Gospel of Jesus the Christ**, Levi, 1907, Devors Co., Marina del Rey, CA.
4. **Atlantis, The Antidiluvian World**, Ignatius Donnelly, 1882, Harper & Row, NYC.
5. **Atlas of the Ancient World**, C. Fagg & F. Clapham, 1979, Crescent Books, NYC.
6. **The Bhagavad Gita**, translated by Juan Mascaro, 1962, Penguin Books, NYC.
7. **The Book of the Damned**, Charles Fort, 1919, Ace Books, NYC.
8. **Children of Mu**, James Churchward, 1931, Ives Washburn Inc, NYC.
9. **Doomsday 1999 A.D.**, Charles Berlitz, 1981, Doubleday & Co., Garden City, NJ.
10. **Fate Magazine**, Sept. 1983, Highland Park, IL.
11. **Forgotten Worlds**, Robert Charroux, 1971, Popular Library, NYC.
12. **The Four Books**, Confucius, various translations and editions.
13. **Gods of Air and Darkness**, Richard Mooney, 1975, Stein & Day, NYC.
14. **The Gods Unknown**, Robert Charroux, 1969, Berkley Books, NYC.
15. **Hitler, The Survival Myth**, Donald McKale, 1981, Stein & Day, NYC.
16. **In Search of Noah's Ark**, D. Balsiger & C. Sellier Jr., 1976, Sun Classic Books, Los Angeles, CA.
17. **It's Still A Mystery**, Lee Gebhart & Walter Wagner, 1970, SBS, NYC.
18. **In Search Of...**, Alan Landsburg, 1978, Doubleday Inc., Garden City, NJ.
19. **Karma Cola**, Gita Mehta, 1979, Simon & Schuster, NYC.
20. **Legacy of the Gods**, Robert Charroux, 1965, Robert Laffont Inc., NYC.
21. **Lost Books of the Bible**, 1926, Bell Publishing Co., NYC.
22. **Lost Worlds**, Alastair Service, 1981, Arco Publishing Co., NYC.
23. **Revealed**, Rev. Dr. Charles Potter, 1962, Fawcett Books, Greenwich, Connecticutt.
24. **The Lost Continent of Mu**, James Churchward, 1931, Ives Washburn Inc., NYC.
25. **Li Po and Tu Fu**, translated by A. Cooper, 1973, Penguin Books, NYC.
26. **The Mahabharata**, translated by Protap Chandra Roy, 1889, Calcutta.
27. **Masters of the World**, Robert Charroux, 1967, Berkeley Books, NYC.
28. **Medieval Legends of Christ**, A.S. Rappoport, 1935, Scribner, NYC.
29. **The Morning of the Magicians**, Louis Pauwels & Jacques Bergier, 1960, Stein & Day, NYC.

30. **National Geographic**, Roy Chapman Andrews, June 1933.
31. **Not Of This World**, Peter Kolosimo, 1971, University Books, Seacaucus, NJ.
32. **On the Track of Unknown Animals**, Bernard Heuvelmans, 1955, MIT Press, Cambridge, MA.
33. **One Hundred Thousand Years of Man's Unknown History**, Robert Charroux, 1965, Robert Laffont Inc., NYC.
34. **The Queen of Sheba and Her Only Son Menyelek (Kebra Nagast)**, translated by Sir E.A. Wallis Budge, 1932, Dover, London.
35. **The Ramayana**, various translations and editions.
36. **The Search For the Twelve Apostles**, William McBirnie, 1973, Tyndale House, Wheaton, IL.
37. **Secrets of the Past**, Reader's Digest, 1980, Berkeley Books, NYC.
38. **Shambala**, Andrew Tomas, 1977, Sphere Books, London.
39. **Strange Abominable Snowmen**, Warren Smith, 1970, Popular Library, NYC.
40. **Tao Te Ching**, Lao Tzu, various translations and editions.
41. **Tibet,** Pietro Mele, 1975 edition, Oxford & IBH, Calcutta, India.
42. **Tibet**, Thubten Norbu & Colin Turnbull, 1969, Penguin Books, NYC.
43. **Timeless Earth**, Peter Kolosimo, 1973, Bantam Books, NYC.
44. **The Travels**, Marco Polo, 1958 edition, Penguin Books, NYC.
45. **2000 AC Distruzione Atomica (Atomic Destruction 2000 BC)**, David Davenport, 1979, Milan.
46. **The Ultimate Frontier**, Eklal Kueshana, 1963, The Stelle Group, Stelle, IL.
47. **Vanished Civilizations**, Max Parrish, 1963, Thames & Hudson, London
48. **Vymaanika-Shaastra Aeronautics**, Maharishi Bharadwaaja, translated and published 1979 by G.R. Josyer, Mysore, India.
49. **The World Almanac Second Book of the Strange**, 1981, NYC.
50. **The World's Weirdest Cults**, Martin Ebon, 1979, Signet Books, NYC.
51. **The World's Last Mysteries**, Reader's Digest, 1976, Pleasantville, NY.
52. **The World Alamanac First Book of the Strange**, 1977, Signet, NYC.
53. **We Are Not the First**, Andrew Tomas, 1971, Souvineer Press, London.
54. **Mysteries of Ancient South America**, Harold Wilkins, 1946, Citadel, NYC.
55. **The Romeo Error**, Lyall Watson, 1974, Hodder and Stoughton, London.
56. **Christ In Kashmir**, Aziz Kashmiri, 1973, Roshni Publications, Srinigar.
57. **Lost Continents**, L. Sprague de Camp,1954, Ballantine Books, NYC.
58. **Science Digest**, August 1981, Hearst Corp., NYC.
59. **Discovery of Lost Worlds**, J. Thorndike Jr.,ed., 1979, American Heritage, NYC.
60. **The Spear of Destiny**, Trevor Ravenscroft, 1982, Samuel Weiser, NYC.
61. **The Unknown Life of Christ**, Nicholas Notovich, 1894, Paris. Republished with additional material in 1980 by Leaves of Healing Publications, Santa Monica, CA.
62. **Magic and Mystery in Tibet**, Alexandra David-Neel, 1929, Dover, NYC.

63. **Himalayas: Abode of Light**, Nicholas Roerich, 1930, Roerich Museum, NYC.
64. **The Tibetan Book of the Dead**, W.Y. Evans-Wentz, 1927, Oxford Press, London.
65. **Raja Yoga**, Yogi Ramacharaka, 1906, Yogi Publication Society, Chicago.
66. **Analects**, Confucius (Kung-Fu-Tzu), various translations & publishers.
67. **Chuang Tzu**, Chuang Tzu , various translations & publishers.
68. **The Dictionary of Imaginary Places**, A. Manguel & G. Guadalupi, 1980, Macmillian, NYC.
69. **Shambala**, Nicholas Roerich, 1930, Roerich Museum, NYC.
70. **The Lost Ship of Noah**, Charles Berlitz, 1987, Putnam, NYC.
71. **The Maldive Mystery**, Thor Heyerdahl, 1986, Adler & Adler, Bethesda, MD.
72. **Jadoo**, John Keel, 1957, Pyramid Books, NYC.
73. **The Encyclopedia of the Strange**, Daniel Cohen, 1985, Avon Books, NYC.
74. **The Dark Gods**, A. Roberts, G. Gilbertson, 1980, Panther, London.
75. **Secret of the Ages**, Brinsley Le Poer Trench, 1974, Pinnacle, NYC.
76. **Lost Cities**, Leonard Cottrell, 1957, Robert Hale & Co., London.
77. **Living With the Himalayan Masters**, Swami Rama, 1978, Himalayan International Institute of Yoga Science & Philosophy, Honesdale, Pennsylvania.
78. **The Silk Road**, Irene Franck & David Brownstone, 1986, Facts On File Pub., NYC.
79. **Tai Ki**, Kuno Knobl, 1975, Bantam Books, NYC.
80. **Life and Teaching of the Masters of the Far East**, Vol. 1 - 5, Baird T. Spalding, 1924, DeVorss & Co. Santa Monica, CA.
81. **Pathways To the Gods**, Erich von Daniken, 1982, Berkley Pub., NYC.
82. **A Search In Secret India**, Paul Brunton, 1935, Dutton & Co., NYC.
83. **The Secret of the Hittites**, C.W. Ceram, 1956, Alfred A. Knopf, NYC.
84. **The Luck of Nineveh**, Arnold Brackman, 1978, McGraw Hill, NYC.
85. **The Mysticism and Magic of India**, Ormond McGill, 1977, Barnes & Co., Cranbury, NJ.
86. **The Fringe of the Unknown**, L. Sprague de Camp, 1986, Prometheus, Buffalo, NY.
87. **Spaceships in Prehistory**, Peter Kolosimo, 1975, University Books, Seacaucus, NJ.
88. **Ruins of Desert Cathay**, Vol. 1-2, M. Aurel Stein, 1912, Macmillian, London.
89. **Anti-Gravity & the World Grid**, D.H. Childress, ed. 1987, Adventures Unlimited Press, Stelle, IL.
90. **The Bridge To Infinity**, Bruce Cathie, 1983, Adventures Unlimited Press, Stelle, IL.
91. **Pale Ink**, Henriette Mertz, 1953, Swallow Press, Chicago.
92. **UFOs Over Modern China**, P. Dong, W. Stevens, 1983, UFO Photo Archives, Tuscon, AZ.
93. **Heart of Asia**, Nicholas Roerich, 1930, Roerich Museum, NYC.
94. **On Eastern Crossroads**, J. Saint-Hilair (H. Roerich), 1930. Roerich Museum, NYC.

95. **The Genius of China**,Robert Temple, 1987, Simon & Schuster, NYC.
96. **No Friend For Travels**, A.J. Wightman, 1959, Robert Hale, London.
97. **Vimana Aircraft of Ancient India & Atlantis**, David Hatcher Childress, 1991, Adventures Unlimited Press, Stelle, IL.
98. **Prophesies of Melchi-Zedek In the Great Pyramid & the Seven Temples**, Brown Landone, 1940, Landone Foundation, Orlando, FL.
99. **The Power Places of Central Tibet**, Keith Dowman, 1988, Routledge & Kegan Paul, London.
100. **The Deep Well**, Carl Nylander, 1964 (Sweden), 1969, Allen & Unwin Ltd.London, U.K.
101. **The Lost World of Agharti**, Alec Maclellan, 1982, Souvenir Press, London.
102. **The Indus Civilization**, Sir Mortimer Wheeler, 1953, Cambridge University Press.
103. **Buried Treasures of Chinese Turkestan**, Albert von Le Coq, 1928, George Allen & Unwin, London.
104. **Dolmens Pour Les Morts**, Roger Joussaume, 1985, Hachette, Paris.
105. **Ancient India**, E.J. Rapson, 1914, Oxford University Press, London.
106. **The Indo-Sumerian Seals Deciphered**, L.A. Waddell, 1925, London.
107. **Chinese Geomancy**, Derek Walters, 1989, Element Books, Dorset.
108. **The Religions of Tibet**, 1970, Giuseppe Tucci, University of California Press, Berkeley & Los Angeles.
109. **The Edicts of Asoka**, Edited by Nikam & McKeon, 1959, University of Chicago Press.
110. **Secret Doors of the Earth**, Jacques Bergier, 1975, Henry Regnery, Company, Chicago.
111. **Jesus In India**, Hazrat Miraa Ghulam Ahmad, 1908 (1970 publication), Islam International Publications, London.
112. **Where Did Jesus Die?**, J.D. Shams, 1945, Unwin, London.
113. **The Great Archaeologists**, edited by Edward Bacon, 1976, Illustrated London News.
114. **Myths and Legends of China**, E.T. Werner, 1922, London.
115. **The Traveler's Key to Northern India**, Alistair Shearer, 1983, Alfred A. Knopf, NYC.
116. **The Archaeology of Ancient China**, Kwang-Chih Chang, 1963,1977, Yale University Press.
117. **Delhi & Agra, a traveller's companion**, Michael Alexander, 1987, Atheneum, NY.
118. **The Empire of the Steppes**, René Grousset, 1970, Rutgers University, NJ.
119. **The Way To Shambhala**, Edwin Bernbaum, Ph.D., 1980, Jeremy P. Tarcher, Inc. Los Angeles.
120. **Sungods In Exile: Secrets of the Dzopa of Tibet**, Karyl Robin-Evans, 1978, Neville Spearman, Suffolk, England.
121. **Thailand**, Archaeological Mundi, 1978, Nagel Publishers, Geneva.
122. **Treasure**, Ed. by B.A. Tompkins, 1979, Times Books, NYC.
123. **Easy Journey to Other Planets**, Swami Prabhupada, 1970, Bhaktivedanta Book Trust (ISKCON), Los Angeles.
124. **The Silk Road**, Irene Franck & David Brownstone, 1986, Facts

On File Pub., NYC.

125. **From Earthquake, Fire & Flood**, R. Hewitt, 1958, Scientific Book Club, London.

126. **Life and Teaching of the Masters of the Far East**, Vol. 1 - 5, Baird T. Spalding, 1924, DeVorss & Co. Santa Monica, CA.

127. **Pathways To the Gods**, Erich von Daniken, 1982, Berkley Pub., NYC.

128. **A Search In Secret India**, Paul Brunton, 1935, Dutton & Co., NYC.

129. **The Mysticism and Magic of India**, Ormond McGill, 1977, Barnes & Co., Cranbury, NJ.

130. **The Fringe of the Unknown**, L. Sprague de Camp, 1986, Prometheus, Buffalo, NY.

131. **Spaceships in Prehistory**, Peter Kolosimo, 1975, University Books, Seacaucus, NJ.

132. **2000 Years of Space Travel**, Russell Freedman, 1963, Collins, London, UK.

133. **The Naga King's Daughter**, Stewart Wavell, 1964, Athenuem, NY.

134. **Altai-Himalaya**: A Travel Diary, Nicholas Roerich, 1929, Roerich Museum, New York.

135. **Anti-Gravity & the Unified Field**, D.H. Childress, ed. 1990, AUP, Stelle, Illinois.

136. **Hindu Ameirica**, Chaman Lal, 1960, Bhavan Book University, Bombay.

137. **On the Trail of Ancient Man**, Roy Chapman Andrews, 1926, Doubleday, NY.

138. **Compassion Yoga, The Mystical Cult of Kuan Yin**, John Blofeld, 1977, Allen & Unwin Publishers, London.

139. **Yantras or Mechanical Contrivances in Ancient India**, V. Raghavan, 1956, Indian Institute of Culture, Bangalore, India.

140. **The Mongols**, David Morgan, 1986, Blackwell Ltd., Cambridge, MA.

141. **The Devil's Horsemen**, James Chambers, 1979, Atheneum, NY.

142. **In Secret Tibet**, T. Illion, 1936, Rider & Co. London. Reprinted by Adventures Unlimited Press, 1991, Stelle, Illinois.

143. **Darkness Over Tibet**, T. Illion, 1937,Kegan Paul, London. Reprinted by Adventures Unlimited Press, 1991, Stelle, Illinois.

144. **Tents In Mongolia**, Henning Haslund, 1934, Kegan Paul, London. Reprinted by Adventures Unlimited Press, 1991, Stelle, Illinois.

145. **Men & Gods In Mongolia**, Henning Haslund, 1935, Rider & Co. London. Reprinted by Adventures Unlimited Press, 1991, Stelle, Illinois.

146. **The Great Chinese Travelers**, Edited by Jeannette Mirsky, 1964, University of Chicago Press, Chicago & London.

147. **The Gobi Desert**, Mildred Cable, 1942, Beacon Press, Boston, Mass.

148. **The Religions of Tibet**, Giuseppe Tucci, 1970, Routledge & Kegan Paul, London.

149. **Occult Reich**, J.H. Brennan, 1974, Futura Books, London.

150. **The Dark Side of History**, Michael Edwards, 1977, Stein & Day, NY

151. **Treasure**, B.A. Tompkins, 1979, NY Times Books, NYC.

152. **Myths and Legends of China**, E.T.Werner, 1922, Graham Brash Pty., Singapore.

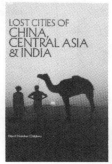

In Secret Tibet

The first two books in the new *Mystic Traveler Series* from Adventures Unlimited Press are very special reprints of rare travel books that first appeared in the 1930s. The author, **Theodore Illion**, was an incredibly resourceful and daring English-German gent. He not only spoke Tibetan, but travelled to Tibet in disguise during a time when foreigners were forbidden entrance. His remarkable adventures make this one of the most exciting travel books ever published.

ADVENTURES UNLIMITED PRESS • **0-932813-13-5** • Theodore Illion • 6x9 • 210pp • 5 b&w photographs, 5 maps • **$14.95**

IN SECRET TIBET

Theodore Illion
Mystic Traveller Series

Darkness Over Tibet

The second volume of **Theodore Illion's** recounting of his travels to Tibet in the 1930s. Here, he journeys through exceptionally remote regions of Tibet, is invited to a secret undergound city, and barely escapes alive to tell his tale. The text is accompanied by maps and illustrations.

ADVENTURES UNLIMITED PRESS • **0-932813-14-3** • Theodore Illion • 6x9 • 210pp • 5 b&w photographs, 5 maps • **$14.95**

OCCULT SCIENCE

Vimana Aircraft of Ancient India & Atlantis

This may be the most controversial science book ever written! To the established scientific community the idea that ancient Indians flew airships of a technology equivalent to our own would be too fantastic to discuss. Yet, several ancient sources show a type of airship called the Vimana, allegedly developed more than 10,000 years ago in the ancient Rama Empire of India. **David Hatcher Childress** has compiled references to the Vimana in ancient and recent literature. Diagrams and photos of airships accompany Childress's lively discussion.

ADVENTURES UNLIMITED PRESS • **0-932813-12-7** • David Hatcher Childress, Introduction by Dr. Ivan T. Sanderson • 8x10 • 280pp • 15 b&w photographs, 15 maps •   **Paperback, $15.95.**

VIMANA AIRCRAFT OF ANCIENT INDIA & ATLANTIS

By David Hatcher Childress
Introduction by Ivan T. Sanderson

VIMANA AIRCRAFT OF ANCIENT INDIA & ATLANTIS

by David Hatcher Childress.
Introduction by
Dr. Ivan T. Sanderson.
This may be the most controversial science book ever written! To the established scientific community the idea that ancient Indians flew around in airships of a technology equivalent to our own would be too fantastic to discuss. This thick and well illustrated volume is a virtual compendium on the fascinating subject of "Vimana" aircraft, a type of airship allegedly developed more than 10,000 years ago in the ancient Rama Empire of India and the "Atlantis". Contains just about every reference ever made to vimanas and "vailixi" (as the Atlantean versions of these aircraft were suposedly called) in ancient and recent literature. Diagrams and ·photos of airships, plus the entire 4th Century B.C. text on Vimanas, the *Vimanika Shastra* text translated by Dr. Josyer of the University of Mysore. 320 pp, 8x10 tradepaper, photos, diagrams & illustrations. $15.95 January Publication.

VIMANA AIRCRAFT
OF ANCIENT
INDIA & ATLANTIS

PASSENGERS PLATFORM

PASSENGERS PLATFORM

CONTROLLING PLATFORM

PITHA

By David Hatcher Childress
Introduction by Ivan T. Sanderson

NEW!

NU SUN:
Asian American Voyages 500 BC
by Gunnar Thompson.
This large and attractive book tells the true story of ancient Chinese voyages to North America and the amazing account of their colonial settlements. Incredible revelations about the mysterious origins of the Mayans and the Taoist source of Chinese & Mayan religious symbolism. More than 500 illustrations of actual artifacts. 240 pp, 8x11 Hardback. Profusely illustrated, with bibliography & index. $23.95

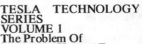
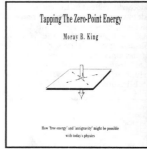

ANTI-GRAVITY & THE UNIFIED FIELD

edited by David Hatcher Childress. Is Einstein's Unified Field the answer to all of our energy problems? Explored are the controversial subjects of how magnetism, electricity and gravity manifest from a Unified Field around us, UFO propulsion, gravity control, vortex technology, suppressed inventions, Nikola Teslas anti-gravity airships, anti-mass generators, gravity waves and free energy are all dealt with in depth. A bit of humour is added in the end with the comics section. 307 pp 100's of Photo's & Drawings, 7 X 10 Tradepaper. $14.95

TESLA TECHNOLOGY SERIES VOLUME 2 BOUNDARY LAYER BREAKTHROUGH.
THE BLADELESS TESLA TURBINE

by Jeffrey Hayes.
The amazing Tesla turbine is the world's most efficient engine. This book traces the history and developement of the bladeless turbine by Nikola Tesla and Jake Possell. Though these are 20 times more efficient than conventional turbines, they are barely known to the scientific world, advanced technology that is 90 years old! 184 pages, 6x9 tradepaper, illustrated with rare photographs & diagrams. $19.95

THE BRIDGE TO INFINITY:
Harmonic 371244
by Captain Bruce Cathie.
Cathie's fourth and latest book on his popular theory that the earth is crisscrossed by an electromagnetic grid system. The book includes a new analysis of the harmonic nature of our physical reality, acoustic levitation, harmonic receiver towers, UFO propulsion, and demonstrates that today's scientists may have at their command a fantastic store of knowledge with which to advance the welfare of the human race. 200 pp, dozens of photos, maps & illustrations, 6x9 tradepaper, $11.95.

EXPLORING INNER AND OUTER SPACE
A Scientist's Perspective on Personal and Planetary Transformation.
by Brian O'Leary, Ph.D.
A remarkable synthesis of of physics, space science, and self discovery, scientist and former NASA astronaut O'Leary takes bold steps beyond the rigid borders of his discipline. He probes consciousness research, energy fields, UFOs, Beam Ships, the mysteries of Mars, the search for extraterrestrial life, the living earth and its monumets and more. 182 pp, 6x9 tradepaper, 12 pages of photos. $12.95

ALIEN BASES ON THE MOON
by Fred Steckling.
This is a pretty strange book! As the title says, this is a book about weird stuff on the moon. It is jam packed with official NASA Apollo photographs and area maps of the Moon that show various craft, robot vehicles and their tracks, pyramids. Readers can examine the full page photographs themselves and decide whether or not there are structures on the Moon or not. Steckling analysed over 10,000 photos, and came up with some startling conclusions. Who is on the Moon? This book can help you decide for yourself. ISBN 0-942176-00-6, 191 Pages, 125 Photographs in color & b/w, 5 x 8 tradepaper. $12.95.

TESLA TECHNOLOGY SERIES VOLUME 1
The Problem Of Increasing Human Energy
WITH SPECIAL REFERENCE TO THE HARNESSING OF THE SUN'S ENERGY by Nikola Tesla. Originally published in June, 1900 in CENTURY MAGAZINE, this book outlines Tesla's Master Blueprint for the World: includes chapters on the transmission of electricity through the earth without wires, the secret of tuning, the electrical oscillator, unexpected properties of the atmosphere, strange experiements and more. 92 pages, 6x9 tradepaper, illustrated with rare photographs & diagrams. $9.95

WAITING FOR THE MARTIAN EXPRESS
Cosmic Visitors, Earth Warriors, Luminous Dreams
by Richard Grossinger.
A thoughtful, balanced and wide-ranging assessment of the New Age: shamans, prophecy, gurus, spirits, extraterrestrials, crystals, enviromental awareness, telepathy and the whole issue of debunking the New Age. Martial Arts, vision quests, Martian structures, aboriginal elders, time warps and more. 169 pp, 6x9 tradepaper. $9.95

TAPPING THE ZERO POINT ENERGY
by Moray B. King.
The author, a well-known researcher, explains how "free energy" and "anti-gravity" might be possible with todays physics. The theories of the zero point energy show there are tremendous fluctuations of electrical field energy imbedded within the fabric of space and how in the 1930s the inventor T. Henry Moray could produce a fifty kilowatt "free energy" machine; how the Pons / Fleischmann "Cold Fusion" experiment could produce tremendous heat without fusion; how certain experiments might produce a gravitational anomaly. 6x9 tradepaper, 170pp, illustrations, diagrams, bibliography, $9.95.

EXPLORING INNER AND OUTER SPACE
A Scientist's Perspective on Personal and Planetary Transformation.
by Brian O'Leary, Ph.D.

A remarkable synthesis of of physics, space science, and self discovery, scientist and former NASA astronaut O'Leary takes bold steps beyond the rigid borders of his discipine. He probes consciousness research, energy fields, UFOs, Beam Ships, the mysteries of Mars, the search for extraterrestrial life, the living earth and its monumets and more. 182 pp, 6x9 tradepaper, 12 pages of photos. $12.95

WAITING FOR THE MARTIAN EXPRESS
Cosmic Visitors, Earth Warriors, Luminous Dreams
by Richard Grossinger.

A thoughtful, balanced and wide-ranging assessment of the New Age: shamans, prophecy, gurus, spirits, extraterrestrials, crystals, enviromental awareness, telepathy and the whole issue of debunking the New Age. Martial Arts, vision quests, Martian structures, aboriginal elders, time warps and more. 169 pp, 6x9 tradepaper. $9.95

THE MONUMENTS OF MARS
by Richard C. Hoagland

In 1976, NASA sent four Viking spacecraft to Mars, to photograph the planet and set landers on its surface to test for the presence of life. On July 25, a lander photographed a mile long peculiar-looking mesa resembling a human face. Through careful analysis of the Cydonia region, the author has uncovered other monuments and structures, including what is possibly an underground city. Why has NASA denied the existance of the artifact? Who were the "Martians?" How does the existance of the "face" change our entire history? 432 Pages, Photos & Illustrations, 7 x 10 tradepaper, $14.95.

THE MONUMENTS OF MARS
Cassette Program
with Richard Hoagland.

A 60 min. cassette companion on the startling discovery of pyramids, structures and a "face" on Mars, plus the struggle to get NASA to show any interest in this important discovery. Includes a chart with nine photos and explanations of the Martian structures. 60 min. One cassette with chart in 4x6 box. $10.95

PLANETARY MYSTERIES
by Richard Grossinger

This anthology opens with an illustrated guide to a bizzare and controversial discovery – a mile long face on the surface of Mars, a massive statue flanked by pyramids and a wall. Dan Noel's dicussion of megaliths and mythic signifigance of the space age follows. Richard Grossinger reports on a visit of an Australian Aborigininal holy man. José Argüelles explores the numerical and fractal mysteries of the Mayan calendar in a long illustrated piece. Also included are The Recollection of Osiris by Normandi Ellis, Artic Explorations by Elisha Kent Kane and more. 272 pp 6 x9 Tradepaper, illustrated with photos and diagrams, $12.95.

ALIEN BASES ON THE MOON
by Fred Steckling.

As the title says, this is a book about weird stuff on the moon. It is jam packed with official NASA Apollo photographs and area maps of the Moon that show various craft, robot vehicles and their tracks, pyramids. Readers can examine the full page photographs themselves and decide whether or not there are structures on the Moon or not. Steckling analysed over 10,000 photos, and came up with some startling conclusions. Who is on the Moon? This book can help you decide for yourself. 191 Pages, 125 Photographs in color & b/w, 5 x 8 tradepaper. $12.95.

LOST CITIES OF NORTH & CENTRAL AMERICA

DAVID HATCHER CHILDRESS

The fifth book in the Lost Cities Series.

We have been getting orders for this book for the last three years, and finally we are going to get it into print. So hold onto your armchairs, for the adventure isn't over yet, and those that can't get enough of lost cities and ancient mysteries can sink their teeth into another volume… Maverick archaeologist Childress continues his world–wide odyssey in quest of the fantastic mysteries of the past. In this exciting book, discover a sunken city in Guatemala, Sumerians in Nicaragua, secret Mayan cities in Mexico, tunnel systems in Arizona, gigantic pyramids in Illinois and even sunken structures in Wisconsin. Join him in search of legendary cities, vast gold treasure, jungle pyramids, ancient seafarers, and living dinosaurs. Soon to be an international television show. 416 pages, 6x9 paperback, illustrated, ISBN 0-932813-09-7, $14.95 (code: NCA)

STONE FRIEZE FROM MAYA RUINS AT TIKAL, GUATEMALA.

MEN AND GODS IN MONGOLIA

HENNING HASLUND

The third book in our Mystic Traveller Series

First published in 1935 by Kegan Paul of London, this rare and unusual travel book takes us into the virtually unknown world of Mongolia, a country that only now, after seventy years, is finally opening up to the west. Haslund, a Swedish explorer, takes us to the lost city of Karakota in the Gobi desert. We meet the Bodgo Gegen, a God-king in Mongolia similar to the Dalai Lama of Tibet. We meet Dambin Jansang, the dreaded warlord of the "Black Gobi". There is even material in this incredible book on the Hi-mori, an "airhorse" that flies through the air (similar to a Vimana) and carries with it the sacred stone of Chintamani. Aside from the esoteric and mystical material, there is plenty of just plain adventure: caravans across the Gobi desert, kidnapped and held for ransom, initiation into shamanic societies, warlords and the violent birth of a new nation. 358 pages, 6x9 paperback, illustrated, 57 photos, illustrations and maps, $15.95. (code: MGM)

MERCURY

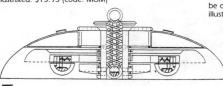

VISIONARIES, MYSTICS & CONTACTEES

UFO PHOTOGRAPHS AROUND THE WORLD VOL. I

UFO PHOTOGRAPHS AROUND THE WORLD VOL. II

UFO CRASH AT AZTEC

OUR COSMIC ANCESTORS

Emblematic image of the earth as medium between light and darkness, from Majer's *Scrutinium Chymicum*, Frankfort/M., 1687

THE 6000 YEAR OLD SPACE SUIT

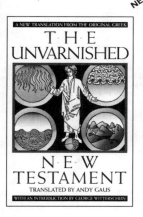

CONSPIRATORS' HIERARCHY:
The Story of the Committee of 300
DR. JOHN COLEMAN.

NEW

This documented book is about a powerful group of international bankers, industrialists and oil magnates trying to control the world. Chapters include information on past and present institutions involved with the so-called Committee of 300 as well as legal associations and banks that were or are now under their control. An interesting conspiracy book, and a book that names quite a few organizations, companies and individuals as part of a vast and evil conspiracy to suppress certain types of technology while promoting alternatives. Includes an index and a table of the Committe of 300 in the back. 288 pages, 6x9 tradepaper, illustrated, with index. $16.95. (code: CHR)

PRINCIPIA DISCORDIA
MALACLYPSE THE YOUNGER WITH AN INTRODUCTION
BY OMAR KHAYYAM RAVENHURST

NEW

This is the bible of Discordianism that provided the framework for Robert Anton Wilson's Illuminatus! trilogy, with an all new 34 page introduction by Omar Khayyam Ravenhurst. In this irreverent and funny philosophy-conspiracy book, you will learn the hidden secrets behind: The Law of Fives; The Sacred Chao, Starbuck's Pebbles, the Curse of Greyface and more! 120 pages, 6x9 paperback, illustrated. ISBN 0-9626534-2-x. $9.95 (code: PRD)

ZENARCHY
KERRY W. THORNLEY

NEW

Zen is meditation. Archy is Social Order. Zenarchy is the social order which holds Universal Enlightenment prerequisite to abolition of the State. Thornley, the co-founder of the humorous pseudo-religion Discordianism, fills the pages with wit and wisdom of Ho Chi Zen, a familiar character to readers of **Cosmic Trigger** and the **Illuminatus!** trilogy. A combination of entertaining thoughts and Zen koans. 119 pages, 6x9 paperback, illustrated, $9.98 (code: ZEN)

Kerry W. Thornley

THE GEMSTONE FILE
EDITED BY JIM KEITH.
WITH COMMENTARIES BY ROBERT ANTON WILSON, KERRY THORNLEY, LEN BRACKEN AND MORE!

NEW

Since 1975, conspiracy researchers have circulated **A Skeleton Key to the Gemstone File,** a document detailing sinister connections and murderous international plotting since the turn of the century. (See **New Books**, page 6). 224 pages, 6x9 paperback. ISBN 0-9626534-5-4 $14.95. (code: TGF)

AWAKENING THE THIRD EYE
DR. SAMUEL SAGAN.

NEW

Dr. Samuel Sagan, the founder of the Clairvision School in Australia, gives a practical and detailed discourse on mind power and the development of "Spiritual Vision." The book gives an understandable description of etheric forces and not only shows one how to open the third eye, but how to tune into land energies and how to dowse ley lines; how to perceive and free energy circulations in the meridians; techniques to enhance daily awareness and presence; and a whole range of techniques of psychic protection and grounding. 308 pages, 6x9 paperback. $14.95 (code: ATE)

THE IDLE WARRIORS
KERRY W. THORNLEY

NEW

Recently featured on "A Current Afair," this book is a portrait of Lee Harvey Oswald written before the assasination of President John F. Kennedy. Subpoenaed by the Warren Commission and stored in the National Archives since 1965, this book finally emerges from obsurityl This astonishing book is a look at Oswald by a fellow Marine and examines his odd "defection" to the Soviet Union after being "released" from military service."The Idle Warriors turns out to be a genuine historical artifact." —Jonathan Vankin, author,— **Conspiracies, Cover-Ups and Crimes.** 202 pages, 6x9 paperback, $10.95. (code: TIW)

AMERICAN DISCOVERY
The Real Story
GUNNAR THOMPSON.
Thompson's second book is a state-of-the-art overview of ancient voyages to America, beginning with the Native Americans and continuing through Amerigo Vespucci. The book features Old World art in America, ancient maps of America, chapters on native tribes; Phoenicians; Norse; Celts, Britons, Irish & Welsh; Greeks, Jews & Romans; Japanese; Hindus; Indonesians; Sumerians; Chinese; Black Africans; Scots, Basques, & Portuguese; Polynesians; Egyptians & Arabs. Archaeologist Thompson explores the reasons why Old World voyagers sailed to America and their impact on native culture. Diffusion of plants, diseases, languages, symbols, races, religion, metals, and civilization are examined.100s of illustrations and photos. ISBN: 0-9621990-4-4, 400 pages, 6x9 hardback, Profusely illustrated, bibliography & index. $17.95. (code: AMD) Publication date: November, 1992.

THE MYSTERY CAVE OF MANY FACES
A History of Burrow's Cave
RUSSELL BURROWS & FRED RIDHOLM.
This hardback book tells the incredible story of how Russell Burrows discovered a cave of thousands of fantastic artifacts in April of 1982. The cave's walled up entrance in a remote valley of southern Illinois kept one of the most astonishing archaeological discoveries hidden for approximately 2000 years. This discovery, and photos of the artifacts, have created a sensation in the archaeology field, and some well-known scholars, such as Barry Fell, have declared much of the collection to be a fake. Others, such as Joseph Mahan, maintain that the thousands of ancient Hindu, Egyptian, Sumerian and other artifacts, are genuine, and that the cave is but one of a number of such caches. This book chronicles the exciting discovery of the cave, the trials and dangers of getting the story to the public, and a brief description of some of the many artifacts found inside, including statues, coins, engraved tablets, various texts and more. Well illustrated with photos and drawings of the artifacts from the cave. 254 pages, 6x9 hardback, Profusely illustrated, bibliography & index. $24.95. (code: TMC)

HOLY ICE
Bridge to the Subconcious
FRANK DORLAND.
The world's formost crystal expert, Frank Dorland, brings us this definitive work on rock quartz crystal. Dorland bridges many topics, including the famous crystal skull found at the lost city of Lubaantun, ancient magic lore concerning crystals, crystal healing, and the making of artificial rock crystals, and most importantly, Dorland discusses the matter-of-fact uses of crystals in high technology. In an important chapter for the New Age scientist, Dorland discusses crystal oscillators, crystal autoclaves, and Catoptromancy (we didn't know what that was either). Divination, charging crystals, crystal balls, chakras, and more. 193 pages, 6x9 tradepaper, illustrated with drawings & photos, bibliography & glossary. $12.95. (code:

THE LOST PYRAMIDS OF ROCK LAKE
FRANK JOSEPH.
Ancient pyramids are found beneath Rock Lake in Wisconsin! Atlantis researcher Joseph searches a Wisconsin lake for underwater ruins using high-tech equipement and scuba divers. Evidence shows that the structures beneath Rock Lake are astronomically orientated to the other pyramids and mounds in the vicinity. Nearby are the huge pyramids of the Sun and Moon at Aztalan. The book discusses such controversial topics as Atlantis in Wisconsin, and the monster of Rock Lake, and has plenty of good illustrations. 6x9 trade-paperback, 240 pp, Illustrated, $12.95. (code: TLP)

NATIVE AMERICAN MYTHS & MYSTERIES
VINCENT H. GADDIS.
Before the dawn of the Egyptian and Mesopotamian cultures a great archaic civilization, advanced in medicine and agriculture, and highly skilled in mathematics and astronomy, flourished in the Americas. The tribal shamanic knowledge links Native Americans today to this spiritual past, many thousands of years old. Divination and healing ceremonies, the Shaking Tent mystery, Navaho feather magic and other traditions all portend a great knowledge lost to the European colonizers. One chapter in this fascinating book is on underground tunnel systems hidden in the American landscape. 184 pages, 6x9 paperback. Bibliography and Index. $12.95. (code: NAM)

WIZARD OF THE UPPER AMAZON
F. BRUCE LAMB.
In 1907 Manuel Cordova was on a rubbercutting expedition deep within the Amazon jungle where he was captured by the Huni Kui, an isolated tribe with an incredible knowledge of tropical plants. Under the tutelage of their ancient and wise chief, Xumu, Manuel was telepathically given an ancient shamanic knowledge through the use of the hallucinatory drug Ayahuascar. Similar to Castenada's work, Wizard of the Upper Amazon is exciting and fascinating! 420 pages, 6x9 paperback. $12.95 (code: WIZ)

RIO TIGRE AND BEYOND
The Amazon Jungle Medicine of Manuel Cordova
F. BRUCE LAMB.
Rio Tigre & Beyond is the second volume in the life of Manuel Cordova. It includes accounts of Cordova's daring adventures through dangerous jungles in search of medicines and knowledge, his initiation into a Freemasonry lodge deep in the Amazon jungle, and the remarkable herbal cures that he learned. 420 pages, 6x9 paperback. ISBN 0-932813-06-2. $12.95 (code: RIO)

THE LOST CITIES OF CIBOLA
RICHARD PETERSEN.
This well illustrated and researched book brings together such different topics as ancient structures and canals in Arizona (Cibola), the giant heads of Easter Island, Ice Age deposits in Iowa, and strange vitrified geological formations in the American Southwest, to formulate a theory of a comet catastrophe that destroyed the advanced civilization of Cibola. Included is information on the "Seven Cities of Cibola" and why much of the country around southern Arizona and New Mexico is vitrified. 252 pages, 6x10 hardback, 65 rare photographs, maps and drawings, $24.95 (code LCC)

NU SUN
Asian American Voyages 500 BC
GUNNAR THOMPSON.
This large and attractive book tells the true story of ancient Chinese voyages to North America and the amazing account of their colonial settlements. Incredible revelations about the mysterious origins of the Mayans and the Taoist source of Chinese & Mayan religious symbolism. Similarities between ancient Asian sculptures, pyramids and temples and those of ancient Meso-America are explored in great detail. The startling parallels between ancient Taoist motifs and those used by the Mayans are enough to convince even the most die-hard sceptic. More than 500 illustrations of actual artifacts. 240 pages, 8x11 hardback, Profusely illustrated, bibliography & index. $24.95. (code: NUS)

THE SECRET
America in World History before Columbus
JOSEPH B. MAHAN.
This hardback book by respected historian Mahan of the Yuchi Indian tribe in Georgia, tells of the ancient sun kingdoms in America and their relationship with Old World cultures. The book goes into detail about about ancient Hindu, North African, and Mediterranean voyagers to North America and the legacy that they left. Being a Yuchi Indian himself, Mahan is in a unique position to show the heritage of the pyramid-building civilizations of the Mississippi, Ohio and Southeast U.S. as it relates to the Sun Kingdoms of the ancient world. 247 pages, 6x9 hardback, illustrated with drawings & photos, bibliography & index. $22.50. (code: SEC)

DRAGON TREASURES
Chinese explorations in America Before Columbus
EDITED BY DONALD CYR
Did the ancient Chinese sail regularly to the Americas in ancient times? Chinese map of the world from 2250 BC, ancient books on expedition to America and more are all profiled in this large format book. 112 pages 8x10 paperback, 100 photos, illustrations and maps. $9.95 (code: D

NIKOLA TESLA ON HIS WORK WITH ALTERNATING CURRENTS

AND THEIR APPLICATION TO WIRELESS TELEGRAPHY, TELEPHONY, AND TRANSMISSION OF POWER
LELAND I. ANDERSON.
In this thick, large format book, the many patents of Nikola Tesla and his wireless electrical devices are explained and illustrated. Learn that what is science fiction today was reality in 1910! Chapters include information on the Wardenclyffe Tower on Long Island that was to broadcast free power to the East Coast; Supreme Court documents on the dismantling of the equipment; and diagrams showing the velocity of light hitting the earth. Hundreds of photos, patents and illustrations on Tesla's fantastic science. A must for any free energy or Tesla buff. Includes Supreme Court documents on the trial of Nikola Tesla and his controversial free energy devices. 237 pages, 8x11 paperback, profusely illustrated. $44.95. (code: NTAC)

TESLA TECHNOLOGY SERIES VOL 1:

The Problem of Increasing Human Energy & the Wireless Transmission of Power.
NIKOLA TESLA.
Originally published in June, 1900 in Century Magazine, this small book outlines Tesla's master blueprint for the world. It includes chapters on the transmission of electricity through the earth without wires, the secret of tuning the electrical oscillator, unexpected properties of the atmosphere, and some strange experiments. 92 pages, 6x9 paperback, illustrated with rare photographs & diagrams. $9.95. (code: TESL)

TESLA TECHNOLOGY SERIES VOL. 2:

Boundary Layer Breakthrough: The Bladeless Tesla Turbine
JEFFREY HAYES.
The amazing Tesla turbine is the world's most efficient engine. This book traces the history and development of the bladeless turbine by Nikola Tesla and Jake Possell. Though these are 20 times more efficient than conventional turbine, they are barely known to the scientific world, This advanced technology is 90 years old! 184 pages, 6x9 paperback, illustrated with rare photographs & diagrams. $19.95. (code:

INTERNATIONAL TESLA SYMPOSIUM PROCEEDINGS

EDITED BY STEVEN R. ELSWICK.
The best collection of Tesla material currently in print, it includes papers on the transmission of electricity through the earth without wires, Tesla and particle beam weapons, advanced gravitics, levitation, Maxwell's lost Unified Field theory, radiant energy, Tesla Coils and much more. 21 articles in all, a must for any serious Tesla student! 304 pages, 9x11 hardback, illustrated with rare photographs & diagrams. $49.95. (code: ITS)

ETHER TECHNOLOGY

A Rational Approach to Gravity Control
RHO SIGMA.
Before the term "Quantum Field" there was the "Ether". Written by a well-known American scientist under the pseudonym of Rho Sigma, this brief book discusses in detail international efforts at gravity control and discoid craft propulsion. Includes chapters on Searle discs, T. Townsend Brown, Ether-Vortex-Turbines, and more. Foreward by former NASA astronaut Edgar Mitchell. 108 pages, 6x9 paperback, illustrated with photographs & diagrams. $9.95. (code: ETT)